S A D E

SADE

A BIOGRAPHICAL ESSAY

Laurence L. Bongie

The University of Chicago Press
Chicago & London

LAURENCE L. BONGIE, F.R.S.C., is professor emeritus of French at the University of British Columbia, and an Officer of the *Ordre des Palmes académiques.* He is the author of a major study on the philosopher Condillac; of *Diderot's femme savante; David Hume: Prophet of the Counter Revolution;* and *The Love of a Prince: Bonnie Prince Charlie in France, 1744–1748.*

The University of Chicago Press, Chicago 60637
The University of Chicago Press, Ltd., London
© 1998 by The University of Chicago
All rights reserved. Published 1998
Printed in the United States of America
07 06 05 04 03 02 01 00 99 98   1 2 3 4 5

ISBN: 0-226-06420-4 (cloth)

Library of Congress Cataloging-in-Publication Data

Bongie, Laurence L.
  Sade : a biographical essay / Laurence L. Bongie.
    p.   cm.
  Includes bibliographical references and index.
  ISBN 0-226-06420-4 (hardcover : alk. paper)
    1. Sade, marquis de, 1740–1814.   2. Authors, French—
18th century—Biography.   I. Title.
PQ2063.S3B59   1998
843′.6—dc21
[B]   98-25227
                                                     CIP

⊗The paper used in this publication meets the minimum requirements of the American National Standard for Information Sciences—Permanence of Paper for Printed Library Materials, ANSI Z39.48-1992.

Contents

Preface

Although the whole of Sade's life and works is touched on in this study and a detailed chronology has been provided for the guidance of readers unfamiliar with the marquis' personal events, I have not set out to write a full-blown biography of the man who at one time was discussed mostly in horrified whispers but whose writings in the last half century or more have achieved a widely acclaimed position in the canon of world literature. Not surprisingly perhaps, Sade the man, celebrated as the apostle of untrammeled individual rights, as a giant of philosophical thought and a martyr to freedom of conscience, has shared in that rehabilitation.

My purpose in this biographical essay, to which I have appended a free-ranging postscript on Sadean criticism, will be to test the validity of those remarkable claims. As befits both the ambitions and methodology of the essay genre—pretending to no higher title than an imperfect thrust at the subject—I have in the course of this exploration allowed myself a fairly unconstrained itinerary, being concerned less with orderly procedure and full ceremonial coverage of territory than with the freedom to linger at times over certain key features of the Sadean landscape and to give other aspects such as the notorious Marseilles affair, Sade's confinement at Miolans, or his relatively uneventful final years at Charenton little more than a passing glance. My journey, for all that, will not shrink from its formal responsibility to reach an identifiable destination, and I give fair warning at the outset that few of my conclusions are likely to please the divine marquis' more devoted champions.

A major premise—at one time viewed as commonsensical and self-evident but nowadays condemned in some critical circles as lamentably unschooled—underlies my basic approach to the subject, namely, the assumption that there is a person behind the text and that it is both legitimate and useful to seek a linkage between an author's life and writings. Sade's biography throws important light on his fiction, just as his fiction significantly draws upon and illuminates his singular life. What the marquis did or personally conceived of doing in real life is intimately connected to the actions of his fictional monsters for whom—it is important to note—*conceiving* and *doing* are one and the same. And just as the mental process of imagining or conceiving in real life is not hampered by what is either probable or possible, so too are the *actions* of Sade's characters for whom no physical limitations exist. This absence of boundaries, impediments, and limits of any kind becomes in fact the defining attribute of the Sadean novel whose monster characters are entirely creatures of action and physical excess, who can *do* everything to their victims that can be *conceived* and even, some would say, that cannot be conceived. It is this equation of real-life *conceiving* and of fictional *doing* that forms the nexus of Sadean life and literature. Sade's monsters thus do not, in any ultimate sense, exemplify art separated from life; indeed, one imagines that the marquis, like one of his most redoubtable modern defenders (Annie Le Brun; see the appended critical postscript), would have been profoundly irritated by Roland Barthes' cooptation of his monsters as mere text ("*écrite la merde ne sent pas*"). However tentative the marquis' real-life coprophilic forays may have been, they nevertheless provide one of many verifiable links in a life-and-literature connection and prove as well that within the Sadean universe all is not simply discourse, that shit—Barthes' quip notwithstanding—*is* intended to smell, in the same way that dismembered, disemboweled, and sodomized infants or gouged and mutilated mothers torn to shreds by vicious dogs and even more vicious sons are meant to be taken by Sade's reader as something other than play tokens in an elaborate word game. But even setting aside all such considerations of formal intentionality, the simple act of writing for Sade (and for Sade more than for most authors) necessarily implies some form of self-expression and some kind of intimately personal—indeed, pedagogical—communication to an implied reader.

To write about Sade's life is, essentially, to seek explanation. I begin that search in Part I by focusing almost exclusively on the marquis' parents and more generally in Part III on his mother, though not because I embrace the tempting etiologies of psychoanalysis, however popular such "explanations" as the negative Oedipus complex have become among the critics and clinicians who have attempted to account for the man's central anomalies. Total forbearance in the matter has not been possible, however, anymore than I have been able to restrict as I would have preferred all behavioral analysis in this essay to what I believe Proust disapprovingly called *la psychologie plane.* I have also been inclined throughout to favor a rather classical view of the passions, acknowledged as the dominant motor of our lives that can nevertheless be lived deliberately, responsibly, and lucidly in a world where the "subconscious" remains an overworked and perhaps even an unproven hypothesis. Sade, one of humanity's most arrogantly lucid and intelligent specimens, lived just such a "passionate" and deliberate life of body and mind. His self-awareness and lucidity, his constant claims to moral authenticity, did not, however, prevent him from also being one of the most obnoxiously adolescent, opportunistic, tantrum-prone, egotistical, self-absorbed, puffed-up hollow men of his age, the very epitome of bad faith, and, as if that were not enough, the author too of the most monotonously egregious, long-winded pornographic novels imaginable, all richly interlarded with a preachy, secondhand ideology that he frequently pilfered from thinkers far more original and coherent than he.

But to return to the question of explaining the man and to my initial focus on the parents, I set out in that general direction because, despite the pioneering contributions of Maurice Heine, Gilbert Lely, Jean-Jacques Pauvert, and especially Maurice Lever, biographical scholarship has so far been able to tell us little if anything about the marquis' early childhood, of that period in his formative years when primary nurturing placed its own indelible—if largely accidental—stamp on a nascent personality already no doubt substantially programmed by genetic predisposition. It is during this period, Sade's first four or five years of existence, and again during his beginning adolescence, that his mother's presence may have impinged critically on his life; in this regard I offer a few significant archival discoveries that help to flesh out the picture of a shadowy maternal figure who has remained to this day such a mystery. Also included in this first section that has less to do with the marquis himself than with his antecedents is some extended new material concerning his father, a polished but ineffectual and curiously petty courtier-libertine, very much a creature of his times who was the lifelong object of his son's overt affections but whose profligate tendencies and lack of personal integrity may have had an important effect on the marquis' adolescent development. Unfortunately, despite the fresh data provided on both parents, it remains obvious that we still know far too little about Sade's early years, not enough, certainly, to "explain" the man—indeed, barely enough at times to describe him. Here, conjecture, whose proper task in biography is to ask rather than answer questions, still plays an uncomfortably important role. With respect to the mother, however, it seems nevertheless safe to infer from the obsessively grim treatment afforded women victims in both the marquis' life and literature, and especially from the disgust and obscene hatred for mothers constantly preached in the novels, that the most telling abnormal developmental factors probably go back to this early period, that they were in some way essentially mother centered, and that their effect was decisive.

Whether the marquis was more the creature of anomalous nurture than singular nature will never be known but—and here I must disclose another premise of my study—even if one day we were able to grasp the totality of these relevant causal factors, it would not follow that to explain all and understand all is to forgive all. Despite the bluster and bravado of his efforts to transmute his particular psychopathology into a proud ethic of authenticity, Sade, as an intelligent, civilized, and essentially sane human being capable of subjecting himself to moral scrutiny and of leading an examined life, did have his options, including the option of denying himself the "pleasure" of inflicting his fantasized cruelties and indignities on helpless fellow creatures. That, of course, is a proposition he vigorously contested with what he thought to be unassailable logic, preferring always to shift responsibility for his actions onto others. A fair number of respected thinkers today seem to find themselves in total agreement with Sade on this point.

And further to that point, here too is no doubt the place to declare that I have found little evidence to support the claims, frequently advanced since the time of Apollinaire and the surrealists, that the marquis de Sade deserves to be honored as the archetypal freedom fighter, a martyr of conscience and "the freest spirit who ever lived," a culture hero who sacrificed his personal liberty to the unrelenting critique of all social constraints that diminish the irrepressible human element, restoring thereby to civilized man the strength and health of his primitive instincts. Anyone familiar with the biographical facts of the case should be astonished—if not amused—by the poet Paul Eluard's insistence that the marquis was a heroic figure imprisoned nearly all of his adult life because of his "desperate struggle in defense of absolute justice and equality." The corollary to such lyrical fantasies is Sade's own assertion that his (relatively comfortable) prison years in the Bastille and in Vincennes represented a case of "philosophy clapped in irons." That too is nonsense, if for no other reason than the simple fact that Sade's "philosophy" first saw the light of day in writings published after his release from prison, unless, of course, we are to construe his earlier propensity to abuse prostitutes as the Sadean equivalent of writing Paine's *The Rights of Man* or perhaps even Kant's *Critique of Practical Reason.* Sade's confinement as a privileged aristocrat in the Bastille, surrounded by books, furnished with writing materials and many little comforts, visited regularly after a time by his wife who in exchange for the vilest verbal abuse dutifully brought him his reading materials and his fruit baskets, his favorite jams and his anal dildos, in no way reminds us of Nelson Mandela's many long years of hard labor with little more than a single sisal mat for a bed in a damp six-by-nine-foot prison cell on Robben Island. Sade's aristocratic rank, buttressed by the wealth and legal connections of his in-laws, routinely and repeatedly made it possible for him to escape the ignominy and horrors of his century's ordinary criminal justice. His fetters were the fetters of favor, and when the ancien régime (with his family's approval) imprisoned him by means of an essentially protective *lettre de cachet,* it was not for his "philosophy" but because of his criminal sexual abuse of unconsenting victims, almost always lower-class women. Sade, to put it in the simplest terms, was a "sadist." His crimes of violent cruelty, aggravated as they were by the element of chronic recidivism, would probably be deemed in most legal jurisdictions today to be as transgressive and punishable as they were in eighteenth-century France.

Sade may well have achieved in recent years, thanks to his various hagiographers, a front rank in the pantheon of Western writers, including recent canonization in the most respected and successful French collection of great authors, the Bibliothèque de la Pléiade, but that remarkable achievement in no way alters the fact that, despite his many grandstanding protestations and grandiloquent claims to principled integrity, much of his life—and most flagrantly his career in the Revolution—was lived as a lie. Though extolled as the greatest (and most slandered) of literary geniuses, as history's only true revolutionary, he is frequently revealed by both his acts and his words to be a hollow opportunist, a weathercock in his political principles (his integral atheism excepted), a largely unoriginal thinker, and a tiresome—and tiring—pornographer. Curiously, many of his admirers have been quick to deny that he wrote pornography—even though he himself, more than once, happily admitted to the fact.

It is possible that the acclaim currently enjoyed by Sade's fiction will not endure at present levels, although contemporary critics, with some notable exceptions (the final position of the late Octavio Paz being a strikingly lucid example), still seem endlessly forgiving of the clumsy didacticism, the many plagiarisms, and the monotonous pornography that mark much of the marquis' formal writing. In his introduction to the Pléiade *Oeuvres* (I, liii, lv), Sade's recent editor Michel Delon suggests, for example, that it is only the "hurried reader" or the "pornography amateur" who will find the marquis monotonous or boring. With similar indulgence, he subsequently goes on to describe Sade's plagiarisms as gestures of philosophical solidarity with his brothers in combat and as illustrations of a dynamic "collage artist" at work.

A more likely development in Sade's future literary fortunes might involve increased recognition that it is really the marquis' correspondence—most notably his prison letters—that deserves to be honored as great literature and accorded some measure of the praise that has been lavished almost superstitiously on his novels. These impassioned letters that constantly invent and reveal the man, overflowing with sarcasm and anger, filled with lies both to himself and to others, poured out in molten rhetoric, humorous at times if nearly always tinged with prison paranoia, will no doubt remain his most lasting literary achievement, his true masterpiece. A parallel with certain characteristics of Rousseau's celebrated *Confessions* inevitably comes to mind.

It seems to me, on the other hand, that Sade as novelist and thinker has been taken much too seriously of late. Perhaps the time has come to reconsider the frequently mocked comment that Anatole France made more than a century ago (see Appendix II) to the effect that one is not necessarily required to look upon a text by Sade as the equivalent of a text by Pascal. Sade's rehabilitation has since that time become a self-sustaining industry. This essay is intended as an informal but reasoned (and soberly provocative) attempt, based on original archival research and close reading of the primary sources, to redress the balance. In an ultimate sense, it addresses issues of bad faith rather than "evil," and it most certainly does not call for a return to the benighted censorship of a bygone era that too often did not know either how to live and let live or how to stay out of the bedrooms and bookstores of the nation's consenting adults. Rather, it urges careful appraisal of the man along with close analysis of the Sadean text, inviting readers to challenge, when the imperatives of civility and reason dictate, a prevailing orthodoxy that has blurred not only the distinction between literature and pornography but, far more important still, the line of demarcation between the legitimate ethics of personal authenticity in all its self-regarding variants and an uncaring, destructive subjectivity, solipsistic in essence and grounded in the polity of the jungle.

Vancouver, April 1998

Introduction

Dead center in the *siècle des Lumières,* the high point of the Enlightenment, on Monday, 6 July 1750, five-thirty in the afternoon, a large crowd of onlookers is gathered at the Place de Grève in Paris to witness the burning at the stake of two young workmen, Jean Diot and Bruno Lenoir, for the capital crime of sodomy. Seven cartloads of prime firewood and two hundred bundles of straw and kindling will provide the fuel.

A police patrol had surprised the two *in flagrante delicto,* full action in broad daylight, on a public thoroughfare, the rue Montorgueil. The punishment was astonishingly harsh for the day: "An anachronistic accident," writes the historian Michel Rey.[1] "Totally puzzling," agrees the Sadean scholar Maurice Lever.[2]

It was indeed an extremely rare event. In all, seven "sodomites" were burned at the stake in Paris during the eighteenth century, the last being the Capuchin monk Pascal, in 1783. With all the other cases, there had been critically aggravating circumstances: sodomy coupled with murder, rape, abduction. . . .[3]

The lawyer Barbier noted in his journal one month before the 1750 double execution that the public expected the uncommonly severe sentence of burning at the stake to be stayed, even though the flagrancy of the crime was unusual. The sentence would be reduced, he speculated, for reasons of prudence, given "the indecency of such examples which acquaint many of our youth with what they have never heard of before."[4] Moreover, the effrontery of the culprits' actions had been helped along apparently by a little too much wine.

Barbier later notes that the original sentence of execution was carried out to set an example: "All the more," he continues, "since it is said that this crime has become very common and that many of the prisoners in Bicêtre are there for that reason." The lawyer's next observation tells us a good deal about the social hierarchy of the ancien régime: "Since these two workmen had no connections with any persons of distinction, either of the Court or the Town, and since they apparently implicated no one else, the example has been made without any risk of further repercussions." Happily, the vice in this case—once thought of as *le vice noble*—had not in fact publicly involved any members of the upper classes. No awkward mixing of social strata was associated with the crime, and the risk of widespread scandal was not present as it had been, for example, a quarter of a century earlier in the notorious Deschauffours affair when as many as two hundred persons of all ranks had been implicated.[5]

And let it not be said that pity was wanting in the most enlightened and culturally refined capital of the eighteenth-century world. The two young workmen, tied securely to sturdy posts erected on the Place de Grève, were mercifully strangled before the straw was set ablaze. Moreover, unlike what had been required at the 1726 execution, the sentence was not proclaimed by an official town crier, "apparently to spare the public the name and designation of the crime."[6] The whole business, in short, was neatly and efficiently disposed of: no lengthy investigations, no dragged-out disclosures of messy details, no public focus on powerful figures; administratively, it had been a quick, clean, surgical strike.

In sharp contrast with the treatment meted out to the two unfortunate workmen, police files concerning the arrest of sodomists in Paris around this same time make it amply clear that most run-of-the-mill cases were disposed of quietly and in a far less radical fashion.[7] People of wealth or rank usually escaped arrest entirely. A year before the 1750 burning, police inspector Louis-Alexandre Framboisier, in charge of the sodomy detail and sundry other matters,[8] had expressed regret, for example, in a letter to his superior Nicolas-René Berryer, the lieutenant général de police, that he could do nothing about a certain Duval, the *capitation* tax collector: "The high office he holds has prevented my sending him to prison as he deserves." He was nevertheless hopeful that M. de Bernage, the prévost des marchands (effectively, the mayor of Paris), would have a quiet word with this privileged "*infâme.*" Despite warnings, as one of the administration's leading tax officials, Duval simply thumbed his nose at Framboisier: "My moral character, my conduct and the duties of my office place me beyond the reach of your investigations."[9] As for less privileged transgressors, a week or two of imprisonment (sometimes considerably more in the case of a repeat offender) and a severe reprimand followed by a *soumission* (a signed declaration of repentance along with a promise not to reoffend) generally resolved matters. A wide array of social classes and occupations figure in Inspector Framboisier's files: soldiers and shopkeepers, shoemakers and pastry cooks, day laborers and notaries, not to mention a goodly number of clerics. Perhaps the largest contingent of offenders was made up of domestic servants whose masters, alerted by tearfully contrite appeals, frequently intervened by writing petitionary letters to the lieutenant général de police, attesting to the sterling qualities and absolutely indispensable services of the unlucky delinquent.

A particular case that seems to have escaped the notice of historians who have carried out research in this area is that of Antoine Leclerc, a cook by trade, charged on several occasions with having committed sodomy, most notably on 28 April 1749 with an unconsenting person, one Jacques Charpentier, a minor functionary in the grain trade. The not entirely "classic" incident according to the victim's testimony apparently took place in the following manner: Leclerc and a pastry cook named Guillaume Martin, having first lured Charpentier to Martin's room on the Place Baudoyer (dangerously close to the place of executions at the Place de Grève), bolted the door and then pinned their unsuspecting guest down on the bed. "With Martin holding the aforementioned Charpentier by the head," continues the police report, Leclerc brutally sodomized him twice, paying no heed to Charpentier's deafening screams that Leclerc was hurting him "too much." When it was all over, Martin "went off to fetch a bottle of wine which all three then proceeded to drink."[10] We see that the case has its ambiguities; indeed, it is further complicated by the fact that Charpentier, in addition to being something of a true amateur whose despairing parents eventually asked to have him incarcerated for life in Bicêtre (or even transported to a distant penal colony), was a police informer or *mouche*.[11]

My attention was drawn to the case in the police archives less by such anomalies than by other considerations. Antoine Leclerc was, in fact, known to the police as a chronic offender, and his name comes up in a number of interrogations, revealing many previous incidents. Most recent among these was his scandalous participation in a semipublic masturbation contest with two other habitués of the notorious cabaret "À la Côte de Rheims" on the rue du Faubourg Saint-Antoine. Urged on by a circle of presumably like-minded enthusiasts, Leclerc, along with Jean Martin, wine merchant, and the elder Lefèvre, a dealer in used clothing, had hit upon a novel means to determine which of the three should pay the wine bill. By common consent it was decided that "the last to ejaculate would pay the reckoning."[12] The detailed outcome of that sporting event is not revealed in the police file, but, in any case, the authorities were by now more concerned with Leclerc's involvement in the Charpentier assault. Brought in for questioning, he at first denied everything, even after being confronted with his accuser. Finally, he confessed, but only, as the official report goes on to note somewhat ominously, "when the facts were proved to him." It is after his transfer on 28 May 1749 from the relatively gentle surroundings of For-l'Evêque prison to the living hell of Bicêtre that he attracts our special interest.

The usual letters petitioning the chief magistrate on the prisoner's behalf, employing all the clichés of the genre, may be found in Leclerc's dossier, including one from no less a personage than Louis de Talaru, marquis de Chalmazel, chief steward of the Queen's Household, who requests that "some indulgence" be accorded this "young lad whose character may have been blackened by evil companions but not rendered criminal." Not surprisingly, in an age when social connections were of the greatest importance, Chalmazel is also careful to point out that Antoine Leclerc's brother was a loyal officer of the queen's household.[13]

But it is a long-overlooked letter from the wayward cook's employer that is of particular interest: Antoine Leclerc, sodomite, rapist, and an apparently serious contender in the competitive sport of public masturbation, was (and had been for several years, it turns out) in the domestic employ of Marie-Eléonore de Maillé de Carman, comtesse de Sade, mother of the future "Divine Marquis." The comtesse's note on the occasion of her cook's arrest, something of a rare find in that very few of her letters have surfaced in the archives to date, is short and direct and conveys an unmistakable tone of authority that suggests the writer was not anticipating even the remotest possibility that her request to the police would be denied or even delayed:

Glatigny, 2 June [1749]

My cook, Leclerc, left my service and ran off to Paris to play the libertine. I have learned, Sir, that you have punished him for it and that he is now in For l'Evêque prison. He has written to me of his misfortunes, his disgrace and his repentance which I judge to be sincere. Since he is an excellent cook and much needed by me here in the country, I request that he be returned to me. I shall be obliged to you for it.

I trust that you will grant me this kindness as well as that of believing me to be entirely, Sir,

Your most humble and obedient servant,
Maillé de Sade[14]

The comtesse's letter, brief and totally without the usual fulsome pleas-antries, stands in sharp contrast to typical models of the genre. In similar circumstances, the marquise de Mézières, writing to Berryer about her sodomitical laquais Bazile, respectfully assures the chief magistrate that the offending domestic "will never again set foot in my house!" Echoing such sentiments, the présidente de Lamoignon informed the magistrate that her similarly inclined cook Goblet had been shown the door the moment she learned of his evil deeds: "I dismissed him immediately, not wishing to have in my house anyone guilty in any way of anything reprehensible." The comtesse de Valencey, faced with the same problem, chooses to be more nuanced but is still clearly anxious to show great deference to Berryer's magisterial authority. She would never, she assures him, have been able to convince herself that her faithful servant, François Duquesnel, was guilty of such infamies had he not confessed! She would, of course, dismiss him, "if the magistrate absolutely required it." [15] The celebrated novelist, Cré-billon *fils,* also pleads in the usual style of Berryer's petitioners: his excel-lency will know that he, Crébillon *fils,* holds his excellency in the highest regard and thinks of him as entirely "good and wise." His humble peti-tioner will "dare to hope" that the exalted magistrate "will look favorably upon this his most humble supplication." As for the marquis de Ximenès, a less talented writer than Crébillon *fils* but a greater libertine, he proffers unctuous thanks to the chief magistrate after his own rascally cook, Nico-las Hussenot, is released from Bicêtre: "I hope that my personal example and the pardon that you have granted him will place him once more on the path of virtue; if he again goes astray, I shall dismiss him from my employ." [16]

The subtext as much as the text of Marie-Eléonore de Maillé's note to one of the most powerful representatives of state authority in the whole of France tells us something very important about this little-known mother of the marquis de Sade and the society into which her son was born. Her letter is not petitionary in tone, nor is it directed to a social equal. Her communication is coded, rather, in the brusque protocols of the old feudal nobility. One notes the correctly polite but firm manner of someone who had grown up in the Hôtel de Condé among princes of the blood royal. She thanks a state functionary for doing his duty as expected and then concludes by claiming as a matter of course a recognized prerogative. Her servant's crime, even though it involved both sodomy and rape, becomes secondary to the process, is itself reduced to a trivial level of reality: An-toine Leclerc had been "playing" the libertine, *faisait le libertin,* rather like "playing" the fool, an injudicious but relatively innocuous bit of theater; it was only right and proper that the lieutenant général de police, carrying out his assigned, constituted duties, should have been involved in apprehending and punishing the culprit initially. However, courtesy now required that the arrant knave be promptly returned to his masters. There was no need for the state, for centralized authority, for the intruding apparatus of justice, to intervene further in the matter. The "family," it was understood, would take care of it. The comtesse's letter leaves no room for hesitation or dissent on Berryer's part. Indeed, he would be expected to recognize in the very brevity of her text its most important message.

It would not be the last time that this mysterious mother of Donatien Alphonse François, marquis de Sade, would find herself writing in haughty style to the king's authorities on behalf of someone who had run afoul of the law. Coincidentally, on the very day she wrote in defense of her cook, her son celebrated his ninth birthday.

Part One

ANTECEDENTS

*C'est une terrible femme.
Son fils en tiendra.*

[She is a dreadful
woman. Her son will
be like her.]

One

M Y S T E R I O U S   M O T H E R

Mysterious mother? All of the marquis' biographers insist on the point: "What we know about the comtesse de Sade can be said in two pages," writes Jean-Jacques Pauvert in a three-volume biography that devotes more than seventeen hundred pages of text and notes to an engrossing account of the life of Marie-Eléonore's notorious son.[1] Although my own study will bring to light roughly double the number of known letters by her, Pauvert's description of the information desert that surrounds the marquis' mother can still be accepted with only minor quibbles.[2]

Maurice Lever's authoritative biography, based on newly accessible family papers that he is currently in the process of publishing,[3] has filled in a number of critical gaps in our information relating to Sade's later adolescent years. Most important, Lever has thrown much new light on the close, "symbiotic," emotional, and intellectual relationship between Donatien and his father, Jean-Baptiste, comte de Sade, who turns out to be a very different and much more significant figure in the life of his notorious son than was previously supposed. But while Lever is able to speak of the "omnipresence" of the father in Sade's life and works, of his defining influence on his young son's imagination and sensibility, the Divine Marquis' most complete and most objective biographer to date notes that the father's role necessarily takes on even greater significance and visibility in that "the mother is *practically nonexistent.*"[4]

Our ignorance regarding this "figure three-quarters hidden in the darkest of shadows" (again Pauvert) is especially critical regarding the emotional side of things: "We do not know if he loved his mother, just as we know nothing of the feelings she may have had for him."[5] I have been fortunate enough to turn up a few new items hidden away until now in the archives, but the surviving major gaps in the history of a well-known family that enjoyed high status in the nation's capital during the marquis' early years still remain a matter of puzzlement and surprise. Indeed, what Simone de Beauvoir wrote on the subject of Sade's childhood nearly a half-century ago, well before the extensive biographical investigations of Lely, Pauvert, and Lever were carried out, remains basically valid even today. It is still true, despite all of the necessarily speculative inferences—Klossowskian or other—that we are tempted to draw from Sade's fiction and from the monstrous victim roles assigned to hated mothers in *Justine, Juliette, La Philosophie dans le boudoir,* and *Les 120 journées de Sodome,* that the real-life sources of those undeniably pathological phantasms remain largely hidden. It is also still true, as Simone de Beauvoir pointed out, that it is "only *a priori,* and following on certain general concepts, that we suspect the importance of Sade's relationship with his father [thanks to Maurice Lever, less true today] and his mother [still an enormous problem!]; the particularizing detail of their rapports escapes us. Sade when we first discover him is already formed and we do not know how he has become what he is. [. . .] Because of this unfortunate gap, knowledge of Sade's innermost being will forever be denied us; all explanations will leave behind a murky residue that only his early childhood history might have illuminated."[6] Beauvoir had in mind especially the missing psychophysiological facts that presumably gave rise to the writer's real-life sexual aberrations, multiplied a thousandfold in the grotesque excesses of his fictional monsters, the Noirceuils, Blangis, Gernandes, and others. But, apart from any prudent skeptical doubts we may have regarding the possibility of eventually identifying "causal" factors that explain the writer's singular imagination, it must be acknowledged that even some of the most basic physical facts of Sade's childhood are as totally unknown today as their aforementioned "psychic" equivalents.

Inescapable, too, is the fact that these glaring material gaps have been for the most part glossed over by all of the marquis' biographers at some point or other. When, for example, did Donatien's supposed "mother deprivation" begin? How much time in the 1740s did the "absent" Marie-Eléonore actually spend away from her infant son? Did she not see him, visit with him at all, during the five or six years he is assumed to have been continually away in Provence—that is, before he was brought back to Paris at the age of nine or ten in 1749 or 1750? When did the mother and father separate permanently, and when, especially, did Marie-Eléonore retreat to an apartment in the Carmelite convent on the rue d'Enfer? Biographers have varied in their guesses on that last critically important point by as much as ten years! Was young Donatien one of the six hundred or so boarders during his school years at Louis-le-Grand (1750 –1754), or was he a day pupil? If the latter, did he live with his mother at the nearby convent apartment, or with his father at a succession of residences, or solely with his tutor the abbé Amblet in the rue des Fossés Monsieur le Prince? Did not even one small oasis of maternal affection shelter him for a time in the vast "emotional desert" that is generally presumed to have environed his childhood and early adolescence? Was he not brought back to Paris even once, perhaps for a holiday visit, in the late 1740s? Did Marie-Eléonore never travel to Avignon where her son was staying with his paternal grandmother—a woman she got along with very well—or to Ebreuil where he lived for some time with his uncle, the abbé Paul Aldonse de Sade? The abbé was Jean-Baptiste's youngest brother. He was also a libertine priest who always had a couple of willing wenches hanging about the house, a situation that did not escape the notice of his precociously alert young nephew who probably took full advantage of every furtive opportunity to observe the good life. "Is his castle a seraglio?" the nephew would later mockingly ask. "No, better still, it is a brothel."[7]

Early abandonment by the mother has been an entirely standard if extremely problematic cliché of Sadean biography. My study will provide some new evidence to show that at least during the first four years of his life—critically important developmental years in the eyes of most psychologists—the young marquis probably did enjoy the presence of a loving (if chronically ill) mother. The evidence of paternal affection or at least attention during this same time is, however, rather less clear.

Sade himself, in several pseudoautobiographical passages of his novel *Aline et Valcour* (less "pseudo," we shall see, than has frequently been thought), is chiefly responsible for starting the "psychological orphan" rumor: "Abandoned in early childhood, having lived only to suffer . . ."— such is the hero Valcour's lament to his friend Déterville in the last letter of this epistolary novel published in 1795.[8] Similarly, in real-life correspondence from his Vincennes prison cell, Sade occasionally harks back to these early years, proudly recalling his ingrained, deeply defiant nature. Strictness had never succeeded with him, and punishment would never cow his rebellious spirit: "Such is my character which has not changed even from the time I was a child—Amblet *who raised me* can vouch for the fact."[9] Ignoring here the incontrovertible fact that he was at least nine years old by the time the abbé Amblet first came on the scene,[10] the marquis suggests that his tutor, rather than his mother and father, was responsible for his primary upbringing.[11]

Clearly, far too many pieces of this intricate biographical puzzle are still missing to allow for much in the way of firm conclusions on the subject, but what we do know at least gives rise to legitimate speculation. While it is true that children in eighteenth-century aristocratic families often saw more of their wet nurses, tutors, and governesses than they did of their parents—without for all that ending up as sadists—it is not clear that Sade himself escaped suffering ill effects from such usual arrangements. We shall see that more than once in later life he complained bitterly about the entire notion of absent parents. Given the theme of violent mother hatred that runs insistently throughout his novels, and given too his undeniably pathological behavior toward women in certain circumstances, the question of his own mother's "absence" or "presence" during his early childhood must obviously be addressed.

➤

What, then, do we really know about Marie-Eléonore de Maillé de Carman, comtesse de Sade? Born in Paris in 1712, she could count among her ancestors Claire-Clémence de Maillé de Brézé, niece of Cardinal Richelieu and wife of the Great Condé. Her lineage made her something of an aristocrat's aristocrat, collaterally related to France's reigning Bourbon family through one of its most powerful branches. Indeed, her privileged pedigree, contrasting with the Maillé family's relative penury and her very modest dowry prospects, must have seemed a heavy burden when she came to weigh her chances for a good marriage. When she was sixteen and freshly out of the convent (where one of her closest friends was Marie-Anne de Nesle, the future duchesse de Châteauroux and mistress of Louis XV), her mother, the marquise de Carman, was named lady-in-waiting to the fourteen-year-old Caroline-Charlotte, princess of Hesse-Rheinfeld-Rothenburg, who was on the point of becoming the second wife of Louis-Henri, duc de Bourbon, prince de Condé. "Monsieur le Duc," as he was called, was the great-grandson of the illustrious seventeenth-century general. With his mistress Mme de Prie he had governed France as prime minister after the death of the Regent in 1723.

For Marie-Eléonore's mother, the privilege of exercising her *dame d'honneur* duties at assemblies in the vast apartments of the Hôtel de Condé or at Monsieur le Duc's magnificent château at Chantilly appears to have been a mixed blessing, and it was not long before many small but vexatious problems arose, directly related to her own hyperacute sense of belonging to the highest nobility. There is little doubt, too, that such class consciousness eventually emerged as one of her daughter's most fundamental personality traits. Elaborating and reviewing fastidiously tiny social distinctions and degrees of noble ancestry was both a solemn science and a common pastime of ancien régime blue bloods. It was also a thorny problem that constantly plagued the protocol officers of Versailles, giving rise to the many hilariously petty quarrels over precedence and ceremonial privilege that we find recorded in exquisitely monotonous detail in the pages of the duc de Luynes' court *Mémoires*.

For Marie-Eléonore's mother, the critical problem had arisen because Monsieur le Duc's teenaged wife, the duchesse de Bourbon, received numerous visitors, all distinguished, of course, but obviously few were of more distinguished birth than her own *dame d'honneur!* What was a justly proud and dignified lady-in-waiting to do? How to attend to those duties involving the presence of her social inferiors without violating her own deeply ingrained sense of high birth and the immutable fitness of things?

Even Monsieur le Duc saw the difficulty and delicacy of poor Mme de Carman's dilemma. Responding in a letter of 17 July 1729 to a dignified and spirited protest from his poor but proud cousin, this former prime minister, a leading prince of the blood and still one of the kingdom's most powerful personages, made every effort to mollify the wounded sensibilities of his wife's lady-in-waiting. He began by requesting, almost apologetically, that she continue to make the necessary sacrifice of accommodating his wife's outside visitors of "lesser distinction." It was a matter, after all, of noblesse oblige. "I know more than anyone that you are of better birth than many of the ladies who are allowed to call on Madame la Duchesse. But since you have been good enough to accept to be her lady-in-waiting, no one will attribute the attentions you show them to anything but politeness on your part, and it will always be supposed that what you do for 'Madame whoever,' is in no way done as a duty towards her." As for his young wife's cohort of palace ladies as opposed to those from "outside," Monsieur le Duc was categorical and soothing: "It goes without saying that you are to be granted precedence everywhere and at all times."[12] Marie-Eléonore, dreaming of one day succeeding her mother in these exalted functions, no doubt observed the process closely and stored it all away for future reference.

One of Monsieur le Duc's favorite hangers-on and a frequent visitor to the Hôtel de Condé was the witty roué and polished *petit-maître,* Jean-Baptiste Joseph François, comte de Sade. Born in Mazan in 1702, this scion of an old Provençal family had come up to Paris before his twentieth birthday, determined to enlarge his social horizons and succeed either in an army career or in the diplomatic service. His progress in the latter area seemed for a time most promising and even included the prospect, as he later claimed, of being sent as ambassador to St. Petersburg. It is known that a secret mission took him to England at one point, for we find him on

12 May 1730 in London at the Horn Tavern in Westminster being initiated by the Duke of Norfolk into the Society of Freemasons, along with the celebrated writer Montesquieu.[13] The author of the *Lettres persanes* was thirteen years Jean-Baptiste's senior, but the two men had already shared a certain number of common experiences in the fashionable circles of Paris, including, possibly, liaisons with one or two Condé princesses. In fact, almost immediately after its anonymous publication in 1725, Montesquieu's second notable literary work, the *Temple de Gnide,* was recognized by the capital's cognoscenti as an allegorical representation of life at Chantilly. To the author's delight, it was even much praised (after some hesitation) by Monsieur le Duc himself, who probably was aware that his sister, Mlle de Clermont, a great beauty of the day, had almost certainly inspired the work's discreetly erotic representations of courtly goings-on, confirming for many the suspicion that she had already rewarded the fortunate Montesquieu with her favors. Jean-Baptiste, for his part, had little affection for the celebrated Bordeaux writer who, despite the opposition of Cardinal Fleury, Monsieur le Duc's successor as prime minister, had somehow managed to get himself elected to the Académie Française. In matters of trivial literary composition, the young comte de Sade, though undeniably talented, clearly lacked the *gravitas* and scholarly focus of his rival. Though he too had his literary ambitions, such pinnacles of good fortune as membership in the French Academy would forever elude him, and only after many bitter years of frustration in various areas of endeavor did Jean-Baptiste de Sade finally succeed in resolving the problem of chronic career failure by drastically lowering his expectations, or at least by assuring everyone that the world's honors and baubles were of no interest to a man as truly worthy as he. Meanwhile, he played to perfection the role of a modest and unobtrusive courtier, reputedly the best informed and wittiest of antechamber gossips and a past master at teaching the intricacies of the quadrille to the daughters of the great. His greatest ambition of all was to seduce as many high-ranking ladies of the court as possible, but here too he refused to confine himself to such single-minded revelries, displaying as well—though very privately—equal virtuosity as a bisexual. There is every probability that his versatility in this regard initially served him well in gaining crucial diplomatic career contacts with such powerful kindred spirits as the future cardinal Henri-Oswald de La Tour d'Auvergne, archbishop of Vienna, and other senior diplomats like Anne-Théodore de Chavigny.[14] Interestingly, his chief patron, Monsieur le Duc, was also known for his occasional experimentation along similarly unorthodox lines.

Such variant behavior on Jean-Baptiste's part was not, however, without some danger, and more than one police report of the day illustrates the extent to which he seemed prepared to risk arrest by the sodomy patrol while engaged in low-life soliciting in the public gardens of Paris or even in the more direct purchase of a male prostitute's services. One incident that took place in the Tuileries Gardens on 9 September 1724 when he was residing at the Hôtel de Bretagne on the rue de Seine shows a degree of involvement in active homosexuality that goes well beyond, I think, what Maurice Lever has characterized as representing little more than an "aristocratic caprice" evincing the comte's desire to escape "the monotony of common eroticism" by playing a kind of game "made more exciting because it was forbidden." [15] On the day in question, Jean-Baptiste, repeating an offer he had already extended at the same location several days earlier to the same person, expressed a keen inclination to "put it" to a young stroller behind some bushes in a quiet corner of the gardens. To his dismay, he discovered that the attractive youth was a police decoy! His offer, moreover, had apparently been prefaced with the usual "infamous remarks," the sodomy squad's euphemism for such standard soliciting code phrases of the day as "Are you of a mind to?" "Is it good and hard?" and "Is it a truly big one?" Jean-Baptiste had also informed the young man that although he had only shortly before been masturbated by another obliging stranger, he was yet of a mind to take him to his nearby rooms to spend the night were it not that he wished to hide his inclinations from his servants. It was at that point in the encounter that the decoy signaled to officer-of-the-watch Haymier, who was waiting in ambush close by. On learning that the *infâme* he had just arrested was a nobleman—indeed, one who claimed to be a relative of "Mme la duchesse de la Roche-Guyon"—Haymier released the twenty-two-year-old count on the understanding that he was to turn up as required before the magistrate. By coincidence, only three days earlier, one of Jean-Baptiste's future in-laws, the marquis de Maillé, a colonel in Monsieur le Duc's cavalry regiment, had accosted the same decoy but had (all the while attempting to insert his hand into the young man's breeches) made it clear that "his sole pleasure was in diddling thus, and that he did not like *putting it*." [16]

Jean-Baptiste's commitment to "the philosophical sin," as it was called in more elegant settings, obviously went well beyond the tentative experimentation of the fashionable young noblemen at the court who, around this time, were known to have indulged in some of the more preliminary exercises of the sport with the teenaged Louis XV. Indeed, according to the marquis d'Argenson, it was because of Cardinal Fleury's determination to "shame" his royal master onto the heterosexual straight and narrow that the infamous Deschauffours was burned at the stake in the Place de Grève on 24 May 1726. [17] On the other hand, Jean-Baptiste de Sade's anomalous penchants, though well documented, were certainly far less adventuresome than the later singularities of his celebrated son. Moreover, although his homosexual exploits continued to be the subject of police interest for more than twenty-five years after the Tuileries incident,[18] they clearly never distracted him in any permanent sense from his lifetime preoccupation with high-style heterosexual seduction and the unremitting hunt for "*bonnes fortunes*," as he liked to call his many feminine conquests.

It was about five years after Monsieur le Duc's second marriage—in 1728[19] to his child-bride German princess—that Jean-Baptiste, having already bedded a goodly number of his patron's distinguished relatives, set his sights on Caroline-Charlotte, Monsieur le Duc's much neglected young wife. The enterprise was not without its political and personal risks. Though he had but one eye—the result of an old hunting accident—Monsieur le Duc was far from blind. He was also extremely jealous (though he himself kept a mistress) and took great precautions to isolate his bride from contact with other men.

In a fascinating autobiographical fragment recently brought to light by Maurice Lever, Jean-Baptiste relates with much brio and candor how he nevertheless succeeded in carrying out his daring conquest.[20] To achieve his end, he hit upon the scheme of proposing marriage to Marie-Eléonore de Maillé de Carman, the daughter of Caroline-Charlotte's (alas, recently dismissed) lady-in-waiting. He had, of course, weighed the fact that Marie-Eléonore, now twenty-one, was without fortune. Admittedly, as a "career move" it would involve considerable risk, a personal sacrifice, even. On the other hand, she was attractive enough, and marriage to this fresh and innocent Condé cousin would advantageously ally his less distinguished provincial title with the junior branch of the reigning Bourbons and the princes of the blood. Eagerly conspiring in the scheme, Caroline-Charlotte, not yet twenty, successfully persuaded her unwitting husband to look favorably on the proposed marriage of his proud and pretty cousin to the gallant cavalry captain. Every detail of the would-be lovers' adulterous conspiracy was worked out to perfection. Monsieur le Duc could certainly be counted on to accept his wife's supplementary suggestion that, once married, Marie-Eléonore should be appointed Caroline-Charlotte's *dame de compagnie* to replace her mother; it would be a fine wedding present. Naturally, as the official lady-in-waiting, the young comtesse de Sade, along with her husband, would have to occupy an apartment in the palace very near that of the princess. There was a back stairway through which Jean-Baptiste could gain secret access to Caroline-Charlotte's wardrobe closet and "potty" room, a perfect trysting place! Only the wardrobe maid would be in on the secret. Of course, Jean-Baptiste at the same time made a special point of assuring Monsieur le Duc that this marriage to a woman of distinguished lineage but, alas, of so little wealth (yes, it would be quite a sacrifice!) was chiefly intended as a mark of his personal fealty and allegiance to his dear patron. In return for this lie, the enterprising comte de Sade received from Monsieur le Duc what turned out to be an equally fraudulent promise of a colonel's rank in his very own cavalry regiment.

Everything went as planned. Voltaire, one of Jean-Baptiste's many social acquaintances, sent his anticipatory congratulations in the form of a poem that hailed the young libertine's good luck on acquiring with one stroke both a "novice beauty" and brilliant career prospects in the military.[21] The marriage was celebrated on 13 November 1733. Monsieur le Duc now stayed only rarely at the Hôtel de Condé but journeyed in from Chantilly to do the honors, and it was Caroline-Charlotte herself who ceremoniously conducted the shy young bride to the marriage bed.

Jean-Baptiste narrates the scene with obvious relish: There he was, already waiting between the sheets when his innocent young bride, trembling with emotion, was brought to him, still clinging to the reassuring hand of her mistress and begging the princess not to leave her. At that very moment, he suddenly experienced an extraordinary surge of erotic rapture, the thrill of a multiple-partner fantasy! His young wife was beautiful enough, of course, but the presence of the princess added so much to his excitement that he proceeded rather more hurriedly and eagerly than he would have had she not been there just before.[22] Best of all, very soon after that, the princess made good on her promise and granted him what the age was pleased to designate as "the ultimate favor." According to Jean-Baptiste, Monsieur le Duc's young wife cuckolded her one-eyed husband with extraordinary ardor, appetite, and enthusiasm.

All precautions were taken to hide the affair, but unfortunately for Jean-Baptiste, Marie-Eléonore soon discovered the guilty lovers' secret. "There is nothing that a jealous woman cannot find out!" the comte noted with philosophical resignation years later. Marie-Eléonore did not confront her husband. She suffered deeply and in silence. One day in his presence she sadly exclaimed that it was her misfortune to love and not be loved in return. Jean-Baptiste solemnly reassured her, protesting his innocence—and carried on merrily with the affair. At the same time, he kept a sharp eye out for any additional *bonnes fortunes* that chance might steer his way.

But soon it was the princess's turn to be jealous. During a friendly probing conversation with her new lady-in-waiting, Caroline-Charlotte learned from the still naive and unsuspecting Marie-Eléonore a number of intimate details about the wedding night. As she listened, the princess grew pensive, then more and more irritated. From Marie-Eléonore's unwary account, she concluded that Jean-Baptiste had displayed with his wife on that occasion a remarkable versatility and a variety of imaginative techniques that she was fairly certain he had not been thoughtful enough to share with her during their own lovemaking. She tearfully confronted her lover on the subject and was only partly reassured when Jean-Baptiste, roaring with laughter, pointed out that Marie-Eléonore had been such an inexperienced ninny on her first night, that she was simply incapable of recognizing what was either usual or innovative in matters of sexual intercourse. Mollified but not entirely convinced, Caroline-Charlotte made Jean-Baptiste promise that he would sleep "less regularly" with his wife and even that he would henceforth remove himself to a separate bedroom. Jean-Baptiste promised and obeyed.

As time passed, Marie-Eléonore, "in a frightful state of hurt and sorrow," continued to say nothing, fulfilling her conjugal duties when called on, but the magical love marriage was now dead for her. "From that day onward," regretfully noted the comte many years later (*regretfully*, but he continued to pride himself on his inconstancy[23]), "her friendship, which would have given me more happiness than all of my *bonnes fortunes*, was entirely lost to me."[24] In fact, Jean-Baptiste and his fine mistress were fortunate that only Marie-Eléonore had learned of the affair. Six years later the pretty princess, who was apparently endowed with an unusually healthy sexual appetite (we have Jean-Baptiste's expert opinion on this), became involved in an even riskier secret liaison, this time with the young marquis de Bissy (already colonel of his regiment while Jean-Baptiste continued to cool his heels as a captain). Unfortunately for Caroline-Charlotte, this time Monsieur le Duc had his newest pair of antlers awkwardly pointed out to him by one of his valets, who was encouraged to tattle, according to the usually reliable testimony of the marquis d'Argenson, by the now supplanted and dangerously compromised comte de Sade! Fearing the worst, Louis XV immediately ordered de Bissy back to his regiment, pointedly at a time when all the other colonels were being allowed to continue enjoying the comforts of the capital.[25] The injured husband, meanwhile, gave orders to have the back stairway sealed off and the princess moved to an apartment with barred windows. The possibility that even more dangerous consequences would result from Monsieur le Duc's wrath (in the process of extracting a confession, he had threatened to hang the complicitous wardrobe maid) became a matter of worried speculation and concern well beyond the private enclosures of the Hôtel de Condé: "There is grave danger," d'Argenson noted in his journal, "that this pretty princess will be shut up in some dreadful castle for as long as her husband lives."[26]

Marie-Eléonore's silent, seemingly almost numb reaction to her husband's infidelities reveals yet another fundamental trait in her character. Though she was deeply saddened and humiliated, her pride and sense of dignity were such that she continued to keep the hurt to herself. The entire Hôtel de Condé seemed to be disintegrating before her eyes. The Condé family's political fortunes had been on the wane already for a number of years, and the place was turning into a veritable zoo of crapulous behavior, domestic vendettas, and sundry madness. She herself clearly had no taste for the overt libertinism of these *royals*—the notorious "Clermonts" and "Charolais," male and female, who carried on in this vast palace where her own charmingly handsome and wittily false Jean-Baptiste amused himself alternately with sodomizing the kitchen staff and dazzling the mistress of the house with his sexual sophistication. Her solution was to soldier on with her official duties, keeping up appearances and protecting what really mattered most to her: family honor. Already driven by Jean-Baptiste's defection into a kind of psychological withdrawal, she was determined nevertheless to play out her assigned role and to accomplish that double duty expected of her as a nobleman's wife—namely, producing a male heir, the recognized primary goal of marriage among the great, and advancing her husband's diplomatic or military career. Later, ground down by chronic illness, her brood mare functions completed, she would be allowed to retire physically and emotionally to a convent retreat, leaving her dissolute husband to pursue his dissolute ways. She could not have guessed, of course, that the gravest injuries to family honor were yet to come and that they would arise not from the actions of her libertine husband but from horrendous scandals that would shock the nation, generated by the behavior of her even more dissolute son.

Two

A DIPLOMAT AND HIS WIFE

Marie-Eléonore, by all indications, took her family duties and marriage loyalties very seriously, and she worried herself sick when, scarcely six months after the wedding, Jean-Baptiste had to leave for his regiment then involved in the siege of Philippsburg on the Rhine, one of the significant battles in the dragged-out War of the Polish Succession, which his distinguished companion in arms (and fellow libertine) Maurice de Saxe later described as "too short."[1] Even with such highly placed friends, Jean-Baptiste soon discovered that his marriage was unlikely to bring him the brilliant military career he had hoped for. Monsieur le Duc had not followed through on his promise of a regimental command, and, equally frustrating, yet another of his powerful protectors, the foreign affairs minister Chauvelin, had recently sent the disappointing news that he had been unable to obtain for him a much coveted commission as *guidon* in the corps of Gendarmes. The rank of *guidon* was not quite the equivalent of Monsieur le Duc's promised colonelship, but it would at least have made him a member of Louis XV's senior officer class.[2] In fact, Marie-Eléonore's husband, a mere captain of dragoons when she married him, was destined to remain a captain of dragoons for the rest of his active military career, a situation that was not substantively changed by his acquiring in 1738, at enormous personal expense—involving the investment of 135,000 livres—the honorary title of lieutenant général de Bresse, Bugey, Valromey, and Gex.

Preoccupied with such matters, Jean-Baptiste seems to have been strangely indifferent to Marie-Eléonore's personal worries about his safety in battle. He regularly neglected to write home. Even his brother the abbé, two days after the French victory at Philippsburg in July 1734, chided him on the subject: "Mme de Sade writes me that she is frantic. You ought to set her mind at ease by writing more often."[3] Back in Avignon, Jean-Baptiste's mother was also worried. Another of her three sons, the chevalier, was at the time risking even greater dangers with the French army in Italy, and she was concerned too about other family matters. It was time to think of the next generation. She hoped that Jean-Baptiste, her eldest, would soon return to Paris: "It is only natural," she wrote to her daughter-in-law on 2 October 1734, "to want him to be employed this winter in giving me heirs. [. . .] I have been writing to urge him to apply for leave, but all to no avail."[4]

Producing that proper male heir was to take, however, a little longer than expected. Marie-Eléonore's first child, a daughter, was born in 1737 and died two years later but not before being baptized with the name Caroline-Laure, no doubt to honor in part the de Sades' legendary ancestor of Petrarchian fame, the beautiful Laure de Noves, but also to reflect Marie-Eléonore's continuing sense of loyalty toward her mistress despite what had gone on between Caroline-Charlotte and Jean-Baptiste in the wardrobe maid's closet. Now a mother herself, the princess had happily agreed to be the baby girl's godmother, and Monsieur le Duc obligingly stood as godfather. Finally, on 2 June 1740, the prayers of all were answered with the birth of Donatien Alphonse François. A third and last child, another girl, was born 13 August 1746 and survived only five days.

Meanwhile, Jean-Baptiste's alternate career aspirations in the diplomatic service were not forgotten. In 1737, another of his current patrons, Amelot de Chaillou, himself protected by the powerful minister de Maurepas, was named to succeed Chauvelin as minister of foreign affairs. After winning a few minor diplomatic assignments, Jean-Baptiste's big opportunity came in 1741 with his appointment as *ministre plénipotentiaire* at the court of the elector of Cologne. It was not the ambassadorship he had been hoping for, but Cardinal Fleury himself tried to soothe the comte's anxieties by pointing out that "one has to start somewhere," promising to take better care of Jean-Baptiste's fortunes when the right moment came. The promise, coming as it did from a nearly ninety-year-old prime minister who was not long for this world, was obviously less than reassuring. Unfortunately, that "right moment" never came, and Marie-Eléonore, once so ambitious for the advancement and honor of her family, so confident that her handsome and clever spouse possessed all the qualifications needed to succeed, was eventually forced to the conclusion that Jean-Baptiste was really no better at being a diplomat than he was at playing the role of husband. But the time for that dismal conclusion would not come for a few years yet.

On learning of Jean-Baptiste's appointment to the elector's court at Bonn, the marquis d'Argenson, who several years later would himself supplant a disgraced Amelot as foreign minister, expressed serious doubts about the wisdom of naming the comte de Sade to such a strategic posting. The new envoy was yet another of those Versailles-haunting *"petits-maîtres,"* a typical courtly coxcomb possessing "some wit but little substance."[5] French national interests in the German states deserved more competent management.

Although events would eventually prove d'Argenson right, the comte was initially a great success in Bonn. He managed in his usual manner to charm the elector, Clement-Augustus, at the same time as he displayed great skill in countering the rival political machinations of the elector's anti-French and pro-Austrian ministers. The German political scene had become increasingly unstable since the death of the Emperor Charles VI in October 1740. Jean-Baptiste's mission, defined in February of the following year, was to ensure that in the matter of succession the elector would support the candidacy of his brother elector, Charles-Albert of Bavaria, rather than vote for Austrian interests and the husband of Maria Theresa.[6] In that regard all went well, and the new emperor was crowned Charles VII in February 1742. As for Clement-Augustus, archbishop-elector of Cologne, Jean-Baptiste found him to be very much a man after his own heart, especially since he did not allow the fact that he was an archbishop to interfere with his addiction to gambling, wenching, ceremonial balls, theater, and other gracious social entertainments. Unfortunately, he was also somewhat unstable and capricious.

Louis XV's new *ministre plénipotentiaire* was not quite an ambassador and lacked an ambassador's budget, but he was determined from the beginning to entertain in a style that few ambassadors could afford, thus making a big impression not only on the elector and members of his court but also on the senior officers of the French army encamped nearby and all the distinguished visitors from Paris who happened to turn up in Bonn. Such extravagance—well beyond Jean-Baptiste's means—was interpreted by Clement-Augustus as the sincerest proof of personal trust and friendship, and he was more than pleased to return the compliment. As for persuading Clement-Augustus to conform to Versailles' diplomatic requests, Jean-Baptiste found that he had only to ask and his every whim was immediately satisfied: "I am in great favor here; the Elector showers me with kindnesses," he informed his superiors in the ministry. Occasionally, France's plenipotentiary and His Serene Highness would even embrace, Jean-Baptiste beginning, it seems, by clasping His Serene Highness's knees. Then they would shed tears of joy, and His Serene Highness would insist on lavishing gifts. Did the dear comte de Sade have any personal favors to ask? His wife's younger brother? Why, of course! The worthy chevalier de Maillé would be most welcome to come and join his marvelous brother-in-law in Bonn. Yes, His Serene Highness would be more than pleased to grant the young man a nominal position in his court, and when it was time for him to return to Paris, there would be a parting gift of three thousand livres, all for the dear chevalier. And was the French prime minister, cardinal Fleury, really that anxious to have His Serene Highness's pro-Vienna minister Stephné out of the way? It would be done at once! "I had only to speak," Jean-Baptiste boasts in his report to Amelot. "He leaves for Manheim tomorrow. And if removing him from Bonn is not enough, I shall see to it that he is ruined as well!"[7] So pleased, indeed, was Clement-Augustus with his French envoy that he even offered to ask Louis XV to allow the good comte de Sade to remain at the court in Bonn *forever.* Jean-Baptiste inwardly shuddered at the thought but pretended to be ecstatic. What a delightful prospect, indeed! Regrettably, much as he wanted to stay—yes, *forever*—he would one day have to return to his dear family.

In truth, Jean-Baptiste had much more ambitious plans. He was building for the future, and that future did not include the provincial tedium of Bonn.

A newly discovered letter written to Jean-Baptiste by one of his distinguished French visitors, François Poisson, throws some light on the wider ambitions of Marie-Eléonore's husband and the extent to which he had become a roaring social success during his first year in Bonn. It also shows him well on his way, finally, to building up a broad power base back in Paris. Great things could be in store, his correspondent hinted, for the comte de Sade. Princes, foreign ambassadors, the richest financiers in the French capital were singing his praises:

> *Paris, Sunday morning*
> *26 November 1741*
>
> Dear Sir,
>   To begin with, a fine compliment: your ears must be ringing for I speak endlessly of you. You may very well retort that I should mind my own business but it would be wrong of you since my business is to speak both my heartfelt sentiments and the truth. I dined the day before yesterday at the home of monsieur Pâris de Montmartel in the company of three Condés or, rather, three members of the House of Condé. Yesterday, I dined with the prince of Grimberghen and others at the home of monsieur Lenormant de Tournehem. We spoke only of you, Dear Sir, of your kindnesses and generosity toward all the many French visitors who constantly invade your household in Bonn. When I had finished reciting my entire litany on that subject, along with my thoughts and my predictions, everyone was of the opinion that I was right and that you should be supported. All of which goes to show that I am not wrong. It is my consolation. [. . .][8]

The letter goes on in that cordial vein, and we see Jean-Baptiste strategically poised on the very threshold of success, having gained the confidence of France's most powerful financial cartel whose rule would soon be made all the more secure by the triumphant accession of their "daughter" to the royal bedchamber at Versailles, it being the case that each of the three financiers—Jean Pâris de Montmartel, François Poisson, and Charles-François Lenormant de Tournehem—could with equal verisimilitude and probability claim to have fathered Jeanne-Antoinette Poisson, future marquise de Pompadour. As for her "public papa," François Poisson, he had, in fact, recently been in Bonn on a government mission. The elector had given him a treasured portrait of himself and invited him to attend the February 1742 coronation of his brother as emperor. Jean-Baptiste had made all the arrangements. Poisson makes it clear in the letter that such efforts were much appreciated and would never be forgotten. The comte de Sade was also to understand that the powerful *fermier général,* Lenormant, "desires greatly to make your acquaintance and to drink a toast with you, as does Pâris de Montmartel whom you should choose as your banker—*and that for reasons known to me.*" It was the strongest of hints. What more could an ambitious diplomat of modest means ask? Jean-Baptiste had, in fact, just been given a golden invitation to seek renown and riches by the very persons who, with a simple stroke of the pen, could grant his every wish.

One last remark in François Poisson's letter reveals that Marie-Eléonore had also played an important part in providing the marvelous hospitality enjoyed by the well-connected visitor to Bonn. He closes his letter by asking Jean-Baptiste to pass on his compliments to his dear wife the comtesse and to remind her that her new friends back in Paris were most anxious to know whether they could be of any service to her in the capital.

Marie-Eléonore's arrival in Bonn in the early fall of 1741 had not come about in the happiest of circumstances. Monsieur le Duc had died rather suddenly on 27 January 1740, leaving a severely ailing though much relieved young widow and a son, the four-year-old prince de Condé, Louis-Joseph de Bourbon. Few at the Hôtel de Condé mourned the duc's passing, mainly, it seems, because of the huge fuss he had made at the time of the Bissy affair—as if, the lawyer Barbier dryly observed, some kind of law exempted great princes from being cuckolded![9] In his own journal, d'Argenson notes that there was speculation at the time that *la petite duchesse,* as the princess was called (Monsieur le Duc's mother being still alive), would become Louis XV's new mistress,[10] but Barbier's diary entry concentrates on the disturbing rumor that Caroline-Charlotte's illness was widely thought to be of suspicious origins. Could it be that agents of Monsieur le Duc had been assigned to carry out his plan of vengeance from beyond the grave? Gossipy accusations became indeed so common that immediately after the princess's death on 14 June 1741, an autopsy was performed in the presence of a dozen physicians, "because of the unpleasant rumors that had been circulating about her on account of Monsieur le Duc."[11] The results, however, proved disappointing for the rumormongers: the beautiful twenty-six-year-old princess had succumbed, in fact, not to poison but to the lingering aftereffects of childbirth. Her brother-in-law, the comte de Charolais, named guardian of the orphaned prince, had been Caroline-Charlotte's staunchest defender during the time of her greatest troubles with her husband, and he now insisted that her death be marked by all the trappings and ceremony of a royal funeral. Awkwardly, the great magistrates of the Parlement of Paris—required by protocol to attend the holy water ceremony as a body rather than as individuals—refused to make the necessary collective gesture. Charolais, notorious for his savage temper as well as his vices, threatened dire consequences. Finally, to settle matters, Louis XV issued a *lettre de cachet* ordering members of the nation's highest court to obey. The Parlement grudgingly complied on 23 June, and members of all the other judicial courts immediately followed suit. The next day, the Feast of Saint John the Baptist, a gigantic evening procession of heralds, mounted officers, more than three hundred torch-bearing attendants, and dozens of carriages drawn by horses decorated in silver-trimmed black velvet, solemnly made its way along the rue Saint-Jacques to the convent of the Carmelites where the body of the princess was finally laid to rest.[12] Marie-Eléonore was, of course, among the mourners in attendance. Perhaps she decided at some point during the doleful ceremony that this same Carmelite convent would one day be her own place of retreat, should it ever become necessary for her to withdraw from the world.

With the untimely death of her mistress, Marie-Eléonore had lost her most important ally at the Hôtel de Condé. Her friendship with the princess had grown very close over the years despite the initial awkwardness of the younger woman's adulterous affair with Jean-Baptiste. As proof of her own deep affection for her loyal *dame de compagnie*, Caroline-Charlotte at her death left Marie-Eléonore a special bequest of diamond jewelry.[13]

Materially, Caroline-Charlotte's passing was a catastrophe for the de Sade couple: Marie-Eléonore's official position at the Hôtel de Condé had provided the security of free board and lodging for herself and her son, a clothing allowance, plus a generous annual stipend of three thousand livres.[14] Fortunately, as a loyal companion to the late princess, she was viewed with favor by the comte de Charolais and given permission for the moment at least to go on living there, helping out with the young prince de Condé's upbringing. The atmosphere was nevertheless heavy with tension and conflict and the situation quite uncomfortable. The unpredictably ferocious Charolais stormed about, dismissing right and left many of the old attendants as well as dozens of hangers-on and what he liked to call the "putrefying remains" of Monsieur le Duc's era. Vindication of the dead princess's memory was only part of Charolais' motivation; he was also engaged in a violent feud with his mother, the dowager duchesse, the person whom he most hated in the world. . . .

In Bonn, the news of Caroline-Charlotte's death came as a severe shock to Jean-Baptiste, but it was not sentiment for an old mistress that was uppermost in his mind. All he could really think of now was the monetary loss and the inevitable impairment of his long-established Hôtel de Condé connections. It was just one more item to add to what he saw as an accumulating pile of bitter disappointments. Marrying the penniless Marie-Eléonore had been a high price to pay for a bit of furtive slap and tickle amid the commodes in the wardrobe maid's quarters. And then there were all those empty promises by the late Monsieur le Duc. His immediate reaction on hearing the news was less than gracious: "The death of Mme la Duchesse is an enormous bother to me," he complained in a letter to his superiors in Paris. *"Here am I, encumbered now with a wife!"* [15] He would need more money if he had to support Marie-Eléonore and bring her to Bonn. And could not Monsieur le Cardinal at the same time add a little something for his brother the abbé who was also a heavy burden on his budget? In response, Fleury obligingly increased Jean-Baptiste's stipend by the same amount—three thousand livres—that Marie-Eléonore had just lost in salary. He also assigned a small benefice pension worth two thousand livres to the playboy abbé, not quite enough to suit Jean-Baptiste, but Fleury insisted that he wanted to see some evidence of improvement in the abbé's notoriously loose morals—at the time frequently on display in the capital—before he committed even more of Heaven's largesse to the cause.

And so it was that one day in the autumn of 1741, Marie-Eléonore packed all her winter clothes and, probably leaving her sixteen-month-old son behind with a nurse at the Hôtel de Condé, set out to join her husband in Bonn. Jean-Baptiste was less than enchanted by the prospect of seeing his wife appear on the scene. Access to his "lucky conquests" had been plentiful in Bonn, and, apart from adding directly to his expenses, her presence would undoubtedly cramp his style somewhat with the ladies. Of course, the still attractive Marie-Eléonore could also prove useful to him; she got on well with people and would almost certainly add much-needed distinction to the elector's court. She could also help him entertain visitors from Paris and especially the wives of those senior French officers who wanted to brighten up the sedately Teutonic gloom of the place with dancing, fashionable *promenades,* and other social activities that, it was generally agreed, could be animated in that superior manner only by those familiar with the refinements of the French court. As soon as Marie-Eléonore arrived, Jean-Baptiste made it a point of vanity to show her off, sparing no expense, much as when he used to make all the husbands (and some of the wives) in their Hôtel de Condé circle furious by the way he would practically ruin himself "so that she could put on a finer display than the others." [16] Ostentation was important and Jean-Baptiste's basic rule in human relations had always been to place style above substance, *paraître* before *être*. All the same, he resented his wife's presence, the physical cost, the personal intrusion. . . . To make matters worse, he was experiencing occasional bouts of ill health, and things were starting to go less smoothly with the elector, who, though he was still convivial most of the time, was sometimes extremely fickle and moody. On top of all that, Jean-Baptiste was having trouble with his staff. To his embarrassment, he had been forced to dismiss one of his secretaries, the nephew, unfortunately, of a good friend in Paris, on the grounds of laziness and incompetence. That left him with a twenty-year-old substitute, Henry Baumez, an irritatingly affectionate little show-off, originally from Montpellier, irrepressibly bright and impertinent, who kept demonstrating to his master that he did not know his proper place.

Much of the time during that winter of 1741–1742, Jean-Baptiste was extremely bad tempered with Marie-Eléonore. Nearly everything she did seemed to irritate him. When spring came, he insisted that she return without delay to the Hôtel de Condé in Paris. She pleaded to stay on. In her role as wife and hostess had she not been helpful to him in his delicate negotiations? Everyone had been so kind and welcoming toward her, including the elector. She had made so many good friends. But it was all to no avail; Jean-Baptiste refused to budge. When she finally did leave, in early June 1742, he was scarcely speaking to her.

The following two letters written by Marie-Eléonore after her return to Paris to Henry Baumez in Bonn have only recently come to light. They are set apart here because they add considerably to the small stock of her known correspondence and provide some of the most significant information discovered so far concerning this "mysterious mother" of the marquis de Sade. In some respects, they also throw a quite different light on the marquis' father, revealing a much more petty and mean-spirited man than has been hitherto suspected. Best of all, one of these precious letters yields up the only absolutely certain information that has surfaced to date concerning the marquis' early childhood, including probably the first formally recorded words of the future author of *Les 120 journées de Sodome*. In this last regard, the letters, valuable in themselves, also provide much-needed hard evidence, entirely lacking until now, that authenticates one of the most frequently—and speculatively—quoted "autobiographical" passages in Sade's novel, *Aline et Valcour.*

The first of Marie-Eléonore's letters to Baumez, written about five weeks after she arrived back at the Hôtel de Condé, is filled with concern about Jean-Baptiste's health. He has still not written, and she is worried. Significantly, he has been writing to his brother the abbé who is residing in Paris at the time and diligently ministering to both the spiritual and other needs of various distinguished and less than distinguished ladies of the town.[17] It is clear from several references in her letter that Jean-Baptiste's bad temper and sullen uncommunicativeness continued to be a problem even weeks after her departure from Bonn and that now, left to fend for herself, Marie-Eléonore was in fairly difficult financial straits:

Paris, 7 August 1742

I am worried by what you tell me of M. de Sade's illness. He has sent me no news of himself and so I am especially obliged to you. Has he not taken the waters? I urge you to take good care of him always and to let me have news of him regularly. I have not answered all of your letters because of the great cost of the post. The abbé has not mentioned receiving anything from you. M. le maréchal de Maillebois wrote to me that M. de Sade would be returning to Paris at any moment but there is no talk of that here. For the sake of his health I wish indeed that he were here. I very much fear that the air there is not good for him. He should write and tell me if he wishes me to speak to M. Amelot for I am most anxious about him.

I quite expected that my packing cases would not arrive in good time. I pray Heaven they get here safely. Unless proper precautions were taken, I very much fear they will have been opened; if so, my poor garments will all be ruined and I cannot afford to buy others.

Tell M. de Sade that I sold my coach as well as his berlin, both of which were falling into ruin, to a saddler who, most reluctantly, allowed me eight hundred francs for the two. He did not, in fact, want them at any price but did it to please M. d'Auteuil in the hope of receiving an order from him for a new coach for M. le prince de Condé. M. d'Auteuil advised me to keep the two small horses for myself and to sell the other two for which I have been offered only one hundred *écus.* I shall give that sum as well to the saddler, making a total of eleven hundred francs, enough for a berlin that is well upholstered and almost new. It will be there for M. de Sade to make use of when he returns but there is still another seven hundred francs to pay. According to everyone I have consulted on the matter, the transaction was not a bad one since both of the vehicles I sold were truly decrepit and falling apart. I do not know whether M. le comte will approve of what I have done. I doubt it for he does not always approve of what I do and that vexes me greatly since I am always trying to do my best in all things. Please convey to him my most tender sentiments and send me news of his health.

Tell him that my son thrashed M. le prince de Condé and took away all of his toys, shouting all the while, *Out of there, you child, you!* For all that I have tried, I have never been able to make him call the prince anything else. [. . .] [18]

There before our eyes our first image of the little marquis and his first recorded words! Until now, the capricious gods of the archives have refused to surrender anything earlier than 1753—eleven years later—when we hear Donatien's sentiments being directly quoted by his father's mistress, Mme de Longeville, so delighted that her lover's thirteen-year-old son has so readily accepted her as a *seconde maman*. By then, the austerely proud and loving Marie-Eléonore had become a hated *mère obstacle* in the confused psyche of the adolescent marquis, now totally a creature of his doting father's manipulations.

An eleven-year gap—how one would like to fill in the interval with more such letters! Barely out of his infancy, at a mere two years and two months of age, the little marquis already seems to be acting out the characteristically belligerent, larger-than-life scenarios of his later years. His pugilistic triumph over the prince de Condé, a solemn boy, unusually tall for his age, who would be celebrating his sixth birthday just two days later,[19] was destined to become an important family and personal legend, enshrined in an anecdote that was probably repeated to him many times by his mother. She relates the story here with obvious relish and certainly with more pride than distress. Even grumpy Jean-Baptiste must have been amused. *Her* son, her golden-haired, blue-eyed son, so winningly audacious with his baby talk, so adamant, had made a great show of "character," had cowed and bullyragged the lord of the castle, a prince of the blood, no less, who, the following Sunday, was to be officially presented to the king at Versailles! "My son . . .": Sade's biographers have become too used to imagining the mother speaking lines assigned to a quite different character, but there is no "distant, indifferent and absent" mother to be heard here. In later years, the marquis would recall the incident—or at least the oft-told family anecdote that scarcely embroidered it—as something that had always formed an integral part of his self-image, satisfying proof that right from the beginning he had been his own man, "the freest spirit who ever lived," a force of nature, intransigent, adamant, incorrigible—"this creature who cannot be controlled," in the despairing words of the Bastille's governor in 1789. Of course, by the time the marquis included the story in *Aline et Valcour,* the political landscape had changed radically. The Revolution was in its sixth year, and his youthful victory over a six-year-old prince of the blood was opportunistically adapted to the current *sans-culottes* mode by the simple insertion of a patriotically fierce republican variant. The original source—a defining moment in the life of the marquis de Sade—nevertheless remains unmistakably recognizable:

> Born and brought up in the palace of the illustrious prince to whom my mother had the honor of being connected and who was about my age, I became the object of zealous efforts to link us together so that being known to him from childhood I would be able to enjoy his protection throughout my lifetime. But my vanity of the moment which as yet understood nothing of this calculation took offence one day when, during our childish games, he attempted to take something of mine, and even more because he no doubt thought his many illustrious titles and his exalted rank gave him leave to do so. I retaliated with many repeated blows, paying no heed to any other considerations, stopping only when force and violence were employed to separate me from my adversary.[20]

Marie-Eléonore goes on with her letter to Baumez, asking him to pass on her fond greetings to her brother and to all those "ladies and gentlemen of Bonn," especially her good friend Mlle Nothaft. Then she signs off with the greatest simplicity: "Votre servante, Maillé de Sade."

Three weeks later, Baumez received another letter from this woman whose voice and intimate sentiments have eluded us these many years. She has had one curt communication from Jean-Baptiste in the interval but nothing reassuring on the subject of his health and no acknowledgment of her news about happenings at the Hôtel de Condé. Her relationship with Jean-Baptiste's mother is revealed to be still very close, a continuing link that was to prove especially important when, in less than two years, illness and probably pressure from her husband would persuade her to allow Donatien to be shipped off for a time to Avignon to live with his grandmother. But this second letter also shows even more plainly the continuing deterioration of the marriage. Jean-Baptiste, still surly and uncommunicative, has not responded concerning any of the matters she has raised. Worse still, behind her back, he has complained peevishly about her to his brother, telling the abbé how furious he is with her for spending money on a coach. As if she had spent the money for herself alone! When he returned to Paris (soon, she hoped), would he not need it himself to get about decently? Meanwhile, did he really expect her to go about on foot? She cannot imagine what she has done to put him in such a constantly sour mood; he is forever finding fault with her and it is all so strange. . . . She has almost no money to take care of the day-to-day necessities. Her baggage has still not arrived. If her winter clothes have indeed been lost in transit from Bonn, she will be unable to afford the cost of replacing them, and it will be just like the year before. Then she adds one more reproachful observation: in his most recent letter, Baumez has described the lavish social entertainments hosted by Jean-Baptiste subsequent to her departure. How ironic it all was! The comte had ordered her back to Paris against her will, supposedly because her presence in Bonn was costing him too much money. She had tried to stay on, citing the ways in which she could be useful to him, offering to help out personally in the running of his household. Again, he would have none of it.

Such direct and unguarded confidences made to a twenty-year-old secretary reveal not only Marie-Eléonore's total and uncomplicated commitment to Jean-Baptiste but also something of her essential *aloneness* as a wife. Jean-Baptiste, we can be certain, was more irritated than flattered by such obtrusive fidelity. His wife had been gone for already more than two months, but the bragging libertine could only congratulate himself on being rid, at least for a time, of this boringly constant, loving, and loyal wife.

Paris, 29 August 1742

I did answer your letter, Monsieur. I cannot understand why you say you have not received it. I am obliged to you for sending me news of M. de Sade and delighted to learn that he is feeling better. I believe, however, that he will recover totally only when he returns and I truly wish that he were here. I asked M. Amelot the other day if he would be coming home soon and he told me not for a while yet.

It was very wrong of you to write to my mother-in-law that M. de Sade was ill. You could have told her he was ill, but not in the way you did. Your letter, which she sent on to me, gives the impression that he is at death's door. You are never to write like that again! The poor woman is overcome with anxiety. Moreover, if M. de Sade has been as ill as you indicated to his mother, why did you not inform me of his condition? Who could be more concerned than I and yet you always wrote me quite the opposite, that he is well! That vexes me greatly, Monsieur. I do not wish to have any of M. de Sade's indispositions hidden from me, and you simply must not torment his mother to no purpose as you did. Send me news of him, then, and tell me about his condition. Although I have heard from him since, his mother's letter made me most anxious and—let us not beat about the bush—if his illness does linger he absolutely must come back. You may show him my letter and I shall expect your reply on this.

Please convey my greetings to all the ladies and gentlemen of Bonn and especially to Mlle de Nothaft. My cases have still not arrived and nothing has been heard of them at the Hôtel de Maillebois where they were sent. No one even knows what that could mean. Pray, bestir yourself so that I can have them soon, and let me know to whom I should apply for news of them. Have Bequelin look into it. It is dreadfully cold and I have no winter coat. Here am I once more as I was last year. I knew that this is what would happen.

I have just received your letter. The abbé has also had one from M. de Sade who appears to be furious with me for borrowing the money from M. Lambert to pay for the berlin I bought. What was I to do? I cannot obviously go on foot here! However, if it angers him so much, he has only to say the word and I shall sell it. I cannot imagine what I have done to him but he certainly treats me most strangely. He would have done better to keep me in Bonn. I could have spared him many exertions when the army was there. The honors of his house would have been done to the best of my ability. But such was not his wish. I am most obliged to you for your detailed report on the entertainments. They appear to have been quite lavish and I cannot see that my not being there has saved M. de Sade any expense. Mme de Belle-Isle chose a better way and closed up her house as soon as she heard that the army would be passing through. M. de Sade would have been wise to do the same.

If you like, you can send him my letter. Let me have news of his health; it worries me greatly.[21]

Jean-Baptiste had indeed been seriously ill during the spring of 1742 and was unable for a time to join the elector on a tour of his dioceses. These annual ceremonial visits tended to go on for months at a time and presented good opportunities, during stays at one or another of Clement-Augustus's many fine palaces, to influence his political leanings. Each of the foreign diplomats vied for a place in the official entourage, and those ministers unfriendly to France, taking advantage of Jean-Baptiste's forced absence, had been trying very hard to undo his earlier good work.[22] Happily, Louis XV's hefty subsidies, paid promptly each quarter by the charming M. de Sade, continued to be highly persuasive counterarguments. Clement-Augustus was pleased to remain loyal to France—or at least neutral during the current hostilities—as long as a goodly supply of *louis d'or* kept flowing into his coffers.

Still, Jean-Baptiste had been unable to put out of his mind the thought of finally obtaining a diplomatic posting more worthy of his rank and talents. Bonn, for all its strategic importance in the Austrian war, was not an embassy. He was still counting on the old cardinal and, more immediately, on Amelot and, of course, on Amelot's own powerful protector, Maurepas, to put things right. Maurepas himself had acknowledged Jean-Baptiste's New Year's greeting with reassurances that he was keeping a close watch on the situation; everything had gone well so far, and he was certain that the future would measure up to the comte's expectations.[23] Jean-Baptiste nevertheless decided to ask for leave. Too many interesting things were going on in Paris for him not to be there. Fellow diplomats like Louis-Augustin Blondel, chargé d'affaires at the court of the elector of Mainz, warned him, however, that his chances for getting leave were poor; his presence in Bonn was absolutely essential: "both political and military considerations require it."[24] Blondel's prediction proved correct, but Jean-Baptiste continued to ask nonetheless.

In July, still ailing, Jean-Baptiste took the waters, and by September he was able to join the elector on his major Westphalian tour, taking with him a half-dozen of his own servants while leaving the others in Bonn along with his bumptious secretary, Henry Baumez, who was left with complete instructions on how to look after not only the official diplomatic mail but also umpteen personal matters. Jean-Baptiste's orders arrived back in Bonn regularly: the secretary was to send his master a dozen shirts—they simply did not know how to launder properly in Westphalia! Baumez was *not* to rent a sedan chair, and he was *not* to buy the winter's supply of jams. Paris might be coming through with Monsieur le Comte's leave or, better still, an ambassadorial posting. The master would be needing his fine red suit for the St. Charles Day ball, the special brimmed hat with gold ribbons; and, oh, yes, he also wanted his Persian fabrics brought to him by one of the servants, not those he had purchased in Bonn and not the tapestry ones either, but the others. And would Baumez also find out whether the elector's fine dress shoes were ready for delivery? No, Mme de Sade had not yet received her goods, and how could "poor Baumez," fool that he was, possibly imagine that the kind of people *he,* a mere nobody, was acquainted with in Paris would know *anything at all* about whether Monsieur le Comte was to be given an embassy!

Entrusted with all these chores and many more, Henry Baumez was not, however, entrusted with the keys to Monsieur le Comte's study. He was to ask La Jeunesse, the comte's most trusted valet, who would let him in if it was absolutely necessary. That little restriction was intended to put the lowly secretary in his place; how not to be condescending, after all, toward this irritatingly young upstart who seemed prepared to accept all manner of verbal abuse, not to mention low (and infrequently paid) wages, in return for the privilege of serving such a worthy master. And, above all, Baumez was not to get any grand ideas about being important in the larger scheme of things. He should remember that he was really a nobody who was being honored by his worthy master as a somebody: "You are neither my first assistant, nor my second, but someone I hope to render capable of at least something, and that is why I must scold you." Baumez should not complain, moreover, about being left behind in Bonn. While his master was on tour with the elector, was he not, after all, being honored with the care of his master's special errands, almost as though he were a *résident des affaires de France?* "You have never had such a fine role to play in all your life. Instead of reproaching me, you ought to thank me." And, one more thing: the wig powder purchased for his master had too much lime in it. As a result, thanks to his disgracefully incompetent secretary, Louis XV's *ministre plénipotentiaire* at the court of Cologne was having to go about with peeling skin on his face![25]

Visibly present in the Jean-Baptiste de Sade–Henry Baumez master-servant relationship is a certain familiar Almaviva-Figaro dynamic that is well brought out in the following draft of a playful note from Baumez to one of his female admirers. Safely out of earshot, Baumez gently twits his absent master, his *"adorable maître,"* as he mischievously calls him. Baumez, Marie-Eléonore's confidant, is obviously much at ease with the ladies, to such an extent that Jean-Baptiste may have even viewed the younger man as a rival, a threat to the success of his own lecherous forays below stairs and into the town. Baumez was boarding at the home of a "charming embroidress,"[26] but the object of his most ardent affections was a certain Mlle Kaukol, the young woman to whom the letter in question seems to be addressed. The junior secretary hopes to marry her. His good master has promised to see to all the arrangements, but there are troubling indications later in the correspondence that Monsieur le Comte has half a mind to exercise at some point, Almaviva fashion, his *droit du seigneur* in the matter. The relevance of this last notion to the marquis de Sade's biography will become apparent in a later chapter.

[Bonn, October–November 1742]

Madam,

It has been such a long time since I have heard from you and since you have heard from me.

It is because I am afraid I bore you and so I deny myself the pleasure of writing, sparing you in that way the distress of reading gibberish. [. . .] I can already hear you saying as you yawn, *"What a nice child, he is!* . . ."

Did you know that I have become a minor minister? Indeed, yes, that is how it goes! Given time, one becomes something. Only the first steps are difficult. It's child's play, once one is used to it.

And do you think I could so easily have forgotten the axioms of my opera? No, Madam, [. . .] one must incur pain before gaining pleasure. Yes, Madam, I am now a minor minister, replacing my *adorable master* who has been in Westphalia with His Electoral Highness these past two months, leaving me here to direct matters in his absence. I am called upon to decide on everything. I write to the Court; I communicate with M. Amelot. Here am I, deep in the affairs of state as if I had been doing it all my life. Won't little brother be amazed when he hears about it![27] He will have difficulty believing it, as I do! But it's true, nonetheless. My *adorable master,* who has every reason to be pleased with me, wrote to me recently:—*How is it, my dear Baumez, that you pine for my presence? You should think yourself most fortunate and hope that I remain away forever since you occupy my place and you have never played such a fine role.*

—*That is true, I replied, but I would much prefer to play the role with you. Moreover, I have never discussed my salary with you; I find it rather slender and were it not for my good master's friendship which I value above all, contrary to expectations, there would be little enough to set aside, since 300 livres is not much. [. . .]*[28]

It was indeed not much, but in closing, to impress his lady even more, the minor minister reveals that he has had a small bonus of a hundred livres, plus a fine present consisting of a ring and a small silver case that he has just had engraved with his coat of arms. His coat of arms? Had he known, Jean-Baptiste would have choked with derision! But he now had more serious matters to think about. A new source of hope for his career came in November when an important change took place at Versailles that had everyone talking: Louis XV suddenly dismissed his longtime mistress, the comtesse de Mailly, and replaced her with her sister, the marquise de La Tournelle. Marie-Eléonore's old convent friend, in other words, had just become the most powerful woman in France, the *maîtresse reconnue* if not yet *déclarée* of Europe's most powerful king. The entire affair had been expertly stage-managed by the duc de Richelieu, the man whom the new royal mistress addressed as "uncle." Less than a year later, full recognition came with the *tabouret* and the title duchesse de Châteauroux.

Jean-Baptiste could not have hoped for a more promising shift in fortune. Now more than ever he realized that it was not a time to be wasting away invisibly in Bonn, catering to the volatile whims of the feather-brained archbishop elector and trying to outsmart these hostile German ministers. Unfortunately, there was one small complication: his immediate protector, Amelot, and especially Amelot's own patron, Maurepas, were not allies of Richelieu, the new power broker at Versailles. The comte de Sade hesitated: should he trade immediately on Marie-Eléonore's providential connection with the new mistress and risk offending Amelot? After some hesitation, he decided to avoid any awkwardness; it was, after all, properly up to Amelot to place him. The post of ambassador to Venice was coming vacant, it would be perfect for him—well suited, he modestly observed, to the "mediocrity" both of his talents and of his purse.[29] Three powerful ministers—Fleury, Maurepas, and Amelot—had solemnly promised to look after him. He would be patient and wait.

The bad news came directly from Cardinal Fleury himself. Others, it seems, were in line for the Venice posting. Indeed, that particular embassy had been promised already for some time. Not to worry, though! "We are pleased with your services and I shall not be found lacking in good will when the time comes for me to demonstrate, Monsieur, all of my sentiments for you."[30] Such reassurances from the ailing nonagenarian (who would die of old age less than two months later) did nothing to hearten Jean-Baptiste. Suddenly, he felt overcome by an angry sense of betrayal. In a bitterly candid letter to Amelot, sent at the end of December 1742, he blurted out his feelings: Why was he always being singled out as the perpetual victim of broken promises? His ambitions had been frustrated at every turn! He had made great sacrifices, and prominently listed among these was his marriage to Marie-Eléonore, embarked on, he crudely admits, purely for reasons of personal advancement. She herself obviously counted for nothing in his eyes. The whining, resentful voice of the real Jean-Baptiste, no longer hiding behind lofty protestations of indifference to vain success, comes through loud and clear:

> For twenty years I served as a captain of cavalry but I was refused the *croix de Saint Louis!* For five years running, I kept ready the sum of 10,000 royal *écus* to acquire a regiment but my application went unanswered. *Finally, tired of waiting and without any hope that help would be forthcoming from the Court, I married!* For a dowry, my wife brought me only the promise of a regiment of Condé dragoons. Everyone knows what came of all that for me. [. . .] The diplomatic corps was my last hope. I applied and you accepted my services but, once again, my hopes were dashed when I learned that I was not to be named ambassador straightaway, unlike some others whose birth, knowledge, and talents appeared not to be superior to mine. When you offered me this posting you did me the honor of telling me that one must begin somewhere. . . . I am, however, the only one who was required to make such a beginning. My eagerness to serve His Majesty was too great not to accept whatever was offered me but I fear that my humility has done me harm and that one so humble may have seemed to you unworthy of the highest positions. M. le cardinal told me I would be here for only a short while and that he would soon place me more fittingly. [. . .] The Elector was

anxious to ask the Emperor to invest me with his Order, a distinguished decoration to which a stipend is attached. His Majesty refused me permission to accept. The Venice embassy falls vacant. With the greatest alacrity I solicit the posting. I am refused. My misfortune follows me everywhere. [. . .] Championed and protected by you, I have lost all hope.[31]

Jean-Baptiste sent his long litany of complaints to his patron at a time when conventional New Year's greetings would have been more the order of the day. He closed by adding that all he really aspired to now was untroubled retirement from the world. That statement, of course, was empty rhetoric. His ambitions were undiminished; confidence in his good friend and patron Amelot was shaken but remained basically intact. Of course, since so much depended on the strategies and vagaries of patronage, he might have to start betting on more than one horse. . . . He had been too patient as he watched lesser men pull ahead of him.

Three

DESPERATE MEASURES

Bad luck continued to dog the comte de Sade as he entered his third year of service at the elector's court in Bonn. First of all, Cardinal Fleury died on 29 January 1743, and with him expired all the promises he had made and the reassurances he had given. To make matters worse, Jean-Baptiste now found himself caught up in a high-level power struggle at Versailles: Louis XV's new mistress and her versatile impresario, the duc de Richelieu, seemed bent on annihilating the Maurepas-Amelot power base on which he had for some time been totally dependent. D'Argenson notes retrospectively in his journal that Richelieu's "ruling passion was to cause the downfall of M. de Maurepas, and getting rid of M. Amelot, he liked to say, was at least putting out one of Maurepas' eyes."[1] Reviewing the state of French diplomacy during the period before he himself took over as foreign minister from Amelot, d'Argenson also made it clear in the same memorandum that he had not modified his original low opinion of the *petit-maître* de Sade, unwisely appointed by Amelot to represent French interests in Bonn. While it was true that the comte de Sade had at first made good progress with the elector, nothing truly substantial had been accomplished, and then very serious difficulties had arisen, the elector having gained after a time the shocking impression that France's plenipotentiary was guilty of committing "a number of base and self-serving transgressions."

The fact was that by the beginning of 1743, despite the pleasant entertainments and the continuing *bonnes fortunes* he boasted of to correspondents,[2] Jean-Baptiste was thoroughly fed up with his Bonn assignment. It was a diplomatic dead end and an intolerable drain on his personal finances. In this last regard, truth to tell, he had begun after the first year to cast about for ways to make up his losses, employing stratagems that were not entirely in keeping with normal accounting procedures. He had not forgotten either the importance of keeping his options open, and to this end he managed a quick trip back to Paris in late April and May 1743, returning to Bonn in early June, ready, despite a sprained ankle, to join the elector on his annual tour. By mid-August, however, French diplomatic relations with Clement-Augustus suffered a serious chill, provoked in part by deliberate tardiness in the payment of the elector's subsidy. Paris had ordered a stiffening in policy, intended as a warning to Clement-Augustus to cease his behind-the-scenes dalliance with Vienna and London. By October the chill had turned personal as well, and soon it became clear to Jean-Baptiste that it was not just the elector's pro-Austrian ministers but the elector himself who would be delighted to see the back of him. Of course, all that fitted in well enough with Jean-Baptiste's own plans. In December he announced his departure for Paris, putting about the story that he had been recalled definitively by Versailles. In fact, he had discreetly arranged only an informal leave with his superior Amelot even though his secret intention was to leave Bonn forever. It was an ingenious way for him to have his cake and eat it too. By telling the elector that he had been recalled and would not be coming back, he was making himself eligible to receive, along with an official acknowledgment-of-recall letter (*lettre de récréance*) from Clement-Augustus to Louis XV that he was to hand in to the ministry on his return to Paris, the standard farewell present, normally a gift worth thousands of livres. He was, of course, aware of the dubious legal and ethical implications of this little ruse, but he justified it to himself with the thought that he would, after all, be recuperating only what was his due, a much needed reimbursement of all the personal expenses he had incurred while carrying out his official duties. The fact that he seems to have been strangely unconcerned about the possible risks of discovery suggests how certain he felt that he could count on his friend Amelot's discreet connivance in the scheme.

Everything went almost as planned. On 31 December 1743, Jean-Baptiste was duly handed his *récréance* letter by one of the ministers, the elector himself having deliberately chosen to ignore the occasion. As for the all-important present, Clement-Augustus unfortunately proved to be even more wily than the departing diplomat. A present was indeed delivered (to add to the insult, by the minister Stephné, Jean-Baptiste's old Vienna-leaning enemy), but it was a paltry thing, not diamond jewelry such as Marie-Eléonore had received personally from Clement-Augustus when she had sadly taken her leave eighteen months before, but a very ordinary snuff box. It was an unimaginable affront! The elector let it be known at the same time that a "proper" present might be forthcoming as soon as payment of his equally "proper" French subsidy was unblocked. Outmaneuvered and furious, Jean-Baptiste disdainfully left the snuff box behind in Bonn with his secretary Baumez, along with instructions to return it to the Clement-Augustus in the least polite manner possible—by local mail.[3]

Jean-Baptiste returned to France very much in a huff but immensely relieved to be finally rid of an unwanted posting. Not only had it brought him little profit, it had kept him away from Versailles and had isolated him from valuable career opportunities. Of course, his situation was now highly irregular. Soon after arriving back in Paris, he confided the awkward circumstances of his departure to Amelot, who immediately advised him to regularize his situation by returning the *récréance* letter forthwith to Bonn. Reluctant to give up that easily, Jean-Baptiste decided instead to wait a while. Yes, he would return the letter, but not right away, not until the elector came through with the "proper" present. Meanwhile, with the tacit approval of the minister, he quietly continued to draw his salary. At the very least, the Ministry of Foreign Affairs surely owed him that much for all the trouble and expense he had been put through. As for his Bonn duties, yes, Baumez could surely look after routine matters. He had promised him an annual stipend of three thousand livres; the impertinent fellow hardly deserved that much, but Jean-Baptiste privately promised himself to reduce that sum eventually to something more in keeping with what underlings are worth. In any case, he would be in no hurry to pay him; meanwhile, with his salary of twenty-four thousand livres continued, he would be pocketing at least eight times that amount in Paris, and with none of the bother.

His own ambitious career plans were still uppermost in his mind, but now Jean-Baptiste also had something new to think about: assuring the future of his son. It was time to take charge himself of Donatien's education, to begin to instill in him the essential elements of manly comportment and rational thinking. The boy had already been too long under the narrow-minded supervision of his mother, "the invalid," as Jean-Baptiste liked to call her. Moreover, with his unruly and fiercely independent character, Donatien had apparently been wearing out his welcome at the Hôtel de Condé of late. It would be prudent to settle him for a time nearer to his paternal roots where he could acquire a proper sense of his seigneurial destiny and be introduced to his loyal Provençal "vassals," giving them at the same time an opportunity to pay respectful homage to their young lord. The ultimate fortunes of the entire family rested on the shoulders of this precious male heir, and such matters required careful planning and control.

So far no documents have come to light to explain why Donatien was sent off at the age of four to live with his grandmother in Avignon, but perhaps Jean-Baptiste's reasoning had run along such lines. One senses that it would have been mostly the father's decision and that Marie-Eléonore, chronically ill and a constant target of her husband's complaints and disapprobation, would not have been permitted much of a voice in the matter. Jean-Baptiste did, however, consult regularly with his brother on important family business, and there is no doubt that the abbé agreed that Donatien should go to Avignon for a while. The abbé, no longer an admirer of his sister-in-law, would see to everything. In fact, it was already time to be thinking ahead about a prestigious future marriage for the boy.

It was probably also with such considerations in mind that the abbé, around the time of Jean-Baptiste's December departure from Bonn, signified support for his brother's plan to purchase a new title for himself as head of the family. For a mere twenty thousand livres the comte could become a "prince of the Empire." It would cost a pretty penny, and both Louis XV and the Emperor Charles VII would have to give permission, but it would be well worth it. In fact, the abbé had recently discussed the advantages of such a move with the leading expert in these matters, the duc de Richelieu. The consultation had taken place in Montpellier where the duc was attending the Languedoc provincial assembly meetings, and Richelieu had signified his total agreement. There was no doubt, he assured the abbé, that the title of *prince d'empire* would add luster and prestige to the de Sade family name. Jean-Baptiste should not hesitate: "It is an extremely illustrious rank in the Empire. You would be held in high regard in France; it would guarantee you a major embassy, win you the *cordon bleu* sooner than otherwise, smooth the way for your son to make a most distinguished marriage and be a source of many charming and pleasant things for you."[4] The famous duc and the abbé had in fact managed to identify at the conclusion of their chat in Montpellier several of Jean-Baptiste's most cherished ambitions: an embassy and the *cordon bleu* for himself and the assurance of a *grand mariage* for Donatien.

Unfortunately, the comte de Sade never managed to become a prince of the empire, and many other bitter disappointments also lay ahead. These were all the more difficult to bear since no one kept more abreast than Jean-Baptiste himself of the honors that everyday were showered on men he saw as less worthy than himself. And not even *men,* some of them! Fronsac, the duc de Richelieu's son, was given his regiment and a colonel's rank at the age of six. Donatien's solemn playmate, the prince de Condé, had received the order of the Golden Fleece before he was four! (Yes, and for all that anyone knew, he himself, the longtime lover of Caroline-Charlotte, may have been the father; the prince certainly bore no physical resemblance to Monsieur le Duc. . . .[5]) As for the *cordon bleu,* Jean-Baptiste was incensed when he learned that Louis XV intended to award that prestigious decoration to the young marquis de Bissy, the very man who had supplanted him as Caroline-Charlotte's paramour: "This favor has taken Paris by surprise and distressed many courtiers," he wrote to his friend, the marquis de Poyanne. He then added to those sour grapes a pious topping of bad faith: "Apparently all one needs these days is scheming ambition in order to make very rapid progress."[6]

On unauthorized leave in Paris all through 1744 yet drawing his full salary, Jean-Baptiste did eventually send his *lettre de récréance* back to Baumez in Bonn with detailed—and very devious—instructions on how it should be returned to the elector in such a way that the waters would be well muddied, leaving the impression that Amelot had refused to accept the document since there had been no present attached for the comte de Sade. Subsequently, he suggested other imaginative scenarios, all designed to exonerate him from potential charges of professional wrongdoing. Baumez could let it be known that the French authorities had not allowed Jean-Baptiste to present the letter since "proper" formalities (again the missing present) had not been observed. Another possibility was to suggest that the comte de Sade had innocently mistaken the French king's intentions when he informed Bonn that he had been recalled: he was actually supposed to leave Bonn "definitively" only after his replacement had been named. Finally, Jean-Baptiste resorted to what can only be described as desperate prevarication: Baumez should simply hint to one of the ministers that his master had, in fact, not even taken the letter with him to Paris; he had left it in Bonn while he awaited clarification. Then Baumez was to suggest with a knowing wink that the comte de Sade, realizing that his salary would be terminated the moment he handed in the document, had deliberately made no mention of it once he reached Paris. Presumably, Clement-Augustus would recognize approvingly in such a mercenary stratagem the rascally tactics of a kindred spirit. In the end, much to Jean-Baptiste's displeasure, Baumez did nothing, fearful of the consequences to himself. The result was that during the entire year 1744, Louis XV was under the impression that he still had a *ministre plénipotentiaire* (currently on leave) assigned to the elector's court, while the elector held an equally firm belief that the envoy he had come to detest had been definitively recalled and, providentially, was gone forever.[7]

In fact, Jean-Baptiste had other reasons to feel uneasy about the anomalous situation he had got himself into. Even before his return, the ministry had identified troubling discrepancies in his budget accounts and had carried out various audits concerning his administration of official funds. In March 1743, for example, he had been obliged to apologize for a book-keeping "oversight"; later audits refer to the "disorder" and "vagueness" of his accounts. Requests from the ministry for clarification were prudently left unanswered or were answered in such a way as to obfuscate rather than inform: "You have not given me an easy task, Monsieur," comments one official to his superior, "when you asked me to examine M. de Sade's correspondence to determine what remains to be paid of our subsidy to the Elector of Cologne. I cannot for the life of me understand how anyone can write as unhelpfully as he does. It is a hodgepodge without rhyme or reason." Some funds appeared to have been simply divvied up like war booty between the French envoy and the elector! Elsewhere, the same auditor notes that three thousand livres had simply vanished into thin air.[8]

It is likely that creative bookkeeping—reimbursing himself for what he considered to be legitimate expenses—rather than petty larceny was the source of the comte's difficulties, and it is equally probable that Amelot was aware of these irregularities and was prepared to overlook them. Unfortunately, Amelot, much to Maurepas' displeasure and Jean-Baptiste's consternation, was abruptly dismissed by Louis XV at the end of April 1744. Finally, Jean-Baptiste was confronted with the full realization of the extent to which his career was in jeopardy. His first thought was to regularize immediately his situation by ending his "leave" and hurrying back to Bonn; he had not, after all, handed in his *récréance*. It was only then that he learned that the foreign ministry, now under direct administration of Louis XV himself, had no intention of sending him back. He was in limbo.

None of these matters helped to soothe his irritation as he continued, meanwhile, to address self-serving instructions to his unofficial stand-in back in Bonn. Baumez was being so infuriatingly pretentious as he went about (skillfully, though the comte would not admit as much) the diplomatic tasks his master saw as so much above the knave's station. With his very first letter back to Bonn after his arrival in Paris, Jean-Baptiste decided to cut the impertinent jackanapes down to size. He also did not want him corresponding any longer with Marie-Eléonore.

Paris, 24 [January 1744]

[. . .] I received yours of the 14th, very long as usual. You could have cut out all of the polite nothings at the beginning where you hope I have arrived, you hope it with all your heart, you are impatient to have news of me, and the time spent without me seems like an eternity. As you yourself know, all that is meaningless verbiage *and you might refrain also from writing to Madame who doesn't care a fig about your letters.* It vexes me that you returned the present to *M. le grand maître*[9] personally. It was not fine enough for that![10]

There was indeed little that Jean-Baptiste did not find fault with. Baumez's gentle reminder to Jean-Baptiste that he had not as yet been paid any salary was an irritation, almost a deliberate provocation! And he was certainly no longer inclined to facilitate Baumez's marriage to the comely Mlle Kaukol as he had originally promised, not at least until their accounts were straightened out. Did Baumez really think he deserved a stipend of eight francs per day simply for looking after his master's routine chores? (It goes without saying that the master made no reference to the fact that back in Paris he was himself illegally drawing full salary, ten times that amount, for doing absolutely nothing.)

Versailles, 16 March [1744]

It was very wrong of you to allow Mlle Kaukol to leave before we have come to an arrangement. I wrote you my conditions for being obliging enough to take her into my service. I stipulated that our business should first be settled and also that you were to send me my papers. You did send the account but I had hoped that in the meantime you would have decided to be reasonable and not ask me for eight francs per day despite everything I had already said to you about that.[11]

The comte's essentially bullying and mean-spirited nature—revealed really for the first time in these letters to his secretary—becomes more and more apparent in the correspondence, suggesting a possible new source for the equivalent haughtiness toward social inferiors later so flagrantly exhibited by his notorious son. For Jean-Baptiste, the thought of this underling Baumez strutting about in Bonn, ostentatiously taking care of business and arrogantly giving his betters advice, was simply infuriating. Did he not realize that any good that happened to come his humble way could only be the result of his master's patronizing forbearance and generosity?

[early April 1744?]

If things don't turn out as you wish, my dear Baumez, you must blame yourself. You continue to indulge your foolish ways and this ruins my plans for you. From the moment I left, you began strutting about like a minister. You have tried to show off as such in the antechamber and the chapel. You have rented sedan chairs to maintain your dignity. All that you have done has been worthless and made you a laughing stock. I have always warned you about putting on airs and about your vanity which will be the death of you. You were very wrong to lend—the moment I was gone—anything at all to M. de Nehaus. You could easily have said that everything is packed up and that you did not have the key. Of course, you did it in order to look important and to seem to be in charge of everything.

What could be more fatuous than Baumez advising M. Amelot about what His Majesty should do! It is the worst thing you could have done for yourself, not only now but later even; people will not forget that piece of imbecility. I had thought of leaving you as resident in Bonn and even diverting a thousand francs from your stipend to give to M. Berne to watch over your conduct for a year or two. I did not tell you about it because I feared you would immediately take on airs and start talking in ministerial tones and committing blunders, for I knew what would happen. "Don't put ideas into his head," I thought to myself; "given the uncertainty of success, such ideas might unhinge his feeble mind. . . ."

I will *certainly not* send you an authorization giving you your entrees everywhere. I don't care a fig if you have entrees.

And what will you do, my poor Baumez, and what will become of you? You may be obliged to take a clerk's position somewhere and you'd be lucky to get one, since it is not certain that I will be given a posting. And if I am posted, I may well need a secretary I can count on and who isn't forever being an idiot. One must not think of rising up unless one can maintain the position. Why have I not allowed my people to address me as *excellency?* It is because once I am back in Paris, I will no longer be able to use the title. If I am named ambassador I will obviously accept the title because then it would be mine forever. You should follow my example: nothing makes me self-important.

[. . .] Have one of the servants sleep in your room. I know that if you heard a noise you would be too afraid to get out of bed to see what it was.[12]

Not surprisingly, after Amelot's dismissal the comte's general mood grew even more sour and his tone with his secretary even more bullying.

Worried that he no longer had Amelot to cover for him, Jean-Baptiste reluctantly sent back to Baumez the *récréance* letter he was supposed to have remitted to Louis XV months before. The secretary's apparent success at replacing him, deliberately stealing glory from his master, was irritating in the extreme. To prove just how incompetent the conceited coxcomb was, Jean-Baptiste decided to favor him with a "helpful" analysis of his writing style, adding a commentary on the secretary's most recent diplomatic report to the ministry:

Paris, 30 [May 1744]

Your letter to M. du Theil is quite ridiculous You were at Brulh for a moment only yet you say that *the envoy from Hanover, judging by his conversation, is very polite, very witty and has very fine manners.* First of all such things are of no interest to anyone. Moreover, it takes months of observation to judge a man's wit and you, in any case, are not up to attempting the task. You could say, "He is reputed to be witty but I am unable to judge." Again, one does not say that a *man* "has very fine manners." You write that *you were unable to judge whether he was extremely solicitous.* I should think so! In the two hours that you were there what could you have seen? You say: *I do not believe he could join in the heron shoot since he is so myopic he needs a magnifying glass.* These are such trifling matters, not worth mentioning and quite ridiculous. *Both M. de Nehaus and I noticed the heavy silence.* That means you were ill-received but, in any case, here you are putting yourself on the same level as M. de Nehaus, as if you were equals. Your intention quite obviously is to convey the sense, "We, the ministers for France and the Empire, . . ." Fatuousness creeps into your letters without your noticing it. If only you wrote as I told you to, just the news, without ever referring to yourself, you wouldn't be so ridiculous, as are all of your letters from start to finish.

Ask someone else to run your errands; I will do no more for anyone! It is a waste of money. People ask me to do these chores to escape having to pay and yet you still expect me to do other people favors! Don't be in such a great hurry to pay the rent; you will pay before leaving but I certainly do not owe fifty *pistoles.* Again, you are merely trying to put on airs of generosity. [. . .]

I am sending back the letter I was given for His Majesty when I left Bonn. Its acceptance was deemed inappropriate. Give it back to *M. le grand maître,* saying only that I did my best to have it accepted but it was refused because proper procedures had not been followed. [. . .] [13]

The comte's petty jealousies are even more visible in a July letter to Baumez that again reflects his irritation with reports of his secretary's success. He was aware that senior French diplomats in the field were now making no secret of their satisfaction with his informal stand-in. Charged with a special mission to Bonn in May 1744,[14] the diplomat Blondel, for example, praised Baumez in a letter he sent to the secretary from Frankfurt on 18 June: "In my report to the court concerning my mission to Bonn I acknowledge in full what I owe to your energies and efforts *and I have made no secret of this in my letter to M. de Sade.*"[15] Equally irritating to Jean-Baptiste was the fact that Baumez was hesitant about returning the *récréance* letter to the elector. He had even suggested that grave dangers were attached to such a move, but the comte was having none of it. A little fancy footwork and a modicum of misrepresentation on Baumez's part would solve everything. Above all, Baumez should not even think of consulting the ministry on the subject!

Versailles, 28 [July 1744]

[. . .] This letter is a *récréance* that the Elector had delivered to me believing that I was leaving for good and which I should not have accepted since no present accompanied it. M. Amelot warned me about it when I arrived and instructed me to return it. Since I was still under the impression that the present was forthcoming I kept it. [. . .] There is no point consulting the court about it since I should not have received the letter in the first place. All you can do is inform M. Stephné that I left the letter he had given me for His Majesty with you, since I did not wish to have it without knowing His Majesty's clear intentions regarding my return to Bonn. [. . .] You can also say that it is a matter of self-interest for me since my stipend would cease from the moment I received my *récréance*. [. . .]

Once more the master pointed out to the lowly servant that he should not put on airs or think that he was anything but an office boy who had been asked to forward the mail:

I am very well informed about the court's thinking with regard to the Elector and I know they have no wish to send an envoy. That is why they leave you there. Not wishing to send anyone, they make do with you and are pleased to have someone of no consequence who can forward the news. [. . .] I very much fear that your grand notions deceive you and that you will find yourself between two stools, with your arse on the ground. All these ministers who address you as chargé d'affaires will not care a fig about you or about finding you a new posting when you are gone from there. [. . .]

Jean-Baptiste had long since given up the house he had been leasing from countess von Plettenberg, wife of the former minister, but he had been in no hurry to pay the rent still owing. He guessed that sooner or later the elector would have paid it, and it irritated him considerably when he learned that his secretary had taken it upon himself to settle the debt. Poor Baumez! He was so lacking in the finer skills of a gentleman! And he was wasting paper, too, writing too often and leaving wide margins—especially at the top of the page, as if he were addressing a social equal:

> If you hadn't been in such a great hurry to pay Mme de Plettenberg the Elector would have taken care of it. It does no harm for a minister to leave debts behind; it shows that he was a generous spender. The Elector himself was in my debt for six months and he still owes me. But you thought it would look bad for you if I had any debts.
>
> Do not write to me so often. Do not leave a margin and do not begin so far down on the page. You are wasting paper and it will not change the fact that our ranks are not equal.
>
> [. . .] I advise you to mail your reports less frequently. When you have really nothing to say, you send platitudes. Of course, the postmaster will be less impressed with you if you receive fewer letters. No matter how much I tell you, you do not change and the slightest thing spoils you and turns your head. I'm sorry, for I do like you and you are a good lad. [. . .][16]

That little pat on the back, condescending and paltry though it was, shows nevertheless the extent to which a now much threatened Jean-Baptiste recognized that he needed Henry Baumez in his camp. The dismissal of Amelot had not entirely destroyed all of his hopes for an embassy. He could count, after all, on the good will of Louis XV's new mistress, the duchesse de Châteauroux. With the help of his wife, to whom he had apparently confided nothing of his difficulties in Bonn or the exact nature of his leave, Jean-Baptiste set about cultivating Marie-Eléonore's old school friend. Of course, matters could not be rushed; the royal mistress was still consolidating her own political power base, and he knew that there would be many claims on her patronage. Still, though she received few visitors, Mme de Châteauroux had already let Marie-Eléonore know that she would make an exception for her and her diplomat husband. In May 1744, while the new *sultane* was staying at the home of the financier Pâris-Duverney in Plaisance, she invited them both to come and see her. "She has given us permission to visit her there as often as we please," Jean-Baptiste wrote with great satisfaction to his friend the marquis de Poyanne. It was a critical time for the nation still caught up in an interminable war. Louis XV had just left for the army, and his mistress was waiting impatiently for permission to join him.[17] To be allowed to visit with her at such a time was no small honor. Even the marquis de Poyanne, himself one of those admitted to Louis XV's inner circle, was duly impressed: "Being among the chosen few is a real feather in your cap."[18]

Four

THE END OF A
PROMISING CAREER

Things had looked very black to Jean-Baptiste after Amelot's forced departure from the scene, but with Louis XV's new mistress apparently determined to make his fortune, everything seemed auspicious once again. Then, yet another catastrophe struck, leaving Jean-Baptiste's already tattered career prospects in pitiful shreds. On 8 August 1744, Louis XV fell gravely ill at Metz. To the enormous scandal of many, the royal mistress and her sister, the duchesse de Lauraguais, both warmly supported by their mentor the duc de Richelieu, were allowed to remain at Louis XV's bedside. It was even rumored that the two sisters had jointly provoked the king's exhaustion and illness through unremitting sexual shenanigans on the preceding evening.[1] Convinced that he was on the point of death, Louis was finally persuaded by his confessor to send the sisters away, to express publicly the most profound regret for his wicked ways, and even to beg the queen's forgiveness in public for the scandal and grief his infidelities had caused her in recent years. So great was the anger and moral indignation of the inhabitants of Metz that the duchesse de Châteauroux and the duchesse de Lauraguais narrowly escaped being stoned by the mob and had to be smuggled out of the city behind the closed shutters of the local governor's carriage.[2] It was a serious setback for the Richelieu camp, and many believed that the duchesse de Châteauroux's fortunes had been irremediably damaged.

Weighing the probabilities and basically convinced that this was indeed the case, Jean-Baptiste once more decided to hedge his bets and even indulged his ready wit by retailing some of the nastier anti-Châteauroux gossip that was going around, not to mention circulating to friends the poet Piron's waggish ode on the convalescing monarch's royal turd.[3] At the same time he visibly shifted some of his loyalty to the newly energized queen's party. In the eyes of many, Metz had reinstated the retiring and timid Marie Leszczynska to her proper place, but even well before the king's illness, Jean-Baptiste had been prudently ingratiating himself with Louis XV's neglected spouse as well as her father, Stanislas, the exiled king of Poland who held court at Lunéville. Soon after his return from Bonn, for example, he arranged to have himself invited along on several of the queen's countryside excursions during which he was fortunate enough to serve as one of Her Majesty's equerries. Marie Leszczynska had also begun to invite him to her high-stakes gaming parties, and his friend de Poyanne teased him a little on the point: "She must be madly in love with the thought of your going to see her."[4]

But Louis XV recovered, and more uncertainty followed. Almost immediately, His Most Christian Majesty came to regret the indignity of his act of contrition in front of the gaping masses at Metz, not to mention his panicky repudiation of all fleshly joys. The big question now was would he take Mme de Châteauroux back? The royal mistress herself was very confident on the matter as she charmingly explained to her "dear uncle" (and former *partie carrée* partner), the duc de Richelieu: *"Naturally, while his mind is weakened by illness, the King will be filled with thoughts of religion, but I wager that as soon as he has recovered a little, thoughts of me will be going pitter-patter in his head."*[5] Jean-Baptiste, writing in late August 1744, saw the problem in essentially pragmatic and personal terms: if Louis XV on recovery chose to give up having mistresses entirely, the decision would probably be best for the nation. "On the other hand," he added, "if he were to go back to having one, I would be quite chagrined if it were someone else. [Mme de Châteauroux] was with Mme de Sade at the convent and has always been a very good friend to her. I myself was fortunate enough to do one or two small favors for her with Monsieur le Duc,[6] and she has always shown me gratitude and kindness; she has asked Mme de Sade to let her know what favor she should request from the King for us." Of course, Jean-Baptiste added glibly, it was "sentiment" rather than any hope of a benefit accruing to himself that so attached him to her.[7]

A few weeks later, Jean-Baptiste announced to a correspondent a significant piece of news: the king, fully recovered, had indeed called back the disgraced mistress. "We shall soon see Mme de Châteauroux once again at court." And then a darker note: "Those who offended her must be quaking in their boots; I doubt if she will forgive them."[8] No shrinking violet, the duchesse had a reputation for what the marquis d'Argenson described as "brutality" and "a mercenary spirit,"[9] but Jean-Baptiste could not have suspected at the time the direct relevance of his gloomy observations to his own career prospects. Ever the witty courtier and society tattler, he himself had been one of the offenders who had doubted rather too publicly that the duchesse de Châteauroux could ever regain power after her ignominious fall from grace at Metz. In fact, by mid-November, the duchesse was entirely reinstated in the heart of Louis *le bien-aimé,* and when she died, very suddenly on 8 December, her royal lover was stricken with grief.

Jean-Baptiste meanwhile was still in diplomatic limbo, still waiting, but now with rapidly diminishing optimism, for assignment to the distinguished posting he had originally hoped to gain from Amelot when he abandoned Bonn the year before. No successor to his former protector had yet been named, and he was becoming concerned. Would the new minister be another helpful crony like Amelot? He could only hope! Now in his correspondence with Baumez he made grudging efforts to adopt a more conciliatory tone. He spoke of his genuine regret at not being able to pursue arrangements for his secretary's marriage to Mlle Kaukol. As for the continuing problem of Baumez's salary, yes, he really did want to settle matters—if only Baumez would be *reasonable.*

8 October [1744]

I was extremely sorry, my dear Baumez, not to be able to see you married off to Mlle Kaukol. I have always had it in mind that things could change and that is why I believed it best not to reveal your intentions. You can be certain, in any case, that, as soon as an opportunity arises, I shall try to show that family how much I am their friend. I very much hope to be able to do the young lady a favor for I have always held her in high esteem. If her mother no longer wishes to keep her at home I could place her in service with my wife, a position that would be most suitable for her.

I enclose the letter of recommendation you ask for. Paying you on a monthly basis is what I would prefer. That would put an end to our quarreling. Write and tell me what you think is a necessary and fitting stipend.[10]

Try as he might, however, Jean-Baptiste found it impossible to sustain for long this new note of civility toward the cocky young secretary who more and more was putting on the airs of a proper diplomat and solemnly exchanging news and views with ministry representatives. Baumez had even asked for (and received from the ministry, to Jean-Baptiste's astonishment and irritation) his own cipher code. The comte responded to the news with sarcasm; for good measure, he then proceeded to humiliate his subordinate by informing him of his own rather special plans for the fair Mlle Kaukol. Finally, he passed on a message of greetings from Marie-Eléonore, still condescendingly referred to as "the invalid":

Paris, 26 [October 1744]

[. . .] What a fine fellow you are! So many things received "by order of the King": a cipher code, news of Madame's death,[11] news of the King's departure! . . . None of that will get you very far. I say to you once again, stop making a spectacle of yourself and ruining your prospects.

[. . .] The invalid sends her greetings. [. . .] I received your letter today. You ask what will be Mlle Kaukol's position. You must know that here we have only chambermaids. She will be distinguished from the others, of course, by our particular friendship for her but she shouldn't hope for anything else. Her wages will be fifty *écus* plus twenty sous per day for food if she objects to eating with the other servants, and she will have an annual clothing allowance. That is the best we can do for her. If I'm given an embassy, I'll take her along as my *gouvernante* [housekeeper] if she is agreeable to that. I cannot afford more at the moment despite our friendship for her. As for the trip, she can leave when she wishes. [. . .][12]

"I'll take her along as my *gouvernante*"—Jean-Baptiste's cavalier comment must have come as a shock to the young secretary whose plans to marry the woman in question had been so recently dashed. The comte's words also clarify the current state of his relationship with Marie-Eléonore: *gouvernantes* looked after the households of unmarried men, widowers or bachelors, and it was usually assumed, if they were young, that they took care of their "single" gentleman's routinely utilitarian bedroom needs as well. But more is revealed here than a lord and master's callousness toward a discarded wife or a lowly servant. His remark also provides the only proof that has so far come to light of the essential lie young Donatien lived with as a child, the lie that his mother effectively chose to "abandon" him to follow his father. In *Aline et Valcour,* Sade's hero states that he had been sent off at an early age to stay with "a grandmother in Languedoc" because his diplomat father had been posted somewhere and his mother, as a matter of course, accompanied him.[13] Perhaps that was precisely the scenario presented to the little four-year-old when, one day in July 1744, he learned that he would soon be leaving on the long journey to Avignon with his uncle the abbé. The Kaukol *gouvernante* reference in the new correspondence makes it perfectly clear, however, that Jean-Baptiste had not the slightest intention of allowing his wife to accompany him on any future diplomatic missions. Similarly, he had earlier forced Marie-Eléonore to return home from Bonn, much against her will. Marital alienation and a deliberate decision to remove his son from *l'invalide's* influence had no doubt also played an important part in the decision taken only a few months earlier to send Donatien to live with his own relatives. Whether the little marquis was aware of this disunited family situation at the time is not clear. Significantly, when he later came to write *Aline et Valcour,* the notion of domestic conflict is absent from the hero's autobiographical narrative.

The remaining months of 1744—the very year Jean-Baptiste had been counting on so much when he unceremoniously deserted his post in

Bonn—brought him still more bad luck. In mid-November, Louis XV finally got around to appointing Amelot's successor, and Jean-Baptiste learned to his horror and disgust that the new minister was to be none other than the marquis d'Argenson, his greatest detractor. He immediately confided to a friend his low opinion of the new minister: "Few men are less capable and I doubt if he will survive in that position for long." Jean-Baptiste's prediction concerning the length of d'Argenson's tenure proved quite wrong, however, and with the passage of time his low opinion of the man got even lower: "Not only is he without wit, talent and dignity, his tenure in that position is nothing short of obscene." [14]

D'Argenson, for the moment completely unaware of the fact that Jean-Baptiste had fiddled his departure from Bonn, was nevertheless not about to send the comte de Sade back to Cologne, a posting he considered far too important for such a foppish amateur. Still, he felt that it was vitally important to have someone representing French interests at the elector's court. Within a week of being appointed and with the express approval of Louis XV, the new foreign minister quietly shunted aside the comte de Sade and invited an old acquaintance, the abbé Aunillon, to accept a discreet mission to Cologne. In a "Memorandum concerning my appointment to the court of the Elector of Cologne," Aunillon fills in the rest of the story:

> I pointed out that I knew the comte de Sade was currently accredited as His Majesty's envoy at the Elector's court. M. le marquis d'Argenson answered that M. le comte de Sade had been in Paris for more than a year and seemed in no hurry to return to Bonn; indeed he had not even come to see him. At that time, it was not yet known at the French court, nor was I aware of the fact, that M. de Sade, having had a personal quarrel with the Elector nearly fifteen months earlier, had taken leave without His Majesty's authorization and had received his letter of *récréance* which he had in fact not remitted to His Majesty; so that he was enjoying in Paris both the honor of his posting and his salary, something that was not discovered until March 1745, when the Elector learned that the count was being sent to his court to deliver His Majesty's condolences on the death of the Elector's brother, the emperor Charles VII. The Elector immediately dispatched a courier to His Majesty requesting that he not send the comte de Sade and begging to be excused for not receiving him at his court if by chance he had already left Paris by the time his courier arrived, which indeed is what happened. [15]

Jean-Baptiste, as Aunillon indicates, had indeed finally received the much awaited call to return to Bonn as soon as news of the emperor Charles VII's death on 20 January 1745 reached Paris. D'Argenson himself chose to be "too busy" to see him, and consequently Jean-Baptiste received his instructions from the ministry's principal clerk, Le Dran—instructions, it has been suggested, that were entirely sham in nature and designed to divert attention from the real negotiations that were already being carried out in secret by the abbé Aunillon.[16] Jean-Baptiste had, in fact, got wind of Aunillon's confidential mission sometime in January, a week or two before any question of his own recall arose. He immediately fired off a letter to Baumez, angrily accusing him of betrayal and disloyal cooperation with his rival Aunillon. He also repeated the charge that Baumez was being, as usual, ridiculously obsessive about the trivial matter of unpaid wages. In a draft reply that has survived, Baumez protested both his innocence and his continuing loyalty, but he also cursed the day he had ever set foot in Bonn. At last, the worm had turned.[17]

As unaware as Jean-Baptiste himself was of the entirely peripheral nature of her husband's mission, Marie-Eléonore was no doubt much relieved to learn that the comte's career was *finally* off to another brilliant start. Perhaps this time, true recognition would be his reward! Her own family pride in what seemed like such a favorable turn of events is well summed up in a congratulatory letter to Jean-Baptiste from her brother, the comte de Maillé:

> It was with great pleasure, my dear brother, that I learned of your departure for Bonn. I have every confidence that your presence there will convince the Elector once more of the advantages of good relations with France. It is our destiny to be the making of emperors and with the election of this one your embassy is assured. You can see how your merit and talents are known, since it is to you they turn when things get difficult![18]

"A maker of emperors"! The purely ostensible nature of Jean-Baptiste's mission along with the catastrophic events that awaited him on the road to Bonn would soon invest almost every word of his brother-in-law's letter with the cruelest irony. News of his impending arrival reached the elector's court in Bonn on 6 February, provoking an immediate protest in the strongest terms from Clement-Augustus, who informed Louis XV by special courier that *any* emissary His Most Christian Majesty wished to send him would be most welcome, *except* the comte de Sade. Warned of the awkward situation that was developing, Baumez immediately dispatched his own couriers to intercept and warn off his "adorable master," but it was too late. Within only a few miles of his destination but still outside the territories of Clement-Augustus, Jean-Baptiste was waylaid by the troops of the Empress Maria Theresa, arrested, and soon after taken as a prisoner of war to the *citadelle* of Antwerp.

It was only now that the full consequences of the comte's malfeasance with respect to his recall letter came into play. Still unaware that their representative had long since taken definitive leave of Clement-Augustus, officials at the French ministry demanded that the elector of Cologne honor the normal obligation to protect a diplomat duly accredited to his court. The elector, only too pleased to learn of Jean-Baptiste's bad luck, refused to ask the Austrians for his release; the comte de Sade's misfortunes, he pointed out, had nothing to do with him. The gentleman in question was no longer accredited to his court, and the arrest had not even taken place on his territory. To leave no doubt in the matter, a copy of the 31 December 1743 *lettre de récréance* that Jean-Baptiste had received under false pretences and had also failed to remit on his return to Paris was immediately couriered to Versailles, leaving the French ministry without a leg to stand on. Baumez, perhaps to protect himself from any charges of connivance (and no doubt also to secure his place as secretary to the comte's replacement, the abbé Aunillon), did not help matters much when he sent copies to d'Argenson of the comte's highly compromising correspondence on the subject, revealing at the same time the deceitful nature of Jean-Baptiste's claim that he had had to keep up an expensive house and an entire team of servants in Bonn even after his return to Paris, thereby justifying his salary continuance. As Baumez very carefully (and no doubt perfidiously) explained, his master had, in fact, long since given up the rented house in Bonn and had also sent away the servants. And, yes, one more piece of awkwardness to report: his dear master had not yet seen fit to pay his faithful secretary his wages or even to reimburse him for out-of-pocket expenses incurred in the service of His Most Christian Majesty.[19]

Given these shocking revelations, it is not surprising that after an initial show of diplomatic concern, neither the marquis d'Argenson nor Louis XV seemed very worried or even unduly annoyed by the arrest of their *envoyé extraordinaire*. To Marie-Eléonore—kept totally in the dark by everyone—the foreign ministry's indifference seemed incomprehensible. Surely there was some mistake, all that confusion about the nature of Jean-Baptiste's leave the year before. Surely Amelot would be able to clear up the matter in minutes! D'Argenson, in fact, had already ordered a search of Amelot's files and had found nothing to exculpate the comte de Sade. Suspecting Amelot's connivance in "all this gibberish and confusion,"[20] the foreign minister in the end tactfully suggested to Marie-Eléonore that she contact his predecessor directly. Her account of what followed, addressed on 25 February 1745 to one of d'Argenson's clerks, not only suggests the certainty of Amelot's complicity but also reveals the strength of her own naive faith in the integrity of a husband who had obviously been less than candid with her about this and many other matters:

> I inquired of M. Amelot, as M. d'Argenson suggested, whether he could remember having sent permission to M. de Sade to take leave, before his departure from Bonn. He answered that he recalls sending M. de Sade a leave authorization but he cannot remember the precise terms of it, whether it was a definitive leave or only permission to return to Paris for a time, in which case M. de Sade's accreditation at the Elector of Cologne's court would still be in effect. I believe that is indeed the case since M. de Sade was paid his stipend as His Majesty's representative in Cologne during the entire time he was back here and it seems to me that he left again with the same title. He did not receive a present from the Elector and there is no proof that his leave was definitive. Would you not have in your files a copy of M. Amelot's letter to M. de Sade sent at the time of his return? M. d'Argenson spoke to me yesterday of a letter written by the Elector on 31 December 1743 which begins in these terms: *Sire, M. le comte de Sade has informed me of your Majesty's orders for his return. I was most touched, etc. . . .*
>
> Could you not, Monsieur, send me a copy of that letter? It might serve to jog M. Amelot's memory and he could then provide clarification concerning what M. d'Argenson wishes to know. [. . .][21]

Amelot, famous for his phenomenal memory if little else,[22] did not, of course, need any reminding of the relevant circumstances. An office notation on Marie-Eléonore's letter indicates that no action was taken on her request. Out of delicacy, it was no doubt decided to spare her the embarrassing truth about her husband. The "31 December 1743" letter was, in fact, a copy of the original *récréance,* recently forwarded by the elector to Louis XV as damning proof against her husband.

Ill informed but stubbornly loyal, Marie-Eléonore now began a lonely uphill struggle to have her husband freed. Officials in various ministries, influential friends, even Jean-Baptiste's captors were bombarded with letters, all to little effect. D'Argenson, though he had at first seemed concerned and had assured her that she could count on him, now decided to let matters take their course as more and more evidence of the comte's dubious activities—possibly including outright pilfering—continued to accumulate. Spring and summer passed, and nothing happened. By September 1745, Marie-Eléonore's frustration with d'Argenson and his associates had reached its peak, and she was now even losing patience with Jean-Baptiste himself. Why had he not taken proper travel precautions? How could he have got himself into such a pickle?

Another of Marie-Eléonore's surviving letters provides a rare opportunity to hear once more her distinctive voice, blurting out to her husband a mixture of hurt family pride and scolding concern. Even if he had contributed in some way to his own misfortune (and she still knew little of the true circumstances), the shameful neglect of his case by the ministry was outrageous; it was yet another humiliation imposed on their family. That was not, she sharply pointed out, how the maréchal de Belle-Isle's recent release had been handled! *He* had a way of making himself seem indispensable; Jean-Baptiste would do well to learn from the maréchal's example:

> The more I think of it, the more angry I am that you chose to set out without a passport when you left for Bonn. You must have known what would happen if you were captured and that what was done for M. de Belle-Isle would not be done for you. You must be reconciled to the fact that, no matter what he does, *he* always finds a way to be seen as a man who is indispensable. The other day I encountered all the ministers except M. de Maurepas at his house and he was closeted for four hours with M. d'Argenson of Foreign Affairs. There is talk of a congress and everyone says that Belle-Isle will attend as plenipotentiary. You are wasting your time there in Antwerp. If negotiations do get under way you could be making much better use of yourself. Couldn't you do something at your end to obtain your freedom? M. de Belle-Isle worked harder to gain his own release than anyone else. Seeing you wasting your time there makes me so angry![23]

De Belle-Isle, "an indispensable man"—how Marie-Eléonore would have liked to hear those same words said about the comte de Sade, her husband! She goes on in her exasperation: Yes, of course, she had kept on hounding d'Argenson, de Stainville, anyone who might help! Yes, of course, she had written to Prince von Kaunitz, a favorite of Maria Theresa and governor of the Austrian Netherlands. And, no, she had not forgotten to mention the damaging effect all this was having on her unfortunate lawsuit:

> Do you imagine that I did not write and tell M. de Kaunitz that your imprisonment was the reason why I lost my lawsuit? I wrote him five or six times that our affairs were suffering badly because of your being a prisoner. The truth is, as I have discovered, that you would be freed if representations on your behalf were made from here. [. . .] I do not know what to make of all that. M. d'Argenson in the beginning showed a great deal of interest in the matter and then suddenly he let it drop. I want him to tell me why, and I intend to speak to him again on that subject. It makes me so impatient! You can be certain that sometimes, when I leave his office, I am absolutely furious.

Other details follow—some of a practical and mundane nature. She has been ill. She has heard from Jean-Baptiste's mother (who by now was looking after little Donatien). Then more admonitions and gentle wifely reproofs, a bit of court gossip, and a closing as domestically affectionate and prosaic as one could wish:

> Have you remembered to write to your mother? You can do so through M. du Chayla and you really must send her news of yourself. She is much happier hearing from you directly. Let me know how your eyes are. You must be careful not to strain them. You will no doubt answer that it cannot be helped, there being nothing to amuse you except reading and writing. But I hope they have now given you a little more freedom. The comte de Saint-Germain promised me that he would see what could be done. Leave has been canceled for all the officers in the Flanders army, which makes one think that there is something in the offing. If Antwerp is besieged, you would be freed immediately. I have been hoping it would happen for some time now. [. . .]
>
> I believe we shall be appealing our case once more to the Council. This cursed lawsuit is costing me a great deal of money and M. de Nicolai is a dreadful adversary to have to contend with.
>
> Goodnight, Monsieur le comte. Write to me, I beg you.[24]

If on 24 November 1745 the comte was finally released, conditionally and on his honor, after nearly ten months of fairly comfortable internment, it was almost entirely thanks to Marie-Eléonore's unremitting efforts to pressure the French foreign minister into making the required gestures. Vienna was at last convinced that the French court actually cared about the fate of her unfortunate husband! Once safely back in Paris, the comte, suitably grateful, thanked his wife by immediately getting her pregnant. The pregnancy, Marie-Eléonore's last, was difficult, and a daughter, Marie-Françoise, was born several weeks prematurely, on 13 August 1746. She died five days later.

Well before then, however, Jean-Baptiste had gone back to playing the polished libertine, sending witty little notes to his latest mistress, expressing his tenderest passion, and adding in the best stylistically precious tradition of the day that he had now totally forgotten the chains of Maria Theresa's prison and could think only of the cherished bonds that tied him to his newest love.[25] The occasion for such a pretty compliment was the lady's fleeting indisposition, but there is little evidence that Jean-Baptiste was at the same time much concerned with Marie-Eléonore's increasingly frequent bouts of severe illness. Various correspondents throughout 1746 mention her fragile health, and more than one playfully chides him for not passing on their greetings and best wishes to her.[26] Perhaps Jean-Baptiste's neglect in the matter can be attributed to mere habituation: Marie-Eléonore had, after all, been less than well almost from the first days of their marriage.[27] In any case, it was not an issue that was very close to his heart. There was now little left of the marriage. Given the atmosphere of alienation and "the invalid's" delicate health, it seems probable that Jean-Baptiste decided that his son, now already six years old and presumed to be happy in his adopted surroundings, should continue to reside with members of his own family in Provence where a doting grandmother, several maiden aunts (most of whom had taken the veil), and the boy's jolly uncle, abbé of the church and lecherous Petrarchian scholar, were collectively only too pleased to go on taking care of the little marquis who was destined one day to succeed his father as head of the clan and carry on the family's honorable name.

And Baumez? He continued, of course, to irritate his former master exceedingly. In a letter sent to Maria Theresa's unlucky prisoner in the *citadelle* at Antwerp in July 1745, one of Jean-Baptiste's correspondents commiserated on the subject: Yes, Monsieur le Comte certainly had every right to be furious with "this snotty little secretary who was making his way," having transferred his loyalties to the abbé Aunillon. The ingrate! And after everything Monsieur le Comte had done for him!

But, as it turns out, Henry Baumez, part "minor minister" and part resourceful Figaro, was guilty of a much greater offense than lack of gratitude toward his master. Much cleverer than his master gave him credit for being, Baumez, beginning already in 1743 when Jean-Baptiste took his first leave from Bonn, had embarked on the lucrative career of selling the unsuspecting comte's diplomatic secrets to the English. It was probably the abbé Aunillon who first suspected that Baumez was a spy. After Aunillon's first year in Bonn, he and Baumez had their own falling out, probably involving rivalry over a mistress. Jean-Baptiste, for his part, seems never to have caught on to the enterprising secretary's game, any more than he ever became aware of the fact that his supposedly thick-witted underling had been poking fun at him for some time. Fate, however, finally caught up with Henry Baumez in April 1747 when he suddenly found himself in the Bastille, charged with espionage. He died seven months later, still in prison, after suffering a mysterious illness. No one since then seems to have had a kind word to say in his favor, but perhaps we now know enough about his brief encounter with an overweening and mean-spirited master to find some mitigating elements in his decision to turn to amateur crime.[28]

Five

A Mystery Explained

Despite her faltering marriage and serious health problems, Marie-Eléonore continued in the following years to press for her husband's career advancement. Ministry officials were forcefully confronted. Was there not a proper embassy available for the deserving comte de Sade? Perhaps an opening of some importance with the army? At one point the comtesse even reminded the foreign minister that he had the honor of being related to her and that he should consequently make a better effort. D'Argenson's replies were always smoothly reassuring but left no doubt about Jean-Baptiste's real chances: ministers can make suggestions; it is the king who decides.

> *Marly, 19 January 1746*
>
> I have received, Madame, the letter you did me the honor of writing to me. Pleasing you would be, of course, a matter very close to my heart but I cannot guarantee either the means or the opportune time. During the few occasions that I am able to present to His Majesty the candidacies for employment of his various subjects, it is always the Master who chooses, as is only right. His Majesty knows the character and special aptitudes of his subjects better than anyone else at court. I would be charmed to be of some help in obtaining for M. de Sade what he deserves for his activities and recent sufferings in the service of His Majesty. The honor I feel in being connected to your family is an additional motive that impels me always to seek eagerly for ways to convince you of the respectful attachment with which I am, Madame, your very humble and very obedient servant.
>
> *D'Argenson*[1]

The comtesse, who in her habitually forthright style sometimes asked correspondents to sign off without the usual flourish of compliments,[2] probably found it difficult to stomach such a perfectly fulsome example of epistolary decorum. As for Jean-Baptiste, he pretended that he was too noble minded and disinterested to push matters himself. D'Argenson had called him in after his liberation from the Austrians, but instead of commiserating, the foreign minister had actually given him a humiliating reprimand. Then he had had the audacity to cut off his pay. Finally, he had told Jean-Baptiste that, far from deserving a reward, he deserved to be punished.[3] Jean-Baptiste retaliated by denigrating the foreign minister behind his back at every opportunity, especially in letters to trusted friends, always taking care to underline his bravado with the comment "I would not dare say this if I wanted an embassy."[4] It was a bad-faith comment at best, for the truth was that he still wanted an embassy more than ever. To the abbé he displayed the same gift for self-deception, boasting of his "character that knows not how to grovel" and his "aversion for the role of courtier." There was now a new *sultane favorite* governing France, Mme de Pompadour, daughter of his old acquaintance, François Poisson. Jean-Baptiste bragged discreetly that if he wished, he could easily profit from the new mistress's accession to power. "I think she will want to be helpful to everyone; I could prove it if I wished," he intimated somewhat mysteriously to his brother, and then went on to hint at even more:

> I did her father a favor and she feels all the more obligated to me because I ask nothing of her gratitude in return. She has given me permission to visit her at Choisy: I have made the trip several times; I have slept there. She treats me well and, if I wished, I could deem myself to be in favor but I shall take no advantage of that fact. Obligingness which is natural with me when I am with friends demands too high a price when it seems to depend on servitude. I was not born to be a courtier; I like to say what I think and do as I please.

Jean-Baptiste, rather like his son in later years, was fond of assigning himself dramatic *beaux rôles,* but he was obviously more of a frustrated courtier than he cared to admit. "I do not know," he assured his brother, "whether I shall be given a posting; but one thing is certain: I shall not ask."[5]

But the plain truth is that Jean-Baptiste *did* ask, almost everyone and at every opportunity. He even asked his enemy d'Argenson, directly and repeatedly. He also asked de Noailles, de Saxe, anyone in a position of power.[6] Finally, d'Argenson felt obliged to make the situation as plain as he could:

> *Bouchout, 2 June 1746*
>
> It is certainly with much distress, Monsieur, that I see you blaming me for your current lack of employment. I have the honor from time to time to place before the king the Foreign Affairs candidacies of his subjects, and it is His Majesty's discernment that decides with justice and reason the identity of those who are most suitable.
>
> No one, Monsieur, is more than I have the honor of being, your most humble and most obedient servant.
>
> *D'Argenson*[7]

Despite the stark clarity of that response, Jean-Baptiste was still inclined to think that his blocked career was attributable entirely to d'Argenson's malice. He consoled himself with the thought that the foreign minister could not continue in the post forever. Biding his time, he carefully tended his Versailles network of cronies, and it was with great relief and anticipation that he learned in February 1747 of his enemy's replacement by one of his old friends, the marquis de Puisieux. He immediately sent a memo to the new minister, depicting his past services in the most favorable light, claiming four years of service in Bonn (rather than the actual two), and omitting any reference to the embarrassing *récréance* letter or the various audits carried out on his suspect accounts. D'Argenson, he implied, had deliberately tried to discredit him in order to give the position to one of his own favorites, the abbé Aunillon. During his confinement at Antwerp, for example, his dear wife had gone to great lengths to try to persuade d'Argenson to request his release, all to no avail. Could he not now presume upon his long established friendship with the new minister to set things right?[8]

To Jean-Baptiste's total astonishment, Puisieux's response was anything but reassuring. Finally, the truth dawned on him: somehow, he had become unemployable! There were obviously mysterious reasons behind this unhappy situation, reasons that went much deeper than any surviving bureaucratic misgivings about his questionable conduct during the Bonn posting. What could these be?

It was Jean-Baptiste's brother who finally discovered the solution to his puzzle. In 1748, four full years after the death of the duchesse de Châteauroux, the abbé was having a friendly chat in Montpellier with his sometime companion in debauchery, the *maréchal duc* de Richelieu. Richelieu had once hinted to him that he knew why the comte de Sade's career was blocked. Questioned subsequently on the subject by the abbé, Richelieu revealed the horrible truth: Jean-Baptiste's secret enemy was none other than Louis XV himself!

Writing from Narbonne on 15 December 1748, the abbé immediately passed on this astonishing piece of intelligence to his brother:

> I spent a few days in Montpellier with M. le maréchal de Richelieu who was more friendly than ever. I had for some time been troubled by something he had casually mentioned to me concerning you. I asked for details. He told me that you had lashed out furiously at him and at Mme de Châteauroux, that you had done so in the presence of several of that lady's friends who subsequently informed her of it. She was all the more incensed by it since she had resolved to make your fortune and that of your wife who

was her special friend. She mentioned the incident to the King who, ever since then, has been much indisposed toward you. I assured him most emphatically that you could not have done such a thing, that it was pure calumny, that you had always seemed to me to be much attached to Mme de Châteauroux, and that you were incapable of ingratitude. That was all I could get out of him.[9]

Shaken by Richelieu's revelation—coming as it did from a man who was uniquely qualified to know—indeed, who had been the duchesse's protector and mentor and who was himself still one of the most powerful and feared personages in the kingdom—Jean-Baptiste immediately wrote back asking his brother for more details. The abbé replied by return post from Ebreuil on the twenty-sixth of the following month. Since the matter was extremely delicate and the mails were increasingly insecure, he decided to use a thinly disguised word cipher to camouflage the identities of the persons involved:

> I can tell you nothing more about what you wish to know. I have no details. The man who leaves for England told me only that his master was much resentful of you because of certain things you had said about the dead woman. I attempted to defend you. He laughed in my face and assured me that it was true. He himself seemed very bitter about it. That is all I know. From what you tell me, I cannot see how you could ever be employed. If you thought as I do, you would find that a comfort, and if I strike you as being distressed by it all, it is because I think it distresses you and that you do not think as I do.[10]

The problem of dating the two letters just quoted is of critical importance and in itself provides a cogent example of how little we still know about the marquis de Sade's family background. It also highlights some of the treacherous difficulties associated with editing correspondence, especially when much of it is anonymous and bears no indication of the year or perhaps even the month of composition. The following rather detailed exegetical interlude provides a much needed solution to the puzzle; with apologies to the nonspecialist reader, I place it here rather than in an extended note.

In his recent biography *Sade* (1991), Maurice Lever dates the first of the two letters just quoted, the abbé de Sade's "15 December" Narbonne letter to which I have assigned the year 1748, as belonging to the year 1744 (p. 57 and p. 671, n. 34), no doubt on the grounds that Richelieu had indeed presided at the meetings of the provincial *états* of Languedoc in November–December 1744 (he arrived back in Paris on 24 December),[11] and the duchesse de Châteauroux had died on 8 December of that year. Quite naturally, Lever dates the "26 January" Ebreuil letter, alluding to "the man who leaves for England" (Richelieu), "his master" (Louis XV), and "the dead woman" (Mme de Châteauroux), as "26 janvier 1745" (p. 57), seeing it as an answer to Jean-Baptiste's concerned request for a more detailed explanation of the disturbing comments reported in the 15 December letter from Narbonne. Consistent with that 1745 dating for the second letter (p. 672, n. 11), Lever quotes (p. 62) another passage from this same 26 January "1745" Ebreuil letter that refers to the arrival at Ebreuil of one of the most important personages involved in the marquis de Sade's life and career, the abbé Amblet, Donatien's newly hired tutor, who, it has been established,[12] was born in 1716 and who is therefore described by Lever as being "twenty-nine years old" at the time:

> M. Amblet has arrived, dear brother. His journey went very well. I do not know him yet so I am unable to give you my opinion of him. All I can say is that he is quick-witted and gentle. If I'm not mistaken, you have come up with an excellent find for your son. I shall soon be able to send you a more definite opinion. Meanwhile, I am delighted to have him here. He has begun his tutoring apprenticeship by undertaking to teach Italian to a lady of my acquaintance and he seems to be going about it quite successfully.[13]

It is here that the plot thickens, for Lever, by choosing January 1745 as the date for this letter, has implicitly cast aside one of the old pivotal "facts" of Sadean biography, suggesting something quite new—indeed, revolutionary—concerning five or six critically formative years of the marquis' childhood, beginning with the summer of 1744 when Donatien was taken to the Avignon region to be honored by his "vassals" at Saumane, after which he is presumed to have remained in Languedoc for the next five years, solely in the care of his paternal grandmother and his many aunts, or else with his uncle, the dissipated abbé de Sade, that uncle being, in the words of Sade's other major biographer, Jean-Jacques Pauvert, "his only masculine reference point."[14] Conclusions of a most serious nature have been drawn from this anomalous, female-dominated childhood environment. But with Lever's 1745 dating of the Ebreuil letter, the influence of the new tutor could presumably now be seen as countering the effect of this insalubrious family mix, fully five years earlier than has normally been thought! Lever does not insist on the implications of the dating, although it would seem that a tentative reevaluation of the various personality-shaping influences that guided and perhaps malformed the childhood development of Donatien Alphonse François de Sade might have been legitimately explored at this point.

But let us return to the problem of dating the abbé's two key letters to his brother in Paris. When, two years after his 1991 biography, Maurice Lever published the first volume of the *Papiers de famille: le règne du père (1721–1760)*, the same critical problem of dating the two letters in question arose once again, and this time a different solution was proposed. What I have designated as the December 1748 Narbonne letter is still maintained as "15 December [1744]," but the "26 January [1745]" Ebreuil letter, even though it is quite obviously a return-mail follow-up to Jean-Baptiste's response to the abbé's 15 December Narbonne letter, is now supplied with a suggested new date, "[1750]"—that is, *five years later,* and the abbé's mention of the tutor Amblet's arrival is footnoted with the indication that "the abbé Jacques-François Amblet, born at Annecy on 19 January 1716 [. . .] was hired around 1750 as private tutor to Donatien Alphonse François, then aged ten," 1750 being the year the young marquis began his studies at the Collège Louis-le-Grand in Paris. This substantial correction to the previous dating has, of course, the effect of bringing Lever into line with what biographers have traditionally stated to be the case, as well as with the usual interpretation of the supposedly "autobiographical" revelations made by Sade himself in *Aline et Valcour* in which the hero Valcour notes that after his lengthy stay with an overfond grandmother in Languedoc, he returned to Paris to take up his studies "under the guidance of a man who was both firm and intelligent, well-suited to mold my youth. Unfortunately for me, I was not with him for a long enough time." [15]

The conventional view that Donatien's tutor Amblet was hired in 1750 and was responsible for bringing him back that year to Paris to begin his studies at Louis-le-Grand is no doubt responsible for Lever's 1993 shifting of the Ebreuil letter from January [1745] to January [1750]. Perhaps there were difficulties, too, in trying to imagine how Richelieu in January 1745 could have been ciphered as "the man who leaves for England," since it was only in January 1746 that a frustrated Richelieu, heading an expeditionary force of twelve thousand men, found himself on the French coast waiting for the winds, the sea, and the English navy to allow him to cross the channel to help put the Young Pretender, Charles Edward Stuart, on the usurped throne of his ancestors. As for the Narbonne 15 December letter, it could only have been after much hesitation that it was, in 1993, maintained at the 1744 date. [16] Certainly, the abbé's reference to having "for some time been troubled" by what Richelieu had hinted to him concerning Jean-Baptiste's shattered career prospects is somewhat puzzling in a letter supposedly composed as early as December 1744. Moreover, if the context involved in any way the sudden death of the duchesse de Châteauroux on 8 December, it seems doubtful (though not impossible) that the news could have reached Montpellier "a few days" before the fifteenth of the month. It is also not an easy matter to harmonize with such an early date the reference "ever since then," suggesting as it does an already extensive duration period for Louis XV's displeasure.

But the conclusive proof that the 15 December "1744" letter was in fact written four years later, in 1748, lies elsewhere and, indeed, is maddeningly simple: If we look at it again, we note that the abbé de Sade speaks of having "spent a few days in Montpellier with *M. le maréchal* de Richelieu. [. . .]" The key to the puzzle lies in the title the abbé employs. It was, in fact, only in October 1748 that Richelieu, the immensely popular hero of the Genoa campaign, was finally granted the coveted *maréchal's* baton that had so long eluded him. On his triumphant return from Italy that year, he had stopped off in Montpellier to preside as usual over the *états* meetings of Languedoc, arriving back in Paris on 25 December 1748.[17] Of course, that means that the Ebreuil letter, an obvious response to the 15 December Narbonne letter, was written not on 26 January 1745 or 26 January 1750 but on 26 January 1749, all of which provides the young marquis de Sade with a tutor, if not for five additional years, at least for one year more than has been generally thought. Nor is there any possibility that the 15 December Narbonne letter could have been written even later—that is, in December 1749 rather than 1748—since Richelieu, for that session of the Languedoc *états* meetings, did not leave Paris for Montpellier until January 1750, the assembly having been postponed until 19 January 1750 to accommodate the intendant Le Nain, who was slowly recovering from the amputation in early September 1749 of a gangrenous right arm.[18]

The implications of this new dating, made possible by the clarification of one tiny but critical fact, throws some new light on the tenacity of Jean-Baptiste's active career ambitions as well as on Louis XV's singular determination to hold a personal grudge. More important, however, the proof it provides of a tutor's arrival in Donatien's young life already by 1749, at least one year before his probable return to Paris, leaves room for additional speculation regarding the psychological dynamics of this formative period—about which, everyone agrees, we still know far too little.

↣

And so it was that only late in January 1749, more than five years after his witty tongue and sotto voce comments had cost him the friendship of the king's mistress, did Jean-Baptiste de Sade, frustrated soldier and diplomat, learn that there could be no future for him in Louis XV's France. With his special talent for making a virtue out of necessity, he put up a good show of shrugging off disappointment. Setting aside for the moment his diplomatic ambitions, he continued to cultivate his senior army connections as he played the role of the fashionable courtier on the fringes of court life at Versailles. In the retailing of high-quality gossip, he was still deemed to have few equals, and, of course, the *grandes dames* of Versailles still looked on with gushing approval as he demonstrated the art of the graceful ballroom pirouette to their little daughters. He deserved better from life but consoled himself by secretly nurturing his inner bitterness. At the same time, he outwardly proclaimed himself fortunate enough to be entirely immune to the slavery of ambition, free to be his own man as he bathed in life's endless stream of pleasures.

Those pleasures continued to include, of course, his serial *bonnes fortunes;* in this regard, he continued to trade on his celebrated imprisonment and on the elegantly apposite metaphor that went with it: "I am once more in shackles [. . .]," he exulted to one of his correspondents. "Guess who has now cast her magic spell over me." [19] It was clearly very important for him to be able to boast to others about such exploits: "My confession is done," he confided to another. "Forgive me the error of my ways. Confessing my sins is no doubt my greatest crime. But how can I refuse you? In any case, my little adventure has already caused such a deal of chatter. . . . I have passed it on to so many confidants." [20]

"So many confidants"—we can guess that Marie-Eléonore did not escape hearing frequent rumors of her husband's well-trumpeted feminine conquests. On the other hand, it is far less likely that either she or the *grandes dames* of Versailles would have heard much about the comte's parallel "lucky encounters" below stairs at the Hôtel de Condé where he continued to pursue the pleasures of sodomizing laquais, pastry cooks, and sundry male prostitutes invited for expeditious visits to the de Sade apartment. We know that Antoine Leclerc, brother of an officer in the queen's household, party animal, and excellent cook (we recall Marie-Eléonore's testimonial), had been with Jean-Baptiste for some years, but he was obviously not an exceptional presence in the de Sade household. Several of the comte's other servants, along with their master, are named in police reports around this time, and it seems entirely likely that Jean-Baptiste had selected at least some of his domestics on the basis of their bona fide sodomitical credentials and trusted connections with the town's network of male homosexuals, commonly branded unspeakable degenerates (*infâmes*) by the authorities.

François Le Poivre, a journeyman harness maker and male prostitute who was later obliged to become a police informer, was first introduced to

Jean-Baptiste's household staff by the older Goblet, a cook in the employ of the présidente de Lamoignon and an associate of Antoine Leclerc. Goblet made a business of discreetly procuring young tradesmen for such well-known *amateurs* as the comte de Sade, the tax official Amelot, son of the magistrate of that name, and the notorious collector of the *capitation* tax, Duval. One of Le Poivre's best customers around this time was the bishop of Fréjus, Martin du Bellay, diocesan successor to the late cardinal Fleury, who frequently officiated at the queen's special religious ceremonies at Versailles. Bishop du Bellay's cook Hulin, along with Caillet, his *valet de chambre,* and his lackey Clermont were all known to have participated from time to time in the pleasures of their episcopal master, a situation that was probably not very different from that which prevailed in the Hôtel de Condé apartment of the comte de Sade where Leclerc the cook, the footman Thomas Beguet, and at least one other servant were known to the vice squad as members of the network. Police records indicate, in fact, that Le Poivre serviced the bishop (both actively and passively) early in 1749 soon after one of his (passive) interludes with Jean-Baptiste in the seclusion of the Hôtel de Condé apartment. Characteristically perhaps, Jean-Baptiste's modest payment of six livres for that particular session of buggery was less than half what the bishop handed over for precisely the same service, and it seems that Marie-Eléonore's inveterately grumpy husband also failed to be as cordial as the high churchman who accompanied his payment with equally generous compliments, even extending a gracious invitation to Le Poivre "to come back to see him often." [21]

How much Marie-Eléonore at this time knew or cared about what was going on either above or below stairs in their vast apartment is not clear. We have Jean-Baptiste's word for it that her early discovery of his infidelities with Caroline-Charlotte had cost him "her entire friendship." It is likely that his habitual dalliance with the household lackeys and male prostitutes, if she was aware of it, would have also cost him some of her respect. The totally dissolute atmosphere of the Hôtel de Condé, aggravated by intrigue, cruelty, and the near-certifiable madness of several of the principal occupants, must have made the place seem less and less a safe or sane haven either for herself or for her son. Given her various domestic problems, her illness, and her continuing lawsuits, perhaps the thought occurred to her that little Donatien might just as well continue staying on with his grandmother in Provence.

In one key respect, however, Marie-Eléonore's sense of solidarity with Jean-Baptiste as chief custodian of the family's fortunes never wavered. Undoubtedly, the abbé's recent revelations concerning Louis XV's enmity jolted her. As a result of Jean-Baptiste's imprudence, family honor had once again been besmirched and trampled on. She had hoped that her husband, starting out under the protection of Monsieur le Duc, would one day achieve a brilliant position among the nation's leaders. Instead, her marriage had brought her only a faithless fop, repudiated by everyone who counted. Her family pride and her personal loyalty were such, however, that, despite everything, she could not bring herself to give up on all of her ambitions for her husband and for the family. That would remain the case even after she formally separated from Jean-Baptiste. As late as 1756, for example, when the French under the duc de Richelieu were engaged in the Minorcan expedition, she complained bitterly to the war minister, the comte d'Argenson, as well as to his nephew, the marquis de Paulmy, angrily pointing out that her husband, who desired only to serve His Most Christian Majesty, had once more been passed over in favor of lesser men. De Paulmy's response to this persistent poor cousin of the *princes du sang* was deeply apologetic: "Nothing will be nearer to my heart than the wish to convince you of the full extent of my good will in everything that may be agreeable to you." The young de Paulmy was obviously as adept at composing pleasantly meaningless phrases for Marie-Eléonore's benefit as his father, the retired foreign minister, had been. But it all came to the same result. The answer was still no.

Jean-Baptiste-Joseph-François, Comte de Sade (1702-1767), father of the Marquis. Detail from a portrait by Jean-Marc Nattier.

Marie-Éléonore de Maillé de Carman, Comtesse de Sade (1712-1777), mother of the Marquis. Detail adapted from an anonymous miniature.

Donatien-Alphonse-François, Marquis de Sade (1740-1814) in his early twenties.
Detail from a drawing attributed to Charles-Amédée-Philippe Van Loo.

Grand M.^{tre} de France
Louis Joseph de Bourbon Prince du Sang
né et titré Prince de Condé

Coat of Arms of Donatien's playmate at the Hôtel de Condé,
Louis Joseph de Bourbon, Prince de Condé (1736-1818)

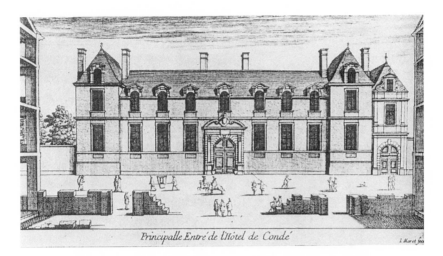

View of the main entrance to the Hôtel de Condé in Paris, birthplace of
the Marquis de Sade. Early engraving by D. Marot.

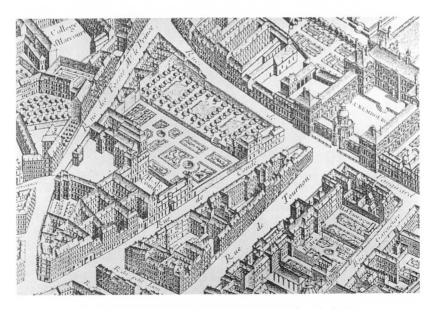

Detail from the Plan de Louis Bretez ("Plan de Turgot," 1739), showing
the Hôtel de Condé and adjoining gardens.

Louis II de Bourbon, "the Great Condé" (1621-1686), Marie-Éléonore's distinguished ancestor. Engraving by Balthazar Moncornet.

Part Two

TRANSGRESSIONS

Ce n'est point ma façon
de penser qui a fait mon
malheur, c'est celle
des autres.

[It is not my way of
thinking that has caused
my misfortune; it is that
of others.]

Six

MASTER AND PUPIL

Access to the family papers recently published by Maurice Lever, though it has significantly enriched our understanding of many aspects of Sade's later adolescent years, has added surprisingly little, unfortunately, to our knowledge of the even more important formative period that preceded. Here, we still seem to have to depend for most of the "facts" on one brief page of treacherously fictional "autobiographical" narrative in the novel *Aline et Valcour*. It seems evident, first of all, that most of the relevant family papers are still missing. Volume I of Lever's *Papiers de famille,* for example, provides barely five pages of correspondence for the year 1748; barely nine pages for 1749, a total of eight in 1750 (one of which, as we have seen, belongs to the year 1749), three for 1751, and eight for 1752—and this during the period that saw such significant events as the formal separation of Jean-Baptiste and Marie-Eléonore, Donatien's acquisition of a tutor, and, especially, his return to Paris for schooling at Louis-le-Grand. We still do not know where, how, or with whom he lived once he was back in Paris, and it is not even really clear where Jean-Baptiste and Marie-Eléonore normally resided during this period. One major biographer has stated that the comtesse retreated to the Carmelites on the rue d'Enfer "probably around 1747 or 1748,"[1] whereas another speculates that the move occurred more than a decade later, "around 1760."[2] Letters in the *Papiers de famille* are silent on the matter though they do suggest that the couple continued to share, perhaps as late as 1752, independent use of the Hôtel de Condé apartment in addition to their recently acquired country house at Glatigny near Versailles. Jean-Baptiste is occasionally asked by correspondents to pass on personal greetings to his wife, but at times he seems to be quite ignorant of Marie-Eléonore's movements or whereabouts. We know that for a considerable period of time in the early 1750s he used the Glatigny house as his main Versailles headquarters, while his town residence was somewhere in the vast Luxembourg complex, just next door to the Hôtel de Condé. Most of the time he kept moving around, dutifully following the court's seasonal rituals of transplantation to Compiègne or Fontainebleau. Sometimes he simply stayed for extended periods with friends, old mistresses for the most part like Mlle de Charolais, the sister of Monsieur le Duc. "You flit about in such a sprightly manner that I no longer know where to meet up with you," chided Mme de Longeville, another of his sometime mistresses, one day in August 1753.[3]

As for Donatien, though he may have resided with his father some of the time between 1750 and 1754, especially during the summer vacations when Jean-Baptiste would take him to the Champagne countryside to stay with Mme de Longeville, still it seems most likely that the boy, soon after his return from Provence, became a full-time boarder at Louis-le-Grand, staying only intermittently during the school year either with his mother at the Hôtel de Condé or with his tutor Amblet in the immediately adjacent rue des Fossés Monsieur le Prince. Most of that, unfortunately, is still a matter of speculation. If, as some biographers have suggested, Donatien was never a boarder but only a day student at Louis-le-Grand, then he probably resided mainly with his mother before her move to the Carmélites apartment and chiefly with Amblet afterward.

A basic incompatibility of temperament between Marie-Eléonore and her husband, no doubt present from the beginning, deepened over the years, aggravated by her increasing bitterness and disillusionment with the comte's libertinism, his career failures, his constant gambling debts (by his own admission he had been obliged to "torment" her for loans on occasion),[4] the whole exacerbated by her own chronic ill health and a disenchanted sense that she had paid dearly for the honor of being the wife of this witty, handsome, exquisitely polished but dissipated and shallow wastrel. It is likely, on the other hand, that Jean-Baptiste went about explaining to all of his friends and relatives who cared to listen that most of his marital problems were caused by Marie-Eléonore's "changed" character, she having become "fretful," "high-strung" and "difficult."

It had not always been that way. In the early years of the marriage, Jean-Baptiste's brother, the gallant abbé, used to scold him for neglecting to send him news of his beautiful young wife: "You have a wife whom I like very much but it has been ages since I have heard her mentioned."[5] By 1750, however, the abbé had suffered a radical change of heart. Responding to a suggestion from Jean-Baptiste that he come to Paris "to unite our revenues and live together," his brother politely declined with the observation, "You have a wife whom I would find rather more difficult to live with than with you. It is hard for me to imagine we could survive for very long together."[6] Jean-Baptiste obviously made no secret of his difficulties with "the invalid," and he was never at a loss when it came to finding ways to cast himself in the *beau rôle* in the eyes of their common friends. It seems likely that this was also the course he followed with his impressionable adolescent son who soon came to share his father's view of a bad-tempered, "interfering" mother, this vigilantly devout matron who constantly scolded on the themes of discipline, family duty, and fidelity, complaining all the while that she was getting little respect or gratitude for her efforts to prevent the boy from becoming a perfect replica of his dissipated father.

Again, with so much of the evidence missing, we can only speculate on these vitally important matters, but my guess would be that it was not so much Donatien's supposed resentment of his mother's *absence* during this time, not so much the frequently posited "emotional desert" that nurtured in the adolescent marquis the seeds of his retaliatory "sadism," the urge to punish maternal power and women in general,[7] but rather Marie-Eléonore's *presence* as a blocking maternal authority figure whose stiff attitudes and moralistic actions would eventually be mirrored in the character delineations of those severe, "Argus-eyed" mothers in *Justine* and *Juliette*,[8] women who are so "deservedly" and routinely abused, lacerated and murdered by their demonic, pleasure-seeking sons and daughters.

How different Marie-Eléonore must have seemed in the eyes of the little marquis from his doting, fondly indulgent papa, "the most tender-hearted father in the whole world, [. . .] the tenderest of all fathers and the best of all friends"![9] Though indulgent to a fault, Jean-Baptiste would have angrily brushed aside any reproving matronly accusations that he was schooling his adoring son in debauchery; no, he was merely guiding this appreciative youngster toward a life of "virtue without austerity" in a world where the most important rule of conduct was to "follow the dictates of good form." The comte was very much a man of his milieu: manners outranked morals, appearances transcended reality, and sincerity was at best a tactical ploy.

The adolescent Donatien, highly intelligent and acutely sensitive, would have been quick to pick up on the destructive tension between his alienated parents, and Jean-Baptiste's easy-going permissiveness, so ready to adapt to the boy's own expanding intellectual and emotional horizons, would have made it very easy for the son to choose consistently the father's side. Entering his teens, Donatien probably saw his father more as a companion, a friend, rather than as a parental authority figure. Moreover, he rather liked all those other women he saw hanging about in his father's circle of friends—warmly supportive, sensual women who always seemed ready to play the role of *secondes mamans,* to fill in where Marie-Eléonore had been found wanting both as a wife and as a mother. These indulgent surrogate mothers, cuddling and fussing, had been a fact of Donatien's life nearly from the moment he had arrived in Avignon at the age of four. Everyone had leaped at the opportunity to comfort the little "orphan," first and foremost his grandmother whose "excessive fondness," [10] to quote Valcour's own words, spoiled him rotten. Then it was the turn of Mme de Saint-Germain, the lively young governess who helped out when he stayed with his uncle at Ebreuil. She was a pleasant, quick-witted, and loving woman, someone he would continue to call his dear *maman* for the rest of his life. Even his mother-in-law, Mme de Montreuil, the archetypal monster-mother of his prison correspondence and novels, began her relationship with the marquis as a much cherished *seconde maman.* Indeed, he found her strong maternal protection to be the only redeeming feature of that unwanted marriage, and it was he who deliberately sought her out from the start as a substitute mother: "Oh! with what joy in times past did I address you as mother! It was to you, as my mother, that I had come with my entreaties." [11] It was an attachment he later turned violently on its head, but in the beginning it too had followed the old adolescent patterns established long before with the approving complicity of Jean-Baptiste.

Maurice Lever's new utilization of the Sade papers, through no fault of the author, cannot quite live up to the claim that his biography has now made "familiar" Donatien's youth, "from about his eleventh to his eighteenth year." [12] But even with so many family documents missing, Lever has managed to break much new ground in the use he has made of the correspondence exchanged by Jean-Baptiste with Mme de Longeville, the comtesse de Raimond whose letters throw at least some indirect light on the marquis' relationship with his mother during this period. Mme de Longeville, three years younger than Jean-Baptiste, regularly hosted Donatien and his tutor Amblet during summer vacations at her modest country château where she readily assumed, with her lover's approval, the role of substitute mother. A letter she writes to Jean-Baptiste on 8 September 1753 could not be clearer in this respect: "Alas, *our child* has gone and we are left much saddened. He has a heart, that charming child! I'm told that he was weeping when he said goodbye to me, though he hid his tears." [13] Two weeks later she is proud to inform Jean-Baptiste that little Donatien treats her "like a real *maman*": "I love him too, as if he were my own child. I want him to love me as if I were his *maman,* for I love being loved." [14]

It is not difficult to imagine the confused and hostile feelings the thirteen-year-old boy would bring back with him to Paris when he returned to the cheerless apartment of the woman his papa liked to call "the invalid." She was so disapproving, so totally different from the others, so ready always to make life miserable for all concerned. In a sense, his papa's flagrant infidelities were a just "punishment" for the straitlaced Marie-Eléonore, almost a gesture of solidarity in support of his own struggle for liberation from matriarchal tyranny.

Jean-Baptiste imposed neither physical nor moral strictures on his son. When Donatien was thirteen, his overfond father decided that it would be a good idea to rent a *petite maison* for him not far from the college. Donatien would have his very own playboy hideaway! By coincidence, it was the same little house where the comte de Clermont—another of those worthy Bourbon-Condé *princes du sang*—used to lodge the famous *danseuse* la Camargo. The comte found it amusing to watch his son perform in that celebrated setting, play-acting (both he and Donatien loved the theater) the role of the apprentice libertine as he and his papa entertained Mme de Longeville and her attractive friend Mme de Vernouillet at fashionable suppers. The proud father could not help noticing that his precocious thirteen-year-old was already feeling intense carnal passion for the shapely Mme de Vernouillet, once the mistress of the duc de Richelieu—and, of course, of Jean-Baptiste himself. It was especially fascinating to note that the delightful lady in question was herself not entirely indifferent to the situation and that she in turn playfully flirted with the boy "while she waited," as she archly remarked, "for him to grow up." [15]

Donatien did not have to wait very long to "grow up." During his last year at Louis-le-Grand, he probably became a day-student but remained at the same time essentially free of his mother's frowning vigilance when Jean-Baptiste decided to set up the *petite maison* as his son's occasional domicile and arranged for Donatien to take some of his meals there, presumably under his tutor's supervision. *Petites maisons* would, in any case, soon become a standard fixture in the life of the marquis de Sade, and it is not clear how many others he had access to in the next ten years before he finally acquired the one near the rue Mouffetard where, in October 1763, he would inflict his singular horrors on Jeanne Testard, thereby earning the first of several prison sentences for criminal sexual abuse. By then he was truly "grown up." Indeed, he had already used the rue Mouffetard hideaway in June of that same year, scarcely two weeks after marrying Marie-Pélagie de Montreuil [16] in a ceremony that had to be delayed for a time while he waited for a stubborn case of gonorrhea to be treated.

Of course, his dear and tender papa had taught him much in the in-

tervening decade, doing his best all the while to keep both himself and Donatien at a safe distance from the righteous scoldings of Marie-Eléonore.
The comte had always made it a point to foster a sense of moral emancipation in his son, to free him from "superstition," "prejudice," and any
sense of guilt or constraint in the exercise of his sexual freedom. In fact,
Donatien had already celebrated his eighteenth birthday when his father,
in a *billet-doux* to Mme de Longeville in which he lightheartedly reviewed
his own lifetime of lucky conquests, specifically alluded to his ambitions
for his son regarding this all-important question. Fidelity in matters of the
heart, he graciously informed her, deserves neither our respect nor our
praise. It was not one of the lessons in life that he had chosen to teach his
son, and he had made that decision quite deliberately. A time comes when
one must have done with stale compliments and conventional protestations of unending love:

> Would to God I had never loved anyone but you. But how can one *not*
> be unfaithful, my sweet? Only fools remain constant. One must never cease
> to love what one has truly loved but one must also take advantage of all new
> opportunities. We become more worthy of being loved as a result. M. de
> Richelieu would be only a mediocre man if he had only one woman to his
> credit. When women chase after him, do you imagine it is that wrinkled old
> prune that they pursue? Not at all! They are chasing after the lover of a hun-
> dred women! They think they become more attractive by adding their
> names to his list of conquests. They do it not for the pleasure but to enhance
> their reputation. [. . .] I have met up with faithful lovers from time to time:
> they are so gloomy, so sullen that they inspire fear. *If my son were to choose a
> life of constancy, I would be outraged. I would almost prefer to see him become
> a member of the Academy.*[17]

A time was fast approaching when the master would take considerably
less pride in his pupil's infidelity, but for the moment at least, Jean-Baptiste
was entirely pleased with the progress his apprentice libertine had made.
What the father's lessons in the traditional arts of sybaritic dalliance do not
account for, however, is the soon to be revealed darker side of his offspring's libertinism, more deeply rooted, one suspects, in the troubled and
ambivalent relationship of the son with his mother, going back to a much
earlier time when at the age of four or five he found himself abruptly torn
from his most vital emotional roots, abandoned apparently by this nurturing angel who had suddenly banished him from her presence.

It was probably then, very early on, that the "absent mother" trauma
(if trauma there was) had its most devastating effect. Almost overnight,
Donatien had found himself an "orphan," deprived of all "control" over

the mother who until then had always been there to respond lovingly to his every need, his every willful gesture. It was that same angry *control,* coercive and punitive, that he would later seek to regain over women in the manipulative dominance fantasies and coercive acts that are the very essence of both his sexual and literary expression.

More speculation, of course. At the same time, we have only faint impressions of Marie-Eléonore's own thoughts and feelings regarding her son's upbringing during the later adolescent years when Jean-Baptiste's influence seems to have taken over entirely. That she still attempted from time to time to intervene in her son's life despite her husband's sustained efforts to reduce her role to insignificance can be deduced from several remarks gleaned in the surviving correspondence of the young marquis' various substitute mothers. Donatien's former governess Mme de Saint-Germain, like her neighbor Mme de Longeville, warmly welcomed "*her* child's" visits to the country. At the end of one of her letters, she too writes of her reluctance to send the darling little angel back to Paris. If only he could stay with her a little longer! But apparently the stern will of the comtesse, Donatien's mother, had to be satisfied in the matter. This most cherished of Donatien's substitute mothers, the woman whom the marquis even thirty years later would describe to his wife as "the woman whom I love most in the entire universe, after you, and to whom I owe everything that a son can owe to his mother," [18] is almost frantic in her pleadings to keep her dearest treasure with her just a bit longer:

> Would you really be so cruel as to rob me of *my child,* to snatch from me the only pleasure I have ever asked from you as a favor? Leave him with me a little longer. *If I had the honor of Mme de Sade's acquaintance I would write to her and beg. Do it for me!* The court and the town provide you with so many amusements and distractions that you can surely give up for my sake the bourgeois pleasure of having your child with you. [. . .]
>
> I await your reply. It will decide my destiny. You will answer when you choose to but I declare to you that I will not let my child leave until I hear from you. I cannot believe you would be so inhuman as to refuse me this. [19]

We can well imagine how Donatien, just entering his teens and torn by parental conflict as well as the emotional turmoil generated by an already ambiguous attachment to these substitute *mamans,* would balk at returning, even for short stays, to the austere atmosphere of his mother's apartment at the Carmelites. The place, exuding that sickly fragrance of illness and religiosity he associated with old women, reminded him of nothing so much as death. [20] Soon the army and the freedom that marked the military rites of passage to noble manhood would rescue him from all that.

Of course, it would mean leaving his "tender papa" and his wise tutor Amblet behind. But glory awaited! Soon, he would excel as a soldier, qualifying superlatively, according to his army records, under two not entirely unrelated categories: "very unbalanced" and "very brave."[21] Incredibly, even now his interfering, eternally fretful mother was trying to put obstacles in his way. Despite his dear papa's efforts to gain him a place in one of the best regiments, she almost ruined everything at the last minute. Jean-Baptiste's good friend, the marquis de Poyanne, still a powerful figure at court, had offered Donatien a junior commission as a *cornette* in the Carabiniers regiment and a position as one of his aides de camp. It was a splendid opportunity; the Carabiniers were one of the most distinguished and dazzling of all the regiments. It is true that their casualty numbers were appallingly high: "It was rarely spared and it was frequently placed in harm's way."[22] But both the sixteen-year-old Donatien and his father—determined that his son's military career would succeed where his own had failed—saw de Poyanne's offer as a golden opportunity. Not so Marie-Eléonore, unfortunately, and she did not hesitate to let her feelings be known in the right quarter, as we learn from an embarrassed letter written to Jean-Baptiste by the corps' commander: "Madame de Sade seems not of your opinion, my dear comte, and I would be risking her full anger if I took her son along with me to a place that displeases her. You know how attached I am to her and I would be most sorry to be a party to anything that causes her displeasure. I have not seen her since you wrote me. [. . .] I had already done everything I could to convince her."[23] Again, the interfering mother!

This time, however, Donatien prevailed, and soon there arrived in the post from Mme de Longeville what must have been a very welcome show of substitute maternal solidarity for both father and son. From her letter we can deduce that a noisy family dispute had taken place on the issue and that Donatien on this occasion may even have broken openly, if not irrevocably, with his mother. Of course, everyone sympathized with poor Jean-Baptiste: "You have had to endure Mme la comtesse de Sade's ill humor once again. Her intentions are good, I think, but the damage is done. People with quick tempers do get off on the wrong foot and there is no going back."[24] The "quick-tempered people" referred to are presumably an emotionally overwrought Marie-Eléonore and her equally volatile son, the "damage done" being probably a memorably ugly confrontation between the two, crowned by fiery outbursts and the exchange of harsh words that would not soon be forgotten or forgiven. But still Marie-Eléonore refused to budge, and the matter was left unresolved. Two weeks later, Mme de

Longeville returned to the point: "What have you decided to do about that child? In short, with the best intentions in the world, his mother is still working against your interests. Ah, what *love!*"[25] There is little doubt that Mme de Longeville had hit upon the right word, and we can indeed be certain that the mother's overriding motivation in all this was a profound love for her son. But the son, impulsive and hostile, perceived it as suffocating and meddling intrusion. In the end, father and son prevailed—that was normal for the times in such matters—but in the process of winning this victory the son undoubtedly added more resentment and anger to the bitter disaffection he already felt toward his mother.

Years later, the marquis inherited these family papers, and there is evidence that he diligently worked his way through them, putting them in order and identifying each correspondent when he could with such notations as "From my uncle, the abbé de Sade, to his brother," "From my father to the bishop of Orléans," and so forth.[26] Maurice Lever, who has published the papers, even refers to the "meticulous devotion" with which the marquis "kept, annotated and saved from destruction the slightest paternal madrigal, the most inconsequential note from relatives, distant or near."[27] Lever makes the point that such care constitutes proof that Sade never ceased to claim membership in his family milieu and, contrary to legend, never abandoned a spiritual solidarity with his ancestral roots. One cannot really disagree, at least insofar as Jean-Baptiste's paper legacy is concerned. On the other hand, the apparently almost total and highly suspicious absence in these archives of any personal letters written either by or to Marie-Eléonore strongly suggests that, as he played out the role of family archivist, the marquis, when it came to preserving materials relating to his mother, saw fit to be highly selective in his archival duties. During the stormy interlude involving Jean-Baptiste's choice of the Carabiniers regiment, for example, we are allowed to hear something of the mother's voice but only as it is filtered through the words of Jean-Baptiste's mistress or echoed in the letters of the marquis de Poyanne. Here, as for other events, the archivist-marquis eventually found himself in a position to edit his life as it suited him, free to wipe from the biographical record any particularizing details that troubled him regarding the mother he had somehow grown to hate. That he actually did suppress her letters and "edit her out of existence" would not be in the least surprising: full control and manipulation of the data of his world, the studied positioning of all the actors involved in every scene, the arbitrary assignment of predetermined roles to friends and enemies—all that was as much a part of his dramatically structured life as it was of his fantasized literature.

At least, he had the opportunity. Whether he, in fact, did manipulate his parental realities in this way is again a matter of pure speculation. Perhaps his mother's letters simply vanished in some other fashion? But the puzzling fact remains that most of Marie-Eléonore's correspondence that has so far come to light has been found not among the family papers but in archives to which the marquis never had access, letters addressed by her, for example, to the police authorities, the war office, or the foreign ministry.

What would have been the marquis' motivation in scissoring his mother out of his life? Would it have been to suppress all annoying evidence of the lingering presence in his world of a woman he disliked and had to punish for some reason, perhaps for having "abandoned" him during his early childhood? Was it to wipe out any later evidence—and evidence there was—of her annoyingly persistent concern for his welfare, along with all signs of maternal love and any indications that he owed her in return, if not a son's love, at least filial gratitude? This intensely obsessive, antimaternal, antigratitude theme is preached with suspicious frequency and insistence in his fiction. We shall return to the question, for it is clearly in Sade's troubling novels and not in what little has survived among the relevant family papers that substantial evidence of his darker manipulations of Marie-Eléonore's "reality" can be found. That central reality looms larger than any other Sadean theme in the background of his fiction, secretly shaping the destinies of his obscenely tortured mother characters, conjured up initially from the deepest and earliest layers of the writer's sensibilities, and confounded, finally, with blatant demoniacal images of his hated mother-in-law whom he would eventually come to blame for all his misfortunes.

Seven

SURPASSING THE MASTER

The young marquis, headstrong, sullen and spoiled, sexually precocious and very bright, acquired his vices early and for the most part not accidentally. The process was as much an emotional act of rebellion against authority, especially maternal authority, as it was part of his intellectual emancipation from what all his life he would call "the prejudices [superstitions] of childhood," the oppressive mind shackles of religion that he consistently decried in all of his writings. Religion poisons childhood; religious mothers poison the minds of their children. The sovereign remedy is atheism and defiant, deity-taunting sexual extravagance. Indeed, free thinking and free loving are one. All of Sade's "pedagogical" sexual monsters associate superstition with childhood, and several of his protagonists refer explicitly to having freed themselves of sexual and religious superstition already by the age of twelve or thirteen.[1] We may guess that in Sade's own life the corresponding years, 1752 to 1753, scarred by the trauma of separating parents, were for him a critically important time of rebellion, and we can safely assume that the chief target of his defiance at that time was not Jean-Baptiste, his philosophical emancipator and boon companion, but the devout and disapproving mother who had gone off to bury herself in a dreary convent retreat. The father, we know, encouraged his son's accelerated liberation, proud to see him following so closely in his own footsteps.

Soon, however, Donatien's rapid "progress" along such lines became worrisome, and by the time his pupil was sixteen even the master was becoming concerned. There were such temptations in the army, for example. Jean-Baptiste fretted about the usual whoring, gaming, and sundry related pastimes of junior officers. It was not long, moreover, before he became suspicious that there might be something worse, beyond all that. Donatien was showing signs of irresponsible and unbridled libertinism, even an uncaring alienation from his father. The comte shared his worries with Mme de Longeville who, exercising her functions as mistress and *seconde maman*, tried to reassure the father: "It is certain that as he grows older your moral teachings will come round again but, unless we are born with it, we acquire wisdom only at our own expense."[2] She agreed that the dangers were many. In addition to the common passion for gambling, there were, of course, loose women; both vices could be as catastrophic for a young gentleman's purse as they were dangerous to his health. Finally, apparently echoing one of Jean-Baptiste's specific concerns, Donatien's substitute mother also wondered whether there might even be something more unwholesome, errors of a kind that nature, she was convinced, does not teach. Probably unaware of her old lover's own occasional indulgence in the "unnatural" errors she had in mind, Mme de Longeville tried her best to allay the father's suspicions. Not for a moment could she bring herself to believe that their dear "child" had any true inclinations for such "horrors." Donatien had always been so attracted to pretty females. . . . And as for his libertinism in general, she recommended a patient and leniently casual approach. Of course, if the dear lad were to catch a venereal disease, it should be attended to at once. For the rest, Jean-Baptiste should continue to play the understanding father and tolerant friend: "If you are too severe with him, he might become disgusted with women. But they say it is no safer with the others."[3]

What Jean-Baptiste and Mme de Longeville did not know, even if—as seems the case—they had their suspicions, was that the young marquis de Sade by this time had very probably already become the "rather good-looking bugger" he would recall himself as being in later years.[4] His sexual initiation presumably had taken place while he was still at the college of Louis-le-Grand, perhaps even before his fourteenth birthday while he was still one of the approximately six hundred boarders who inhabited that vast and populous scholastic warren along with a nearly equal number of Jesuit tutors and hundreds of servants. Certainly there would have been no lack of opportunity! It is almost as a matter of course that the marquis in his correspondence employs the verb *to molinize* (from Molina) as an equivalent of *to sodomize,* and it is not merely a coincidence that one of the more ordinary characters in *Juliette,* for example, speaks of anal sex as one of those "school boy habits which I am not surprised to see continued in later years and which I myself, like the others, still have."[5] In the absence of explicit evidence, all that is, of course, conjecture, but a document first brought to light in 1991 by Maurice Lever (although he chose not to expand on it specifically) may provide a certain measure of corroboration.

While relating the circumstances surrounding the seizure in manuscript form of Sade's last major work, *Les Journées de Florbelle,* during a police search at Charenton on 5 June 1807, Lever refers to a report by Dubois, prefect of police, in which the officer records having discovered among various documents of the prisoner de Sade a brief autobiographical fragment "wherein the author recounts his first experience in debauchery before embarking on the career in which he made such rapid progress. He tells how, after being sodomized from five o'clock in the morning until eight, guided unremittingly by the principle which directs him to choose an intermixture of impiety and licentiousness, he went to confession and took communion, after which he abandoned himself during the rest of the day to the most outrageous forms of dissipation."[6] A busy fun-filled Sunday at Louis-le-Grand? We shall probably never know for certain, and, of course, the narrative in question, now lost along with the destroyed manuscript of *Les Journées de Florbelle,* may have been nothing more than a stray fragment from the marquis' literary portfolio, set aside for some reason by the novelist. If that is the case, Maurice Lever deserves to be congratulated for his caution and prudence. But given all that we do know about Sade's own particular tastes and what he himself tells us about life with the Jesuits at Louis-le-Grand, substantially confirmed by other testimony of the period,[7] it is difficult to reject entirely the possibility that the document described by the police in 1807 may have been a precious fragment of Sadean autobiography, perhaps a page from the marquis' retrospective journal musings that were unfortunately destroyed in great part while he was a prisoner at Charenton[8] and all the more significant in that the passage in question deals with a crucially significant but little known period of the marquis' life. If additional "corroboration" of our speculation is required, perhaps the following passage from Sade's letter of July 1783 to his wife Renée-Pélagie, spewing out his usual anti-mother-in-law venom from his prison cell in Vincennes, will be helpful:

> Don't forget the nightcap, the spectacles, the six blocks of wax, the *Confessions* of Jean-Jacques [Rousseau], and the jacket that M. de Rougemont assures me you have. [. . .] I kiss your buttocks most cordially and the devil take me if I don't honor them straightaway with a good wag of the wrist! Don't go telling the Présidente, please! She's a good Jansenist who disapproves of *molinizing* women. She claims that *M. Cordier* has never *poked* her anywhere but in her propagation vessel and that whoever strays from that vessel deserves to boil in Hell. But I was raised by the Jesuits and taught by Father Sanchez that *swimming in a vacuum* is to be avoided as much as possible because, as Descartes has said, *nature abhors a vacuum,* and so I find I cannot *fit in* with *maman Cordier's* way. You, on the other hand, are a philosopher. You have a most delightfully attractive *wrong way,* and warmth in the *(cor)rectum* so that I can indeed *fit in* very nicely with you.[9]

Although there is a slim possibility that if one day the detailed staff records of Louis-le-Grand are recovered, we would find the name of *le Père Sanchez* on the list of the five hundred or so early-rising *précepteurs* at the famous school, it is far more likely—the anachronistic Cartesian allusion notwithstanding—that Sade is referring here to Thomas Sanchez, S.J. (1550–1610), Spanish casuist, sometimes described as the Thomas Aquinas of sex, whose *De matrimonio* (1598), though written for the use of confessors and directors of conscience, addressed the pious task of examining the full gamut of imaginable sexual practices in such earnestly salacious detail that it attracted the prurient interest of learned readers throughout Europe and was reputed to surpass even the best Italian examples of the pornographic genre. Whether young Donatien actually managed a furtive look at Sanchez's in-folio volumes while he had access to the vast Jesuit library at Louis-le-Grand (the work was eventually placed on the *Index Librorum Prohibitorum*) or only much later, the question of its possible notional influence on his own various and distinctly "nontheological" compendia of sexual "delights" (e.g., the "six-hundred different dishes" introduced in *Les 120 journées de Sodome*) might be worth exploring.[10]

Despite Jean-Baptiste's growing concern about his son's precocious gambling and whoring in the army, he never wavered from his basic goal of ensuring Donatien's success in a career in which he himself, despite a lifetime of effort, had suffered only defeat and exclusion. The disgrace of the minister Maurepas and subsequent weakening of the queen's party, following closely on the abbé's discovery early in 1749 that his brother was indeed "unemployable," had only helped to make Jean-Baptiste's own prospects even more of a lost cause. It was a bitter pill to swallow, but, as much of the comte's surviving correspondence testifies, such impediments did not stop him from systematically hounding the powers of the day in an attempt to wheedle special favors for his son. At one point he seems even to have dedicated Glatigny, his attractive country residence near Versailles, entirely to this purpose. From the time it was acquired in 1746, the house had served as a convenient showplace where both Jean-Baptiste and Marie-Eléonore entertained guests from the court. The comte had purchased the property from the estate of the dowager duchesse de Ventadour, governess to the royal children and the woman whom Louis XV always addressed, up until the time of her death, as "dear *maman*." [11] Distinguished guests came for visits, including, in the spring of 1749, the queen's father, King Stanislas of Poland.[12] Indeed, there is every chance that His Majesty had several opportunities to sample some of Antoine Leclerc's excellent cuisine before that particular member of Jean-Baptiste's versatile kitchen staff set off for Paris to play the libertine. Like her father (and unlike her husband!), the queen of France was still something of an admirer of the comte de Sade, and one day in July 1755 she too quietly took refuge at Glatigny. She had gone there, as she later informed Jean-Baptiste,[13] to escape the constant ringing of church bells at Versailles on the occasion of Mme de Mazarin's funeral. The following year, Marie-Leszczynska assured the comte that she hoped to visit again, this time to have a closer look at all the improvements he was making to the house and grounds.

Marie-Eléonore, for her part, seems not to have used Glatigny much after the couple's formal separation, which probably took place in 1752. In November of that year, Jean-Baptiste decided that he would sell the place if he could find a buyer[14] and, not long after, the duchesse de Mirepoix made him an offer of twenty thousand *écus*. It was a handsome price and Jean-Baptiste was eager to accept, but Marie-Eléonore, the comte later explained bitterly to a correspondent, was underhanded enough to ask the duchesse to withdraw her offer, "which distressed me no end," Jean-Baptiste confessed.[15] Their marriage by then had become little more than an armed truce, and Marie-Eléonore's stubborn tendency to put obstacles in his way regularly infuriated the comte. Her opposition to the sale had been, of course, strictly a matter of financial prudence. Though he possessed extensive land holdings in Provence, Jean-Baptiste actually was drawing little financial benefit from them at the time: "I have estates," he exclaimed in exasperation one day to his brother the abbé, "but all I harvest from them is trouble, lawsuits, difficulties, and no revenue."[16] For Marie-Eléonore, on the other hand, Glatigny unsold represented greater security than any potential cash proceeds from its sale that would have been quickly squandered in the hands of her profligate husband and son. As a result of this stalemate in the couple's financial negotiations, Jean-Baptiste was reduced to using the house for his normal residence. It was only several years later, after the outbreak of the Seven Years' War, that he came up with the notion of exploiting Glatigny as part of a scheme to accelerate Donatien's career in the army.

That career had begun in 1754 when Donatien took premature leave of the Jesuits at Louis-le-Grand to join the elite cavalry school of the Chevaulégers. After twenty months, he was enlisted with the Régiment du Roi as an unpaid sublieutenant, but it was not until January 1757, after a fiery confrontation with Marie-Eléonore, that he finally gained his first substantive position as *cornette* with the Carabiniers. In an age when military rank depended on the gift of favor and personal wealth almost as much as on birth, Donatien's junior officer status was necessarily modest, a *cornette* being basically still the equivalent of sublieutenant. All of which makes more astonishing a legend that has flourished in the hands of various biographers (including, surprisingly, Maurice Lever) regarding the military exploits supposedly carried out by the adolescent marquis de Sade only a few days after he turned sixteen. He was then still a mere "unstipended sublieutenant"[17] in the infantry Régiment du Roi. Unaccountably, however, biographers have credited him with leading a heroic charge of several companies in the duc de Richelieu's celebrated capture of Port-Mahon on 27–28 June 1756. Lever's account reads as follows:

Our Cherubino received his baptism of fire there. For a first attempt it was a masterstroke, and it is with justifiable pride that, like Rodrigue, he might have exclaimed:

> *Je suis jeune, il est vrai, mais aux âmes bien nées*
> *La valeur n'attend pas le nombre des années.*
> [I am young, 'tis true, but in well-born souls
> Valor awaits not the reckoning of years.]

Caracoling at the head of four companies of Hainaut, Soissonnais, and Cambis grenadiers, Lieutenant de Sade executed gallant acts of prowess during the particularly perilous attack on the Queen's Redoubt. The *Gazette* recounts his exploit as follows: "At ten o'clock at night, all batteries having ceased firing, the marquis de Monti, on the signal of one cannon firing and the discharge of four bombs from the signal tower, came out upon the enemy at the Strughen and Argyile fortifications, while the marquis de Briqueville and *the sieur* de Sade carried out a fierce attack on the Queen's Redoubt which, after encountering very heavy and fairly deadly fire, they succeeded by direct charge and escalade in taking."[18]

There is, of course, no possibility that Donatien, still the most junior of officers and actually posted at the time with others of his regiment in provincially peaceful Abbeville, could have been present at the siege of Port-Mahon hundreds of miles away in the Mediterranean, carrying out the senior leadership functions of a lieutenant-colonel heading several *companies* of grenadiers in such a critically important attack. The source of the confusion is made clear in the duc de Richelieu's own report of the great French victory that was rushed to the court at Compiègne by his son Fronsac on 10 July 1756. The heroic "sieur de Sade" in question, specifically identified in Richelieu's report as a lieutenant-colonel in the marquis de Briqueville's regiment, was one of Donatien's distant cousins from the d'Eyguières branch of the family, which provided both the army and the navy of prerevolutionary France with several distinguished senior officers.[19]

Also enjoying the tranquillity of the Picardy countryside during the time of Richelieu's far-off victory was Jean-Baptiste, hovering like a mother hen on the periphery of the Abbeville garrison in an effort to keep his hell-raising son out of trouble. When he was not spying on Donatien's recreational pursuits, the comte busied himself as usual with writing long gossipy letters to his friends in Paris or complaining to Mme de Longeville about Donatien's increasingly sullen behavior toward him. On a lighter note, he informed her that he was staying at the residence of the princesse de Rache, a remarkable woman whose custom it was to offer herself to all newly arrived overnight gentlemen guests. The season of lucky conquests, of *bonnes fortunes,* had not yet passed him by! "She claims as a right that those who stay with her in her château owe her the courtesy of the first night. The following day, she makes four or five of her female attendants available, each extremely attractive, who succeed her in these honors without it causing any ill humor on her part. *She finds me not too old and my son not too young.*"[20] Young Donatien must have been impressed with that general scenario, perhaps even to the point of exploiting it years later in his fictional depictions of sexual orgies shared by fathers and sons.

Although Jean-Baptiste by 1757 had pretty much given up all hope of ever playing any substantial role himself in either the diplomatic or military service, his lofty ambitions for Donatien's advancement continued to rise. His ultimate goal was, of course, the acquisition of a regiment for his son, the very honor Monsieur le Duc had defaulted on in his case. He realized, naturally, that one had to begin with something more modest. In a letter that year to the new war minister, the marquis de Paulmy, he spoke directly and eloquently of his own failed career, striking—for transparently rhetorical purposes—a note of uncommon sincerity: "I cannot blame Dame Fortune; she singled me out in the crowd, extended a welcoming hand, but found me so puny and frail that, after attempting to raise me up, she let me fall back to the ground again. There I remain, without complaint."[21] No, he was not soliciting for himself, he assured de Paulmy; "and as for my son," he added adroitly, "he deserves nothing yet." Just the same, he invited the minister to come and visit him at his humble Glatigny "hermitage."

In addition to being the war minister and a great libertine, well known in all the more distinguished brothels of Paris, de Paulmy was a learned man of letters (we owe the Bibliothèque de l'Arsenal to him) and thus merited in Jean-Baptiste's eyes just such a display of his rhetorical talents in the subtle art of wheedling. But soon, quite shamelessly, the comte abandoned subtlety and began systematically offering his country residence at a highly attractive rental to every leading French military commander who might be in a position to advance Donatien's promotion. Among the first he approached was the recently appointed minister for the navy, François-Marie Peirenc de Moras, who in May 1757 was persuaded to rent Glatigny for the tidy sum of one thousand *écus* per annum, "entirely furnished with decently upholstered pieces,"[22] Jean-Baptiste agreeing to continue paying for the gardener. Unfortunately, de Moras, "very wealthy, [. . .] fastidious and lazy," according to Barbier,[23] displayed such incompetence at running the French navy that only one year later he was prevailed upon to resign honorably, in lieu of being fired. Jean-Baptiste then generously offered Glatigny to the marquis de Poyanne, Donatien's commander in the Carabiniers. Poyanne, accompanied by the duc d'Orléans visited the house, thought it very pretty indeed and thanked the comte in his best polite style, "a million times over." Unfortunately, a million thanks was the best he could do to accommodate Jean-Baptiste's wishes with respect to Donatien's advancement, he too regretfully finding himself obliged to decline.[24]

Undaunted by such a polite brush-off, Jean-Baptiste next attempted to interest Louis-Hyacinthe Boyer de Crémilles, the newly appointed deputy-war minister. De Crémilles' guarded response to the comte's "gracious offer" to let him stay at Glatigny makes it amply clear that by now the father's ulterior motives had become only too transparent at the war office. First, the maréchal de Belle-Isle's deputy expressed his deepest regrets at being unable to accept such a generous offer. He would, he insists, have accepted in an instant, but—what bad luck!—he had already completed arrangements for renting a country house—not as nice, of course, as Glatigny— just moments before Jean-Baptiste's gracious offer arrived. . . . De Crémilles then came straight to the heart of the matter. He was duty bound to remind his generous correspondent that "with regard to your son," the new war minister, the maréchal de Belle-Isle, had made it abundantly clear that he alone had sole responsibility for granting "all favors." [25]

Not to be stopped so easily, Jean-Baptiste immediately turned his attention from the deputy to the *maréchal* himself. De Belle-Isle, already warned of the comte's motives, was in turn driven to reject, again with many thanks, "the obliging offer" of the Glatigny residence: "I would not have hesitated an instant to make it my first choice had I been even slightly tempted to take a private house," explained the maréchal who was busy losing one of French history's most important wars, "but such a retreat would be of little use to me now that I have less time or inclination than ever before for leisurely pursuits." [26] A few months later it was the turn of the maréchal d'Estrées, another of France's foremost military commanders of the day, to decline. [27]

Only fifty-six but convinced that he was on the threshold of old age, increasingly disappointed with the life of a fading courtier at Versailles, feeling, as he confessed one day to a friend, "too old to dance," Jean-Baptiste finally decided in the spring of 1758 to leave the capital and re-turn—for how long he was not sure—to his Provençal roots. He had done everything he could to ensure Donatien's progress, including making him-self slightly ridiculous by following his regiment round the countryside to various postings, living in residences close by the garrison to keep an eye on his son's physical safety and morals. His precautions, he realized, had been for the most part futile, but now matters were out of his hands and he could leave: "One must not grow old in Paris," he wrote to Mme de Longeville. He was depressed. What folly it had been to devote his life to seeking happiness at court! Only slavery could be found there. Of course, he might have to come back one day to take care of Donatien who had now left for serious battle with the Carabiniers in Germany. Meanwhile, he could try to help his son in other ways, by putting the neglected family es-tates in order. He owed it to Donatien: "It is a very pleasant occupation," he told his old mistress, "to be working for a son who is dear to me." [28]

As for Marie-Eléonore, now totally ignored and brushed aside by husband and son alike, she seems not to have played even the smallest part in any of these grand calculations.

WAR AND MARRIAGE

Not long after Donatien's departure with his new regiment, events conspired to bring Jean-Baptiste and Marie-Eléonore once more into brief contact. News reached Paris of the catastrophic defeat of the Carabiniers at Krefelt on 23 June 1758. The fighting had gone very badly for the French. The maréchal de Belle-Isle's only son, the comte de Gisors, had been killed along with many other officers, more by far than in any other regiment involved in the battle. Marie-Eléonore was visiting friends at Maisons near Saint-Germain-en-Laye at the time, and great efforts were made to contact her there to make certain she knew that Donatien had escaped the massacre. The young cornet was indeed safe, but it had been a very close thing; years later he would recount (with a modicum of misrepresentation) that de Belle-Isle's son had been "killed, ten paces from me, at the battle of Krefeld." [1] De Gisors, in fact, died of his wounds three days after the battle, on 26 June 1758. [2]

There is every reason to believe that Donatien conducted himself during his true baptism of fire with the kind of bravery he later ascribes to the hero of *Aline et Valcour:* "The campaigns began and I dare say that I acquitted myself well. The rashness native to my character, the fiery spirit that was naturally in me, only added a greater degree of force and intensity to that ferocious virtue we call courage." [3] Admittedly, his heroism had probably not measured up to that of another eighteen-year-old Carabiniers cornet during the same engagement, a certain de Ballioud whose exploits on that day—carrying the standard as he galloped through the enemy lines, rallying his disheartened troops, capturing an enemy battery and slaying several enemy gunners, not to mention taking a Hanoverian colonel prisoner, and, finally, returning to safety with his men—had made him something of an instant legend back in Paris. The comte de Clermont, at the first opportunity, informed the maréchal de Belle-Isle of the young man's heroism and requested that he be given a company of cavalry, the corresponding rank of captain, and the *croix de Saint-Louis,* France's highest military decoration. With de Belle-Isle's blessing, Louis XV did even better than that: he made de Ballioud a colonel, gave him a regiment, the *croix de Saint-Louis,* and a pension of eight hundred livres.[4] It is no small indication of Jean-Baptiste's tenacity (as well as his brazen cheek) that, even while the tributes were pouring in from all sides for de Ballioud, he continued to push the maréchal de Belle-Isle very hard on Donatien's behalf, asking the war minister to overlook the ordinary rules of promotion policy and to grant his son special favor. And while he was at it, Jean-Baptiste also decided to ask the grieving maréchal for that same *croix de Saint-Louis* for himself, in spite of the strict rule that excluded the candidacy of anyone not on active service.[5]

It was only in April 1759 that the comte finally succeeded in purchasing (for the handsome price of thirteen thousand livres) a company for Donatien who thus became, if not a colonel, at least a dashing cavalry captain, more ready than most, apparently, to throw himself into the thick of things, on or off the battlefield. His reputation among his fellow officers in the highly competitive arena of recreational dissipation was formidable. Captain de Sade, it was agreed, possessed a body that was "fearsomely combustible," and *Woe betide the German girls!* would surely be the order of the day. Much to his father's chagrin, Donatien had also become an inveterate gambler and was accumulating more than the usual number of "debts of honor." Jean-Baptiste was both furious and disappointed; Donatien had solemnly promised him so many times that he would be prudent and moderate. But by now the comte was beginning to fathom the true nature of the promises his little rascal of a marquis so easily made. He summed it up in a letter to his brother the abbé: "What he says and nothing comes to the same thing."[6]

Donatien's army career ended abruptly in March 1763, one month after the Treaty of Paris put a merciful end to a disastrous war. Not long before, Jean-Baptiste had dined with the officer responsible for discipline in his son's regiment, and, much to his chagrin, Donatien's name had come up more than once in a very negative context. Some of the stories about him were quite horrifying, and the doting father finally realized he was no longer dealing with mere youthful high spirits and the sowing of wild oats: "Everything he says about him is rather frightful," he noted in a letter to the abbé.[7] In fact, the young marquis' reputation as a libertine with aberrant tendencies had by now achieved a degree of notoriety that extended well beyond the confines of his regiment, even to the offices of the capital's vice squad.

Increasingly ill and ill humored, Jean-Baptiste had once more come up to Paris to watch over his wayward son. Marie-Eléonore, meanwhile, kept very much to herself behind the secure walls of the Carmelites, shielding herself not only from her husband's almost constant jeremiads but also from the sly cajoling and clever blandishments that Donatien, who had succeeded so well over the years with Jean-Baptiste in this respect, was now occasionally trying out on her. It had not been all sham with his father. He still felt genuine affection for Jean-Baptiste, the only person who had ever managed to provoke in him the slightest twinges of conscience, even if these were very slight twinges indeed. Writing one day to his old tutor Amblet after a particularly dissipated and riotous leave in Paris that had ended rather badly, Donatien cleverly injected elements of remorse into the letter, intending obviously that it be shown to his father: "My many misdeeds during my stay in Paris, added to the way I treated the most tender-hearted father in the world, have caused him to regret having sent for me. But how abundantly am I now punished by remorse for having displeased him and by the fear of losing his friendship forever!"[8] How fortunate that this "tenderest of fathers" was still willing to forgive him! Even now he was making efforts to keep his repentant son's transgressions out of the public eye, and all Donatien would have to do to obtain his dear papa's forgiveness was to show him how sorry he was for his sins: "He has instructed me to make a general confession to him." The efficacy of a full confession, made to an understanding and forgiving father, had been one of Jean-Baptiste's more naive child-rearing nostrums for many years. In the Citadelle of Antwerp in 1745, he had taken an interest in a fellow prisoner, the young comte de Harrach, incarcerated at the behest of a stern father who hoped that such harsh treatment would correct his son's dissipated behavior. Ironically, that early encounter in Antwerp had provided an uncanny foreshadowing of Jean-Baptiste's own future problems with a son caught up even more intensely in the frenzied transports of youth and pleasure. At the time, Jean-Baptiste had composed several stanzas of versified wisdom for young Harrach's benefit, assuring him that the father who was punishing him for his misconduct was, in fact, "tender, though strict." Did the young rascal not see that a heart-to-heart talk with his parent, reinforced by a sincere display of repentance, was the answer to his problem? All he had to do was appeal to his father for forgiveness, acknowledge his sins, and all would be well:

> *Ton repentir saura te rendre un père*
> *Fais lui bien voir ta douleur, tes regrets*
> *Écris, promets, jure, proteste, prie.*
> [Your repentance will regain you a father
> Show him all your sorrow, your remorse;
> Write, promise, swear, affirm and entreat.][9]

For years now, Donatien had been taught that same handy lesson by Jean-Baptiste and had become quite expert in applying it. Yes, of course, he would oblige his tender papa with a full confession! "I shall make my confession," he continued in his letter to Amblet, "and I assure you that it will be sincere; I will dissemble no more with a tender father who is willing to forgive me once again if I confess my faults to him." [10] It was as good as done. Indeed, it was what he had already done many times before. It cost him nothing, and it seemed to give this most affectionate, this most tender-hearted of all papas so much pleasure. Yes, he would provide as much confession and repentance as *dear* papa desired since he *dearly* loved his *dearest* papa, and, truth to tell, he always welcomed such excellent opportunities to play a dramatic role, to hone his skills in the arts of representation, control, and manipulation. With his no-nonsense mother it was a different matter. With her, his little games worked best when he could manage to play the father against the mother, but such occasions of opportunistic mother-son solidarity (as when he managed to get Marie-Eléonore to hire his insolent valet Teissier who had actually brought a legal action against Jean-Baptiste) were fairly rare. Significantly, there is no mention of Marie-Eléonore in the marquis' penitent letter to Amblet. We can assume that contact between mother and son at this time was infrequent.

As the months passed, and despite such assuasive measures, the deterioration in relations between father and son intensified alarmingly. In 1762, Jean-Baptiste moved to a modest apartment in the Séminaire des Missions Étrangères, rue du Bac, more to save money—now in very short supply—than to search for spiritual solace among the young seminarians training to teach the Gospel to the heathen of India. An additional reason was, he informed his sister, the abbess of Saint-Laurent d'Avignon, "so as not to have to take in my son who has greatly displeased me." [11] The polished courtier who used to hold sway in the salons of all the great houses was no more. "For a long time now I have taken little pleasure in society," he assured her. He was seriously thinking of withdrawing from it all. He was fairly certain that he no longer cared about anything, no longer aspired to anything. In a letter written that same year, probably to his aging mother shortly before she died, he sounds totally dispirited: "I intend to retire to some corner of the world where, far from the crowd, I shall direct all my thoughts to my life's end. Soon, I shall bid you an eternal adieu, asking your forgiveness for all the hurt and sorrows I have brought you." [12] Jean-Baptiste had, in fact, given more "hurt and sorrows" to his wife than to any of his own blood relatives, but it is highly unlikely that he ever thought of asking Marie-Eléonore for forgiveness, just as it is highly unlikely that Marie-Eléonore ever received any filial equivalent from her son Donatien.

Jean-Baptiste's new-found spirituality, despite his lifelong obsession with material success and frivolous entertainments, was clearly more than just a rhetorical pose. The plain truth is that after so many happy years of free-thinking and free-loving, he was getting religious! The whole process had come on gradually. Even several years before, Mme de Longeville, had discovered to her delight that he was showing some faint inclinations "to submit to God's will."[13] His mother's death in late 1762 affected him deeply, and he worried afterward that all the sorrows he had caused her might have hastened her end.[14] By the time he got around to writing out his will scarcely two years later, he had become a devout believer: "I pray most humbly that divine mercy will forgive me my sins through the righteousness of our Lord Jesus-Christ his only son, through the intercession of the glorious Virgin Mary and all the saints, living and dead. [. . .]"[15] Donatien would not have recognized in those pious words the style of his philosophical mentor of old. Jean-Baptiste was now obviously prepared to make a commitment that would hold all the way to eternity! When his hour came, it was his intention, he declared, to die "like a true child of the Catholic, Apostolic and Roman Church."[16] He had much to atone for, and he left it to his brother the abbé to determine the precise number of masses that needed to be said for the repose of his soul.[17] When all is said and done, the comte turned out to be such a petty and *normal* man! His son, who quickly surpassed him in all the darker forms of debauchery, would prove to be made of much sterner stuff, especially when it came to staying the course with his passionate and unconditional rejection of all religion.

Lack of ready money and serious illness had been aggravating Jean-Baptiste's depressed state for some time. In 1762 he found it impossible to pay back various amounts borrowed from his aging mother as well as from Marie-Eléonore, even though both of them were themselves desperately short of funds. In February 1763 he was so ill that his servants, in a great fright, sent for a priest to administer the last rites to their master. To the indignation of Jean-Baptiste's friends, Donatien seemed callously unconcerned: "My son has not missed a ball or the theater even once," the comte informed the abbé. "People are indignant. Yesterday he sent word that he would not be coming to see me because he was going on an outing to the country."[18] A surgeon told him that he might die at any time. Finally, even Marie-Eléonore, "who perhaps thought I was more ill than I am," did the unexpected and came to see him.[19] Their meeting did not generate a renewal of mutual affection, but they probably managed to agree that some-thing had to be done about Donatien. For some time now, Jean-Baptiste had been casting about for a suitable marriage for his son; it was the only solution and the sooner the better, if only to be rid of "this little fellow who does not possess a single good quality but has all the bad ones."[20]

Easier said than done! Donatien, not surprisingly, had his own notions about what kind of woman he would marry. A certain Mlle de Lauris, his mistress at the time, had caught his fancy but she, in the end, had other plans. The spurned lover was beside himself with rage. He wept, he begged, he threatened, he wheedled and cajoled, but the young lady re-mained quite unmoved. Finally, in what must be one of the low points in the long history of the love letter as a genre, this presumed descendant of Petrarch's Laura, furious at the thought of losing control over the object of his affections, threatened to inform any potential rival that she had given him gonorrhea (in fact, it probably happened the other way round) and to tell even worse things about her: "*There are, I swear to you, no horrors to which I would not stoop.*"[21] Long before the bitterness of his first prison ex-perience, long before hatred for de Sartine or his mother-in-law soured his passions, the marquis reveals in full flower his characteristic trademark of conceptual excess. But it was all to no avail.

Meanwhile, after much searching and more than one failure (most families broke off negotiations as soon as they learned of Donatien's repu-tation), Jean-Baptiste was delighted to find what he deemed to be a suit-able match. Marie-Eléonore was less impressed with his choice, but even-tually, after weeks of chilly negotiations conducted with the estranged mother through third parties, most of the clauses in a contract for marriage between Donatien de Sade and Renée-Pélagie de Montreuil, daughter of a wealthy *noblesse de robe* family, were agreed on. Admittedly, the Montreuils were of rather recent nobility and could point to few achievements that would be likely to dazzle any self-respecting members of the old feudal *no-blesse d'épée,* let alone a proud descendant of the Great Condé. Whether for that reason or another, Marie-Eléonore proved irritatingly inflexible dur-ing the final discussions. She had every reason, of course, to be nervous about money matters, being only too aware of the extent to which her own financial independence had fallen hostage to the profligacy and irresponsi-bility of both her husband and her son. Stubbornly defiant, the raw energy she displayed in her blunt refusal to be pushed around by Jean-Baptiste on this occasion suggests the extent to which Donatien's own legendary in-transigence, and perhaps even some of his fiery rhetoric, may have owed more to his mother's example than to any other source. Coercive measures, she warned Jean-Baptiste, would never succeed with her: "There will never be cause for complaint with me, the moment you cease grasping me by the throat to make me do the things you want." The defiant rhetoric we later find on nearly every page of the marquis' prison letters seems already present in both the style and energy of her objections. Her dowry and her diamonds, Marie-Eléonore insists, have to be specifically exempted from the marriage contract; nothing will make her change her mind, and that was that![22] For several days she withheld her final consent, each day suggesting a new difficulty: "She is a dreadful woman," Jean-Baptiste wrote in exasperation to the abbé. Then he added several more words that leave us with much food for thought, coming as they do from the one person whose intimate knowledge of both mother and son, though colored by his personal difficulties with each, was second to none: "She is a dreadful woman. *Her son will be like her.*"[23]

Even after Marie-Eléonore reluctantly agreed to sign a modified contract, Jean-Baptiste was extremely worried that something might go wrong at the last minute and ruin everything. The Montreuils were wealthy; the daughter, all things considered, was a fine catch for Donatien — not even ugly! But with so many delays the family might simply give up and start looking elsewhere for a son-in-law. Then how would he get rid of his troublesome son? Happily, as it turned out, the brief pause in the wedding arrangements proved to be a godsend, providing as it did a little extra time for the young worthy to complete his gonorrhea treatment in Avignon before coming up to Paris.

Unlike the groom's apprehensively haughty and high-strung mother, the future mother-in-law — the Présidente as she was called — was delighted with a match that added to the Montreuils' *noblesse de robe* and money credentials the luster of an alliance with distant cousins of the *princes du sang.* Admittedly — yes, it was undeniable — the prospective groom did have a bad reputation. He was apparently a little "wild" and also deeply in debt. But Renée-Pélagie's mother was inclined to view her future son-in-law's notorious libertinism as a matter of boys being boys: "What young man does not commit follies now and then?" she blithely commented to an apologetic, if pleasantly astonished, Jean-Baptiste. The comte could hardly believe his luck.[24]

On the other hand, Mme de Montreuil found Marie-Eléonore's mistrust of her own flesh and blood quite incomprehensible. How could the young man's mother be so suspicious, to the point even of categorically refusing, for example, to make the customary wedding gift of jewelry, handing on the diamonds that had been left to her by Caroline-Charlotte or given to her by the elector of Cologne? Equally exasperating and puzzling to the bride's parents was the comtesse de Sade's insistence that a special clause be added to the marriage contract, guaranteeing that none of her own legal claims on the property of her husband would in any way be nullified as a result.[25] Such distrust and resistance on her part had come about, of course, only after years of financial mischief and mismanagement by Jean-Baptiste. And as for Donatien, Marie-Eléonore's general irritation with him and the insane situations he kept getting himself into was now such that the comte felt it prudent to pass on a warning to his son, who was still recuperating in Avignon from the malady he had shared with the charming Mlle de Lauris: "If my son has not yet left," he wrote to his sister several weeks before the wedding, "tell him that he will have to stay with me; his mother does not want to put him up any more."[26] The comte at the same time also alerted his brother to another danger: "Do not ask my son to transport the plates; he would sell them on his way here. Nothing is sacred to him."[27] He had learned a lot about Donatien since those trusting days when all that was needed to mollify his injured paternal sensibilities was a full confession. Ironically, selling the wedding presents on the way to delivering them had also been the sin of young Harrach, and Jean-Baptiste could probably recall only too well how he had advised his fellow prisoner that he needed only to have a good heart-to-heart with his father to set things right. Now, thanks to the hard lessons taught him by his own prodigal son, he knew better. He even confided to his sister the abbess his misgivings about fobbing off such a potential disaster as Donatien on the Montreuils: "I cannot help feeling sorry for them regarding the acquisition they are about to make and I blame myself for deceiving them about their future son-in-law's character."[28] Oh, indeed, he knew that his brother in Avignon thought he had been too much of a disciplinarian with the boy. The abbé kept insisting that his nephew was really good-natured and "gentle"; no doubt he was still thinking of the little boy he had sent back to Paris a dozen years before. Donatien, *gentle?* Quite to the contrary, he was as uncontrollably pigheaded as he was perverse! "Only his tone is gentle," Jean-Baptiste assured his sister, "but with the smallest things as with the most important, it is impossible to make him change. I think I shall not want to be in Paris for very long once he is here."[29] The comte was now more and more convinced that he could recognize in his son that same passionately uncompromising stubbornness, that rigidity of character he had found so troublesome in Marie-Eléonore almost from the beginning. Yes, Donatien *was* like her; like that dreadful woman!

And dreadful she remained. Just weeks before the wedding, Donatien rather typically had to be rescued from debt collectors. Only a joint underwriting of the debt by both the father and the mother could save the young wastrel from disaster, possibly even debtor's prison. To everyone's astonishment and disbelief, Marie-Eléonore refused to sign. Dumbfounded by such intransigence, the marquis' future mother-in-law tried gentle persuasion; Marie-Eléonore remained unmoved: "But if my son does not pay the debt, my pension will be seized," she objected in her own defense. "Oh! Madame," retorted Mme de Montreuil (who would grow to be very much wiser in the future), "what a bleak picture you paint of your son! If you think him capable of that, then I am most unfortunate to be giving him my daughter. But I have a better opinion of him than you and we will be his surety if you will not, for it is quite shameful to abandon M. de Sade in his present state."[30]

In the months immediately following the wedding ceremony on 17 May 1763, Mme de Montreuil found no reason to change her mind. Her son-in-law admittedly had his faults, but these were clearly more apparent than real. "His heart, deep down," she assured Jean-Baptiste, "is better than it has perhaps been depicted to you, or better than you imagine. His quick temper alone may sometimes give the wrong impression [. . .] but I can answer for his heart."[31] Donatien, we see, had lost no time in finding yet another doting "substitute mother." And, as before, supremely confident in his ability to control others, to wheedle and charm at will, he set about exploiting his new situation to the hilt.

Nine

JEANNE TESTARD

The true character of Donatien Alphonse François, marquis de Sade, became much clearer when, only five months after the wedding, he found himself incarcerated in the royal prison of Vincennes for "extreme debauchery" and "horrifying impiety." The words are those of his father, who during his own youth had himself developed some minor strengths along such lines. Jean-Baptiste was describing what has come to be known as the Jeanne Testard *affaire* that occurred during the night of 18 October 1763 in a *petite maison* near the southern edge of the Faubourg Saint Marceau, just off the rue Mouffetard. The nightlife of the quarter was popular with soldiers, servants, porters, and cab drivers who found a hospitable off-duty welcome there in its numerous cabarets. Disorderly incidents requiring the intervention of police patrols were not uncommon. It was the kind of area Donatien had come to know well as an unruly hell-raising young officer on leave in the capital, though he may also have acquired an earlier familiarity with the neighborhood during schoolboy explorations of the streets around Marie-Eléonore's apartment at the nearby Carmélites on the rue d'Enfer.

Jeanne Testard, a twenty-year-old fan maker and part-time prostitute (she "retailed," to use the expression that was then common in the trade), probably had no qualms about being taken to the Saint Marceau house in a rented carriage by the rather short and stocky, slightly pock-marked, well-dressed young man who had taken care of all the arrangements for the evening's entertainment through the good offices of her procuress, Mme du Rameau. Madame had more than once been good enough to send such well-paying clients her way. Jeanne knew that in the morning she was to receive two *louis d'or* as her share of the take from the strangely silent gentleman sitting beside her. Two *louis*—that was rather more than usual; it meant that her gentleman would be expecting certain rather special "favors," probably something in the Italian style, perhaps something even more fanciful. What she did not know, however, was that a number of the more established bawds of the capital (Mme du Rameau was probably not among them, or perhaps she knew and did not care) had already received warnings from Inspector Marais of the Paris vice squad, strongly advising them not to send any of their "girls" to these isolated *petites maisons* with the individual in question.[1]

The marquis, who had been spending his honeymoon with Renée-Pélagie at Echauffour, his in-laws' country estate in Normandy, had secretly rented the Saint Marceau *petite maison* probably even before the May wedding. He had already been able to put his hideaway to some discreet use in June, displaying thereby his total contempt for the marriage vows he had made, admittedly with great reluctance, only a few weeks before. Now, after an intolerably boring summer with his wife and in-laws in the country, he was back on his own in Paris, on his way down the rue Mouffetard, part of the ancient Roman road south. Calmly sitting beside him in the shuttered fiacre was the hunter's quarry, vulnerable, unsuspecting.

Jeanne Testard's deposition of 19 October 1763 before police magistrate Hubert Mutel takes up the narrative at the point where she and her fine gentleman client entered the little house with its yellow carriage entrance, topped with iron spikes:

> [U]pon arrival, he showed her to a bedroom on the second floor; then, after instructing his servant who had followed them to go back downstairs, he locked and bolted the bedroom door. Left alone with her, he asked first of

all if she was religious, if she believed in God, in Jesus Christ, and the Virgin. She replied that she did and that she observed as best she could the rites of the Christian religion in which she had been raised. Upon which, the individual responded with horrifying blasphemies and abuse, saying that God did not exist, that he had put the matter to the test, that he had masturbated into a chalice which had been in his possession for two hours in a chapel, that Jesus Christ was nothing but a jackass fucker and the Virgin a buggress. He added that he had copulated with a trollop who had accompanied him to communion, that he had got hold of two hosts and inserted them into her private parts before penetrating her, saying all the while, *If you are God, avenge yourself!* He then suggested that they go to the room adjoining the bedroom, warning her that she would see something extraordinary there; she replied that she was pregnant and was afraid of seeing things that might frighten her. He answered that she would not be frightened and immediately took her to the neighboring room, locking the door behind them. Looking around, she was astounded to see hanging on the wall, four bundles of switches and five scourges of various sorts, three with rope lashes and two with metallic strands, one brass, the other steel. Also, three ivory crucifixes, two engravings of Christ, also engravings of the crucifixion and of the Virgin displayed on the walls along with a great number of drawings and prints, depicting nude figures and extreme obscenities. After showing her these various objects, he told her that she had to whip him with the steel-tipped cat-o-nine-tails heated red hot and that he would afterwards do the same to her with whichever of the other scourges she wished to choose. She having refused these propositions, though much pressed, he next took down two of the ivory crucifixes, trampled one of them underfoot and masturbated on the other. On hearing her cries of surprise and horror, he ordered her to trample on the crucifix, pointing out to her two pistols lying on a table, his hand also on his sword, ready to be drawn from its scabbard, and uttering threats at the same time to run her through. Fearing for her life, she had the misfortune to obey, trampling the crucifix underfoot as he forced her to utter the impious words: *You bugger, I don't give a fuck about you!* He even tried to make her take an enema and then defecate on the crucifix, which did not happen because she refused. During the night which she spent with him without food or sleep, he showed her and read to her several poems filled with impieties and totally contrary to religion, which he said had been given to him by one of his friends who was as great a libertine as he and who thought and acted as he did. Finally, the said individual proposed that he take her contrary to nature and even pushed impiety to the point of making her promise that she would meet him next Sunday at seven o'clock in the morning in the same place, to proceed afterwards together to the parish church of Saint Médard for communion. They would take away the two hosts, burn one of them, and use the other to commit the same impieties and profanations he had boasted of carrying out with the aforementioned trollop. She left the house at nine o'clock this morning when the aforementioned Mme Rameau came to fetch her. Before she left, however, and before Mme Rameau's arrival, the said individual had forced her to swear that she would not reveal any of the things that had gone on between them or that he had told her. Lastly, he had required her to sign a blank sheet of paper. . . .[2]

Given the marquis' already well-established notoriety and Jeanne Testard's detailed description of the house and her client, it took Inspector Marais, acting under orders of the lieutenant général de police, Antoine-Gabriel de Sartine, only a few days to determine the identity of the anonymous culprit. An official search in the presence of a *commissaire de police* was carried out at the Saint-Marceau house, where the various sexual props and blasphemous paraphernalia stored there were carefully inventoried and seized. Sartine's next step was to inform his administrative superior, the minister Saint-Florentin, who at the time was with the court in Fontainebleau. Louis XV himself personally looked at the various depositions, and on 29 October 1763 a *lettre de cachet* bearing the king's signature was issued, ordering the marquis' incarceration in the Château de Vincennes where he was to be held for interrogation and indeterminate detention. The process itself was fairly routine—a young libertine of aristocratic birth detained by an essentially protective royal order rather than a police warrant. The case, however, was out of the ordinary in some respects: the young miscreant already had a well-noted police record, and the transgressions reported by the prostitute were extreme.

Before the true gravity of his situation sank in, Donatien no doubt entertained the hope that even a discreetly brief detention at Vincennes could be avoided. This was far from being his first encounter with the police, and he had grown rather accustomed to being simply let off the hook or rescued by Jean-Baptiste from sticky situations. It was merely a matter of making the right gestures: a well-rehearsed show of remorse, one or two crisply indignant and righteous allusions to his recent military service, a few bravely resisted tears, a solemn promise not to reoffend and, especially, not to allow himself ever again to be led astray, either by wicked companions, his youthful passions, or by the sad neglect of his Christian duties. Finally, putting on his most sincere demeanor, he would make his very best show of total inner submission and solemn acceptance of each reprimand and warning. In short, all that was needed was his usual "full confession," this time to the fatherly lieutenant général de police, and it would be over in minutes.

But that was not to be. Sartine, the lieutenant général, and the minister Saint-Florentin, in direct consultation with Louis XV, ruled that the offender could simply not be let off with only a warning. The marquis' violent aggressions, including threats to murder his victim, were shocking enough, but no doubt even more shocking for the times (and more easily proved since the offending book was now in police hands) were the reported blasphemies and the samplings of impious verse, probably draft bits and pieces from Donatien's own miscellaneous compositions, including perhaps an early version of his poem "La Vérité," one of his most prized secret salvos against the deity:

> *Je me masturberais sur ta divinité*
> *Ou je t'enculerais, si ta frêle existence*
> *Pouvait offrir un cul à mon incontinence*
> *Puis, d'un bras vigoureux, j'arracherais ton coeur*
> *Pour mieux te pénétrer de ma profonde horreur.*
> [I would masturbate on your divinity
> Or embugger you if your frail existence
> Could present an arse to my incontinence.
> Then, with a mighty tug, I would rip out your heart,
> The better to thrust into you my deepest disgust.] [3]

In later years, Sade thought up a suitable frontispiece illustration for his poem. At the bottom of the projected print he placed a favorite line from the second-to-last stanza:

> *En nous livrant sans cesse aux plus monstrueux goûts*
> [Yielding endlessly to our most monstrous tastes]

The material reality of the Jeanne Testard interlude had necessarily fallen short of its fantasized conceptualization, but the imagined drawing makes clear what those fantasies may have been: "Above the line of verse, two figures are depicted, a handsome young man, naked, is sodomizing a girl who is also naked. With one hand he seizes her by the hair and turns her face toward him, with the other he plunges a dagger into her breast. Visible underfoot are the three persons of the Trinity and all the childish baubles of religion. Above the two figures, Nature, aureoled and resplendent, places a wreath of flowers on his head." [4]

It was decided that this time the young miscreant—yes, alas, so recently a gallant captain in His Majesty's service—would have to be given at least a taste of corrective incarceration. A little taste, nothing dishonorable and not too severe; and the family should, of course, be given every assurance that the unfortunate matter would be handled with total discretion. The culprit himself was especially anxious on that point.

From Vincennes, in a letter brimming with tearful repentance (he was already something of a master at melodramatic prose fiction), Donatien begged Sartine not to reveal to his family the real reasons for his arrest or the "true nature" of his offense: "I would be irretrievably ruined in their eyes."[5] He asked simply that his wife Renée-Pélagie be informed of his whereabouts. In an earlier letter to the prison governor, he had referred to her as "the person I hold dearest in the entire world," someone whose "counsel, more than anything else, could redirect to the path of righteousness a poor unfortunate whose despair at having strayed from it is without equal."[6] That was laying it on pretty thick! Then, in his subsequent appeal to Sartine himself, he pulled out all the stops:

> Unhappy as I am at finding myself here, Monsieur, I do not bemoan my fate; I deserved God's vengeance and I suffer it. My only thought now is to bewail my sins and abhor the error of my ways. Alas! God could have extinguished my life without granting me time to acknowledge them, to feel them. How I must give thanks to Him for allowing me the opportunity to examine my conscience! Give me the means to do so, I beg you, Monsieur, by allowing me to see a priest. Through his holy teachings and my sincere repentance, I hope soon to be worthy of the divine sacrament, the total neglect of which has been the primary cause of my ruin.[7]

It was a clever letter, clever enough to deceive, ever so slightly, even one of the most insightful Sadean critics of the twentieth century, Simone de Beauvoir, who, after taking particular note of this penitent expression of remorse, comments, "This is not pure hypocrisy."[8] But in fact it could have been nothing else, for Sade at twenty-three years of age had been an atheist already for nearly a decade, and his pleas for a confessor (the Vincennes prison authorities were happy to oblige) represented not only self-serving hypocrisy but a supremely cynical piece of intellectual arrogance based on the belief that he could manipulate, control, and dupe anyone and everyone, even God if he existed, as he would later say.[9] But of course "*ce jean-foutre de Dieu,*" this "jackass-fucking deity," did not exist:

> *Oui, vaine illusion, mon âme te déteste,*
> *Et pour t'en mieux convaincre ici je le proteste,*
> *Je voudrais qu'un moment tu pusses exister*
> *Pour jouir du plaisir de te mieux insulter.*
> [Yes, vain illusion, my soul detests you,
> And the better to convince you of that I here declare
> My wish that you could live one brief moment
> That I might revel in the joy of insulting you the more.][10]

Until the time of this first incarceration at the end of October 1763, the marquis had managed rather well in the arts of deception—and not just with Jean-Baptiste. The army in this respect had not presented much of a challenge, either. It had always been an easy matter to pull the wool over the eyes of his regimental commander de Poyanne who on one occasion, for example, after reprimanding the boyish cornet for his "little follies" in Strasbourg, noted that a visibly penitent Donatien had accepted his remonstrances "with such gentleness" that he had suddenly found himself completely disarmed by the lad.[11] It would not be the last time, moreover, that the marquis resorted to the confessional to dupe his jailers. Ten years later, while confined at the fortress of Miolans, he asked the prison authorities for permission to satisfy his "Christian duties" at Easter. His request was granted immediately, and, soon after, the commandant de Launay was "overjoyed in his soul" at the improvement he was able to detect in the behavior of his prisoner and wasted no time in informing his superior, the governor of Savoy, that the marquis' "mood and behavior had suddenly improved." The governor in turn could only rejoice and agree: yes, the outrageously troublesome prisoner's rapid transformation was "an unmistakable effect of the sacrament's grace."[12] Not two weeks later, profiting from the relaxation of rules that had rewarded his newly submissive attitude, the miraculously transformed marquis managed a clever escape through a latrine window. It was all part of the struggle of the fittest to survive, and in Donatien de Sade's perfect universe only the strong and the daring deserved to survive, unhampered by the meek and the stupid of the earth, those slavish multitudes who at times did manage to gang up in packs, contemptible pygmies bent on doing their miserable best to pull down nature's splendid giants, distorting thereby the natural order of things with conniving laws and cowardly social compacts.

In many ways, the Jeanne Testard affair turned out to be the greatest turning point in the marquis de Sade's adult emotional and intellectual life. Most significantly, it established the permanent foundations of his integral hatred of abstract "justice," of magistrate's law imposed "unnaturally" by an unworthy coalition of the weak on the strong. For the remainder of his life, his monomaniacal hostility toward "legal" justice would be summed up in an ardent hatred of one man: Antoine-Gabriel de Sartine, perceived as the lowest and vilest creature in the universe, the monster who was responsible for ruining his life, whose power as an upstart nobody, a parvenu who was not even a member of the real nobility, symbolized the ruin of the nation itself.[13] It was the magistrate de Sartine who had deliberately *chosen* to send him to prison for the first time instead of doing the gentlemanly thing, instead of graciously allowing his clever young prisoner to triumph once again with his little impostures and pious flim-flam! By insisting, during that grim November interview in the massive inner tower of Vincennes, that justice had to be done without favor, by stubbornly maintaining that even a common prostitute deserved the protection of the law, Sartine was to become the object of Sade's most obsessively venomous attacks for the next half century.

Students of eighteenth-century French literature and the correspondence of Voltaire and Diderot will recall a very different Sartine, the lieutenant général de police who was in fact much admired by the enlightened *philosophes* of the century as both a protector of the *Encyclopédie* and an even-handed administrator of the law: "Oh, What a man! What a magistrate! What a friend!" writes the abbé Galiani to Mme d'Epinay.[14] Voltaire made a point of noting that it was a great consolation "for the true men of letters to have as their protector a magistrate so enlightened, one who is as prudent as he is equitable."[15] Denis Diderot, Sartine's friend of more than thirty years, judged the magistrate to be not only as "tolerant as circumstances allowed" but "very determined to heed only the strictest equity."[16] Again that plodding notion of *equity!* It was precisely the basis of the marquis' hatred of the man! In a rare reference to his 1763 incarceration, made nearly twenty years later in a prison letter to Mlle de Rousset, Sade identifies Sartine as "the greatest enemy I have in the whole world, the man to whom I owe the ruination of my life; who, at a time when I should have inspired solicitude even in a tiger—*twenty years of age, recently married, having, despite my young years, already fought in six campaigns, on the point of leaving for Fontainebleau to meet with the minister who had just promised me a regiment*—yes, I dare to repeat it, a situation that would inspire solicitous concern even in a tiger, this man, seizing upon my troubled situation as a means to further his own career, brought me to ruin, sacrificed me, so that people would say of him: *What an excellent lieutenant de police, he spares no one!*"[17] Of course, what the marquis really wanted instead of equal justice was *favor,* the special treatment owed as a matter of right to the natural leaders of the world, in other words, to deserving members of the old feudal elite like himself.

But if the evil Sartine was guilty of an ill-conceived preoccupation with matters of equity (made still worse by his insolent skepticism in the face of this worthy young miscreant's pleadings, impostures, and shams), all was not yet lost. There was still a powerful figure to whom he knew he could turn—his newest *seconde maman,* Mme de Montreuil. As soon as he was given permission after his arrest to contact someone on the outside, he sent a letter to his mother-in-law. It was she who in turn notified Jean-Baptiste. The distraught father cursed his continuing bad luck and, bemoaning an expense he could ill afford, rushed off to Fontainebleau to plead for clemency on behalf of his "worthless" son.[18] In fact, the ten *louis* he spent on that unhappy excursion—a sum that would have covered his living expenses for two months—were probably wasted. By the time he reached the minister, Madame la Présidente had already taken care of the problem.

Scarcely two weeks after Donatien's incarceration, a royal order arrived at Vincennes commanding his release, essentially into the custody of his in-laws for an indeterminate period of exile at the Montreuils' château in Normandy. Rank and powerful protection had served him well. The legal connections and juridical expertise of his in-laws had been especially effective both in limiting the punishment and in completely hushing up the affair. He had been lucky indeed for despite its increasing tolerance, the *siècle des Lumières* still had its "anachronistic accidents." One has only to think of the barbarous fate that befell the chevalier de La Barre, five years younger than Sade and sentenced to death less than three years later for having committed comparatively innocuous acts of sacrilege—vandalizing a wooden crucifix on a bridge, smearing excrement on a cemetery cross, failing to kneel or to remove his hat when a religious procession bearing the Sacrament passed by, and singing blasphemous songs—not quite equivalent to the acts of sexual and religious terrorism perpetrated by our hero on a plain-thinking prostitute in the Faubourg Saint Marceau. La Barre, despite legal appeals to the magistrates of the Parlement of Paris, did not escape with a mere two weeks of incarceration in a royal prison plus a few months of restful exile in the country. After several interrogations under torture, and despite numerous interventions on his behalf by various important figures, including the bishop of Amiens, he was heinously executed on the market square in Abbeville, after which his torso and severed head were publicly incinerated, along with some of his impious reading materials.[19] The difference? La Barre, though he was connected with the *noblesse de robe,* had little in the way of local protection; both of his parents were dead, and his family roots were not from the region. The contrast with Donatien's fortunes is startling nonetheless. It was not the first time, nor would it be the last, that the young marquis de Sade benefited from privileged treatment for his transgressions.

Without his ever wishing to acknowledge the obvious fact, Donatien had indeed been let off rather easily in November 1763 as a result of Sartine's stern but paternalistic leniency and the discreet use of royal *lettres de cachet,* both to effect his brief incarceration and to order his liberation.

However, even though he had managed to escape publicity, his name was henceforth indelibly inscribed both in the large in-folio ledgers of the police administration and in the memory of ministry officials. Almost overnight, he became a star villain in the records of the vice squad and even more than before the subject of "bad john" warnings among the bawds who ran the capital's protected brothels. Though discreetly hushed up, the 1763 affair laid the foundations for his future legend. Arcueil, his next major scandal, would transform that limited and still largely private legend into a public media event, one that would very nearly cost him his precious immunity from ordinary justice.

But that was still five years down the road. In the meantime, Donatien's new *maman* remained mostly optimistic. She also retained much of her affection for this "little son-in-law," her "funny little boy," as she liked to call him. Writing to the abbé, she happily informed him that his charming nephew had been a source of great joy to them during his country exile. That whole unfortunate Paris business had been a close call, but she and her husband had managed to prevail in the appropriate quarters, and all was now forever in the past: "M. de Montreuil and I did what we would have done for our own son, and what we thought was necessary to avoid any harmful scandal; we fondly hope, moreover, that such courtesies will have their effect on a well-born person."[20] This worthy young nobleman had been spared all scandal, and his prospects for a renewed career in the army had emerged undamaged from the affair. The system had worked as intended. Perhaps Mme de Montreuil even allowed herself on this occasion a secret feeling of pride: after all, did she not have the satisfaction of knowing that her family, though not quite as well born as some, had effectively resolved a very ticklish problem that might well have been beyond the capabilities of those who tended to look down their noses at the nobility of the robe.

Donatien could only congratulate himself on having acquired such an efficacious *seconde maman*. Meanwhile, his real mother, Marie-Eléonore, seems to have remained a perfectly irrelevant figure throughout this period of family crisis. It is very likely, in fact, that she was not even informed of her son's escapade near the rue Mouffetard. On the other hand, only a few weeks after the wedding she had been called on to help out in an important matter that was well beyond the powers of even Donatien's new *maman*— notably, seeing to the arrangements for the court presentation in June of Donatien's young bride. Only Marie-Eléonore with her truly noble ancestry was qualified for the task, an event of momentous significance for Donatien's in-laws. Even so, there were limits to what could be done. Protocol at Versailles required that women of recent nobility like Renée-Pélagie could only be "presented" to the king; they could not, of course, be "greeted."[21] Marie-Eléonore, remembering those glorious days when she was the lady-in-waiting of a great princess at the Hôtel de Condé, would have fully understood the need for such exquisitely fine distinctions.

June 1763, two weeks after the wedding, was also when Donatien made his first "extracurricular" use of the newly rented *petite maison* with the yellow carriage-gate entrance near the rue Mouffetard. He had furnished it entirely on credit. As Jean-Baptiste had grandly informed his secretary Baumez years before, one should never be in any great hurry to pay off debts; debts are the honorable mark of a gentleman who *spends*. The young marquis had learned Jean-Baptiste's lessons in both constancy and fiscal prudence only too well.

Ten

ARCUEIL

Smarting with resentment but sensing no doubt how lucky his narrow escape had been, the marquis spent the winter months quietly playing the role of repentant sinner, wise husband, and grateful son-in-law in his cozy Normandy exile. Despite his bitterness toward de Sartine, he had to concede that Mme de Montreuil had handled the whole business rather well. The *lettre de cachet* procedure, everyone realized, had worked without fuss or scandal. Not a word of anything had leaked to the public, and family honor remained intact. Jean-Baptiste, writing to his brother the abbé, noted that fact with great satisfaction: "Nothing has got abroad so far and since he is in the provinces, it will be easy to quash any rumors that might get started. Do not tell my sisters."[1] The comte's final advice to the abbé was predictable and confirms the true gravity of the offense: "If word gets out, you must deny it."

By April of the following year, Donatien received permission to go to Paris for three months. Within days of his arrival in the capital, having accumulated some ready money as a result of an austere winter in the country, he set about enlarging his libertine horizons, exploring the milieu of the theater demimondaines. The pursuit of actresses and dancers from the Opéra was a standard hobby for the rich and would eventually prove to be far more of a challenge to his purse than the uncomplicated hiring of common prostitutes whom he now seemed determined to reserve exclusively for his darker, more anonymous entertainments. In May, the minister Saint-Florentin informed the family that Louis XV, "with great reluctance," had agreed to allow the marquis to travel to Dijon to be formally received there by the Parlement as lieutenant général for the provinces of Bresse, Bugey, Valromey, and Gex, the honorary venal office that Jean-Baptiste had purchased in 1739 and had signed over to his son in the 1763 marriage contract. It was not until September, however, eleven months after the Jeanne Testard business, that Mme de Montreuil received official notice from Saint-Florentin that His Most Christian Majesty was now willing to rescind the exile order entirely.

With no longer any legal restriction on his movements, Donatien soon returned to his old ways with a vengeance. The Jeanne Testard affair had, in fact, taught him little, and the years that followed abound with the usual follies, debts, and *danseuses*. It was, both his uncle and his mother-in-law now admitted, a rather prolonged "phase." Still, things seemed manageable. The young man simply had to sow his wild oats. "He is right now at the height of his passions," the indulgent abbé confided to Mme de Montreuil in 1766, three years after the Jeanne Testard affair. How right she was to take the long and patient view of things! "He's the sort that has to be dealt with tactfully. It would be dangerous to rub him the wrong way, as his father did; it could drive him to commit the worst possible delinquencies. It is only with gentleness, reason and leniency that we can hope to bring him back to the good path. You, Madame, have gone about that in the best possible way. He has such confidence in you, such respect for you, that, sooner or later, he will be putty in your hands." [2]

Alas, in the case of Donatien Alphonse François de Sade, that was placing far too much trust in the maturing process. His "worst possible delinquencies" were, in fact, becoming more and more a deliberate and consciously chosen way of life. His signal specialty, reflected in an increasingly notorious reputation among the capital's bawdyhouse matrons, was violence toward lower-class prostitutes, women he viewed as a necessary but contemptible form of subhuman life. The vice squad in turn continued to keep itself well informed about his activities—through the use of its many paid informers, certainly, but also with the help of the marquis' unlucky neighbors on the rue de Lardenay in Arcueil who were frequently obliged to suffer through noisy disturbances in the immediate vicinity of his most recently acquired *petite maison* where, already for more than a year, according to one police report, he had been bringing "day and night, persons of both sexes with whom he cultivates lecherous relationships." [3] It was not just a matter of boisterous gatherings, moreover: the marquis was also becoming known for his violent rages, "having abused and physically assaulted various persons." [4] Sooner or later, the police feared, an incident would occur that might result in a major scandal. In a report on the subject dated 16 October 1767, Inspector Marais is almost prophetic:

> We shall soon be hearing more horrors concerning M. le comte [5] de Sade; he has been doing his best to persuade *la demoiselle* Rivierre, from the Opéra, to live with him and has offered her twenty-five *louis* [six hundred livres] per month just to spend her days off with him at his *petite maison* in Arcueil. The lady has rejected his offer since she is already receiving benefits from M. Hocquart de Coubron, but M. de Sade is still in hot pursuit. This week, meanwhile, as he awaits the lady's surrender, he has been pressing Mme Brissault to provide him with girls for his *petite maison* supper revels. Fully aware of what he is capable of, she has consistently refused his requests but he has apparently applied to others who are either less scrupulous or who do not know him and we may thus be certain that before long we will be hearing about him again. [6]

Few of the police reports concerning Sade's sexual violence at this time set the stage quite so aptly for what came to be known as the Arcueil affair that occurred at the house in question not six months later.

The much sensationalized Arcueil incident represents in the marquis' adult career a crisis far more significant in terms of its public consequences than the hushed-up Jeanne Testard affair had been. For really the first time, the forces of public opinion, more and more difficult to smother or control from on high as the century progressed, came to play a determining role in Donatien de Sade's destiny, creating essentially the legendary image we still have of him today. In that respect, the biographical import of Arcueil can scarcely be overstressed. In addition, we owe to it yet another rare glimpse of the marquis' mysterious mother, of her character and ideology. Arcueil, in fact, provided Marie-Eléonore with possibly her last great opportunity to demonstrate to Donatien something he generally seems to have wanted to ignore or deny—that is, her fundamental love for her son.

It had all begun on Easter Sunday, 3 April 1768, at the Place des Victoires, the second Easter Donatien had celebrated in the capital since his father's death on 24 January 1767. The comte had been ill for some time and was staying at one of the de Montreuils' country residences near Versailles, not far from Glatigny which Jean-Baptiste had finally managed to sell in 1761. The end had come rather suddenly, and whether Marie-

Eléonore was able to visit him before he expired is uncertain. As for Donatien, he had gone to see his father five days earlier, showing on that occasion every sign of sincere filial devotion.

One unexpected consequence of Jean-Baptiste's death was an improvement in Donatien's relationship with his mother-in-law, which had been deteriorating for some time. As soon as his exile for the Jeanne Testard affair ended in 1764, the marquis had quickly returned to his usual libertine recreations, and that behavior had not sat well with Renée-Pélagie's mother. However, the manner in which Donatien had been affected by the recent loss of his father so touched Mme de Montreuil that she was now once more completely reconciled with him. She informed the abbé of her renewed confidence, expressing the hope that he would assume the role of father to his late brother's son: "Be a father to him, Monsieur; he will not find a better one than you."[7] Marie-Eléonore, forgotten as a wife and as a mother but in legal terms, at least, still a significant family presence, had figured modestly in the comte's will, which directed pro forma that she should receive his "furnished apartment [. . .] and possession of all diamonds and jewels, plus the carriage and horses she enjoys use of."[8] After her death, the diamonds were to go to Renée-Pélagie. Donatien was designated his father's residuary legatee.

The Présidente had not been mistaken about her son-in-law's deeply emotional reaction to his father's death. Donatien and Jean-Baptiste had had their differences and quarrels, some of them very bitter, and at one point the marquis had even forbidden his father access to the Montreuils' house where he and Renée-Pélagie resided. But the son's hostility had never been more than skin-deep and was now totally forgotten. Long after Jean-Baptiste's death—indeed, for the remainder of his life—Donatien nourished a profound and constant sense of loss for his father: "I still mourn him every day," he wrote fourteen years later.[9] Even in death the comte remained for him a living, forgiving presence, a guardian and protector to be invoked in times of trouble. In contrast, Marie-Eléonore, though alive and residing close at hand, seemed to the marquis a distant being long since departed for another world, her person and maternal functions supplanted at every turn by a succession of other *mamans*.

Preceding that fated Easter Sunday of 1768, there had been no shortage of little scandals as the libertine playboy pursued both the high- and low-class tarts of the capital. Not surprisingly, he had succeeded finally in his extravagant efforts to bring about the *demoiselle* Rivierre's complete surrender, convincing her that she should graciously accept the fistful of *louis d'or* that he, a debt-ridden marquis whose purse rarely allowed him to compete successfully with the big players in the game, insisted nevertheless on dropping into her very welcoming lap. She had been only one of his many publicly noted conquests, a passing liaison that was easily eclipsed by his sustained and often stormy affair with la Beauvoisin, the celebrated *danseuse* whom he even managed to pass off as his wife during one extended visit with her to his La Coste estates. Mme de Montreuil on that occasion had been furious at that deliberate insult to her daughter but found some consolation in the thought that it was always better if such outrageous behavior took place far away from Paris. At all events, when she could, she made every effort to minimize the chances of scandal. She had intervened physically the year before, for example, to put an end to his liaison with Mlle Colet, yet another of these *actresses!* Such besotted episodes with demimondaine tarts usually came to an end only after significant damage had been done to the marquis' purse, his reputation, and sometimes even his health. In this last respect, for example, it is entirely unlikely, despite his blanket claims to the contrary,[10] that he escaped the *demoiselle* Rivierre's clutches in time to avoid what Inspector Marais delicately termed in March 1768 the numerous "compliments she had been distributing" around the time of her parting with our hero. One of the marquis' fellow toilers in the Rivierre vineyard, no less a personage than the prince de Conti, had been obliged to follow up with generous payments for the young lady's medical treatments, not to mention his own. "She would indeed be a very pretty woman," Marais conceded in his report, "if she were healthy."[11]

But now, at nine o'clock on this Easter Sunday morning in the Place des Victoires, just two weeks after the date of Marais' report which serves to remind us that the marquis' name still frequently turned up in the vice squad's files, Donatien Alphonse François de Sade was again preparing for the hunt. This time he was on the lookout for a species somewhat out of the ordinary, someone rather different from those expensive, constantly recycled dancers, actresses and singers who figured so prominently in the large in-folio ledger that Inspector Marais described as his "repertory of pretty women," a cohort of mercenary libertines traded like prize cattle among the high-life wastrels of the capital.[12] No, this particular morning the marquis had in mind a more anonymous quarry, someone quite uncelebrated, a woman from the lower classes and not likely to be a problem of any kind. She would have to be a person of simple religious beliefs, rather plain, perhaps even sexually unattractive but vulnerable in some way and needy enough to be lured by the offer of honest work. Out for the hunt that Easter morning, the marquis' eye fell on Rose Keller, a nondescript thirty-six-year-old unemployed cotton spinner, widow of a baker's assistant. She had just come from mass at a nearby church and had stopped to ask passersby for alms. The hunter, dressed for the kill in his gray frock coat and outsize fur muff, sporting a conspicuously large knife and carrying a cane, instantly recognized in her the quarry he was seeking. In response to his offer of an *écu* (a mere three livres) if she would accompany him, the woman recoiled and immediately protested in a voice that betrayed her Alsatian origins that she was not what he imagined her to be. But the marquis was smoothly reassuring. No, no! It was she who was dreadfully mistaken! He merely wanted to offer her employment. He needed someone to tidy up a room. She had only to follow him.

The Arcueil dossier is thick; its legal depositions are well known and require little more here than an outline of Rose Keller's testimony to the police.[13] The promised employment, it eventually turned out, was in a village well beyond the suburbs. She recalled the long, strangely silent cab ride behind closed shutters to the rue de Lardenay house in Arcueil, then the little darkened room. Without warning, the nightmare began.

Suddenly, the clothes of the terrified victim are violently torn off; the aroused hunter utters threats of death. The victim screams and struggles but is forcibly tied spread-eagled on top of a bed, face down; her midriff is also tied down, flat against the red calico cover. The violent whippings begin. Blood seeps from the raw welts. More death threats follow along with an icy warning to the victim that killing her would be a truly easy matter; her body could be quietly buried in the garden just outside, and no one would be the wiser. More whippings; the blows now rain down at a frenetic pace, falling with increasing force. The hunter's large fur muff, "more white than grey," is placed over the victim's head to stifle her uncontrollable screams. Hot wax (was it white candle wax or the more painful red Spanish variety used for sealing letters?) is dripped into small incisions made with a penknife on the victim's back.

Finally, the patient hunter's reward: The initial screams of the cornered, helpless creature become sobbing, muffled cries for mercy; she begs that she not be killed without having first performed her Easter duties. The remark provokes in the assailant's inflamed imagination a sudden, deliciously blasphemous rush of pleasure. Strangely excited, the torturer insists that he will himself play the sacred role of priest-confessor. Yes, she must confess to him!

Now the victim falls silent. The whipping begins again, and the blows fall harder and faster until, suddenly, a succession of "very loud, very frightening" cries and strange guttural groans rise from the throat of the pant-

ing, sweating monster, his entire body now caught up in a convulsive, or-
gasmic shudder. It is over. The hemp cords binding the victim to the bed
are swiftly cut away. Rose Keller is given a towel and a basin of water to
wash off the blood; her attacker, still sweating, pale, leaves the room, but
not before locking her in. Panic-stricken, working desperately in the semi-
darkness, she manages to unblock a window, then escapes to the courtyard
garden below by clambering down a rope of blankets she has frantically
knotted together. Using a vine trellis as a ladder, she scales the garden wall
opposite, just as the marquis' servant, in hot pursuit, appears, shouting for
her to stop, offering money. Paying no heed, she clambers over the high en-
closure, then tumbles bruised and battered into the street. Almost immediately, she is rescued by a group of women from the village who are out
for a quiet Sunday stroll. The police are called. A long and elaborate investigation begins.

Dismayed that his well-planned psychodrama had gone so awry, worried about the almost certain consequences, the marquis rushed back to
Paris and headed straight for the rue Neuve de Luxembourg where he and
Renée-Pélagie were staying with her parents. We can only guess at how he
represented the day's events to the family, but despite all the self-serving
attenuations with which he undoubtedly garnished his narrative, the full
gravity of the situation became immediately apparent to Mme de Montreuil, who quickly took all necessary steps to limit the damage. Within
four days, her agents, including Donatien's old tutor the abbé Amblet,
managed to make contact with the victim. After many solicitous representations, supported by generous offers of money, they succeeded in
persuading her to withdraw her complaint. The final negotiated settle-
ment, given the victim's material circumstances, was one that could scarcely
be refused: immediate payment of 2,400 livres, plus an additional seven
louis d'or (168 livres) for medical expenses. The marquis later described the
amount as outrageous although, in fact, it represented little more than
three or four months of the part-time stipend he had unsuccessfully offered
the *demoiselle* Rivierre not long before to entice her to spend her off days
from the Opéra with him at this same little hideaway in Arcueil. Amblet
took care of the payment (used subsequently by Rose Keller as her dowry
when she later remarried), and he also managed to get to the Arcueil house
in time to remove any compromising paraphernalia before a formal police
search of the premises was authorized. The old tutor's loyalty to his former
pupil was, as always, without limits. Called on during the later inquiry to
provide a character reference for the miscreant, he would testify that having known the marquis since his earliest childhood, and having been en-

trusted with his education, he was indeed aware that the aforementioned marquis had "a passionate nature that inclined him to seek out pleasure, but that he had always known him to be a very kind person and a complete stranger to the horrors attributed to him in the official complaint." [14] Most important of all, the Présidente de Montreuil, making the best use of her husband's legal connections, arranged to have a *lettre de cachet* issued immediately, preempting the legal situation before the police could get fully involved. The order conveyed to the lieutenant général de police His Most Christian Majesty's wish that her son-in-law be detained forthwith in the distant château de Saumur. Once again a royal command had whisked Donatien safely beyond the reach of ordinary criminal justice. To keep matters even more discreetly in the family, special permission was obtained allowing the abbé Amblet, rather than the usual armed guard, to escort Donatien inconspicuously to his privileged place of confinement. On the way, the marquis wrote a quick note to his uncle, alluding to "an unfortunate business" and adding that his "family" was extending its full support and would be petitioning for his early release. Then, much in the style of Jean-Baptiste's earlier plea to the abbé after the Jeanne Testard affair, Donatien suggested a procedure to be followed in case news of the scandal leaked out: "If word of it gets out down there, you can say that it is false and that I am with my regiment." [15] At the same time, in his most polished penitent tones, he asked his uncle to forgive him for any wrongs he may have done him in the past.

Did the marquis on this occasion send a similar letter to his mother? Had he, in his panic, already talked to her in Paris, appealed to her for help before he was ordered to Saumur? In his mind was she even included in his reference to "family"? No direct evidence has so far come to light suggesting that such contact, penitent or otherwise, took place at this time. We know, however, from a letter written by his old governess Mme de Saint-Germain to her "dear papa," the abbé de Sade, that she was sending him the dreadful news about his nephew at the specific urging of both Donatien's mother-in-law *and his mother*.[16] Clearly, perhaps for the first time in years, perhaps also because Jean-Baptiste was no longer alive and no longer heading the family, someone had informed Marie-Eléonore of events and had asked her to help her wayward son. It was a sign that everyone considered the situation to be very serious indeed. Her intervention, after all, would carry weight in the right places. Thanks to her long-established separation from Jean-Baptiste and subsequent retirement to a convent, she had pretty much escaped the collateral damage associated with Jean-Baptiste's (and now Donatien's) social marginalization. Her de Maillé ancestry still commanded a measure of antique respect at the court. Many times in the past she had vowed to wash her hands of both husband and son; now she could not refuse to help.

Unfortunately for the marquis, and despite the best efforts of the family, exaggerated reports of a horrendous crime recently committed at Arcueil by the notorious playboy-aristocrat Donatien de Sade soon spread like wildfire. Inspector Marais noted the fact in a letter to Saint-Florentin, minister of the king's household, only a few weeks after Rose Keller escaped over the Arcueil garden wall: "Everyone in the provinces has heard the story; it is the talk of the town in Saumur, Lyons, Moulins and Dijon."[17] The old-style social structures that had so easily covered up the entire Jeanne Testard business just five years before were now threatening to fall apart, vulnerable especially to the increasing presence of the popular press. Public opinion, fed by rumor as well as sensational foreign and even domestic underground media reports, suddenly became an influential and uncontrollable factor in the case. What is more, Louis XV and his ministers in Versailles were getting rather tired of hearing about the scandalous antics of this marquis de Sade, the ne'er-do-well son of the ne'er-do-well comte whom Louis had never liked very much—ever since that business with Mme de Châteauroux. But most serious of all, the Parlement, ever jealous of its prerogatives, had rushed to set up a parallel investigation of the case through its own criminal chamber. On 19 April, it issued an independent order for the marquis' arrest, and for a time it seemed unlikely that even the protection of the king's *lettre de cachet* could succeed in keeping Donatien out of the clutches of the Paris magistrates. In an effort to counter the Parlement's move, Mme de Montreuil saw to it that another royal order was issued, transferring the prisoner even farther away from the capital, to Pierre-Encize near Lyons. As a second line of defense, royal letters "annulling" Donatien's misdeeds were also applied for.

The marquis' claim that the family had agreed to rally to his defense seems well supported by the evidence. Mme de Saint-Germain spoke for the entire clan when she informed the abbé that the "horrors that are being spread around concerning this poor unfortunate" simply could not be true. The unlucky lad, by his own admission, was guilty at most of "a foolishly thoughtless action."[18] On the way to Saumur, Amblet, no doubt at Donatien's urging, had written to the former governess, begging her not to abandon "her child." In a short, bewildered sentence she sums up her own feelings and what must have been the sentiments of the entire family regarding Rose Keller's detailed accusations: "If it's true, then he is mad; but it's not true."[19] Like other members of the family, she had taken comfort in the belief that the *lettre de cachet* ordering Donatien's arrest almost immediately after the alleged crime would hush everything up, perhaps even put an end to the whole business, but now it had become public and their dear "child" had become the victim of "public hatred [...] directed against him to a degree that is beyond words." There were even accusations of blasphemy circulating! Was the Easter date chosen deliberately? "They are saying that he carried out this insane flagellation to mock the Passion of Christ." [20] Mme de Saint-Germain and the public of 1768 were, of course, as unaware of the marquis' future writings as he himself was, and those persons who circulated the blasphemy rumor in April 1768 had obviously arrived at their conclusion without the benefit of hearing Sade's fictional heroine Clairwil give her reasons thirty years later in *Juliette* for choosing Easter as the best day for indulging in certain peculiar orgies: "It is an ideal choice of time for our little impieties. . . . No matter what some may think, I shall truly enjoy desecrating the Christian religion's holiest mystery precisely on the day of the year it has set aside as one of its greatest feast days." [21] In the Sadean universe God did not exist, but even for the atheist—indeed, especially for the atheist—there were certain exquisite pleasures attached to acts of blasphemy and sacrilege: "It amuses me; I trample underfoot the superstitions of my childhood, I annihilate them, and it arouses my lubricious imaginings." [22]

Inhabiting a much simpler moral universe, the unsuspecting Mme de Saint-Germain quite sensibly concluded that the bizarre accusations against "her child" had to be false: "All this is simply too ridiculous to be credible." [23] It would all turn out for the best; any move by the Parlement to have the protective *lettre de cachet* revoked in order to hand their darling boy over to the magistrates would fail. Little Donatien would not be the sacrificial lamb, punished for the sins of *others,* the truly criminal libertines like Richelieu's son, the duc de Fronsac, notorious for the scandalous horrors he and his fellow profligates perpetrated in the brothels and *petites maisons* of Paris: [24] "I am absolutely convinced," the marquis' favorite *seconde maman* continued, "that he will stay in Saumur and that he is right now a victim of the public's savagery; M. de Fronsac's affair and so many others are making his seem worse." [25]

Though considerably more aware than Donatien's old governess of what her son-in-law was capable of, the Présidente de Montreuil also discounted the gravity of his alleged offense. He had undoubtedly committed an "inexcusable act of folly or licentiousness," but the whole affair, she informed the abbé three weeks after the event, had been shamefully exaggerated and overburdened with imaginary "horrors." [26] That, of course, was all the reassurance Donatien's uncle needed. Yes, he himself had felt certain all along that his nephew was innocent. "You see, I was right to say that my nephew was incapable of committing the atrocities that public rumor has accused him of, and right to maintain that he could be blamed, at most, for thoughtlessness and imprudence. The Parlement acted rather hastily in issuing its writ which will now have to be set aside, always a costly and unpleasant business. Still, every cloud has a silver lining: this will teach him a lesson for the future." [27] Donatien, in other words, was guilty only of yet another youthful *étourderie*, an act of inadvertent thoughtlessness. It was a comforting notion for the family to invoke, one that comes up frequently in the exculpatory letters of the ancien régime's rich and powerful as they plead with the lieutenant général de police for the release of dear ones, even those detained for the most serious crimes. Crime, in a sense, could be properly defined only in terms of class. The misbehaving scions of good families were frequently guilty of "thoughtlessness" or "carelessness" but only very rarely of "crimes." Even then it was usually because "bad company" had—maliciously or otherwise—led them astray. Their offenses, moreover, rarely sullied "the laws of honor." Bad company might temporarily "blacken," but only rarely could it render "criminal" the son of an influential and well-born family. Two years after Arcueil, Mme de Montreuil still speaks of her son-in-law's involvement in the affair as "an unfortunate business that bad company and an over-heated imagination had got him into." It was, moreover, an affair that had been "slanderously misrepresented in the falsest of colors," which had the effect of transforming an act of "youthful thoughtlessness into a matter of grave concern." As required by the rules of the genre, the marquis' "little" offenses are also described as "errors of conduct that in no way impinge on the laws of honor." [28]

It is difficult to recognize the brutal events of Arcueil in that sanitized scenario; presumably, the "bad company" that led the poor innocent marquis astray at his little house in the rue de Lardenay was the victim herself, she being the only other person present at the scene of the crime, and morally disqualified, of course, by presumptions concerning her status as a whore or, at the very least, as a greedy adventuress. The marquis, all things considered, had merely indulged in a bit of erotic spanking with someone who was, after all, in the business of accommodating such pleasantries; he had been good enough, moreover, to offer the woman generous compensation. Whether Donatien's mother-in-law really believed that version of events, it was the only one consistent with the need to defend family honor. No doubt that was how Donatien himself had presented the matter to his in-laws after racing back from Auteuil to Paris to plead for family solidarity in the uproar that he knew would follow.

Did he also try the same story on his mother? It would have been an especially awkward moment for him, getting his crisply indignant narra-

tion of events under way, solemnly affirming his total innocence in that uncomfortable reclusive setting that reminded him only too well of Marie-
Eléonore's frowning reproofs and irritating lectures of days past. He had
had so little contact with her for such a long time now, and almost none of
that contact had been in any way intimate in nature. Marie-Eléonore had
always been—and still was—so different from his other *mamans.* One
could actually joke a bit—yes, even flirt—with the Présidente. She understood the ways of the world, or at least pretended to, rather more, in any
case, than her ninny of a daughter. Marie-Eléonore, on the other hand, did
not laugh very much. She had never hidden her disapproval of his "bad"
behavior, his gambling, his perennial lack of any sense of responsibility and
accountability—the same old litany of complaints he could remember her
going on about with his father. He now remembered only the good times
with Jean-Baptiste. If only his dear papa were still alive, all would be well.
Certainly, there would be no need for Marie-Eléonore to intercede.

Difficult as it is to imagine a penitent Donatien de Sade making his
way to his mother's apartment to plead in earnestly filial tones for her help,
it may well have happened in precisely that way. Some form of contact,
either direct or indirect, did take place at this time. He had never been
more desperate. Though he refused to concede that he had done anything
wrong, for perhaps the first time in his life he was thoroughly frightened at
the possible consequences. On the way from Saumur to the even safer
haven of Pierre-Encize, he confided his anxieties to Inspector Marais, the
police officer charged with escorting him there. Marais knew so many of
his little secrets. It would do no harm to tell him how he "very much
feared" that a prolonged investigation of Arcueil would dredge up all of his
"past difficulties" as well.[29] The marquis' use of the plural should not go
unnoticed. Clearly, already by 1768, more of these early scrapes and im-
broglios had occurred than Sade's biographers know about today.

Eleven

TIGRESS AND CUB

Inspector Marais occasionally flattered himself that these titled libertine
playboys whom he kept under constant (and fairly obvious) surveillance
were pleased to think of him as a trusted confidant. Some like the notori-

ous duc de Fronsac even jocularly honored him at times with the title of "father-confessor."[1] In a report to his superiors in Paris, the head of the vice squad noted that during the long trip from Saumur to Pierre-Encize, he and the prisoner de Sade had discussed the Arcueil "adventure" in great detail. It was all to little effect, however. In his comments on the subject to the inspector, the marquis apparently made it very clear that he regretted only the fact of his imprisonment: "In his heart he remains unrepentant."[2] He felt no guilt for having treated a whore like a whore; in any case, he assured Marais, Rose Keller was lying; he had only whipped her.

Of course, chatting man to man with a hardened vice-squad inspector as opposed to explaining events to his own family were two quite different matters. How specific had Donatien been in taking this line of defense when, no doubt angry and agitated, he had explained away matters to the Présidente on his return to Paris from Arcueil that Easter Sunday evening? We wonder, too, how Marie-Eléonore reacted a day or two later to his direct or reported protestations that the fuss was about nothing more than a bit of high spirits and tomfoolery with one of those "creatures"? Though she had been living an extremely sheltered existence for some time now, the widow of Jean-Baptiste de Sade could nevertheless be presumed to know a thing or two about what went on in the more eccentric bedrooms of the capital or, at the very least, about what used to go on in the bedrooms, the adjoining potty rooms, and perhaps even the kitchens of the Hôtel de Condé. It was not a puritanical age. Scholars familiar with the detailed files of Marais' predecessor, inspector Meusnier, will recall how openly Helvétius, the former tax farmer and future author of *De l'Esprit,* would admit to visiting his favorite brothels to engage the services of their most talented specialists in flagellation, revealing matter-of-factly at the same time that in his very own home "when he performed his conjugal duties with his wife, her personal maid was required to stand by and whip him during the act, in the same manner that he enjoyed when he took his pleasure with the other women."[3] We know from the poutingly envious remarks of the princess Caroline-Charlotte that Marie-Eléonore had had the honor of experiencing first hand in her own bedroom at the Hôtel de Condé an imaginative variety of sexual exercises inspired by the eclectic tastes of her versatile husband. For the marquis, the huge fuss about Arcueil amounted to nothing more, as he himself wrote later on, than misguided "compassion for a street tart's flagellated arse."[4] Marie-Eléonore would not have used quite the same vocabulary or line of reasoning, but it is probably safe to assume that, given her son's earnest representation of the "facts," she would have been prepared to believe that Arcueil had been nothing more than that and the rest was a monstrously vile distortion of the event. Indeed, she really had very little choice in the matter. How otherwise could family honor, all-important family honor, be protected? Any allegations that ran counter to her son's honor, that could destroy the head of a well-born family, had to be the result of malicious exaggeration and slander. Why then so much fuss about a simple *spanking?*

And fuss there was! Maurice Lever's biography of Sade includes a valuable section on the media's treatment of the event, along with an appendix entitled "The Arcueil Affair and Public Opinion,"[5] illustrating how what went on in the marquis' *petite maison* that Easter Sunday in 1768 was soon transformed into a nationwide scandal, the result, especially, of lurid reports in the foreign gazettes. The effect on the marquis' family was devastating, but, fortunately for us today, it is precisely to such reports that we owe the existence (and probably the survival) of a key letter from the reclusive Marie-Eléonore to the lieutenant général de police Sartine regarding Donatien and his Arcueil difficulties, a letter whose style and subtext go a long way toward supporting the suggestion that she was an important early source of the marquis' own ferocious psychological and ideological energies.

First published by Lely in 1957,[6] Marie-Eléonore's letter, dated 24 May 1768, was written after Donatien had been transferred to the fortress of Pierre-Encize, but before the formalities of his royal pardon or "letters of annulment" were completed. In its impassioned tones we hear the anger and determination of the mother tigress defending her offspring. But more than that, its vehement rhetoric reminds us once again of the antique values and anachronistic class notions that still prevailed in the dying years of the ancien régime among members of the old feudal nobility. Marie-Eléonore, rather like her mother agonizing with Monsieur le Duc many years before over the problem of having to be respectful to visitors of "lesser distinction" at the Hôtel de Condé, here fully betrays the extent to which she and her class had grown out of touch, especially with the emerging forces of public opinion that were reshaping the political dynamics of eighteenth-century Europe. A decade or two later, the style of discourse she employs, despite its laudable directness and honesty, would have been seen as imperiously high-handed, perhaps even caricatural. She writes as follows:

May 1768

Had my health allowed it, I would have had the honor of paying you a visit, but the unfortunate business that has befallen my son has not helped to restore the extremely poor health that has afflicted me for some years now.

All the same, I cannot help but bring to your attention the blackest of slanders that has been publicly circulated concerning my son. For some time I thought these libels would surely have reached your ears and that you would have been so good as to put an end to them, all the more since I had been assured that any talk of this business had ceased. I have just learned, however, that the Dutch gazette has published the vilest possible account of this unfortunate matter. It is an outrage that brings universal dishonor to a person, and the scoundrels who have committed such an odious act deserve to be locked up for the rest of their days. No one can be allowed to sully with impunity the name of someone so closely related to me! At the very least, accusations must be made accurately and these exaggerations must be severely punished. My race has no dishonorable stains to reproach itself for and people must be taught to show regard for a family that is respectable in every way. How dare they speak of mine in such terms! These wretches and beggars deserve to be hanged! I do not know if you have read this Dutch gazette but the account of my son's affair is given with totally false particulars which should not have been published at all but at least they should have told the truth. They deserve to be punished and I request, Monsieur, that you take steps to be informed of the identity of these people who have committed such an infamy. In the first place, the Parlement's inquiry is supposed to be confidential and its proceedings must be respected. The Parlement will be taking action in this matter and not all of the details of its inquiry are accurate. There has been much exaggeration. You will be aware, moreover, of my way of thinking on this: if my son has been at fault to the extent that they say he has, then he should be tried, but without dishonoring him so. That is how I myself would wish to be dealt with. I have always been prepared to pay the price when I have deserved to. That was my way of thinking when I was twelve years old, and it is still how I think today.

Be persuaded, Monsieur, of my esteem for you and I hope you will grant me satisfaction for this extreme outrage. I am convinced that being what you are, you can but approve of my way of thinking. I have the honor, Monsieur, of being very sincerely, your most humble and most obedient servant.

Maillé de Sade

My son is in Pierre-Encize where he will remain, I hope.

We learn a good deal from this letter. Especially, we learn that Donatien Alphonse François de Sade was in some very important ways much more his mother's son than probably either Marie-Eléonore, the "absent" mother, or Donatien, the "mother-hating" son, was prepared to admit. Like the marquis angrily firing off his defiant epistolary salvos from the prison towers of the Bastille or Vincennes, she holds nothing back. Her tone, unfeigning, uncontrived, springs from a confident, even arrogant inner sense of personal integrity and class pride. Her words, more ingenuous and plainspoken than what typically flows from the marquis' practiced pen, nevertheless remind us of his own reckless excess and spontaneity. The unaffectedly haughty reference to these low-born *wretches* who have dared to slander a member of her clan is in the best "Off with their heads!" traditions of the Queen of Hearts: Let them be locked up for life! They have dared to dishonor one of hers, "someone so closely *related to me!*" It is not the individual relationship—the mother defending her son—that is most important here; Marie-Eléonore is essentially defending her clan: "*My race* has no dishonorable stains to reproach itself for." The wretches must be taught respect for "*a family* that is respectable in every way." In fact, life imprisonment is too good for these villains and scoundrels. "These wretches and beggars *deserve to be hanged!*" We are transported back to the glorious days of the feudal lords, to those fabled rough and ready times when swift justice was meted out by the local "sovereign" without the intervention, the fuss and bureaucracy of usurping magistrates, these freshly ennobled grandsons of tradesmen and worse.

There is little doubt that it was from his mother's stiff-necked sense of class, from her plain and muscular discourse, rather than from Jean-Baptiste's weasely and polished antechamber rhetoric, that Donatien acquired early on in life, among the Clermonts and the Charolais at the Hôtel de Condé, his own first sense of belonging to a superior species of mankind, of possessing rights that authorized him to run roughshod over lesser mortals. It was there, as his mother had no doubt rather proudly reminded him many times when he was a small boy, that he had soundly pummeled a prince of the blood, much taller and several years his senior, taken away his toys and abused him verbally: "Out of there! You child, you!" That attack had not been carried out as an egalitarian gesture by a defiant sansculotte in embryo, even if, for a brief time after 1789, Sade would find it opportune to claim that it was. We should not be deceived for an instant by his windy "republican" protestations and even outright disavowals of noble ancestry that all too naturally came to the fore during the bloodiest and most dangerous period of the Revolution. It was only prudent and normal in such times of gore and carnage to blend in with the Terror's howling mobs. But even then the fact of his distinctive heritage, passed on especially through Marie-Eléonore and her celebrated ancestors, had remained clear and distinct. It was his mother's credentials that—both for himself and in the eyes of others—had always underwritten his surest claims to the privileges and honors of his class. The marquis de Poyanne, recommending Donatien for the rank of captain in 1759, underlines the happy fact that the candidate "has the honor of being related to M. le Prince de Condé on his mother's side, she being a Maillé-Brezé."[7] Sade himself, soliciting a colonel's commission in a letter to the Prince de Condé (the well-thrashed child of old), reminds his former playmate that he has the honor "of being related to Your Highness," adding that what he is asking for is "a favor [. . .] that I believe I am owed by right of birth."[8] Even the offending Dutch gazettes reporting on the Arcueil affair make the distinction: "The comte [i.e., marquis] de Sade, scion of an illustrious Avignon family and *privileged to belong to the highest nobility. . . .*"[9] In *Aline et Valcour,* the marquis himself makes this significant distinction of scale between his maternal and paternal ancestry: "Connected on my mother's side with the greatest families of the *kingdom,* and on my father's with the most distinguished houses in the *province* of Languedoc."[10] Like Marie-Eléonore, Donatien, too, made easy references to the "rabble," those "wretches deserving to be broken on the wheel," for example, who were his vassals at La Coste.[11] Of course, unlike his mother, he often added an indecent qualifier before the noun, even when referring to his low-born *noblesse de robe* in-laws, the villainous Montreuils whom he despised "like dirt."[12] Indeed, he rarely missed an opportunity to deride the Montreuils, not excepting even his sometimes warmly tolerated but most often derisively scorned Renée-Pélagie: "How your *baseness,* your low birth and that of your parents shows through in everything!" he raged at her from Vincennes one particularly dyspeptic day in July 1783.[13]

One of the few officers in the Bastille who managed to gain a small measure of grudging respect from the prisoner de Sade was the chevalier du Puget, the *lieutenant de roi,* third in command at the prison. Pleased with du Puget's literary talents, the marquis on at least one occasion described him as "the wittiest, most amiable and most honest of men,"[14] high praise that may have emboldened the junior officer to reproach—ever so gently—his irascible prisoner one morning for constantly making insulting remarks about the "low" birth of du Puget's two senior officers, the *gouverneur* de Launay and the *major* de Losme. We should not, suggested du Puget (who would be fortunate enough to escape the bloody fate of his fellow officers on 14 July 1789),[15] pay any attention to a person's ancestry, whether high or low. But the reply of Marie-Eléonore's son was quick and categorical:

> You did me the honor this morning of telling me *that one should pay no attention to what people have been.*
> That is true when their virtues cause us to overlook their birth. In that case, they should attract our esteem, even more than a useless or stupid nobleman who, possessing only the parchment earned by his ancestors, shows himself in society to be so inferior to them. [. . .][16]

Well and good! A concession of sorts. Some of the nobility may have indeed degenerated. However, in a generic sense that did not make commoners any less deserving of contempt, especially such *parvenus* as du Puget's superior officers who, "having recently emerged from the mud and filth, bring to the positions they occupy thanks to their ignoble birth *only the shameful vices of their origin.*" The marquis is pleased to elaborate: De Losme (who, in fact, earned through loyal service in the cavalry both rank and honors well beyond those attained by our haughty hero) is contemptuously dismissed as nothing more than "the son of a gardener from Vitry." Such exemplars of the rising rabble, by definition almost, can never manage to overcome their lower-class origins: "Without their realizing it, everything plunges them back into *the stinking mud pit to which nature has condemned them,* and when they raise their noses above the mire, they resemble to my mind, nothing so much as disgusting and filthy toads who try momentarily to rise from their muck, only to sink back into it once more." [17]

Much breathless nonsense has been written to peddle the view that Sade in the Revolution was the archetypal, freedom-loving republican who exemplified thereby his most cherished and fundamental ideological principles. We shall return to that critically important question later, but the venomous anti-egalitarian rhetoric he employs as his normal stock in trade *before* 1789 (and indeed after that date as well when it was safe to do so) already provides a clear enough rebuttal to the point. This is not to suggest that the marquis' extreme arrogance and Marie-Eléonore's acute sense of class are simple equivalents. It is nonetheless quite possible that the son's own imperious sense of caste was initially conditioned by attitudes first acquired from the mother, a mind-set that evolved somehow into the pathology that is nearly always visible in the aberrant acts of control and punishment he carried out mainly against prostitute victims and other lower-class women. But perhaps the most important point to note here is that Sade himself appears to have associated his class arrogance with his mother. In *Aline et Valcour,* in the same paragraph that begins, "Connected on my mother's side with the greatest families of the kingdom . . . ," the hero (rather predictably in a work that appeared in 1795) speaks of a "ridiculous prejudice" that made him "haughty, despotic and irascible" ("it seemed that everything should give way to me").[18] He traces the source of that prejudice to the Hôtel de Condé: "Born and brought up in the palace of the illustrious prince to whom my mother had the honor of being related. . . ."

Marie-Eléonore's letter of 24 May 1768 (which Sartine answered with the suggestion that it should more properly be addressed to the minister

Saint-Florentin) was not the first she had penned relating to her son's recent affair. Three weeks earlier she had complained directly to the minister that Donatien was being held at Pierre-Encize in a manner scarcely befitting his rank. The letter has so far not come to light, but Saint-Florentin's brief response to it makes it very clear that the comtesse, in formulating her grievance, had unwisely employed her usual blunt style. Given the gravity of the charges, the extent of public outcry and the Parlement's jurisdictional claims, Marie-Eléonore seems strangely unaware of how fortunate her son was to have been rescued from ordinary criminal justice by a timely *lettre de cachet*. Indeed, it is quite probable that Louis XV and his ministers, had they wished, could easily have scored some useful political points merely by throwing the troublesome marquis to the dogs. Saint-Florentin politely acknowledged Marie-Eléonore's intemperate letter but added that, out of prudence, he had not passed it on to the king:

> *May 1768*
>
> What I wrote to M. de Bory [19] was in full compliance with His Majesty's orders concerning M. de Sade. I do not think it would be to M. de Sade's advantage were I to place before His Majesty your complaint concerning your son's treatment at Pierre-Encize. His Majesty might choose to place him in the hands of the Parlement, which would not be advantageous to him. [20]

The veiled threat, in all likelihood personally authorized by Louis XV whom Saint-Florentin consulted on almost a daily basis, had the desired effect. In a postscript to her 24 May letter, Marie-Eléonore signifies her approval of Donatien's incarceration at Pierre-Encize where he was safely beyond the reach of the Parlement's magistrates. On the other hand, her quaintly anachronistic expectation that, like King Canute driving back the waves, the lieutenant général de police could simply "put an end to" all public discussion of her son's case—indeed, that Sartine could somehow institute criminal proceedings against these scoundrels who were churning out slander in the foreign gazettes—bespeaks a surprising ignorance on her part of the complex role "opinion" had begun to play in the affairs of government since her simpler Hôtel de Condé days. That is not to say that her intervention ultimately had no effect; it was probably as much a factor in the final disposition of Donatien's case as the influential legal maneuvering of his in-laws. Indeed, had he been still alive, the much-marginalized paterfamilias, Jean-Baptiste, could not have moved the court as effectively as the mother. The monarchy's ancient feudal substructure still counted for something in 1768 even though it was deeply undermined and well on its way to collapse.

According to inspector Marais, Donatien was hoping that his detention at Pierre-Encize, once the formalities of his royal letters of annulment were taken care of, would be fairly short, precisely because of the minister's "regard for his family." He also expected that, on his release, he would be exiled to his estates, "he himself viewing it as absolutely necessary that he not show his face in Paris for a period of at least two years." Of course, much depended on whether the minister chose, again out of "regard" for his family, not to bring up the matter of all those "past difficulties." [21] As things turned out, Donatien's previous record was kept from the Parlement—if not, obviously, from Louis XV, who by now had heard rather too much about the son of Jean-Baptiste de Sade. The issue of recidivism was especially difficult to ignore and was probably what concerned Saint-Florentin most when, four months later, he informed a tearful Renée-Pélagie that the king had no intention of freeing her husband "for some time yet." [22] On 3 November, Marie-Eléonore also appealed formally to the minister for Donatien's release. Her tone was properly restrained, and Saint-Florentin, after consulting with Louis XV, replied the following day:

November 1768

I have informed the King, Madame, of the letter you honored me with on the 3rd of this month, in which you ask that your son be allowed to retire to his estates on condition that he not come back to Paris without His Majesty's permission. His Majesty has instructed me to inquire of you the precise location of the domicile that M. de Sade has in mind and at the same time he warns you that if consent for M. de Sade's release from Pierre-Encize is granted, he will be confined to his chosen place of habitation by a royal order which will have the same force as that by which he is presently being held at Pierre-Encize. [23]

For the second time, Donatien was being allowed to exchange honorable incarceration for cozy exile. The order to retire until further notice to his estates at La Coste was issued on 16 November 1768. As if recognizing Marie-Eléonore as her son's legal guardian, the minister added to his note informing her of the good news a stern piece of advice obviously meant to be passed on, advice that could have changed the entire course of the marquis' career had he chosen to heed it: "It is his behavior after his release that will determine the degree of liberty accorded him in future, and he cannot pay too much attention to undertaking the necessary steps to repair the past." [24] Marie-Eléonore had given Donatien many such warnings in the past—all to no avail. As before, Donatien, driven by inner compulsions quite alien to prudence, treated the advice with his habitual contempt for pious moralizing. Did he even thank Marie-Eléonore for her help in gaining his release? There is no evidence that he did. Here too he probably followed his old ways. Loyalty to one's self comes first. It is no accident that the *illegitimacy* of feeling gratitude toward mothers eventually became a key theme of his major fiction.

No evidence of any significant intervention by Marie-Eléonore in Donatien's life after the Arcueil affair seems to have come to light. Though only fifty-six in 1768 and hardly the "elderly lady" that Sade's biographers have saluted as the author of the proud and plain letter to Sartine,[25] she seems, perhaps because of worsening health but perhaps also out of despair that Donatien would ever mend his ways, to have withdrawn more and more into her protective retreat on the rue d'Enfer. Family matters still came up occasionally. On 28 June 1769 she was asked to be godmother (M. de Montreuil was godfather) to Donatien and Renée-Pélagie's second son, Donatien-Claude-Armand.[26] Money problems, caused mainly by the marquis' incorrigible spending habits and rapidly accumulating debts, intruded frequently. In 1769, Mme de Montreuil informed the abbé that in the six-year period following her daughter's marriage, Donatien had squandered the enormous sum of sixty-six thousand livres over and above his income, "always for the payment of debts incurred in his dissipations." At the same time, she added, he was "always miserly when it came to supporting his wife or paying for household expenses, and constantly sponging anything he could get off her and me."[27] In his endless scrambling for funds, the marquis spared no one, least of all, it seems, his invalid mother who, despite her hesitations and legitimate distrust, seems to have been ready to help her wastrel son whenever she could. In the end, she even signed over to his advantage most of her own property rights in return for a guaranteed annual pension of twelve hundred livres, a paltry sum that Donatien frequently failed to pay. On more than one occasion it was left to Renée-Pélagie to find some means of borrowing the money required to reimburse Marie-Eléonore "who neither could nor would wait any longer, *she being herself hounded by creditors.*"[28]

It was probably in the context of such financial difficulties that Marie-Eléonore, in July 1769, took the highly unusual step of formally proposing to sell her diamonds to the king. Louis XV declined. Undaunted, she wrote again the following month, offering this time to make an outright gift of the jewels (presumably those given to her by the elector of Cologne) to His Most Christian Majesty's eleven-year-old grandson, the comte d'Artois (the future Charles X). Again Louis declined her offer, as the minister Saint-Florentin crisply informed her on 11 August:

> I have, Madame, informed the King of your offer to donate your diamonds to M. le comte d'Artois. His Majesty will not avail himself of your generosity and he has instructed me to advise you that he will not accept your diamonds, of which, moreover, M. le comte d'Artois has no need, His Majesty having already given him what he requires in this respect.[29]

In the absence of more complete documentation, we can only guess at Marie-Eléonore's motivation here, but the remainder of Saint-Florentin's letter suggests a probable explanation. As she looked about for a solution to pressing money needs, an old injustice came to mind: her husband's unpaid stipend for the period of his imprisonment in 1745! It was still a sore point with her for it was to her personally that d'Argenson, at the time as unaware as she was of Jean-Baptiste's various ruses, had given every assurance that his salary would be continued while he was a prisoner of the Austrians. The issue for Marie-Eléonore must have seemed even more complicated by the "substantial gift of jewelry"[30] she herself had received as a farewell gift from the elector when she took leave of his court in the summer of 1742. Was she now in her straitened circumstances attempting to arrange a kind of quid pro quo "restitution" of the elector's jewelry in exchange for payment of what (nearly a quarter of a century later) she still stubbornly considered to be d'Argenson's dishonored commitment? The remainder of Saint-Florentin's stiffly formal letter rejecting her unusual offer suggests that this was very probably the case: "As to the sum you believe was owing M. de Sade from his stipend while he was minister to the court of the Elector of Cologne, you should direct any inquiries that you may have on this subject to M. le duc de Choiseul."[31]

For a time after his release from Pierre-Encize, Donatien seems to have allowed Marie-Eléonore to continue indulging her motherly attentions on his behalf. Still confined by royal orders to La Coste, his hope was to return soon to active service as a captain in the Bourgogne cavalry regiment. It was simply a matter of waiting for the Arcueil scandal to blow over. Unfortunately, another awkward problem had to be solved before he could effectively take up his military duties: for some time he had been suffering from an acute case of hemorrhoids, severely aggravated by a fistula, not to mention the occasional ministrations of his sturdiest lackey. Until he was cured, sitting a horse as a cavalry officer was out of the question. Happily, another appeal to his mother brought relief: On 30 March 1769, Marie-Eléonore again wrote to Saint-Florentin, asking permission for her son to leave his place of exile in order to come to the outskirts of Paris for discreet medical treatment. The minister's reply granting unofficial permission is dated 2 April 1769:

> I have, Madame, informed the King of the letter you honored me with on the 30th of last month. His Majesty, persuaded that what you write is entirely true, is willing to allow M. de Sade to come to a location near Paris, to some country house where he can receive the treatment necessary for his health and be within reach of medical assistance, but only on the condition that he sees very few visitors and that he will leave immediately for his estates the moment his health allows it, His Majesty's intention being that his original order in this respect shall remain in force. You may notify M. de Sade of this tacit permission so that he can make use of it at the earliest opportunity since the current state of his health requires immediate relief.[32]

Once again, the "absent" mother had been called on to rescue her extraordinary son. As far as we know, it was for the very last time.

BEHEADED AND BURNED
AT THE STAKE

His tacitly authorized medical interlude notwithstanding, Donatien's exile order remained in place, as did the ever-darkening cloud of infamy that continued to hover over his reputation. To Marie-Eléonore it must have been bitterly disappointing to witness her son's inability to assume his proper role in the military, one that was assigned to him by his birthright. The diplomatic service, on the other hand, was not an option. Unlike his father, Donatien lacked both the required social skills and any inclination for that kind of pursuit, a fact that had become evident early on despite Jean-Baptiste's best efforts to parade his reluctant son through the corridors and antechambers of power at Versailles where he had himself lingered so long and with so little success. The Montreuils nevertheless still cherished the hope that their son-in-law would eventually get around to cultivating important court connections. Indeed, they were growing impatient. How long would they now have to wait? Two years after Arcueil, in March 1770, Donatien's mother-in-law decided to test the waters. Her son-in-law's official exile having come to an end, what, she asked the minister Saint-Florentin, were Donatien's chances of being allowed to appear at court?

Saint-Florentin's answer was as exquisitely polite as it was unmistakably negative:

> I have tried, Madame, to sound out the King on the subject of M. de Sade before proposing to His Majesty that he be allowed to reappear at court. It seems to me that the negative impressions His Majesty has formed of M. de Sade at various times are still too recent to be erased. I have consequently not pursued the matter further since I believe he would be ill served by such a course. If he were refused, as seems entirely probable, it would do him much more harm in his regiment. I think that in this matter all our hopes must rest with the benefits to be gained from the passage of time.[1]

Louis XV himself, in other words, would have none of it. By now the son of Jean-Baptiste had surpassed even the father as an object of His Most Christian Majesty's distaste.

Most galling of all for the marquis' entire family, and no doubt especially for Marie-Eléonore if thoughts of her legendary ancestor the Great Condé came to mind, was the humiliating rebuff Donatien received four months later from his army peers when he attempted finally to rejoin his regiment. Little is known about the incident, which may even have ended in his having to fight a duel,[2] necessitating the traditional quick exit from the country (possibly to London) until matters settled down. At all events, the hostile reception he received from his fellow officers in August 1770 clearly underlines the fact that after the Rose Keller affair and in spite of the unsparing efforts of his family, his public image as the ogre of Arcueil had placed him beyond the pale of social redemption. From that point onward, he would find himself set apart, relegated to the margin of things. In a sense he welcomed the rejection. Given his intractable nature, there could be no turning back, no question of personal submission or change on his part. Instead, he would push beyond, defiantly transforming that margin into his own autonomous space, a self-determined isolation in his own moral oasis, entirely under his personal control, where he was free to conceive of unlimited sexual fantasies and even to act these out in real life, as much as he dared.

Donatien de Sade was now thirty years old. More mischance and adversity awaited him and his family in the years ahead. His personal financial problems grew to such unmanageable proportions that at times, while waiting impatiently for money to arrive from his notary or business agents, he would scour the town to find someone willing to lend him even a few livres to satisfy a pressing gambling debt or tailor's bill. In the summer of 1771, like many another spendthrift playboy of the day, he was finally afforded an opportunity to test the joys of debtors' prison in the crowded cells of For-l'Evêque, although not for long and very probably not "on the straw."[3] That same year he was also involved in another serious incident, the precise details of which remain unclear. As in the Arcueil affair, Mme de Montreuil again managed "a prompt resolution," probably by bribing another of her son-in-law's victims to withdraw the threat of charges.[4]

Shortly after his release at the beginning of September 1771—happily, For-l'Evêque, like the Bastille and Vincennes, was not considered to be a dishonorable lockup—Donatien returned with Renée-Pélagie to the family château at La Coste. Soon, they were joined there by Renée-Pélagie's nineteen-year-old sister, the young and pretty canoness, Anne-Prospère de Launay, perhaps already, as Jean-Jacques Pauvert has suggested, Donatien's mistress.[5] Not yet the solitary prisoner of Vincennes and the Bastille but already morally isolated (as much now by predilection as by social rejection) in his defiantly solipsistic world, the marquis seemed increasingly determined in his libertine pursuits to blur the line of demarcation that separated the two key categories of *conceiving* and *doing.* Erotic fantasies had no limits, and the degree to which they could be at least partially acted out, especially in the secure confines of a secret room he had recently set up in his fortress at La Coste, seemed every day more and more feasible. Indeed, he was now well on his way to adopting in his sexual fantasies the one essential slogan of the monsters who would inhabit the blood-soaked landscapes and murderous wastelands of his future novels: *Nothing that causes an erection is villainous . . . ;* buttressed by its corollary: *. . . and the only crime in the world is to deny oneself the pleasure.*[6] The seduction of his sister-in-law the canoness, her almost certain integral eroticization in the process, presented just such a creative challenge to his imagination, along with the opportunity to act out a rich Sadean psychodrama of sacrilegious fantasies and multiple transgressions synergistically enhanced by their imposition on one and the same person, a young virgin promised to God, and a "sister" to boot! Such a rich variety of simultaneously violated taboos— defilement, incest, profanation, degradation, blasphemy, sacrilege—prefigures in this attenuated reality the monstrous joys of Saint-Fond in *Juliette:* "I was a parricide and an assassin, I was committing incest, murder and sodomy, all in the same moment. Oh, Juliette, I have never been so happy in all my life!"[7] In the words of Sade's Dolmancé, "How sweet it is to carry out one's fantasies!"[8] The Jeanne Testard and Rose Keller idylls have already illustrated how inventive the marquis could be. What special games did he propose, we wonder, as he introduced Renée-Pélagie's sister to "sacrilegious fantasies," judged, according to the lessons of Dolmancé, equal in rank to sodomy and "the joys of cruelty" in the experienced libertine's catalogue of erotic delights.[9]

More indicative still of the novels to come, the notorious Marseilles affair that took place during the last week of June 1772 also anticipates some of the psychosexual *tableaux* of *Les 120 journées de Sodome,* rich with artfully choreographed scenes of sadomasochistic flagellation, exhibitionistic sodomy, not to mention what can only be described as a faint-hearted variety of coprophilia, the entire production being liberally spiced with candied cantharides and animated by the robust participation of Donatien's very own, real-life *fouteur,* the pockmarked stalwart La Tour, Donatien's lackey, dubbed for the occasion "Monsieur le marquis," while the real marquis assumed the role of the aptly named, lowly, and submissive valet "Lafleur." In terms of sexual merrymaking, being sodomized by the rough-hewn, lower-class males whom he selected for his household servants was clearly one of the marquis' favorite indoor sports. Once more Dolmancé, the helpful pedagogue of *La Philosophie dans le boudoir,* is at pains to explain: "The question has frequently been asked: *Which of these two ways to commit sodomy is the more voluptuous?* Assuredly, it is the passive, since one derives pleasure simultaneously both fore and aft. How sweet it is to change sex, how delicious to counterfeit the whore, to give oneself up to a man who treats us like a woman, to call that man one's lover, to avow oneself his mistress. Oh! my friends, what sensual delight!"[10] By the time he wrote that, Donatien had already had an opportunity to savor in his father's papers Jean-Baptiste's own elegant encomium on the same subject.[11]

Much of what the four prostitutes involved in the Marseilles affair saw and did during that grindingly busy June day in the rue d'Aubagne must have been fairly old hat to them, although several were clearly distressed by the unusual violence of the whippings, not to mention the reciprocal acts of master-servant sodomy performed with such zest and abandon before their very eyes. Unfortunately for the marquis, two of the women later became violently ill after ingesting a large quantity of his Spanish fly lozenges, cunningly disguised as confectionery sweets. Suspicious rumors of poisoning followed, and the police were summoned. The resulting inquiry and trial quickly turned the affair into a scandal more shocking in its public details than anything the marquis had been accused of before. News of unspeakable actions, widely condemned as even more "atrocious" than Arcueil[12] and amplified by the usual exaggerations and distortions, soon reached Paris. In fact, sensationalistic underground press reports and coffeehouse gossip were hardly needed to intensify and feed the frenzy of public scandal generated by witness depositions that came to light in the course of an expeditious investigation of the affair by the Parlement d'Aix. Matters moved so quickly that there was no possibility this time of avoiding the criminal proceedings that rank and favor had unfailingly spared the marquis in the past. On learning that he was being accused of poisoning and sodomy—both potentially capital offenses—the marquis, accompanied by his valet, immediately took flight. Declared a fugitive, he was found guilty in absentia and condemned to be executed along with his servant La Tour. The sentence was carried out symbolically at the Place des Prêcheurs in Aix-en-Provence on 12 September 1772:

> [A]nd on the twelfth of the said month, the aforementioned marquis de Sade was beheaded, and the aforementioned La Tour, his servant, was hanged by the neck until dead, and then both were cast into the fire and their ashes scattered to the winds by the executioner of the High Court of Justice, and this in effigy. So certified by the clerk for criminal proceedings of the said court.
>
> *Tamisier* [13]

Symbolically beheaded for poisoning and burned for sodomy: In a sense it was a perfect marriage of fact and fantasy! Some have speculated on the basis of a passage in *Les 120 journées de Sodome* that the marquis, safe in faraway Italy where he was traveling with the still besotted canoness, greeted the news of his "execution" with an explosion of sexual rapture: "Everyone knows the story of the marquis de *** who, immediately on learning that he had been burned in effigy, pulled his prick from his breeches, shouting, 'Godfuck, here am I now where I wished to be; here am I covered in infamy and opprobrium; leave me! leave me! I must shoot off!' And he did so, that very instant." [14] One rather doubts that Sade's real-life reaction could have been so instantly focused the moment he heard the news, but the words remind us again, in any case, of how this conscious transposition of *conceiving* and *doing* underlies the fictional universe Sade later constructed from such personal realities.

If we in fact know little about Donatien's reaction when he learned of his emblematic "execution," we know even less about how Marie-Eléonore responded to the lurid reports that most certainly reached her in Paris concerning her son's latest scandal. It would have been too late, in any case, for her or the Présidente to attempt an Arcueil-style rescue operation. In the end, it was left to the unflinchingly loyal Renée-Pélagie to approach the prostitute witnesses in an attempt to buy them off. It is not certain, moreover, that this time Marie-Eléonore would have even wanted to rescue her son. Was Marseilles the last straw for her? There had been so many "last straws" in her life, beginning with Jean-Baptiste's humiliating affronts and scandals going all the way back to their Hôtel de Condé days. It must have seemed obvious to the comtesse by now that her son was, at the very least, disturbingly "different," certainly not just another, more disorderly version of Jean-Baptiste. Perhaps Marseilles finally brought her to the point of accepting that Donatien was not so much slandered or unjustly accused as basically out of control. Was he, perhaps, even mad?

As for the Présidente, we know for certain from her surviving correspondence that Marseilles truly *was* the last straw, probably more because of the marquis' concurrent affair with the canoness, her favorite daughter, than for any concern she may have felt regarding her son-in-law's continuing taste for bordello depravities. She no longer held to the forgiving notion, once so earnestly shared with the abbé, that these transgressions were little more than "thoughtless follies of youth." For the remainder of her life, give or take an occasional tactical concession made in the interests of defending the entire family's honor, Mme de Montreuil saw her son-in-law as someone probably best kept under lock and key. Not to be outdone, Donatien for the next twenty years, with a degree of vituperative rage rarely equaled in the recorded annals of human execration, was pleased to endow this "veritable fury from Hell" with every evil quality under the sun.

And the many scandals that followed, too numerous to explore in detail here? Did Marie-Eléonore even hear about her fugitive son's dramatic escape in April 1773 from the citadel of Miolans? Or the "little girls" affair of January 1775 which occurred during one of his extended incognito sojourns at La Coste? Was it out of a resigned sense of solidarity with her son that she welcomed Renée-Pélagie (no longer willing to stay with her own mother) to her apartment at the Carmelites during her daughter-in-law's occasional visits to Paris? Did she, in her uniquely forceful, honest style, ever write a stinging letter of maternal rebuke to Donatien himself, pointing out the opprobrium and dishonor he had brought down on their "clan"? The answers to these and many other questions may never turn up. They have disappeared, apparently along with virtually all of Marie-Eléonore's correspondence, letters that would normally form part of what seems to have been a fairly well-preserved collection of family papers, selectively culled, one suspects, by the marquis himself.

One very rare and important direct comment by Donatien concerning his mother can be found in a March 1773 letter addressed to the comte Sallier de La Tour, governor of the duchy of Savoy when the marquis—still a fugitive from French justice—was a prisoner at Miolans. It was written only a few weeks before his dramatic escape from the Miolans citadel, and it is difficult to assess the extent to which the important personal characterizations it contains of Marie-Eléonore and other members of his family are distorted by the prisoner's obvious purpose of minimizing past misdeeds and convincing the powerful Sardinian minister that he enjoyed the full confidence of his closest relatives and should therefore be liberated. He was, the marquis declared in his appeal to the governor, the innocent victim of a viciously cruel mother-in-law who, for purely malicious reasons having to do with her desire to break up an affair (the canoness business), admittedly "out of place and untoward," wanted to keep him locked away in prison forever.

The letter has a unique value for us. Unreliable as it may be as a true reflection of his feelings, it is possibly the only surviving direct comment made by Sade about his mother while she was still alive:

> I legally came of age several years ago, Monsieur; it has been my misfortune to lose my father, for I would not be here if he were still alive; *my mother, who is very old and very ill, resides in a convent where she is peacefully living out her last days, totally uninvolved in anything;* my uncles and the remaining members of my family have confirmed to me in writing that they have had no hand in my detention; I have not committed any offense against either the court of France or that of Sardinia; my wife has applied for my release; I am dependent on no one: Who then can keep me here? And who can dare do so without imposing extreme oppression and injustice? [15]

Sade's special gift for autobiographical revisionism, for editing his life as a piece of theater, distributing righteous roles to himself and villainous parts to others as circumstance and opportunity allowed, was already well developed by the 1770s. Soon such obsessive self-referencing, almost always involving a bad-faith interpretation of events, would become his dominant mode of thinking, the entire process made progressively worse by the isolation from normal social contact that marked his prison years. He was no doubt correct in stating to the governor of Savoy that Mme de Montreuil had moved against him without first obtaining a formal mandate to support her actions from the entire Sade family, but the truth is that she could easily have done so, had she wished. It had not been difficult for her to convince the governor that his troublesome prisoner, a fugitive from justice who called himself the "comte de Mazan," was a reprobate of the worst kind, guilty of outrageous debauchery, a freethinking libertine who mocked religion as much as he defied morality. Who in France, with the obvious exception of Renée-Pélagie, would have disputed the necessity of protecting the prisoner's unfortunate family from even greater scandal and public awareness of his crimes?

Still, there may have been as much self-deception as cynical manipulation in Donatien's claim that *his own family*—all those Provençal uncles and aunts—in no way supported his detention. Perhaps he sincerely believed that they too saw him as the Présidente's sacrificial victim? If so, he was seriously mistaken. Just a few years later, even his tolerantly libertine uncle, the abbé de Sade, was unable to contain his joy on learning that his troublesome nephew had finally been locked away in the keep at Vincennes: "The man has been arrested and locked up in a fortress near Paris," he wrote on that occasion to the lawyer Gaufridy. "I can now set my mind at ease and I think everyone will be pleased." [16]

Devastated as she must have been by the shock and stigma of the Parlement's ferocious in absentia sentence and by gossip concerning events deemed to be more dishonorable for the family than even Arcueil, Marie-Eléonore, after the Marseilles affair, very probably no longer resisted the conclusion that her son was a hopeless recidivist who had to be prevented from doing further damage both to himself and his family. When the marquis chose to write his mother out of existence in his letter to the governor, he was, without any doubt, fully aware of her disapproving views. It is even probable that since the scandal of Arcueil she had communicated those views to him more than once, directly by letter and perhaps even by word of mouth. We can accept at face value Donatien's affectionately filial comments regarding his father in this formal letter of appeal: he had made such statements many times before and he would make them again, both in his correspondence and in his fiction. But we can legitimately mistrust, I think, his essentially tactical description of a mother who, despite chronic ill health, was, after all, only sixty-one and still as strong in will as she was sound of mind. Why "*very* old," for example? Why "*very* ill"? Why, especially, "*totally* uninvolved in anything"? The reinforcing adverbs protest too much and scarcely correspond to what Donatien himself knew of Marie-Eléonore's energetically interventionist undertakings on his behalf only a few years earlier. She had never been indifferent to events or uninterested in his conduct or his fate. She had fought for him with spirit and passion after Arcueil. He knew, too, that Louis XV and his minister had seen fit to treat her as the de facto head of the family and had charged her with the duty of passing on an official warning (which he had, of course, ignored)—namely, that whether he spent his future years in prison or at liberty depended entirely on *his* choice of good or bad behavior. There can be no doubt at all that Marie-Eléonore in her usual blunt style passed on that eminently sensible piece of cautionary advice. The only effect had been to remind the balky marquis once again of his rebellious adolescence and the unpleasant difficulties he had had to put up with because of her, until, with the help of his father, he had finally managed to eject Marie-Eléonore from his life, effectively relegating her to the stereotypical role of the hateful interfering mother, purveyor of pious superstitions and destroyer of his pleasures and his autonomy. Yes, if only his dear forgiving papa were still alive to see him through this bad patch. . . .

It would, in other words, be a mistake to place much objective weight on what are apparently the only surviving comments Donatien made regarding his mother while she was still alive. This single line of self-serving text tells us rather more about him than it does about the woman who, during the first four years of his life, had been everything to him, always at his beck and call, entirely his to control, shared with no one, not even with his papa who was away most of the time and almost a total stranger. But then came the great betrayal. With brutal suddenness, he had been spirited away and she was gone. Completely out of it. And completely out of it she should have remained when, as the spoiled young hero, apple of his doting father's eye, he had returned years later with his tutor. Much against his will, he had been forced to live with her for a time. She had made awkward attempts to renew their former closeness, but, of course, he had recoiled, in a kind of horror and disgust. How richly she deserved the punishment his dear papa and all those other *mamans* regularly meted out to her!

Everything after that, the rebellion and transgressions that followed, was in a sense the continuation of that same horror and disgust, an extension of his festering anger with the betraying mother, with all the treacherous whore-mothers, and with the authority figures who claimed the right to punish him for acting out that anger: "*His behavior will determine the degree of liberty accorded him.*" That was the ministry's message—an insolent message, and sent to him through his mother!

Clearly, the prisoner in the citadel of Miolans who was asserting his legal autonomy to the governor of Savoy in 1773 wanted Marie-Eléonore to be completely out of it, "totally uninvolved in anything." Was he not his own master, now that his father was dead? No one had the right to claim any control over him—not his mother, not the French ministry, and, especially, not his evil mother-in-law, the latest maternal tyrant to intrude on his life.

Sade's dismissive statement concerning his mother raises once again a key issue for his biographers. Knowing as we do now how often and with what energy Marie-Eléonore rushed to the rescue of both her husband and her son, it would seem imprudent to conclude, following the lead of most commentators, that such interventions as the letters she wrote during the Arcueil crisis in 1768, were "entirely exceptional."[17] Could it not be the case, rather, that her supposed "absence" in Donatien's life—a standard datum of Sadean biography—comes down essentially to the fact that, at every opportunity, she was deliberately excised by her son, not only symbolically from his moral consciousness but also physically from the family annals?

ALL FOR A DYING MOTHER

Curiously, it is when we come to Marie-Eléonore's death at the Carmelites on 14 January 1777—that is, when she is truly and literally absent from the scene—that the most acute questions arise concerning the nature of the marquis' relationship with his mother. It is then, especially, that our necessarily speculative answers to those questions seem to form such a vital part of any attempt to analyze the man and, equally important, to assess the significance of the tenaciously dominant theme of mother hatred that pervades the Sadean novel.

I shall not review here in any detail events of the years immediately preceding the comtesse's death.[1] Perhaps it is enough to say that the marquis continued in all respects to live up to his now well-defined public character. His escape from Miolans (a few weeks after writing the letter discussed in the preceding chapter) was predictably followed by more—let us use his own word—"heteroclitic" activities, now almost certainly involving some measure of active participation by Renée-Pélagie as well. Seemingly as besotted with the marquis as her sister had been, she was apparently no longer a stranger to what went on in the special room hidden away in the penetralia of the La Coste château. As for the marquis' personal security, the situation was still fairly tense. He had more than once quietly returned from abroad to Provence where he hoped to escape public scrutiny while waiting for things to die down. From time to time, a new accumulation of local gossip and community suspicion posed a threat, and he would prudently leave again for safer climes until things once more settled down.

We rejoin the couple in the autumn of 1776. Having just returned to La Coste after more than a year's absence in Italy, still technically a fugitive from justice, Donatien was planning to lie low for the winter with Renée-Pélagie and await further developments. To help ease the monotony, he had recently decided to invite a very special friend down from Paris. The identity of this mystery man whom he addresses in a letter as "my dear abbé" remains a secret, but, abbé or not, the gentleman in question was obviously the marquis' most trusted companion in debauchery, perhaps the very person, the friend who was "as great a libertine as he," that he had told the shocked and terrified Jeanne Testard about that October evening many years before when he showed her the little book of unholy verses. He was looking forward to the visit; it would be a rare feast for both the intellect and the senses. In all his lifetime, he had never had more than one or two such friends, absolutely reliable lover-companions, intellectual equals, with whom he could speak on the freest of terms as well as share discreetly his more memorable feats of libertine valor. They would be able to criticize each other's literary portfolios, compare recent "exploits," and no doubt even enjoy together some of the novel amenities of the secret room. Certainly, there was sufficient paraphernalia there to impress even the most sophisticated visitor from the capital.

Meanwhile, the vexing consequences of the Marseilles affair and the marquis' legal rehabilitation still loomed large in the background. Various family moves were afoot in Paris to arrange with the Parlement at Aix to have his death sentence for poisoning and sodomy wiped from the books. In Paris, Mme de Montreuil had been working diligently to overturn the verdict, as much, certainly, to protect the honor of her grandchildren as to salvage something of her incorrigible son-in-law's muddied future.

The administrative machinery moved slowly. Convinced that her mother—now less reluctant to hide her basic hostility toward Donatien—was deliberately delaying matters, Renée-Pélagie in January 1777 sent Mme de Montreuil a stinging ten-page letter of rebuke, dictated by Donatien and bristling with wild threats and righteous invective. It was received in Paris on Friday, 17 January. Four days later the Présidente, in a cold rage, wrote to Gaufridy, the marquis' notary and business agent, informing him that she no longer wished to have anything to do with the financial affairs of her daughter and son-in-law. As for Donatien's nasty threats, he should be warned that she knew how to defend herself if she was attacked.

Her daughter's letter, moreover, was inexcusable, even if, as was patently obvious, she had been in this matter no more than the marquis' docile amanuensis.[2]

We cannot determine for certain from this published fragment[3] of the Présidente's 21 January letter whether Mme de Montreuil was already aware by that date of Marie-Eléonore's death, which had occurred at the Carmelites the week before. The funeral had taken place on the 15th, appropriately at the church of Saint-Jacques du Haut Pas, the construction of which during the preceding century owed much to the generosity of Anne-Geneviève de Bourbon, heroine of the first war of the Fronde and a sister of the Great Condé. At last, Marie-Eléonore had gone home to her ancestors.

Donatien probably did not receive news that his mother was gravely ill until around 25 January, precisely at a time when, with his special talent for getting into trouble, he found himself caught up in yet another noisy scandal, the Treillet affair, a series of events that—were it not for the misfiring of a pistol brandished by an enraged father—would have seen the marquis instantly joining his mother beyond the grave, only two days after her burial.

Catherine Treillet (interestingly, she was called "Justine" at the château), a fairly attractive twenty-two-year-old, had been working as a cook at La Coste since November 1776. At about noon on 17 January 1777, her father, a weaver from Montpellier, turned up at the marquis' door demanding that his daughter leave with him immediately. Treillet had just learned that Catherine's employer was none other than the debauched ogre, the dreadful bogeyman whom everyone talked about in the region. Annoyed in the extreme by the intruder's presence, the marquis unwisely refused permission for the young woman to leave, and after physically restraining her, he roughly ejected the insolent interloper from the premises, threatening at the same time to have him jailed until he rotted away if he did not leave his property forthwith. That at least is the version of events the angry father testified to when he made an official complaint to the authorities soon after. In the course of the investigation that followed, the marquis provided a version of events that was quite different and, given what we know of his violent temper and bullying style with social inferiors, distinctly less plausible: "*Without anger, without violence of any kind* [. . .], I escorted him back to the main entrance, advising him that he was going about matters in the wrong way and inviting him to be so good as to wait in the village where word would be sent to him concerning the resolution of his request."[4] That was when, according to the marquis, Treillet, "for no reason at all," pulled out a pistol and fired at him point-blank. Fortunately, only the primer went off but later that same day the irate father returned and fired another shot into the courtyard. Despite the marquis' complaint to the local authorities, Treillet was not arrested. A father attempting to protect his innocent daughter from a monstrous seducer had certain rights, after all, including the right to remove her unopposed from perilous service. The villagers were in total sympathy with the father. They had even assured this madman, again according to the marquis, that he need have no concern about killing the monster of La Coste—"that nothing would happen to him."[5] After winning the battle of local public opinion, the outraged Treillet had gone on to score an even greater victory when he managed to get to the authorities in Aix first to file charges of assault against his daughter's evil employer. Clearly, the life of Bluebeard in this quiet Provençal backwater was no bed of roses!

It was in the middle of this turmoil that news came from Paris that Marie-Eléonore was dying. Despite the Treillet imbroglio and the obvious risks implied by a visit to the capital where an old *lettre de cachet* for Donatien's arrest was still in force, the couple set off in the greatest haste. Did they as they left have any suspicions that a letter recently received from Mme de Montreuil confirming the alarming news might be a trap? It seems that was not the case. As Donatien set out on the wintry road to Paris, his thoughts concerning his mother-in-law would have been ambivalent and mixed—but scarcely as mistrustful and angry at this point as he later chose to remember them. He had already sent her a few days before some account of the Treillet business in case it complicated the negotiations that were under way for his legal rehabilitation. But a suspicion remained: was the Présidente deliberately delaying these negotiations? She was clever. She had an intimate knowledge of the Parlement milieu and would know how legal matters were best conducted. Perhaps the delays represented nothing more than good tactics on her part? Would the Treillet business add to her anger on his account? He was not admitting anything, mind you, but a little hanky panky with the kitchen help—that surely would not bother her. His mother-in-law, he assured Gaufridy, would be the first to understand if—and he was only saying *if*—he had indeed taken advantage of the young servant: "You don't know her very well. Even supposing what you imply, don't assume that Mme de Montreuil would be angry to learn that I have a respectable person in the house who may be pleasing to me. I assure you that she would be the first person to approve, provided no scandal resulted from it."[6] As it turned out, Catherine Treillet, alias "Justine," was not really of a mind to provoke a new scandal. Immediately after being paid her wages on 29 January, the day Renée-Pélagie and Donatien set out from La Coste, she begged Renée-Pélagie to take her along. The arrangement suited both husband and wife: Renée-Pélagie would find good use for an extra servant in Paris since she would be taking up independent residence in a hotel, the marquis having already made it known that, once they arrived in the capital, he wished to be left to his own devices.

Just a week or two before, Donatien had, in fact, renewed the invitation to his mysterious abbé friend to come down to La Coste, but now he found the prospect of getting back to his old haunts in Paris and meeting the "abbé" there instead truly exhilarating. He was rather fed up with his loutish provincial "vassals" and glad to be leaving them behind. They had all been against him. If Treillet *had* killed him, they would simply have shrugged and said it was the wicked ogre's own fault.[7] No generous "republican" sentiments ran through the mind of this future *citoyen* of the Section des Piques as he penned an angry note to Gaufridy before leaving. It would be absolutely essential, he predicted, to come down hard one day on this rabble, "to keep these vassals respectfully in check as they are duty-bound to be." Yes, that was the larger lesson he would draw from this Treillet fracas: "Assuredly, I have been ill-served in this business [. . .] and it is equally certain that I shall not forget it. I have recognized these *Costains* for what they are, wretches all, and deserving of the rack. A day will surely come when I will be able to demonstrate to them my way of thinking and my entire contempt for them. I assure you that if they were ever to be put to the flames, one by one, I would not hesitate a moment to provide the faggots for the fire! They may be certain that when the right time comes I shall not spare them."[8]

The winter roads were bad, and the weather was even worse. By Saturday, 1 February, the chilled and weary travelers had got no farther than the Valence region, where the marquis posted a note to Gaufridy expressing great concern: "Our progress is very slow, my dear lawyer friend, and that is what drives me to despair. But the roads are so bad that it is impossible to make much headway. The weather grows worse by the day and we are finding it all very hard. However, we hope to be in Paris without fail on the 5th."[9] Although there is no reference to his specific reasons for wanting to make such haste, we can safely assume that the marquis' "desperation" arose from a desire to reach Marie-Eléonore's bedside before she expired.

They arrived, unannounced and exhausted, not on the 5th as they had originally hoped but three days later, on 8 February, in the evening. On the 10th, Renée-Pélagie wrote to Gaufridy of their difficult journey: "the roads were dreadful, and we had to have our coach repaired many times."[10] They had gone directly to the Carmélites only to learn that Marie-Eléonore had died three weeks before. According to Renée-Pélagie, Donatien was devastated by the news. During the entire voyage he had been hoping to reach his mother's bedside in time, "and the blow fell all the harder because of that." He had now gone off to stay with a friend, and she had taken rooms at the Hôtel de Danemark, rue Jacob. They had agreed they would not let Mme de Montreuil know of their arrival until Wednesday the 12th. Choosing the right moment to see her would be a very delicate matter.

How genuine were Donatien's filial sentiments as he rushed through sleet and storm over atrocious roads to reach his dying mother's bedside? The answer is far from obvious, given what we know of his actions both before and immediately after learning of her death. However, on this particular occasion the evidence seems to weigh mostly in his favor. Despite being embroiled in the Treillet business, had he not dropped everything at La Coste, leaving his affairs in disorder ("We departed in such haste and left everything in disarray"),[11] and rushed off to Paris in hopes of seeing her once again before she died? But then there were other reasons, too, for hurrying, one being simply the need to get away before there were even more Treillet repercussions. As had happened so often in the past, prudence alone demanded that he make himself scarce for a few months. Local feelings were running high, and the authorities, given his reputation, were unpredictable. There was also the problem of fence-mending with Mme de Montreuil after Renée-Pélagie's angry letter; it was urgent to settle things with her immediately and to placate any feelings of ill will that might interfere with her good management of his legal rehabilitation at the Parlement of Aix, a process that was now potentially jeopardized by the actions of that insolent scoundrel Treillet.

In all probability, both his mother's impending death and these other practical matters were much on his mind as he hurried toward Paris.

And then, of course, there was perhaps the most important reason of all. The explosive volcano of sheer Sadean energy within him had been contained for too long, and he knew it was ready to erupt. In his mind he had already formulated a plan for tasting once again all those special pleasures that only a large and vibrant metropolis like Paris could afford: the most fashionable plays, the latest books, the whores of high, low, and medium style who for the right price could be counted on to accommodate even the most novel tastes of the practiced connoisseur. He had already informed Renée-Pélagie that he intended to be on his own once they arrived. Perhaps he would even rent one of those charming *petites maisons* where more interesting things could go on than even Inspector Marais' spies knew about. Yes, Paris was the place to be in the winter season, competing for the favors of an actress along with the other *grands seigneurs,* with seasoned officers back from the wars and all the other sophisticated roustabouts who haunted the Opéra, the Comédie, the masked balls, and the gaming tables. The winter at La Coste had already been too long, and now, it seems, one was not even allowed to have one's way with the kitchen wenches without becoming the object of impertinent village gossip or the target of some crackpot paterfamilias brandishing pistols. Paris had been his first school of *libertinage.* He knew its darker corners well, and then there would be his old chum to look up—the very one he had just written to again, repeating his invitation to come down to La Coste and share in his simple country pleasures. All things considered and in a manner of speaking, this trip to Paris to see a dying mother for the last time was rather a piece of good luck, as much for the appearance of things as for his less avowable motives. It would be like the old days.

All that by way of introducing one of the most curious and intriguing Sadean letters that has ever come to light. First published by Lely in 1957,[12] it was written probably before noon on the 9th, the day after the couple's arrival, and it presents a key piece of evidence relating to the entire question of Sade's relationship with his mother. More particularly, it calls into question the authenticity and depth of the sentiments he would repeatedly flaunt later on, both in his correspondence and in his fiction, regarding the fateful journey he made to Paris in February 1777 on the occasion of Marie-Eléonore's death, a journey that marked the beginning of his long years of imprisonment. The letter reads as follows:

> The death of my mother, my dear abbé, has brought me here just when you were doubtlessly least expecting it since it was only a few days ago that I wrote you in order to renew my plea that you come down to Provence. The circumstances of this death and the situation with my other relatives with whom I am not yet entirely reconciled oblige me to remain incognito for some time yet. I beg you therefore to tell no one of my arrival. I yearn, nonetheless, to see you, to tell you of my exploits, to hear about yours, and to engage in some of these together with you. The services I requested from you for Provence can now be rendered here, for here we are! I will admit to you, moreover, that I, for my part, am in the greatest need of these services, never having found anyone who can satisfy me in this respect as you can; but if you so require, it will be on condition that I do the same for you and you will thus have no reason to reproach me. Fix a time for me to meet you somewhere that is not too public, or at your place, in the evening. I will be

there very punctually and we can then set out on a little hunting excursion. You can remit your reply to the person who delivers this letter but do not ask him any questions and do not go into any details about me. I'll explain my reasons to you later.

I embrace you with all my heart.[13]

We do not know how the "hunt" turned out or even whether the marquis' four or five days of freedom before his arrest on 13 February allowed sufficient time for its full realization. We can be sure, however, that if it did take place, Inspector Marais, who was made aware of Sade's presence in the capital as soon as he arrived,[14] would have known all about it. Even if the new king, Louis XVI, unlike his late grandfather Louis XV, was rather more interested in amateur locksmithing than in the weekly perusal of spicy police reports on what was going on in the brothels of Paris, his lieutenant général de police still maintained the largest army of informers in existence—"three thousand rogues," as our marquis liked to describe them, whose only purpose, he maintained, was to spy on supposedly free citizens in order to discover how they chose to channel their ejaculations, it being understood that "there are dungeons readied and scaffolds erected for those among these *perfectly free* men who have not yet understood that it is a heinous crime to open the sluice gate to the right rather than to the left."[15] We can guess, and it is only a guess, what specific "exploits" Sade wanted to boast about to his mysterious abbé friend, and the same goes for the mutual services he hoped they could provide each other. The friend was obviously a brother libertine, especially worthy of an invitation to visit La Coste. Though not quite the equivalent of the darkly gothic Silling Castle he would soon be constructing in his imagination as a setting for *Les 120 journées de Sodome,* the marquis' fortress in Provence with its special room was not without its own sophisticated resources. Later, Mme de Montreuil would ask to have the room destroyed,[16] containing as it did dangerously incriminating evidence, "mechanical devices" and other objects, all traces of which were to be buried "a hundred feet below the ground." The various paraphernalia and special items of furniture were, in fact, of such a compromising nature (the Présidente found it inconceivable that Renée-Pélagie could have even known about them) that the lawyer Gaufridy was eventually required to carry out the burdensome task of removing and destroying everything entirely by himself, in a most secret manner and without involving workmen or third parties in any way.[17]

Only four days after Donatien's departure from La Coste, an anonymous letter had been posted from Apt to Mme de Montreuil warning her that her son-in-law's intentions on leaving for Paris were not what he pretended they were, which perhaps also supports our conclusion that he had much more on his mind than the alarming state of his mother's health as he rushed along the wintry roads toward Paris. Mme de Montreuil had in fact no need, as some biographers have concluded, to write a letter of entrapment to entice the marquis to the capital. Nor do I think he himself was drawn there, as Maurice Lever has suggested, by a "suicidal impulse" that caused him to risk the visit that ended in his imprisonment. I suspect that the particular impulse involved was rather more positive, related in some measure to the need to break out of domestic banality and provincial boredom, enhanced by the desire to translate into action those importunate sexual fantasies that had already caused him to extend his original invitation to his abbé friend. These same fantasies are again what persuaded him to send out his rather curious invitation to the hunt perhaps no more than an hour or two after learning of his mother's death. Donatien, one suspects, probably felt more a sense of ambivalent liberation than of unmixed grief when he learned that Marie-Eléonore was already dead and buried. The person who symbolized for him his most deep-seated feelings of repression and constraint was gone. In practical, immediate terms, her disappearance meant that another obstacle had been removed, one that might have delayed or complicated, for example, the little excursion with his friend that he had been planning and anticipating for weeks. And Paris, with all its little hidden corners, those places "not too public," offered opportunities that had been denied him for too many years.

With Marais' police spies on his trail from the very moment his carriage crossed the barrier into the Faubourg Saint-Jacques, it is certain that any fantasies he subsequently acted out, any feats of sexual valor accomplished with his usual lack of discretion, would have come immediately to the attention of the ministry where it was known that "the will of the King" was not in the least inclined to make things easy for the notorious marquis de Sade.[18] He was still technically a fugitive who had escaped from a sentence of death, and if ever his problems with the Parlement of Aix were to be put to rest and his complete legal rehabilitation achieved in the manner that his family wished, he would somehow, everyone agreed, have to be rescued from himself. He would have to show good faith, definite signs of contrition, not to mention a genuine improvement in his behavior over a sustained period of time. The simplest solution would be to arrange for his quiet confinement, at family expense, in one of the royal prisons until all of the formalities were completed. He would have to be patient. Once again, he would have to reconcile himself to those paternalistic benefits afforded his privileged class by the "protection" of one of His Majesty's prisons. The family's sentiments on the matter were known to the ministry as well as to the miscreant marquis. Mme de Montreuil, far from being her son-in-law's enemy, could be counted on to marshal the best legal support for his rehabilitation in Aix, just as she had already done several times before in Paris. She could also be relied on to neutralize, by bribery and intimidation if necessary, any troubling witnesses to that nasty Marseilles business who might be still hanging about. Thanks to her, all traces of compromising "objects" and "writings" had been removed from the locked room at La Coste. Similarly, with the help of Renée-Pélagie and the marquis, she had already managed the year before to have Nanon—one of Donatien's little household sluts and a potential tattle-tale who had stupidly allowed herself to get pregnant by him—locked up on a trumped-up theft charge by means of a conveniently arranged *lettre de cachet*. Luckily, Nanon's baby had obligingly died in the process, and Donatien, as the father, was immensely relieved. For once, the authorities had understood how truly important it was to protect a great family from the rabble.

Of course, when the time came to protect that same family from *him*—indeed, to protect him from himself—such schemes and scenarios seemed rather less appropriate. Mme de Montreuil's carefully worked-out family strategy ("a period of detention will be essential to put an end to his difficulties"), approved even by the abbé Amblet, was not exactly what the impetuous marquis had in mind when he set out for the capital, knowing that he was entering dangerous territory. Everyone knew it would not be an easy matter to convince him that it would be doing him such a great favor to lock him up until all the problems relating to his old death sentence by the Parlement of Aix were ironed out.

The arrest, when it came, was a total shock. Donatien had announced his presence in Paris to his mother-in-law only the day before in a letter that rather pointedly asked her whether she intended to be his "second mother" (now that Marie-Eléonore was gone) or a tyrant. That at least is how he recalled his note a week or two later when he wrote her again from inside the prison walls of Vincennes.[19] Mme de Montreuil had apparently responded very positively with a friendly acknowledgment that the marquis, later on and wise after the fact, claimed he had instantly mistrusted: "I assure you," he later wrote to Renée-Pélagie, "that I was not deceived even for an instant, and you will remember that just moments before your bedroom was invaded by *a gang of scoundrels* who, without showing a royal warrant, claimed they were there to arrest me by order of the King, I was telling you to place no faith at all in that reassuring letter from your mother, that, in fact, her show of warmheartedness was proof positive she was hatching duplicity in her heart."[20]

Leading that "gang of scoundrels" on the evening of 13 February 1777 at the Hôtel de Danemark, rue Jacob, was his familiar arch-enemy, Inspector Marais. Scarcely more than an hour later, Donatien found himself securely locked away in the central keep of the château de Vincennes. Give or take one or two brief interludes of freedom, it was the beginning of a thirteen-year sentence.

LA PLACE DES VICTOIRES

View of the Place des Victoires, starting point of the notorious Arcueil affair.

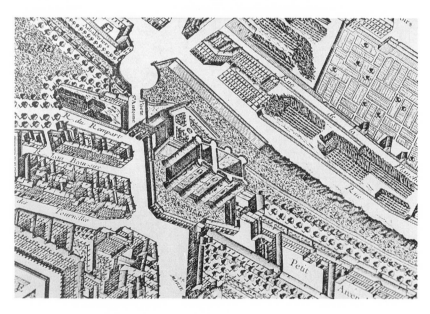

Plan de Bretez detail showing the Bastille and the Porte St Antoine.

Copy of one of the Bastille's keys.

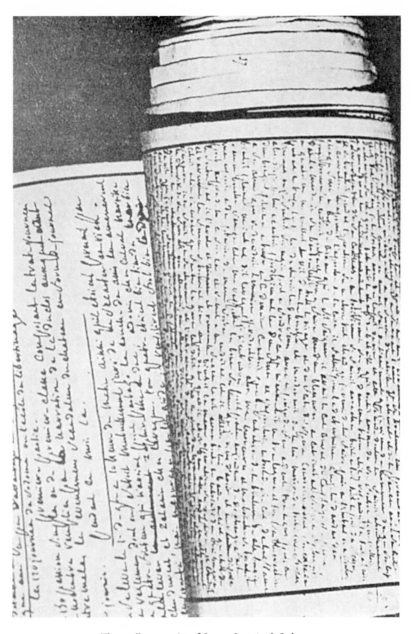

The scroll manuscript of *Les 120 Journées de Sodome*.

Le ciel est-il juste quand il abandonne la vertu
à de si grands tourments ?.....

Illustration from the 1795 edition of *Aline et Valcour.*

Part Three

MOTHERS, WHORES, AND BOGUS POLITICS

*Moi qui duperais le bon
Dieu si je l'entreprenais.*

[I who could bamboozle
the Lord Almighty
if I tried.]

Fourteen

A MOTHER MUCH LOVED?

It is only when we come to Sade's early prison letters, written soon after
Marie-Eléonore's death in January 1777, that we encounter the first references that have so far come to light specifically concerning his professed
feelings for his mother. Unfortunately, these direct, after-the-fact mentions
are of such dubious value that they do little to supplant the need for
even more speculation on a matter that is so central to his fiction. They
provide no reliable evidence, for example, that either confirms or invali-
dates the widely held view that he actively harbored an abiding hatred for
the woman who had brought him into the world. Paradoxically, in fact, it
is precisely when the marquis begins to make explicit and categorical statements on the crucial subject of his mother that the problem of determining the truth, falsehood, coherence, or good faith of what he says really begins. Here as elsewhere he seems incapable of speaking or playing any role
other than the one that is narrowly defined by his immediate purpose. Imprisoned soon after ostensibly putting himself at risk in order to pay a last
visit to his dying mother, he sees himself as suddenly transformed into the
victim of an evil melodrama in which the hero, a quintessentially good son
whose filial devotion was *lifelong,* is tricked and iniquitously oppressed by
his enemies. He goes even farther: it was in fact precisely because he was
such a good son and because he loved his mother with such devotion that
he had suddenly found himself behind prison walls!

The standard biographical view of the matter has been that Donatien
Alphonse François de Sade represents the very archetype of the mother
hater, the malformed product of a negative Oedipus complex. Pierre Klossowski's classic interpretation, though perhaps now something of a termi-
nological period piece, has been adopted more or less in its entirety even

by Sade's most recent and authoritative biographer, Maurice Lever.[1] In terms of developmental conflict, Sade is seen as an exception to the "normal" Oedipal rule: that is, instead of sharing in the common initial conflict of most males that leads to hatred of the father—a conflict deemed by some schools of analytical psychology to be a scientific fact, "duly observed and beyond discussion"—Sade, we are told, provides an example of the opposite, *negative* tendency. The principal events of his life, Klossowski maintains, singularly favored this "much rarer and generally less obvious" behavioral pattern associated with hatred of the mother. Indeed, so many easily recognizable traces of the complex appear throughout his writings that we can legitimately consider it to be "the leitmotif of Sadean ideology."[2] Of course, as Klossowski is quick to point out, it would not be an easy matter to trace to a specific event the exact origin of this pivotal component of the marquis' psychic formation—to a disappointment, for example, that Sade as a very young child may have suffered at the hands of his mother. That initial or triggering event eludes investigation because of gaps in the documentation. But without any doubt, there had to be a *traumatic moment* either motivated by real circumstances or the result of an "interpretation" by the child that would have subsequently reinforced in the son feelings of guilt toward the father for having neglected him. Allying himself with paternal power, the son in the depths of his innermost psyche aggressively resents the guilty mother whose hypocrisy is seen as legitimating any crimes committed against her by the "abandoned" father. Sade's *sadism* is thus reduced to the unconscious expression of this primordial hatred and the pursuit of a mission "to punish maternal power in all its forms and overthrow its institutions." It is only later on in his life when the young libertine comes into direct conflict with his mother-in-law, a mother figure who is "jealous of her prerogatives" and "tyrannically controls her progeny," that the marquis' aggressivity rises to the conscious level and turns into overt "hatred of the matriarchal values: pity, charity, gratitude, sacrifice, and fidelity."[3]

For those who prefer their psychology fancy rather than plain, the Klossowskian itinerary takes us even farther along this road, past such arcane byways as the asocial superego, castration anxiety, and even a Sadean metaphysicoreligious pathology labeled the "loathing of Eve." But on the threshold of the twenty-first century when the very existence of a subconscious appears to be under serious attack, perhaps it is more prudent to continue exploring a more classically familiar road, taking note when we can, however, of those circumstances in what we know of Sade's life that at least seem to support a plainer—if more approximate—application of

Klossowski's analysis. Following that line, biographers have been fairly unanimous in their conclusion that this mother who "barely exists" occupied a position of little importance in Donatien's life, leaving an emotional void that even his "substitute mothers" could not fill. Obliged by a libertine husband to take refuge in a convent, the absent and harshly indifferent mother managed somehow to scar for life the tender psyche of a young, sensitive, and extremely lonely son whose overindulgent father, on the other hand, spoiled him rotten at the same time as he zealously schooled him in the wicked ways of the world.[4]

We can no doubt usefully mull over much along such lines without necessarily wrenching and squeezing even more nebulous testimony from the long-dead marquis' hypothetical subconscious. Some of his early anti-mother developmental influences may have been, moreover, quite direct and unmediated. His surrogate mothers, for example, some of them his father's mistresses or ex-mistresses playing out their active role in the dynamics of family estrangement, did not merely fill an emotional void; they were probably seen by the passionate adolescent as gracious defenders and active allies of the father, understandably inclined to denigrate and deplore in their daily chitchat, perhaps even in front of the child, the narrow, stubbornly principled kill-joy attitudes of the mother, her misguided severity and gloom. It is not difficult to imagine their charitably disapproving whispers, echoing observations similar to those of the comtesse de Longeville:[5] "What are you going to do with that poor darling child? His mother means well, of course, but what a pity!"

Obviously, there is always room for doubt. Do we, for example, in our modish zeal to manufacture victims of early developmental trauma, perhaps exaggerate the deleterious effects of the "absent" mother? It can be argued that even if Marie-Eléonore was as absent as she is sometimes thought to have been, the marquis' experience in this respect was not all that unusual in an eighteenth-century aristocratic family.[6] Sade himself, even when he had some choice in the matter, did not act very differently with his own children. Bourgeois families, more than their noble cousins, tended to keep their children by them, just as it was the bourgeois husband and wife (as the dramatist Nivelle de La Chaussée reminds us) who, by basing marriage on mutual affection, defied most frequently the marital *prejudice à la mode:* "This usage is now found only among the *bourgeoisie.*"[7] Moreover, we now know, thanks to the Baumez correspondence, that Marie-Eléonore was not significantly "absent" during the first four critically important developmental years of Sade's life, although Donatien's sudden deportation to Avignon at the end of that happy period had to have been a palpable shock for the child. Sade himself, in *Aline et Valcour,* seems to put a "normal" construction on his Avignon exile by implying (mistakenly, as it turns out) that it was more a matter of family solidarity, a case of the wife following the husband as a matter of course to his place of employment: "At around that time, my father was employed in diplomacy; my mother accompanied him and I was sent to live with a grandmother in Languedoc."[8]

In fact, by the time Donatien was sent to Avignon the exact opposite was true. Jean-Baptiste was no longer "employed in diplomacy," and normal solidarity between husband and wife had ceased to exist. Perhaps it was the profound estrangement of his parents, so apparent to the astutely observant child when he returned from Provence, that produced the most scarring effects. The returning "orphan" would have witnessed the worst of the separation, the discord, the awkward occasions when Marie-Eléonore, formerly so deferential in the presence of an admired (if no longer adored) husband, showed a new intransigence, became openly outspoken, even a little shrill. At the same time, Jean-Baptiste would have displayed greater indifference, more mocking irony, and, very probably, more of that hitherto unsuspected domestic mean-spiritedness revealed so clearly in the Baumez correspondence. There would have been much wifely hurt and anger at Jean-Baptiste's increasingly blatant infidelities, recriminations at his profligacy, his irresponsible career improprieties and failures. Especially, there would have been unpleasantly obvious disagreements over how Donatien, this only son and treasured future head of the family, was to be brought up. Jean-Baptiste clearly insisted on inculcating his own set of sophisticated "lessons" in life, man-to-man instructions on the need to cast out the bugbears of superstition and religion along with all the frowning bigotries that placed guilty constraints on sexual expression. Marie-Eléonore, on the other hand, would not have made Donatien's precocious acquisition of worldly manners a priority. What was her reaction on learning, for example, that Donatien, at age thirteen, was to have his very own *petite maison* where he could give small dinner parties for those indulgent *mamans* who hugged him so affectionately and teasingly promised to wait for him to grow up to be just like his handsome papa? It is as unlikely that the mother was consulted in the matter as it is unthinkable that she would have assented to it. And no doubt most important of all, Jean-Baptiste and Marie-Eléonore would have disagreed fundamentally on the question of Donatien's religious upbringing. We do not know for certain but it is not unlikely that the woman who eventually took refuge at the Carmelites was at least conventionally devout, perhaps even a bit of a Jansenist, stiff-

necked and strait-laced. As for Jean-Baptiste, though he finally "got religion" in old age, he was at this time (and continued to be well into his
prime) quite the opposite: a fashionable unbeliever, a sophisticated libertine who insisted on teaching his emancipating principles to his son, determined to rid the boy of all the "childhood superstitions" that had no
doubt been piously reinforced by his reverend aunts in Provence and were
again being forced down his throat by that "dreadful woman" who kept
threatening to go off to a convent if her husband did not change his ways.
In short, Klossowskian analysis notwithstanding, it seems probable that
many years in advance of the posited awakening of Donatien's hostile "subconscious" by Mme de Montreuil, Jean-Baptiste's specific and direct lessons had already fostered overt antimaternal feelings in the son.

Sade himself comments from time to time, usually with an all too obvious ulterior motive, on the deleterious effects of parental estrangement
on children. In one of his first letters to Renée-Pélagie from Vincennes, he
speaks of his fear that a sinister move is afoot to separate them: "It would
be the ultimate blow that could be dealt me and, rest assured, I would not
survive it." He goes on to suggest that he is not really thinking of his own
interests here: "I beg you to resist with all your might and to be convinced
that our children would be the first victims of it; *there are no examples of
children made happy by the estrangement of their fathers and mothers.*"[9] Of
course, we have learned to be suspicious any time we find Sade insisting
that he is not thinking first and foremost of his own interests; his entire
ethical philosophy, repeated ad nauseam in nearly every one of his writings,
categorically instructs us to be totally skeptical in this regard. The marquis'
treatment of his own children, moreover, hardly supports the family values
message he preaches here, and it was clearly to his personal advantage to
fight any separation move and to retain Renée-Pélagie as an ally against
Mme de Montreuil. Without her constant loyal attendance to his needs,
her willingness and capacity to soak up his rage and endless insults, would
his mind have remained as intact as it did during all those years in Vincennes and the Bastille? But even if self-serving, his Vincennes comments
on separated parents and his plea for the children cannot help but suggest
the presence of surviving scars, marking emotional upheavals sustained
in adolescence as a result of the increasingly bitter conflict between his
mother and father. The same is true of the not dissimilar "orphan's" en-
treaty regarding the children, sent out a few days earlier to his mother-in-
law: "At least love them, even if you have hated their father. Give them an
education that protects them, if possible, *from the misfortunes that my neglected upbringing has caused for me.*"[10]

Be that as it may, and despite the primary love he must certainly have felt for his mother before he was shipped off to Avignon, the marquis' filial loyalties to his father, from his adolescent years onward, never wavered. Throughout his adult years, he never abandoned the image of his father as his special protector. Both his personal correspondence and his fiction refer to the calamities he would have either initially avoided or ultimately escaped *had his father been still alive.* Not surprisingly, when in 1790 he was finally released from Charenton and faced with Renée-Pélagie's last-minute refusal to cohabit, he would draw an immediate parallel between himself and his "victimized" father whom he now chose to remember as old and failing in health, unjustly left to die abandoned and alone. Was that to be his own unmerited fate as well? "I who married only to have companionship in my house when I grew old, I now find myself forsaken, abandoned and alone, reduced to the sad fate of my father in his last days. Of all the circumstances of old age, it is this that I feared most in all the world." [11] It is a touching speech, and once again the problem is how to take any of it at face value (and most of all, perhaps, his stated reasons for getting married!). He writes this to his aunt, the aging abbesse, in a highly dramatic letter filled with righteously indignant but verifiably false recriminations against Renée-Pélagie and her family, throwing in for good measure an inordinate amount of his usual revisionist blather. The marquis, as always, is playing a role; and as always the question becomes, when do we believe him? When is the role he is playing really his own?

Apart from the instances we have already noted, remarkably few references to Marie-Eléonore of any kind appear in Sade's correspondence, let alone overt and explicit expressions of hostility toward her or toward mothers in general, or direct allusions to her "absence" or "presence" in his life. We do glean here and there, despite Donatien's probable "editing" of the correspondence, a certain amount of indirect evidence that mother and son had their serious disagreements—the already noted indication, for example, that on one occasion she was sufficiently fed up with his behavior to deny him access to the Carmélites apartment. But this was in the heyday of his youthful rebelliousness when even Jean-Baptiste was finally reduced to severing connections with him and given over to thoughts of fleeing the capital to avoid even hearing his son's name mentioned. That unhappy situation reached its most critical point around the time that Donatien married Renée-Pélagie. Immediately after the wedding, and with an astonishing rapidity, he established a warmly complicitous understanding with his mother-in-law. Strong willed and businesslike, the Présidente in turn did her utmost to be supportive and to keep him out of trouble.

There is very substantial evidence—almost all of it in archives that Donatien never had an opportunity to manipulate—that Marie-Eléonore, as with her dramatic intervention in the Arcueil affair, was fully committed to helping her son whenever she could, especially when it came to making sacrifices to advance his military career. A letter of 2 April 1761 to the war minister illustrates the lengths to which she was prepared to go—farther, it seems, than even Jean-Baptiste at the time[12]—to raise the money required to purchase a *guidon*'s commission for Donatien in the corps of Gendarmes, thus securing his future in the army as a worthy descendant of her distinguished soldier ancestor. The letter survives today in the ancien régime's war archives, ironically located in the very château where Donatien, not long after Marie-Eléonore sent it, would be taken to experience his first taste of prison confinement:

> I had intended to write to you yesterday, Monsieur, to inform you that it has not been possible for me to raise the money needed to purchase the *guidon de gendarmerie* commission for my son. I had asked M. de Poyanne to persuade you to give me until April 1st to collect the amount needed but I was unable to tell you yesterday what my wishes were to be in the matter. Given more time, I could have gathered together the necessary sum. I beg you, Monsieur, to reserve His Majesty's kindnesses toward me for another occasion and I ask you for your part to do the same for my son. M. de Sade [Jean-Baptiste] is at Versailles and he will no doubt have seen you and conveyed to you his intentions regarding the *guidon* commission. I can contribute only the letters patent for the office of Lieutenant General of Bresse, valued at 20,000 *écus,* which I would very willingly give anytime it is a question of my son's advancement in the King's service.
>
> Do not doubt, Monsieur, the gratitude, esteem and respect with which I am honored to be, Monsieur, your most humble and most obedient servant,
>
> > *Maillé de Sade*
> > Paris, 2 April 1761
> > At the Carmélites de Saint-Jacques, rue d'Enfer[13]

Other references in the correspondence make it clear that Donatien sometimes called on Marie-Eléonore to lend him money for considerably less worthy ends: "I know, Monsieur," the marquis wrote, for example, to the abbé d'Armand, probably in 1762 or 1763, "how willingly you helped my mother borrow the money when she was looking to send me some. I am again in similar straits—even worse, I dare say!"[14] The sum requested was a mere fifteen *louis,* to be delivered to the bearer of his letter immediately if possible; and if fifteen *louis* proved too difficult to round up, even as little as five *louis* was deemed most welcome. The debt was obviously of a desperate nature, probably the kind that young army officers were pleased to call "debts of honor" after losing all but their shirts at the gaming table. Once again the fact that the marquis felt able to turn to Marie-Eléonore for such emergency funds is hardly evidence that supports the notion of a distant, indifferent, or unapproachable mother—however disapproving she undoubtedly was of his dissolute entertainments.

We know too that Donatien and Marie-Eléonore sometimes talked about conventional everyday matters on those occasions that he stayed with her or visited her at the Carmélites. From Vincennes, for example, he warns his wife on 21 April 1777 to be cautious when entering a certain room in his late mother's apartment where Renée-Pélagie was residing at the time: "I forgot to tell you, after I learned that you were staying at the Carmélites, to keep away from the little room to the right of you as you enter the drawing room. Please remember that it is falling to pieces and that more than ten years ago my mother told me she dared not go in there because the architect told her that it was on the point of collapsing. For my peace of mind, don't set foot in there, I beg you."[15] The remark is workaday and mundane, but it is yet another surviving fragment of evidence confirming that Marie-Eléonore, contrary to the general view, did occasionally have ordinary contacts with her son and from time to time did occupy a place in his adult life.

That Donatien genuinely reciprocated such feelings of affection is, however, less clear. But even without any solid evidence that he did, we cannot be surprised that the theme of his mother's recent death dominates the first letters he was allowed to write from Vincennes after his arrest. Expediency alone, whether or not backed up by sincerity, dictated that such a golden opportunity to capitalize rhetorically on the occasion not be passed up. It was important to show that, once again, he had been made a helpless victim, both by the police and by his evil mother-in-law. She had wickedly profaned a sacred moment of family bereavement; it was almost as though Marie-Eléonore's death was made to order for her plans. Yes, now the conspiracy was absolutely transparent. His mother-in-law and the police, with malice and premeditation, had taken advantage of his devotion and filial love. Like a trusting ninny he had fallen into the trap set by this vile woman who had cleverly used his beloved mother's illness as bait. Once the world learned how great his love for his mother had been, it would know how innocent he was and how treacherously guilty his mother-in-law was. Indeed, how else could the evil Présidente have prevailed? What a despicable trick she had played on a vulnerable, generous, and loving son!

Of all the possible ways that vengeance and cruelty might have chosen, you will agree, Madame, that you have selected the most horrible. I came to Paris to be with my mother during her last moments, my sole purpose was to see her, to embrace her once more if she was still alive, or to mourn her if she was no more. And it was that moment you chose to make me your victim, once again![16]

While the circumstances of the letter's composition naturally provoke the suspicion that the marquis in the passage just quoted is deliberately inflating his filial sentiments, what he writes next must invite our outright disbelief (as well as our unreserved admiration for his melodramatic style), especially when we recall how totally bereft of any sentiments of mourning was his "a-hunting we will go" letter to his abbé friend, written when his mother was no less dead but, of course, before his imprisonment became a factor in the equation. However, writing now from his prison cell, Sade tells his despised mother-in-law that his despair is such and his love for his dear departed mother is such that he wishes to join her in the grave. Yes, the Présidente obviously wanted his death and she would have it: "My situation is horrifying. You know very well that neither my head nor my heart has ever been able to withstand close confinement." He cannot escape physically from the donjon of Vincennes, but no one will prevent him from fulfilling his dearest wish—namely, joining his beloved mother in the only way possible, by doing away with himself:

From the depths of her tomb, my unfortunate mother calls to me; I can see her once more holding out her open arms to me, inviting me to her embrace, to the only haven that is left to me. I am happy to follow her so closely to the grave and I ask you as a last favor, Madame, to have me buried by her side. Only one thing makes me hesitate, it is a weakness on my part, I know, but I must confess it: I would have liked first to see my children.[17]

Readers of Sade's correspondence will recognize here one of dozens of routinely portentous threats to kill himself, scattered liberally throughout his correspondence, all uttered in the most ominous tones and all, without exception, pure hogwash! The marquis, in fact, possessed one of the healthiest instincts for self-preservation and survival imaginable. But knowing that, do we, at the same time as we challenge his patently fraudulent threats to do away with himself, totally discount as merely opportunistic "literature" the loving sentiments he now expresses so ostentatiously for his late mother? There are clearly times when the self-serving "literature" of Sade's correspondence is quite indistinguishable from the "literature" of his novels, when the rhetorical transition from one to the other is seamless. In his fiction, the Paris arrest episode will again be portrayed as an example of "gullible affection" on the part of a too tender-hearted son, a certain "M. de Mézane," described in *Aline et Valcour* as a fugitive from an unjust sentence of the Parlement d'Aix, guilty of nothing more than a few "youthful escapades, entirely excusable at twenty-seven years of age," and guilty as well, of course (the novel appeared during the Revolution), of being a high-minded patriot, having authored a number of antiroyalist pamphlets:

> Despite the danger to himself, M. de Mézane, who had been in hiding for several years, was deceived by his gullible tenderness into coming to Paris to pay his last respects to a dying mother. He had scarcely reached the deceased's apartment when his wife's family had him arrested. His protests against such evil treatment were met with sneering derision and he was cast into a dungeon of the Bastille where he experienced the "great pleasure" of mourning all at once the loss of his liberty, the death of his mother, and the barbarous stupidity of his in-laws.[18]

Aline de Blamont, the heroine of *Aline et Valcour,* is also faced with a similar prison dilemma, unable to escape physically from her father's château, an architectural echo of Vincennes and the Bastille ("more like a fortress than a country house; everywhere, one sees only iron bars, vaulted ceilings and massive doors; everything in this dreadful place blackens the imagination and inspires terror").[19] She, too, determines that physical escape is impossible, her room being more than eighty feet above the ground (approximately the height of Sade's last *chambre* in the Liberté tower of the Bastille). A water-filled moat surrounds the castle. There are guards. Again like the role-playing prisoner in Vincennes, she, too, decides to rejoin her mother by seeking freedom in death: "I shall escape . . . I shall return to my mother's house. . . . They have said that she will no longer shelter me in her bosom but they will be proven wrong."[20] Her sentiments are identical to those described by the marquis after his arrest in February 1777, but her instinct for survival at all costs is far less robust, her principled integrity, her loathing of compromise far stronger. She takes her own life—something Sade could probably never have done—but not before she composes an eloquent piece of literature, entitled "To the spirit of my late mother." It reads almost as though she is copying from Sade's real-life prison letter to Mme de Montreuil:

> At peace in the maternal breast, your unhappy daughter will be safe from the crimes and cruelties of men; in that sacred bosom she will find once more

the calm repose that eluded her in life. Open your arms, my dearest mother!
Open them wide that I may enter. . . .
     Barbarous creatures! They tried to sacrifice me on your tomb. . . . Even
before your ashes were cold, crime had entered their hearts.[21]

Aline leaves instructions for her burial and again fictional literature imitates
what was equally "fictional" life: "I beg, as a last favor, to be buried *next to
my mother.*"[22]

     Direct references to the Présidente's monstrous duplicity and treach-
ery on the occasion of his mother's death continued for a brief time after
his arrest. On 13 March 1777, Donatien began another letter to Mme de
Montreuil in much the same rhetorical vein: "If there could still exist a
glimmer of pity in a human heart capable of betraying in an instant all of
the most sacred sentiments of humanity, [. . .] carrying out the arrest of a
son at the side of his mother's coffin [. . .][23] Similarly fanciful revisionist
elements continued to dominate his self-referencing narratives as the year
progressed. In a letter to an unidentified public official, perhaps the lieutenant général de police, the marquis states that it was news of his mother's
actual death, not of her illness, that had brought him rushing to Paris:
"Summoned here by the death of my mother whom I have been made to
mourn with bitter tears [. . .]" Yes, he had come to Paris to beg Renée-
Pélagie's father and mother to adopt him as their very own, now that death
had robbed him of both his natural parents.[24] Even in his letters to Renée-
Pélagie (who, of course, knew better since she had shared the trip to Paris
with him), he allowed himself to embroider on the event. Was it not while
he was doing his sacred duty, a *sacred act,* that the Présidente de Montreuil
had cunningly enticed him into her snares? "This evil woman wants to
force me to regret, to curse even, the last tributes of respect that I came to
pay my mother. What a loathsome refinement in cruelty! It seems she
wishes to make more bitter still the tears of mourning I have shed."[25] But
now, rather than carry out his threats to commit suicide, Donatien had
found another good reason to stay alive. If he killed himself, was that not
precisely what Renée-Pélagie's evil mother wanted him to do? He would
spite her and live!

     Your abominable mother is most annoyed that I have not yet taken my
     life; it is as if this odious, this infernal monster, set loose against me by all
     the demons of Hell, has declared: "Yes, I want to see you grow to hate every-
     thing that is dear to you; I want to wrench apart all the bonds that might
     link you with others. You loved your mother, you were rushing to her res-
     cue; I want to make you curse her, if I can. You love your wife; I will poison
     her spirit so that her words of comfort will be like so many stab wounds to

your heart. Your children were dear to you; I shall scatter my serpents even over them; it is my wish that they too will revile you."[26]

The parallel claim that he loves his wife reveals, I think, something of the mental juggling that is going on here with regard to his mother as well. From Vincennes, late in 1777 he writes that he loves his wife, "his companion in misfortune, with the greatest excess"; indeed, he would rather lose all his possessions than give her up![27] The statement is categorical, but, like many of Sade's truths, it expresses at best only an ephemeral verity, the subjective truth of the fleeting moment, delivered with all the polemical skills of the clever barrister pleading the morning's case. Tomorrow—perhaps even sooner—there would be other truths to devise and deliver. He needed Renée-Pélagie while he was in prison ("I needed her and feigned accordingly," he later confesses to Gaufridy). She was his only lifeline to the world outside. But very different are some of his statements regarding his wife before his incarceration. In fact, he loved her not at all, he informed his uncle at one point. Even worse, he found it quite impossible to overcome feelings of physical revulsion in her presence, and that had been the case from the moment he first met her.[28] In his correspondence with Renée-Pélagie's mother, the abbé de Sade had been apologetic and had tried to put the matter less brutally: his nephew was, of course, aware of Renée-Pélagie's merits and even felt some respect and friendship for her, but that was all: "He finds her too cold and too devout for his tastes, and that is why he seeks his amusement elsewhere." The situation required patience; one could only hope and wait for "the age of impulsive ardor" to pass.[29]

Whether Donatien felt actual revulsion or merely the absence of attraction for his wife remains a moot point. The character Valcour, the closest approximation we have of an idealized Sadean self-portrait, provides a plausible if rather general and conventional explanation why Donatien might have rejected the wife Jean-Baptiste had chosen for him. Without love, Valcour assures Aline, marriage is nothing more than a vile and mercenary pact, a sordid trafficking in fortunes and family names.[30] But the marquis saw his marriage pact with Renée-Pélagie as vile for other reasons as well, and, especially during his raging tantrums, he took particular pleasure in flinging those other reasons in her face: Renée-Pélagie, to put it bluntly, was beneath him; she came from a class of social upstarts, the recent *noblesse de robe,* and their marriage pact was *vile* precisely because of her ignobility, the baseness of her origins, blatantly obvious in her every act.[31] For Jean-Baptiste, her family's money overruled all such objections, but that argument had not counted for Donatien. In the end, he had been obliged to elaborate a far more convoluted personal dialectic in order to conquer, or at least to tolerate, the intense repugnance he insisted he felt for her. The technique involved a complex semantical manipulation of his feelings, monitored and controlled by self-indulgent but rigorously lucid powers of mind that would surely have invited the applause of more than one of his former masters in casuistry at Louis-le-Grand. He described the entire process to his uncle:

> Well, I did what in truth no honest man should ever do: I allowed my tongue to make a promise that my heart could not keep, and, no longer thinking myself bound by it since it was only a matter of form, I believed that my whole duty consisted in hiding my true feelings. I almost deceived myself, and the obligation to be false, by dulling the true feelings of my heart, by disguising my hatred, caused me to look upon my duty as less of a burden. Weary of such unending constraint, of saying for two years running, *I love you,* without thinking it, I tried to think it in order to feel pleasure in saying it. It was then that I saw things clearly, but, at the same time as I reproached myself for being deceitful, I was planning even better deceptions. However, whether it was because there was now less duplicity, or perhaps because my heart was more completely deceived, I no longer felt the same degree of remorse.[32]

The simple intricacies of what logicians have dubbed the Liar paradox pale into insignificance! In this passage (which deserves more attention than it has so far received), Sade reveals one of his most useful bad-faith methodologies, an invaluable mechanism for lying, not to others—that was mere child's play—but, rather, in a certain sense, to himself, yet all the while not losing sight of the convoluted process that was going on. And, indeed, how could he ever have lost sight of what was actually going on, he who prided himself on his ability to deceive even the deity, if a deity existed? The quintessential Sadean boast still remains: "I who could bamboozle God Almighty if I tried!" We shall have occasion to revisit it later in this study.[33]

If we return now to Donatien de Sade's parallel assertions, "You loved your mother" and "You love your wife," words he places rhetorically in the mouth of a viperous mother-in-law summoned up for the occasion, we have little difficulty accepting the notion that Sade was also capable of applying this same dialectic of lucid self-deception to his feelings for Marie-Eléonore, her death being such a handily exploitable prelude to his imprisonment and such a convenient canvas on which to redraw the realities of his relationship with her. Suddenly, the picture was clear! He was in prison not because of any reprehensible behavior on his part but *because he loved his mother,* a love that the evil Mme de Montreuil had diabolically exploited!

Unfortunately for the image of the marquis as the archetypical good son, time would soon betray the shallowness and patently opportunistic nature of these sentiments. After the initial crisis passed, his correspondence seems to abandon all such references to his mother. Henceforth, his every waking moment would be filled with venomous thoughts concerning his monstrous mother-in-law.

Largely out of mind, Marie-Eléonore was nevertheless assigned a last important role in one of the prisoner's later crises, an epic fit of jealousy that, to the astonishment of his loyal and loving wife, exploded at Vincennes in the summer of 1781 when, in a sudden fury, he accused her of carrying on an adulterous affair with his former secretary Lefèvre. It had all begun with a simple line drawing of Lefèvre by Mlle Rousset, the couple's charming and talented friend who had come up from Provence to stay with Renée-Pélagie. During a visit to the prisoner, Renée-Pélagie had innocently shown the drawing to her husband as an amusing curiosity, but Donatien had immediately flown into a rage, slashed at the portrait with his penknife and stained it with his blood. He then neatly scrawled over its surface the threat that he would one day mutilate this grubby little commoner Lefèvre in like fashion—or hire others to do it—even if it were to cost him a thousand *louis d'or!*[34] The marquis, we see, was being at his aristocratic best, but especially significant are several other haughty observations he scribbled over the partially lacerated drawing, setting out a curiously romanesque defense of his mother's distinguished noble origins. She is referred to as "cousin of the Great Condé," and the marquis momentarily transforms his fit of jealousy into a heroic vindication of the courtly love codes of old. His apparent purpose was to rebut an awkward remark supposedly made by Renée-Pélagie, implying that Marie-Eléonore, years before when she held the position of lady-in-waiting to the princesse de Condé, had succumbed to the charms of the princess's husband, the powerful Monsieur le Duc. In fact, what Renée-Pélagie actually said or did to provoke her husband's jealous rage on this occasion is not entirely clear. It is not easy to imagine why she would have made such a remark to the chronically paranoid prisoner, and it is even less clear how her words could have been maladroitly associated in the marquis' mind with her presentation of Lefèvre's portrait. The prisoner's swift and brutal response reveals, in any case, a noteworthy glimpse of at least one of the fanciful storybook images of Marie-Eléonore that her son had kept locked away defensively in his memory:

> Your analogy is lame, allow me to inform you, Madame la marquise. [...]
> A decent, sensitive woman may have taken pleasure (without any conse-
> quences) in welcoming at her feet a hero's laurels, and the cousin of the
> Great Condé could love someone who was seeking to imitate his ancestors.
> This mother (whom you cause me to mourn still) no doubt had in mind
> what her son would one day write:
>
> > *Si les pardons enfin à nos erreurs sont dus,*
> > *C'est lorsqu'elles font naître, ou payent des vertus.*
> > [If, finally, for our errors, forgiveness falls due,
> > It is when these beget or reward merit.]
> >
> > *Inconstant,* Act II[35]

Did Renée-Pélagie, as Jean-Jacques Pauvert proposes,[36] allow herself, in fact, to make "a timid allusion *in a letter of 1781* addressed to the
prisoner in Vincennes," suggesting the possibility that Monsieur le Duc
courted Marie-Eléonore? If so, the letter in question has apparently not yet
come to light. In any case, Sade's angry rebuttal then goes on to what was
undoubtedly its main purpose, not so much a defense of Marie-Eléonore
but yet another stinging, gratuitous attack on the much abused Renée-
Pélagie, this time for being so contemptuously plebeian, even in her supposed infidelities! Marie-Eléonore's hypothetical romp between silken
sheets with a prince of the blood was hardly to be seen as the equivalent
of Renée-Pélagie's suspected copulation with the low-born *valet-secrétaire*
Lefèvre:

> ... [B]ut she who, either in seeking base revenge or, what can be even
> more sordid, out of a gross and vulgar urge to satisfy her carnal appetites,
> gives herself wantonly to a footman, a peasant of the vilest kind whose fa-
> ther was the recipient of alms from her husband, she, I say, no longer has the
> right even to be called a woman. She becomes no more than a lewd harlot,
> scorned by the universe, a thousand times more contemptible even than a
> creature whose need to earn her bread legitimizes such horrors. Such a
> wretched creature, deserving only ignominy and squalor, is a monster who
> dishonors her children, her husband, and herself. She can claim only the
> right to wallow like a sow in the mire where she sought out the vile instru-
> ment of her crime.[37]

Again in the context of an attack on someone else—his wife this time
rather than the reviled mother-in-law herself—this normally less-than-

devoted son sheds an opportunistic, momentary tear for his mother ("this mother whom you cause me to mourn still"). But the central focus here is not so much on Marie-Eléonore as it is on sexual jealousy, and Gilbert Lely has put forward an ingenious and complex suggestion that Sade's violent reaction on this occasion, fed by ambiguous fantasies concerning the supposed herculean proportions of Lefèvre's penis and recurring dreams of Renée-Pélagie's supposed infidelities, in fact hid an unconscious homosexual urge to be deceived by her. Envious of his wife's pleasure, as well as that of his "rival," the jealous bisexual both abominates and lusts after the illicit thrusts of the alien penis and unconsciously nurtures his jealousy in order to feed the only pleasures allowed him by tortured but ambivalent fantasies of his wife's adultery.[38]

Not the plainest of possible scenarios, that! Still, one is left wondering whether a similar kind of analysis might not be profitably applied to another of the marquis' troubled prison dreams, one he related to Renée-Pélagie from Vincennes on 17 February 1779. This time it is Petrarch's Laura, his direct ancestor according to his uncle's erudite three-volume study,[39] who hauntingly embodies the Sadean image of the mother. His prison dream lovingly evokes the beauty of this maternal specter, Laura, symbol of spiritual perfection and virginal purity. She beckons to him from the tomb. He attempts to follow:

> I console myself here entirely with Petrarch. I read him with unequalled avidity and pleasure. But in doing so, I imitate Mme de Sévigné with her daughter's letters: *I read him ever so slowly, to avoid coming to the end.* How well the work is constructed! . . . Laura makes my head spin. I am like a child. All day, I read her and at night she fills my dreams. Here is a dream I had about her last night while the whole universe was out chasing after amusement.
>
> It was about midnight, I had just gone to sleep, still holding Laura's memoirs in my hands. Suddenly, she appeared before me. . . . I could see her! The horror of the tomb had not diminished the radiance of her beauty and her eyes sparkled as they did when Petrarch sang their praises. She was clothed from head to foot in a black mourning veil and her beautiful blond hair hung loosely over her shoulders. It was as if love, to reveal her as more beautiful still, wished to soften the lugubrious setting in which she stood before me. "Why do you continue to suffer on earth?" she asked. "Come join me. In the immense spaces that I inhabit there is no more pain, no more sorrow or confusion. Take courage and follow me." At those words, I fell to my knees before her and cried out: "Oh, my mother! . . ." Violent sobbing stifled my voice. She held out her hand which I covered with tears. She too was weeping: "When I lived in this world that you now detest, I would

sometimes look into the future; I surveyed the unborn generations of my posterity as far ahead as you and *I did not see you so unhappy.*" Filled with despair and tenderness, I threw my arms around her to prevent her from leaving, or perhaps to go with her, to bathe her in my tears; but the apparition vanished. Only my grief remained.[40]

The image already encountered of the dead mother inviting her son to join her beyond the grave, to exchange the suffering and evil of this world for the peace and tranquility of the tomb, recurs here in an even more intriguing form, and with overtones that are undeniably sexual. The temptation to indulge in arcane and labyrinthine analysis is indeed great. We recall the many references to incest in his novels, usually involving fathers with sons or daughters and frequently brothers with sisters. On the other hand, mother-son relationships, though they occur,[41] seem far less typical. La Delbène's stern caution to mothers in *Juliette* is generally heeded: "Resist the desire. That variety of incest lacks piquancy and can detract from far greater sexual pleasures. Masturbating with your daughter is less hazardous."[42] Our suspicions are instantly aroused. It is rare, indeed, to hear one of the Sadean pedagogue characters, launched in full didactic flight, suddenly cautioning against *any* imaginable form of sexual behavior!

Were repressed incestuous desires a factor in Donatien's early relationship with his beautiful mother? The question, though enticing, is perhaps best left to the musings of those cognoscenti who specialize in subterranean psychic explorations, there being already more than enough telltale surface debris scattered about the wreckage of the divine marquis' life to challenge even the simpler investigative resources of what I have already referred to in the preface as plane psychology.

That being said, it is difficult to escape the conclusion that there remained in the marquis' emotional makeup throughout his life an important void, an unsatisfied maternal need that no amount of substitute mothering could ever satisfy. The marquis had other dreams in Vincennes. One of these was that his old governess, Mme de Saint-Germain, the woman whom even Renée-Pélagie in her letters to Donatien calls "your *maman,*"[43] had died. To the prisoner, the thought of her death was unbearable: "If it is true," he wrote to his wife, "do not tell me; I love her and have always loved her prodigiously. I would not get over it."[44] We believe him, more or less, but we have to note at the same time that Marie-Eléonore was apparently never so fortunate as to elicit a similar tribute from her son. Nowhere in Sade's correspondence, not even in the theatrically overblown ad hoc letters written from prison soon after his mother's death, do we find anything approaching such simple, from-the-heart sentiments about his real mother. What we find is at best a controlled, guardedly neutral tone. The marquis' important "*grande lettre*," written to Renée-Pélagie on the fourth anniversary of his February 1777 incarceration in Vincennes, provides perhaps the clearest perspective on his true feelings toward Marie-Eléonore. In the best tradition of his adolescent "full confessions," what he calls his *grande lettre* purports to tell all, holding nothing back. One by one, he will review his "alleged faults," marshaling after each his denials, his mitigating explanations and best counterclaims. His life, he would have us believe, is an open book. The entire world is invited to scrutinize its every detail, from his childhood on. His tutor Amblet and Mme de Saint-Germain, both still alive, can vouch for the innocence of his earliest years. (Had Marie-Eléonore been still alive, would she, we wonder, also have been cited as a trusted observer and guarantor for those years?) As for his adolescence, the Marquis de Poyanne, who oversaw his military apprenticeship, could similarly testify: "Let them consult and inquire to determine if I have ever given proof of the ferocity attributed to me, and whether certain wicked actions served to foreshadow the crimes I'm credited with." [45] Oh, indeed, there had been the odd lapse. He had transgressed now and then, but his transgressions boiled down to nothing more than normal, workaday libertinism, pure and simple, the kind that all men indulge in "more or less in direct proportion to the corresponding penchants and appetites with which nature has endowed them." And then follows his most famous confession, which, like so many of literature's great confessions, is revealing especially in what it is so carefully crafted to conceal:

> Yes, I am a libertine, I confess it. I have conceived of everything conceivable along such lines, but I have assuredly not done everything I have conceived of, nor shall I ever do so. I am a libertine, but I am neither a *criminal*, nor a *murderer* [. . .] I am a libertine but I have never jeopardized the health of my wife. I have never contracted any of the other libertine disorders that are so often fatal to the fortunes of one's children. Have I ruined them financially through gambling or through other expenditures that might have resulted in depriving them of their inheritance? Did I mismanage my estates while they were still under my control? Did I, in short, show myself capable during my youth of the villainies attributed to me today? Did I not show love to everyone who was owed my love, to everyone I was supposed to hold dear? *Did I not love my father? (alas, I mourn him still, every day). Did I behave badly toward my mother?* Was it not precisely when I came to pay my last respects, when I came to give her a last proof of my affection, that your own mother had me thrown into this horrible prison where she has allowed me to languish these past four years? [46]

In what we may presume to be his most ostensibly candid declaration on the subject, Sade makes a key distinction crystal clear: he *loved* his father; he *did not behave badly* toward his mother. He does not, in short, see himself as a son who *loved* his mother. She had been too much of a stranger to him for that: "Not having had, like you, the good fortune to have raised my own children [. . .]," he once remarked to his lawyer Gaufridy, "I can scarcely insist that they should love me." [47] Filial love was manifestly something he seems to have felt and voiced consistently only for his father, and he never hesitated to express that affection, either before or after Jean-Baptiste's death, even though they had gone through several trying periods when disputes over money had threatened to turn father and son into sworn enemies. In contrast, on mature reflection and in precisely the same context, the most he could muster for his mother was the boast that, effectively, he had not gone out of his way to harm her, a sentiment that scores considerably lower on the scale of fond attachments—rather like the husbandly pride he seems to take, as he continues with his confession, in the claim (doubtful, moreover) that he has never, despite his libertinage, passed on any venereal disease to his wife.

Finally, even a cursory analysis of the views Sade expressed personally—that is, outside his fiction—regarding motherhood would be incomplete without mention being made of a curious letter he wrote in 1803 to Charles Quesnet, the nineteen-year-old son of the woman he lived with after Renée-Pélagie's defection. The Revolution and the Terror had come and gone, Renée-Pélagie had long since walked out of his life, and the hated mother-in-law, Mme de Montreuil, had finally exited his moral universe, having died two years before at the age of eighty-one. [48] In other respects, however, things were back to normal; that is, he was once more behind prison walls, this time for life. Sade had first met the thirty-three-year-old Marie-Constance in August 1790, four months after his liberation from Charenton. A former actress, she had been abandoned, along with her child, by a husband who had gone off to America. [49] The year 1790 had also brought a well-earned liberation for Renée-Pélagie. With Donatien now a free man, she finally, at the age of fifty, screwed up her courage sufficiently to sue for legal separation. Predictably, the marquis chose to feel betrayed, but soon after he met Marie-Constance, "this angel sent to him from Heaven." [50] Salvation at last! Out of sheer gratitude, Citizen Sade took it upon himself to help support her young son and to educate him in "wholesome principles." Part of that salutary education shows up, presumably, in the following letter to this "foster son," a swollen inspirational tract on the subject of motherhood in general. Students of Sade will find in it

sentiments so antithetical to the marquis' "usual" views that they will forgive, one hopes, its quotation here in full:

> Remember, my friend, that your own life came about as part of your
> mother's: the existence you enjoy is, properly speaking, but an emanation of
> hers. Such a thought, in my view, though it derives only from the physical
> world, must necessarily add to the moral sentiments you owe this creature
> who is in so many ways sacred to you! Remember, my friend, that the trib-
> ute of respect and tenderness that you owe her is as nothing when compared
> to the cares she suffered for you. We can never repay, in short, what we owe
> a mother for everything she has done for us since she first gave us life in her
> womb. I have said it to you often: a mother is a friend, given to us but once
> by nature, and when we have had the misfortune of losing her, nothing can
> ever make up for the loss. We can never find anything that takes her place.
> The poisonous barbs of men, their wickedness, their slanders, their vil-
> lainies, wound us at will. We take refuge in the bosom of a friend, of a wife;
> but what a difference, oh, my dear Quesnet! Never do we encounter again
> the selfless attentions of a mother, this precious sensitivity that no selfish in-
> terest can distort. In a word, oh, my dear friend, there is more here than
> simply the hand of nature.[51]

One is flabbergasted! Where in all that magniloquently ultradecent, re-
ligiously inspirational prose, so correctly sensitive in tone that it could—
give or take a few minor stylistic adjustments—be transferred directly to
the modern Mother's Day card, where in all that, one must ask, is the famous negative Oedipus complex? Where is that hatred of all matriarchal
values? The execration of compassion, charity, gratitude, sacrifice, fidelity,
and all the other pieties that are revealed—nay, *demonstrated*—by the author of the Sadean novel to be fraudulent and false?

Elsewhere, obviously, in the *essential* Sadean text—to which we shall
now turn.

Fifteen

MOTHERS MUCH HATED

Much more familiar than the singular letter in praise of motherhood composed in 1803 for young Charles Quesnet, perhaps as a celebratory performance to mark a family occasion, is Sade's diametrically opposed message,

dogmatically propounded, explicitly and aggressively argued, and violently exemplified in all of his characteristic fictional works. The everyday realities and philosophical underpinnings of the Sadean universe leave no room for the gentler maternal pieties.

One hardly knows where to begin exploring that universe. Did the author of *La Nouvelle Justine,* of *L'Histoire de Juliette,* for example, really tell Charles Quesnet that, physically speaking, his existence flows entirely from, is nothing more than, a product of his mother's existence? If so, we are a long way from the equally "physical" explanation of the motherhood phenomenon that we find dealt with repeatedly in the Sadean novel. In *La Philosophie dans le boudoir,* for example, the young and naive Eugénie de Mistival proves herself to be a remarkably fast learner when her two dedicated teachers, Mme de Saint-Ange and Dolmancé, set about educating her in the facts of life. At one point in the lesson she is puzzled momentarily by the precise meaning of the word *fuck;* she wonders whether the union of both the male and female "sperm" is essential for the formation of the fetus? A curious lecture in biology follows, and before we know it we are hearing familiar echoes of Sade's real-life father-mother tensions, distorted by the filtering mechanisms of a Manichean fiction in which the characters are either passive sacrificial victims or voracious immolating executioners.

The transition from life to art is again nearly seamless. From the correspondence we already know how crushing the blow of a father's death can be; the attendant grief lingers forever. In the case of mothers, however, the situation is quite different. Eugénie's teachers, female and male, explain why:

MME DE SAINT-ANGE. Doubtlessly, even though it has been proven that the fetus owes its existence exclusively to the ejaculate of the male, by itself, and without being mixed with the woman's secretion, it would not come to fruition; but that which we supply only prepares the ground, it does not create; it assists creation but is not the cause. Several modern naturalists even claim that it serves no purpose and this has led moralists—ever alert to scientific discoveries—to conclude with a fair degree of likelihood that since the child is formed entirely from the father's blood, he owes affection only to the father. There is some semblance of truth to this assertion and, although I am a woman, I would not think of disputing it.
EUGÉNIE. I find in my heart the proof of what you tell me, Nanny dear, for *I love my father madly and I sense that I detest my mother.*
DOLMANCÉ. This preference is not at all surprising; I have had precisely the same thought. *I am still devastated by the death of my father but when I lost*

my mother, I celebrated with fireworks . . . I heartily detested her. Adopt these sentiments without fear, Eugénie, they come from nature. Formed solely from the blood of our fathers, we owe absolutely nothing to our mothers: all they did was lend themselves to the act, whereas the father solicited it. The father, in short, willed our birth whereas our mothers only consented to it. How different must be our feelings in each case![1]

"Lend herself to the act"—the mother's passivity argues against according any importance to her role. But a different justification for an even more crudely insensitive attack on the mothering function is to be found elsewhere in *La Philosophie dans le boudoir,* one that figures prominently throughout the Sadean repertoire and seems to rest on a curious puritanism directed against the mother, a creature soiled and defiled as a result of her necessarily lubricious participation in the sexual act of generation. Once again the temptation is strong to take up Klossowski's search for covert mechanisms that trigger violent hatred of the mother, perceived as the fallen virgin and wanton whore by the incestuously jealous son. Mme de Mistival, Eugénie's mother, will suffer unspeakable physical torments at the hands of her daughter. Of course she deserves it, and first of all for being so straitlaced: "Shrewish, superstitious, sanctimonious, scolding . . . , and revoltingly puritanical." Eugénie's tutor in libertinism, Mme de Saint-Ange, is willing to bet that this prude, this priggish goody-goody, "has never made a mistake in her entire life. . . . Oh, my dear, how I detest virtuous women! . . ."[2] Eugénie surprises her tutors by declaring that she wants to see the interfering prude dead.[3] Mme de Saint-Ange suggests that her pupil should spare her: "Remember, she is your mother." "Oh, yes, such a fine title!" retorts Eugénie sarcastically, at which point her male mentor, Dolmancé, approvingly introduces the mother-lubricity argument: "Eugénie is quite right. Was her mother thinking of her when she conceived? The wanton allowed herself to be fucked for the pleasure of it, she was certainly not thinking of this girl at the time."[4]

The same refrain will be found in the marquis' other novels—for example, the *Histoire de Juliette,* in which Borchamps asks his son (who has just heaped unspeakable abuses on his mother) if he is capable of helping his father to kill her:

—Do not doubt it, father.
—What! This woman who brought you into the world?
—She labored only for herself; I detest her as passionately as you do.[5]

In *La Nouvelle Justine* we meet the widow Mme de Bressac, whose moral character makes her a kind of cousin of Mme de Mistival:

... a woman forty-five years of age, beautiful still, well-bred and sensitive but astonishingly straitlaced. Very proud of never having made a single mistake in her life, she refused to forgive any weaknesses in others. As a result of this exaggerated strictness, *rather than attracting her son's affections, she drove him from her bosom.* Bressac, we must agree, had many faults, but in what temple will leniency be worshipped if not in a mother's heart?[6]

Mme de Bressac disapproves of her son's profligacy and libertinism. Indeed, he is riddled with all manner of vices: recklessness, neglect of duty, spitefulness, cruelty, atheism, and debauchery. The perfect scoundrel, in short, but emancipated, his own man!

Supreme hatred of his mother was Bressac's primary mania, a hatred founded on principle and buttressed by irrefutable arguments, not to mention the powerful need he *necessarily* felt to rid himself of her at the earliest possible opportunity. Mme de Bressac did everything to bring her son back to the path of virtue, but in her attempts to accomplish this she employed too much severity. As a result, fired up all the more by her strictness, the young man indulged his penchants with even greater abandon, and the poor woman gained from her harassment only an infinitely stronger dose of hatred.[7]

Although she is a wise and pious woman, Mme de Bressac is at a distinct disadvantage in this struggle. It is not merely the fact that her son has a hyperdeveloped aversion to authority; he is also something of a bold and clever philosopher, and she is fully aware that he can defend and "legitimate" every single one of his vices with "unassailable logic."[8] In her attempts to chide him on his misbehavior, she commits the unpardonable sin of employing "the tone of authority." To punish her for such impertinent reprimands, he threatens to force her to witness his sodomistic debaucheries. She essays a restrained and diffident protest. He counters with a brutal rebuff:

—Be silent, madame! Do not imagine that this illusory title of mother gives you any rights over me. Allowing yourself to be fucked in order to bring me into the world is not a great qualification in my eyes. These absurd ties of nature have no hold over a spirit such as mine.[9]

Young Bressac finally decides to do away with this detestable creature and threatens to kill her. The unfortunate mother again asks her son how he can be so cruel to the person who carried him in her womb, nourished him, and cared for him. Coldly, brutally, as he prepares to sodomize her himself—a prelude to having her torn apart by four rabidly vicious mastiffs—the philosopher-son, this "most extraordinary genius ever created by nature," responds:

> —All that means nothing to me; you did not have me in mind when you labored to bring about my existence and the results of a process that satisfied only a cunt has no merit in my eyes. Follow me, whore! Follow me and gainsay no more.[10]

Bressac, as good as his word, finally stabs his mother to death. It would be superfluous to point out that the unfortunate woman expires asking God's forgiveness for her son.

Since the mother's sole motive for engaging in the conjugal act is entirely selfish and lubricious, the child has no obligation to feel grateful to her for bringing him into the world. Nursing her infant is equally a matter of the mother's expedient self-interest: she is not doing something for the child when she suckles him; on the contrary, the child does a favor to the mother who is "driven by a natural inclination to free herself of a secretion that might otherwise become a danger to her."[11] No gratitude is owed women who bring children into the world and nourish them. Even the child's care through to puberty is similarly a consequence of the mother's selfishness, her pride, her vanity, not to mention mere habit. Like the young Donatien brought back from his Provençal exile, the child has no need of a mother's interfering ministrations. Far from being useful to her son, the mother's harassing, faultfinding attentions do great harm; they weaken his healthy instincts; they diminish and devitalize him. Why should he feel love and gratitude after that? By the time he reaches adolescence, if he takes the trouble to do a little critical thinking, he will arrive at some inescapable conclusions in this regard, the main one being that he owes nothing to his mother. Indeed, by definition, she is his enemy: "What will result from his reflections? Dare we say it? Antipathy and hatred for the woman who brought him into the world."[12]

Sade, directly in his correspondence as well as through his fictional characters, hints from time to time that he began his own critical thinking, his emancipation from what he frequently refers to as "the superstitions of childhood," very early on, suggesting even that he had managed to rid himself of these religious and sexual taboos by the age of twelve or thirteen. We may safely guess, I think, that the chief purveyor, defender, and enforcer of those "superstitions" in the eyes of the rebellious thirteen-year-old was none other than his mother, Marie-Eléonore. Eugénie's mother had inflicted the same puritanical indignities on her daughter:

You talked to her about God, as if God existed; you talked to her about virtue, as if virtue was necessary; of religion, as if religion was anything but the imposture of the strongest and the imbecility of the weakest; you talked to her of Jesus-Christ, as if that knave were anything but a cheat and a scoundrel! You told her that *fucking* was a sin, whereas *fucking* is the most delightful activity in life.[13]

Those are the indignant accusations Dolmancé, Sade's libertine pedagogue, hurls in righteous anger at the mother of Eugénie de Mistival. For her maternal "crimes," Mme de Mistival is finally punished in a most graphically horrifying manner (I shall leave aside the details), a punishment that, interestingly, is fully authorized by the child's father. One ventures to think that the ghost of Marie-Eléonore would probably have recognized in Dolmancé's litany of recriminations several distressing echoes of an old father-son refrain. Happily, in return for all her stifling maternal crimes and vigilant attention, Donatien, unlike the fictional Eugénie, had been content merely to thank his mother with uncaring indifference.

The theme of mother hatred is, in fact, treated as fundamental by Sade from the time of his first major novel. Seen as undeniably present in the human makeup, the phenomenon was for him a pivotal truth of nature, fundamental and yet puzzling, something he felt deeply and for which he sought a philosophical explanation. *Les 120 journées de Sodome,* begun in Vincennes around 1782, confronts the problem head-on: La Duclos' introductory narrative is suddenly interrupted by the duc de Blangis, who asks whether her murderous antipathy toward her mother had a specific cause or whether, on the contrary, she felt it to be "naturally in her." For de Blangis the question is basic and essential: "This involves weighing the behavior of the human heart and that is our particular task here."[14] Silling Castle, we are to understand, is primarily a laboratory devoted to the study of human conduct. The duc's question is discussed and then answered fully; it is finally agreed that mother hatred is natural and, of course, legitimate. The consequences are clear: "It is quite insane to imagine that one owes anything to one's mother. What would be the justification for such gratitude? Because she climaxed when she was fucked? Now, *really!*" Mothers conceive for reasons of selfish lubricity, they then cast their children into a world filled with dangers and finally abandon them to their fate.[15] Similarly, the earliest version of *Justine* (originally a longish conte, *Les Infortunes de la vertu,* composed in the Bastille in 1787) sets out clearly de Bressac's harsh arguments and underlines especially the important distinctions—less apparent in the later version—that favor the father:[16]

> But this creature I am attacking is my mother, she carried me in her womb.
> Well, so what about it? Is that trifling consideration supposed to stop me?
> On what grounds, pray? Was she thinking of me, this mother, when her
> lubricity caused her to conceive the fetus whence I came? Do I owe her
> gratitude because she took her pleasure? Moreover, it is not the mother's
> blood that forms the child, but the father's alone: the womb of the female
> shelters, prepares the ground, but supplies nothing, and *there you have the
> explanation why I could never make an attempt on my father's life, whereas I see
> it as a matter of simplicity itself to murder my mother.*[17]

The tiny possibility that there could be exceptions to this merciless
rule is noted: Bressac concedes that there could be times when a mother
might deserve gratitude and perhaps even love. We think of how unsuc-
cessful Marie-Eléonore must have been at eliciting any expression of gratitude or affection from her son despite her many devoted initiatives on his
behalf. The Sadean hero, de Bressac, addresses the question and grudgingly
provides an answer:

> While it is indeed possible that the heart of a child can be rightly stirred by
> some feelings of gratitude towards a mother, it can be only in response to
> her dealings with us when we are of an age to enjoy these. If she has con-
> ducted herself well, we *can*—perhaps we even *must*—love her. If she has
> treated us ill, bound by no law of nature, not only do we owe her nothing,
> but the powerful force of human self-interest dictates that we rid ourselves
> of her, just as it dictates naturally and invincibly that we rid ourselves of any-
> thing that brings us harm.[18]

We have by now fully entered the surreal universe of Sadean victims
and executioners who, if they reflect in some way, as is quite obviously the
case, the realities and fantasies, the actions and ideologies of the author,
do so only indirectly through a kind of distorting, refractive process that
passes them obliquely from one medium or dimension to another. If
Marie-Eléonore in an appropriate time warp had ever found both the opportunity and sufficient stomach to peruse her son's fictional horrors, she
would probably have recognized here and there, if not the specific moral
landscapes of Donatien's fantasized world, at least something of its conceptual topography, perhaps even a child's twisted, fragmentary perceptions of some early Hôtel de Condé realities going back to the time when
the romantically sensitive but passionately self-willed little fellow, his head
filled with images of a beautiful, sometimes elusive and agitated mother,
was tearfully packed off to Avignon.

Not surprisingly, as in La Duclos's case, all of these Sadean mothers who end up being ripped apart, disemboweled, and butchered seem to be benignly warm and comforting creatures who have given no specific cause or excuse for the "natural" antipathy they generate. The mother of Brisa-Testa is typically "gentle, devout and virtuous." Bressac's mother, too, is beautiful, well-bred, and sensitive; she is also, for the most part, "very compassionate" although, Sade writes in 1787, "she injects into her principles and discourse a modicum of severity." [19] Admittedly, in a later version, as if the author is responding to the need to bring more "unassailable" logic to his plot, the words "very compassionate" have disappeared and she is now "astonishingly strict in her morals" and "takes a self-righteous pride at never having made a mistake in her entire life." [20]

In that same romanesque time warp, would Jean-Baptiste not also have recognized something uncomfortably familiar about, for example, the Sadean paterfamilias Borchamps? Borchamps, father of Brisa-Testa, preaches and practices a much cranked-up version of those jolly good-life maxims Jean-Baptiste himself taught and embraced with such zest. And if our two parental shades were allowed to listen in with particular care, would they not make out here and there distant and confused echoes of their own domestic tensions in the scenes of family estrangement that flare up in the Borchamps household, where the dissipations and debaucheries of a freethinking and freeloving father provoke the "small-minded" disapproval of a mother "full of her little ideas"? Mme Borchamps, fearing that their son will become a victim of the father's "frightful libertinism," tries to block her husband's "unprejudiced" ambitions for his children. In the end, she succeeds only in making herself an object of ridicule in the eyes of a man whose goal is to turn his son into a "philosopher" like himself, free of all superstitious moral and religious beliefs. Jean-Baptiste's eavesdropping ghost might also be reminded of the early lessons in life he himself had insisted on teaching his son, again with a view to liberating the boy's mind from guilt-ridden concerns for such false virtues as "constancy." Borchamps' well-schooled offspring become immune to all such weaknesses, "unmoved by either remorse or superstition." [21] Young Brisa-Testa does worry at one point that his mother will be angered by his father's "emancipating" projects. Borchamps' reassuring answer is again one that might well have stirred a dimly refracted reminiscence or two in Jean-Baptiste's spectral memory:

> My friend [. . .] listen carefully to what I have to say to you about that; you have enough wit to understand me. This woman who gave birth to you is perhaps the creature I detest most in the universe. The bonds that unite me to her make me detest her even a thousand times more. [22]

In the end, Brisa-Testa, already his father's pliant catamite, becomes totally persuaded by the same exacting logic employed by de Bressac: Mme Borchamps like all the other mothers "labored only for herself." He eagerly helps Borchamps do away with the woman who brought him into the world, and during the entire blood-curdling process he shows not the slightest hint of remorse. Indeed, the murderous act, shared with the father, becomes an occasion for explosive sexual pleasure.

This deliberate destruction of the Sadean hero's capacity for remorse—all disproportion being maintained in the comparison—is probably not unrelated to some of Jean-Baptiste's earliest ambitions (partly philosophical, partly defensive) to free his son from conventional sexual and religious taboos, including all of Marie-Eléonore's "petty ideas." Seeking an ally, Jean-Baptiste would have explained freely to his adolescent son the grounds for his estranged relationship with Marie-Eléonore. It would have been one of those quietly rational discussions, somewhat in the Borchamps style, pragmatic and man to man rather than father to son. As his clever autobiographical fragment reveals only too well, Jean-Baptiste had a special gift for combining cynical wit and discursive familiarity on such occasions, and we wonder, for example, when it was, precisely, that he showed that entertaining tell-all piece to Donatien, detailing in such a polished and sophisticated manner how he had consented to marry Marie-Eléonore with, to quote his own words, "the sole purpose in mind" of seducing the wife of Monsieur le Duc, his blushing bride's even younger mistress. The son, from the beginning an admirer of stage management, wit, and style, could not have helped but be impressed.

There are risks involved, obviously, in trying to establish such conjectural parallels between the truths of biography and the creative realities of fiction—as Sade himself warns us in his ad hoc polemic with the critic Villeterque, whom he attacks unconvincingly in the same breath drawn to deny with bullying indignation his authorship of such "infamous" and "horrible" works as *Justine.* His critics, Sade thunders, must not be so imbecilic as to forget that "in a dramatic work [. . .] it is the character who speaks and not the author."[23] That rather predictable bromide notwithstanding, it is clearly Sade himself, in his correspondence, in author's notes attached to his fiction, in text as well as paratext and metatext, who invites us to connect character and author, life and art, and to advance our speculations along such trustingly traditional lines. Moreover, many of the collateral arguments (often lifted holus bolus from his favorite materialist philosophers) and much of the formal commentary and validating ideology expressed in the authorial voice and pasted into and around his unrelentingly preachy novels directly parallel, confirm, and support the "fictional" harangues and rationalizations, the outrageously extreme, "unassailably logical" doctrines directly propounded by the monster characters themselves.

Of course, when the Sadean monsters explain that a mother's love for her child, the care and sacrifice she devotes to it, are motivated purely by her own selfish interests, that these maternal virtues are, moreover, the automatic effects of a biological determinism, or, again, when they go on to decree that, this being the case, there is no need for the child to feel gratitude toward the mother, no need to mourn her loss when she dies, we cannot help remembering the one action we know about in Donatien's life that seems to give the lie to such cynicism. Did he not rush off to Paris, ostensibly to be at the bedside of Marie-Eléonore, to see her once more before she expired? No parallel here with the Sadean monster-villains! But then we also remember that he arrived too late, as it turned out, and no mourning seems to have followed—none, at least, until he blew skyward two or three puffs of self-pitying filial smoke from the great keep of Vincennes immediately after his imprisonment when the nearly synchronous occurrence of his mother's death presented such a conveniently exploitable platform for launching an attack on his mother-in-law. We also remember that only a few hours after he learned of his sad loss, he was already making secret arrangements for a modest orgy, involving if not quite Dolmancé's joyful fireworks celebration, then at least a rough equivalent, give or take a few Roman candles: a night of calculated debauchery on the town, a lecherous trophy-hunting expedition in the company of a worthy fellow stalker, "a friend of his who was as great a libertine as he and who thought and acted as he did," to quote once more one of his real-life hunting victims, Jeanne Testard.[24]

Numerous passages in the novels defend such indifference to a mother's death and demonstrate with "irrefutable" arguments the illegitimacy of all mourning for the departed: "What benefit can there be in a sentiment that has no effect whatsoever on the state of the person who has ceased to exist and which disturbs the well-being of those who go on living?"[25] It is not enough to counter with the protest that such traditional truths are not *reasoned* but *felt*. Not at all! Rational logic must prevail in the Sadean universe: "Everything must be subjected to analysis and that which cannot be analyzed must be false." The marquis de Sade, we discover, knew his Condillac as well as his La Mettrie.

Arguments against having feelings of any kind for the dead are stated even more aggressively in *Juliette*. In addition to a solid page or two of "monster-speak" on the subject, the author provides his own note on "the sickening absurdity of mourning the dead."[26] If we insist on making a last gesture on behalf of the dead, it should amount to little more than arranging for the corpse's physical disposal in a location where rapid decomposition can occur to the benefit of the surrounding vegetation—at the base of a fruit tree, for example. In the text of the novel itself, the basic message is the same, even if the tone is more militant and violent. Inside the Sadean universe absolutely nothing is owed a dead mother, neither respect nor esteem, not love, not even memory. And if our entirely speculative suspicions concerning the disappearance from the family archives of Marie-Eléonore's letters are correct, perhaps we may conclude that Donatien de Sade, in this last regard especially, was a man who aspired to practice in real life what he preached in his fiction. After all, respect for the dead and for their last wishes is really a mark of superstitious belief in the odious fables of religion:

> For if we truly believed in the principles of materialism, if we were truly convinced that we are only a sorry composite of material elements, that dissolution is total once we are dead, then it is quite certain that our respect for jumbled bits of matter would strike us as such a palpable absurdity that no one would willingly adopt it. [. . .] Let us be persuaded then that nothing of ourselves survives after we are dead, and that the mortal remains we leave behind on the earth have no more significance than the excrement we deposited at the base of a tree when we were alive. Once firmly convinced of the truth of materialism, we would understand that neither duty, nor respect is owed a cadaver, that—more for us than for the corpse itself—it deserves only to be buried, burned or fed to the animals. But tombs and tributes, prayers and praises, are in no way owed it and are nothing more than homages paid by stupidity to overweening pride, destined ultimately for destruction by philosophy.[27]

Still in her time warp, gasping in disbelief and indignation as she continues to confront the "horrors" of her son's "detestable" novels, our hypothetical ghost of Marie-Eléonore would no doubt also have recognized here and there various scatterings of rebellious discourse angrily shouted at her by her adolescent son who, already at the age of twelve or thirteen, took such overweening pride in being liberated from the shackles of superstition and who had certainly made no secret of that fact either to his mother or in the presence of the other fussing, churchy old women who shared with Marie-Eléonore the faded-flowers atmosphere of the rue d'Enfer convent. Donatien had evolved rapidly after his return from Provence with Amblet, the new tutor who obviously had instructions from the father to take a distinctly latitudinarian approach to the boy's education, especially with respect to religion. Amblet, the learned and tolerant Amblet, had been such a treasure, so clever at navigating the troubled waters that separated the warring worlds of his pupil's mother and father. In later years the marquis would be proud to remember him as the "parent" who, more than either his mother or his father, had raised him, had recognized and respected in him his unconditionally defiant nature, and had rescued him especially from Marie-Eléonore's unrelenting severity. Very early on, the adolescent Donatien had discovered how necessary it was to teach his mother that he was his own man. Later, he would meet many other disapproving authority figures who had to be taught the same lesson—not excluding even Jean-Baptiste at one point. In fact, everyone Donatien de Sade ever encountered in his lifetime, his jailers not excepted, would be required sooner or later to learn that, where he was concerned, any show of severity, of *rigorisme,* only made him all the more determined to be his own man, all the more inclined to be stubbornly rebellious and defiant to the end. Even the governor of the Bastille was finally obliged to recognize that his prisoner was one of those very special creatures who "can never be reduced to obedience."

Hazardous and perhaps even idle speculations? The laws of physics, in any case, will not allow Jean-Baptiste and Marie-Eléonore to go on such retrospective excursions through the universe of the Sadean novel. Perhaps even more to the point, current fashions in literary criticism frown severely on all such ingenuous attempts to confront Sade's fiction with his biographical realities or, rather, with the precious little we know for certain about those realities, about his mother and father, and about Donatien de Sade himself, especially during the two or three critical years that fall on either side of his tenth birthday.

Yet, the fairly musty debate over the legitimacy of searching for bits and pieces of the novelist in the novelist's fiction must surely allow for certain distinctions to be made. Much, after all, depends on *which* novelist and *whose* fiction. Sade, for example, is clearly not like his contemporary Laclos, a true creative genius—not even the current hagiographical fashion has dared to place the marquis on the same level—whose own persona is difficult to find behind the text of that most impersonal of the century's literary masterpieces, *Les Liaisons dangereuses.* Sade's fiction, on the other hand, is rarely allowed to escape the obsessive self-referencing clutches of the man. The author constantly flaunts his ideological presence on the page. Aside from the generally recognized autobiographical elements that we find in *Aline et Valcour* (all biographers cite them, and Marie-Eléonore's new letter to Baumez clearly helps to validate some of the assumptions that have traditionally been made about them), Sade's novels not only are frequently preoccupied with his identifiable "personal" situations (e.g., mother-father animus, the victimized prisoner, arbitrary ministerial processes, etc.) but also, in the tradition of the eighteenth-century philosophical novel, openly and aggressively present themselves as uncamouflaged vehicles for a broad range of the author's pet ideas. Without the benefit of even a clumsy transition, the fictional narration breaks off, and the reader is suddenly confronted by a ponderous tract on one or other of the marquis' favorite themes: determinism, materialism, egotism, atheism, the evils of religion, of jurisprudence, the absurdity of remorse—even solemn minilectures on the correct positioning of the foreskin during masturbation! The great libertine is really an unabashed pedant-pedagogue whose literary productions are so didactically glued to his personal life events that for some of these themes—vilification of magistrates and whores, for example, or scornful denunciations of the legal protections afforded prostitutes in France—it is nearly impossible to distinguish the nuances separating the rhetoric of his personal correspondence from the parallel "monster-speak" of his novels.

It is indeed the reader of the correspondence—Sade's true masterpiece genre—who will be most easily convinced that, on a certain conceptual level, the novelist Sade makes little distinction between art and life. The act of writing emerges as a natural fusion of the two: phrases from the letters are directly transported into both the fictional dialogue and the authorial notes of the novels, leaving us to choose between a correspondence that is sometimes essentially dramatic "literature" and "false to life" and novels that are "true," projecting into fiction real or surreal elements of the author's own identity, milieu, and discourse. Sade's treatment of the key theme of the mother in his fiction, consistently validated by authorial appeals to the standard data of Sadean ideology and science, though it grotesquely magnifies and distorts what we can safely guess were his personal realities, is no exception to the rule.

Sixteen

THE MOTHER-IN-LAW

The search for autobiographical elements embedded in the central matrix of Sade's fiction inevitably brings us to another, more directly traceable, real-life source of the Sadean mother: the marquis' mother-in-law, the

Présidente de Montreuil, for whom he eventually developed a personal hatred that, at least on the conceptual level, surpasses at times even the surreal intensity of loathing directed against mother-victims by the most ferociously vicious monsters of his novels.

As already noted, however, the initial facts of Sade's relationship with his mother-in-law do not fit the classical patterns of antipathy presented later in his prison correspondence and in his novels. Indeed, if Donatien at the time of his reluctant marriage in 1763 saw himself as having one good friend, supporter, and confidante, in either his own or Renée-Pélagie's family, that friend was certainly none other than the bright and attractive forty-three-year-old Marie-Madeleine Masson de Plissay who in 1740 had married Claude-René Cordier de Launay de Montreuil and three years later gained the right to the social title, la présidente, when her husband purchased a high customs and excise judicial office and became one of several présidents of the Cour des Aides in Paris. Paul Bourdin,[1] in the introduction to his invaluable and too often denigrated edition of Sade's correspondence,[2] has left a portrait of the Présidente that captures most of the dynamic characteristics we see reflected in her few surviving letters:[3]

Madame de Montreuil, both in character and intelligence, clearly stands out among the actors in this drama. It is she who directs the action; everyone calls on her for support, even the marquis. Her initiatives provoke both fury and admiration, and everything bends to her will or to her influence. In this cast of characters where each has but one thought or single obsession, she alone is a creature of strength and of action adapted to her times and milieu. She is firm even in her oddities, moderate in her projects, prudent to the point of cunning, yet endowed with more boldness and courage than her fellow-players.

Mme de Montreuil is precise, quick-witted and decisive. She makes up her mind and acts in accordance with all the biases of her class but she controls the impulses that motivate her. She does whatever is needed to achieve her goals and never troubles herself with either the rights or the difficulties of others. She ignores or scorns whatever runs counter to her reason but the means she employs are as flexible and as varied as the definition of her goal is clear. At one and the same time she can charm, intimidate and suborn, making use of every influential connection without obligating herself in return. Though she has at her command all the resources of legal chicanery, she never approaches an obstacle without first carefully reconnoitering the terrain. [. . .] She feels neither regret nor remorse; hatred is foreign to her, as is excessiveness of any kind.[4]

Bourdin's portrait continues in this vein, but I have cited enough of it to suggest why, from the beginning, young Donatien recognized in Renée-Pélagie's mother a worthy ally—indeed, yet another exceptionally understanding surrogate *maman*. The same portrait also suggests why she eventually became in the marquis' eyes his most challenging opponent ever—indeed, one of his greatest enemies.

We recall how Renée-Pélagie's mother, for her part, was equally taken with her new son-in-law. The marriage had distinct social advantages for the Montreuils even if the groom's financial prospects hardly matched those of the bride and despite the fact that the handsome and dashing marquis had a dreadful reputation. In any case, that reputation had already been largely dismissed by the Présidente as undeserved: "Your nephew," she wrote to the abbé de Sade the day before the wedding, "with his gentle, well-bred, reasonable manner, strikes me as a most amiable and desirable son-in-law."[5] Two weeks later, an almost incredulous Jean-Baptiste also wrote to the abbé: "Mme de Montreuil indulges my son's every whim. She is quite infatuated with him. Her family hardly recognizes her."[6] The following week, to his sister in Avignon, the comte notes that Donatien "has completely captivated Mme de Montreuil who, I believe, now regrets having, under his guidance and in connivance with him, made such a scene with me."[7] Donatien, we see, had been clever enough, almost right off the mark, to enlist his mother-in-law as an ally in his latest squabble with his father. Father-son hostility had increased dramatically during the summer months following the marriage, and Jean-Baptiste was even obliged to report to his sister in Avignon that his "unworthy son" had left orders at his in-laws directing the porter to deny him entry to the Montreuil residence in Paris.[8] Most of the quarreling was over money matters related to Donatien's marriage contract, but again Mme de Montreuil, though pained by the constant bickering, confided to the abbé de Sade that she was totally behind her son-in-law and that in this instance she could not find fault "with either the style or substance of his actions." Donatien, moreover, was being so correctly decent about it all. She especially admired the fact that, though he had good reasons to feel hard done by, he had been maintaining throughout a respectful silence in the face of his father's constant complaints to all and sundry about his "ungrateful and unnatural" son. How worried she was for this sweet young marquis! "He being now my son-in-law, his reputation has become a personal matter with me and I must hold it dear." Perhaps her feelings went even deeper: Donatien was so young. . . . And what an endearing little scamp he was! "Here is that *amusing child*— that is what I call my little son-in-law. Sometimes, I take the liberty of scolding him; we quarrel and then we make up immediately. It is never very serious and it never lasts for very long. [. . .] Thoughtless, he most certainly is, but marriage will settle him down."[9] The Normandy countryside where the couple were spending the summer was doing him a world of good: "The calmness of his days here, all part of being in the country, has done wonders for his health. He is putting on weight rather nicely."

At times, however, she wondered whether the salubrious calm of rural Normandy was really quite enough to satisfy the marquis' needs. She asks the question rhetorically in a letter to the abbé, whom she knew to be so wise in the ways of the world and who got along so well with this mischievous "child." At the back of her mind was perhaps an even more specific concern: Was her naive and inexperienced daughter quite up to "satisfying" her passionate young husband? Nicely putting on weight was one thing, but Donatien, the Présidente noted, had a voracious mind and equally voracious appetites: "These are very sharp and need feeding." Whatever the subtext of that remark, Mme de Montreuil was content to be explicit only concerning the restorative charms of country living and her son-in-law's special "appetites" for reading, sleeping in, and stag hunting. Yes, how true was the old saying: "Each stage of life has its favorite toys. . . ."[10]

As we already know, Donatien, unfortunately for all concerned, had other "toys" very much on his mind—as the young prostitute Jeanne Testard was soon to discover.

Jean-Baptiste, writing to the abbé nearly one month after the Jeanne Testard incident, had chosen his words carefully and economically. Of course, both he and the brother he was writing to had had their own embarrassing encounters with the vice squad—but nothing like this! "A rented *petite maison,* furnished on credit, *extreme debauchery* which he carried on there *all alone, in cold deliberation, impieties so horrifying* that the prostitutes felt compelled to make a formal deposition. The culprit has been arrested."[11] In religious and sexual matters, father and son, once so close, had been evolving for some years now in opposite directions. Jean-Baptiste by 1763 had become very much the reformed rake and repentant sinner, whereas his son, having long since progressed beyond the usual limits of "orthodox" debauchery, was now more and more inclined to translate his increasingly anomalous sexual fantasies into assaultive realities, moving steadily from conceiving to doing, and using for this purpose the good offices of those among the bawds of the capital who were willing, despite police warnings, to send their vulnerable young charges to one of his several little hideaways.

Although Jean-Baptiste had finally been made aware by either the minister Saint-Florentin or the lieutenant général de police Sartine of all the sordid details, it is doubtful whether Mme de Montreuil ever learned much that was specific regarding the Jeanne Testard affair or about what had actually gone on during that particular "tart party," to use the marquis' own generic term for his little outings. Certainly, she could scarcely have dismissed as a mere case of boyish high jinks her son-in-law's use of pistols to intimidate his victim, his threats to run the young woman through with his sword, not to mention the curious real-life preview he was good enough to provide of his later fictional scenarios, including the coprophilic abuse of crucifixes, talk of sacramental hosts shoved into various orifices in various ways, sodomy-enhanced blasphemies, and whippings that drew from the victim not only blood but much relished screams of pain. Donatien had himself begged Sartine not to reveal any of the details to his family, and the lieutenant général de police, though he added the report to Donatien's thickening file, seems to have cooperated by doing his part to hush up the affair.

It is nevertheless a tribute to the marquis' boyish charm and his skill in the arts of dissimulation that his rather special "mother-son" relationship with Mme de Montreuil seems to have survived the immediate repercussions of the Jeanne Testard affair largely unscathed. It was still early days for both of them. With Donatien now exiled and calmly relaxing once more in the Normandy countryside and Renée-Pélagie three months pregnant, Mme de Montreuil found herself able to inform the abbé in a letter of 21 January 1764 that her "amusing child" was once more in her good graces. She is cautiously optimistic: "It will be entirely up to your nephew to repair the past by conducting himself irreproachably in the future. We have been pleased with him ever since he was returned to us." [12]

Donatien's conduct in the years that followed did not, of course, live up to that hope. But even though she was to be severely tested in her maternal affections, Mme de Montreuil did not give up easily on this endearing little son-in-law who continued to please her enormously every time he addressed her as "my dear Maman" or asked for her help. When, for example, he required a legal authorization or a signature from the increasingly grumpy and uncommunicative Jean-Baptiste, it was to her that he turned for mediation: "I beg you, Maman, do whatever you can to obtain it." [13] Apart from the fact that its source is not the surviving family archives, it is not clear how that very rare letter, written probably in 1765 and evoking embarrassingly warm images of affectionate filial dependence, managed to escape either Mme de Montreuil's or the marquis' own later purgings of the correspondence. Donatien, certainly, would not have wanted to retain any record of the affection he had once felt (or at least shown) for his mother-in-law, before total hatred of the Présidente finally imprinted on his inflamed imagination the crude Manichaean template that would ultimately shape the Sadean universe.

Meanwhile, the patiently pragmatic mother-in-law in Paris and the worldly uncle in Provence continued to exchange compliments, mutually congratulating each other on their sensitivity in general as well as their superior understanding of the correct way to deal with this naughty little fellow. They agreed that Donatien still needed mothering. That, of course, would be the Présidente's function. The abbé, on the other hand, would take care of all the fathering since Jean-Baptiste had made such an obvious hash of the job. "To keep his light-headed extravagance in check, he greatly needs your advice," Mme de Montreuil informed the abbé. "He trusts you. We have to deal tactfully with him since his first impulse is always violent and therefore to be feared. But when he is encouraged to think things through, he can be reasonable; all he needs is enough time away from any obsessive infatuations to see his way clearly." [14] The abbé for his part prided himself on his ability to show greater understanding than Jean-Baptiste: yes, sweetness and light would surely bring the lad back to the path of virtue. He knew that Donatien trusted and respected his mother-in-law; sooner or later her counsel would prevail. He also knew that his nephew— he had, after all, helped to raise him—was essentially good-hearted and reasonable; she would find that her son-in-law was putty in her capable hands. [15] Quite remarkably, when we think of the depths to which her relationship with Donatien would eventually degenerate, the Présidente seems to have welcomed the notion of playing the delicate role of adviser and confidante to her son-in-law, even to the extent of discussing with solicitous comprehension his lack of physical passion for her daughter and sympathizing with his need to find solace elsewhere. Dear little Donatien! Almost in spite of himself he seemed always to be getting caught up in the evil clutches of those predatory dancers and actresses of the capital, and, of course, the poor boy was not as rich as most of the libertines he had to compete with for these tainted favors. Mme de Montreuil agreed that such problems were not obviously something to be shared with Renée-Pélagie. Occasionally, however, doubts would cast a shadow over her generous meditations. By confiding in her as he did, was Donatien perhaps using her? Tricking her into being an accessory to his transgressions?

Whatever the truth of the matter, the marquis, at any rate, liked to boast that Mme de Montreuil knew all about his little vices and did not really disapprove. The abbé was immensely relieved to learn, for example, that it had been from Donatien himself that she had heard of his nephew's latest infatuation: "He assures me that he has confided in you concerning this lapse. [. . .] I would like to know if that is true for such trust in you would please me and give me hope for the future." [16]

Of course, if Donatien did fully open his heart to his mother-in-law during such trusting interludes (if we are to believe him, they even got around to discussing the rights and wrongs of anal sex [17]), the natural consequence later on when their relationship soured would have been to intensify his hatred of her, his disgust at having colluded in any way with this fury from hell. Especially, he would have been angry at having allowed her to become his ally against Jean-Baptiste during the time when he and this "tenderest of all fathers" had become embroiled in foolish quarreling. All that was forgotten and forgiven after Jean-Baptiste's death. He now remembered only the early bonds of trust, perhaps even the submissive exercise of "general confession"—not to vile priests but to "the most tender-hearted father in the entire world," [18] whose death he never ceased to mourn even though he later elaborated fierce arguments against mourning in general, especially in the case of dead mothers. It is probably no accident that his friendliest years with his mother-in-law coincided with the years of greatest alienation from his father, alienation that was as uncharacteristic and short-lived as it was extreme. In retrospect, it was a heavy burden for the surviving remnants of his tattered filial conscience, even though he eventually elaborated a hardened dialectic in his fiction against the very notion of conscience or remorse.

Her guarded optimism notwithstanding, Mme de Montreuil probably harbored few serious illusions concerning her son-in-law after the Jeanne Testard affair. She nevertheless decided to take a calculated risk. Her hope was that by accommodating Donatien's little vices in the short term she might eventually bring him around to maturity and wisdom. Admittedly, the cost of patience was high, and the limits of her pragmatism and understanding were undoubtedly reached when she learned that the marquis had had the effrontery to pass off as his wife during a visit to La Coste one of his expensive Parisian tarts, la Beauvoisin. "Such public misbehavior," she complained to the abbé, "displayed to his entire province, shows contempt for his neighbors and it will do him irreparable harm if it ever becomes known here, which it probably will." [19] It had been mainly thanks to her that the Jeanne Testard affair was hushed up, sparing the marquis many months of incarceration in a royal prison and possibly even worse. What a strange way he had of showing his gratitude! And he was such a good actor! However, as the incidents multiplied, she was getting the hang of his style: "And then," she mimed in her letter to the abbé, "in a voice filled with conviction, he will bemoan his destiny and the violence of his passions which overwhelm him; he will speak of his sorrow at having caused unhappiness to those close to him." She had heard that well-rehearsed refrain a dozen times already. Donatien was a clever player, but then, as he was to learn in the fullness of time, so was the Présidente. Indeed, her ability to see through his ploys and rationalizations would eventually become his chief reason for hating her. Refusing to be duped by the man whose favorite boast was that he could "bamboozle God" was truly unforgivable.

By the summer of 1765, Renée-Pélagie's mother had just about made up her mind: her calculated risk was probably not worth taking. Donatien was not really trying to reform. His little "I must be what I am" performance, already well on its way to formal elaboration as a full-blown ethic of authenticity, was nothing but a sham, and she was on to it. Her answer was simple: "We are not always masters of our own heart, but we can always govern our conduct." This, of course, was the crux of the matter, a key moral distinction that the Présidente insisted on but that ran counter to the most fundamental tenets of the marquis' deterministic philosophy. Donatien, she finally concluded, had been taking advantage of her generosity; for a time she had flattered herself that yielding to his youthful passions and working to gain his confidence and his friendship would protect him from the "grave dangers he courted with such abandon"—all those mistresses who governed his conduct so despotically, "and what mistresses!" [20] Perhaps it was time to think about cutting the Montreuil family's losses, time to get her daughter away from the clever little monster?

That, as it turned out, would not be an easy task—indeed, it would take nearly a quarter of a century to accomplish—but at least Mme de Montreuil was now well on the way to making up her mind: "As for myself, I shall no longer have anything to do with him," she informed the abbé only a little more than two years after the marriage ceremony; "I am all too convinced that friendship cannot reach his heart." It was becoming apparent that even Jean-Baptiste's harsh corrective methods had worked better than her own indulgent approach: "Strictness was more effective with him than our kindnesses," she conceded to the abbé. [21] Even Donatien's uncle now had to agree.

Events of the next decade were such, however, that Mme de Montreuil, out of concern for the family's honor, found herself unable to stand completely aside. The Arcueil affair and its attendant public scandal would leave her no choice. Like other members of the family she willingly grasped at straws. Was it not possible, for example, that the marquis in that sordid

Arcueil business was mostly innocent? What if Rose Keller *was* merely a conniving prostitute, just as the marquis maintained? Alas, this cunning little devil of a son-in-law could be so convincing at times, just as he had been after the Jeanne Testard affair! There was so much at stake for Renée-Pélagie and the children. But, then again, could he be trusted? It was always the same routine: he would promise solemnly to change his ways, then mention "splendid resolutions and great plans for future good behavior, plans and resolutions that might or might not be sincere." He would flatter himself in any case that he had convinced her. Then, after two or three months, all would be abandoned.[22] The Présidente had written that to the abbé as early as August 1765, intending that her precise words be shown to Donatien, then visiting in Provence, to remind him that she was not in the least deceived by his various subterfuges. In a postscript enclosed with her letter but intended for the abbé's eyes only, she queried her son-in-law's reported boast to his uncle that she was aware of all his "little escapades and was prepared to tolerate them": "What I have said in the three or four letters I have written to him since he left is anything but equivocal and tolerant," she objected. Unfortunately, we do not have those "three or four letters" or the dozens of others that she and Donatien exchanged during this period, and once again we are reminded of the kind of correspondence—whether received from his mother or his mother-in-law—that the marquis probably destroyed when the opportunity to do so presented itself.

Mme de Montreuil was, of course, quite aware of the standard legal remedies available to families in such circumstances. The law allowed fathers and mothers, whether rich or poor, to use forceful means if necessary to correct an offspring whose transgressive activities brought dishonor or the threat of financial ruin either on himself or on the family. The king as father of the nation, acting on the recommendation of the appropriate minister whose intervention was generally initiated by a family request to the lieutenant général de police, had only to issue a *lettre de cachet*. In the case of la Beauvoisin, for example, Donatien could easily have been forcibly removed from the scene. Mme de Montreuil had considered the possibility at the time and had even shared her musings on the subject with the abbé: "The minister would, without hesitation, grant me anything I asked, but that would cause a scandal and do my son-in-law harm. Consequently, it is to be avoided."[23] Resorting to the force of royal authority was a radical solution that tempted the Présidente sorely from time to time during the decade that followed. Fortunately for her own conscience in the matter, Donatien's accumulation of scandals was eventually such that the king's minister, quite independently of any specific family request to lock him up, felt obliged to act. Moreover—and the fact is highly relevant to the marquis' future rages against his much maligned mother-in law and is too often overlooked by biographers—the authorities would not necessarily have released him merely because his family indicated support for such a move.

A "much maligned mother-in-law"? The very notion will strike more than one student of Sadean biography as rather novel, if not downright wrongheaded. And yet there is no shortage of evidence to support precisely such a defense of Mme de Montreuil. Time after time, she allowed herself to give in to generous hesitations, setting aside "firm" decisions to abandon her uncooperative and essentially recidivistic son-in-law to his impetuously destructive ways. By November 1765, for example, only three months after her initial decision to discontinue support, she was prepared to start afresh. There were glimmers of hope on the horizon. Donatien's ruinous affair with la Beauvoisin might just be drawing to a close, after all. Of course, there was always the risk that another of the capital's artistic trollops might immediately get her hooks into him. If only he would show some concern for his wife and, especially, for the family's precarious finances! On that point, were there perhaps some encouraging signs of prudence? "He apparently wants to cut down on his spending," she informed the abbé. Moreover, he was again promising "to conduct himself properly in future"; and he was being so gentle, so gentle and so filial: "I write him extremely harsh letters, I admit, and he replies with such courtesy and gentleness, even with the kind of trust that friendship dictates. But is he sincere or dissembling in all this? Only experience, or those who know him better than I do, can provide the answer."[24]

That learning experience, predictable as was its outcome, turned out to be a long one for both of the self-appointed surrogate parents, the mother-in-law and the uncle. What Mme de Montreuil failed to recognize was that it was not, in fact, an either-or situation as she had suggested, not a matter of whether Donatien was sincere or dissembling. Donatien de Sade had cleverly found a way to be both sincere *and* dissembling, especially in those dramatically structured, exhilarating moments of rhetorical excess that had become second nature to him. When he wished, he could deceive others with remarkable ease, and in the process he found that he could— almost as easily—*almost* deceive himself. He loved role playing, and even when it was his own role he often preferred merely to play it, maintaining a conscious distance from the innermost self he was forever inventing, defining, and trumpeting to the world, yet never really confronting face to face. To his uncle, for example, he sent the humblest of apologies on one occasion for having said very nasty things about him behind his back (but, of course, only after learning that his offending words had unfortunately been brought to the abbé's attention). What nasty things? We do not know, but remarks much worse, it seems, than the caustic observation he had made to one of his aunts, pointing out that his uncle was really in no position to criticize him or to throw stones, seeing that, despite his priestly calling, he always kept a couple of sluts hanging about his house. But whatever those remarks were, when he learned that they had somehow got back to the abbé, Donatien sent his uncle an abject apology. In typical bad faith, however, he refused to accept any personal responsibility for his malicious comments. His verbal transgressions, his show of disrespect, all that had in fact been the fault of la Beauvoisin! He had been blinded by "an infatuation beyond his control." The wicked siren had quite simply turned his head; it was not the real Donatien who had been so disloyal and boorish. His true self was incapable of such evil: "Once restored to my true self, I would not have been capable of such villainous behavior, and now that I am no longer bewitched, I blush with shame and cannot even imagine doing what I did." [25] Then follows an act of contrition modeled no doubt on all the early adolescent confessions he used to like making to Jean-Baptiste: "Please forgive me for everything, I beg you, and believe me when I say that the most intense pangs of remorse among the many I feel as a result of the errors that creature made me commit—the ones that prey most on my conscience—are those that relate to my allowing such horrors to smother in my soul the true sentiments of tenderness and gratitude I shall always feel for you." Well and good! But when the enthusiastic self-applause he could hear resonating in his skull after crafting those elaborately clever lines died down, he simply reverted to more bad faith by revealing his intention to wreak terrible revenge against the person who had blabbed to the abbé about him. And even more characteristic still, within a few short months, he was once again back in la Beauvoisin's mercenary clutches and running up huge debts in an effort to remain a willing prisoner of his passions.

Even though (unlike Marie-Eléonore and Jean-Baptiste) the Présidente and the abbé were fairly much in accord on how to deal with the foibles of their eternally adolescent charge, as Donatien's substitute parents they inevitably found themselves going over the same sterile ground that his real mother and father had struggled through earlier on. Certainly, the most important element in the equation had not changed since those early days when Jean-Baptiste, rather proud of his son's precocious libertine tendencies, wrote in mock severity to his brother that "what [Donatien] promised and nothing at all amounted to the same thing." As they watched the scandals pile up after the Arcueil affair, the marquis' new moral guardians could only have agreed: more police and *petites maisons* problems, more heedless prodigality, more creditors in hot pursuit; then there was that canoness business, the Marseilles affair, the escape from Miolans, the little girls affair, the Treillet affair, not to mention those incidents about which we today seem to know little or nothing but to which police files at the time and the marquis' own letters allude.[26] It was, in short, difficult to escape the conclusion that Donatien's was a hopeless case. He still occasionally called Mme de Montreuil "*maman*," but it had become a matter of pure tactics used mainly in time of need. As wily as he was intelligent, he knew and respected the dynamics of power, and he was certain that the Présidente could protect him—if only she wanted to! Sometimes, he convinced himself that she wanted precisely what he wanted, only she was being devilishly discreet and clever about it. She had to pretend that she disapproved of him and, of course, would not necessarily reveal her hidden strategy to him or appear to act on his behalf in any obvious manner. In 1778, for example, when the details of his legal "vindication" at Aix-en-Provence had been completed, and after his daring escape from Inspector Marais' custody on the way back to Vincennes, it suddenly seemed crystal clear to him that Mme de Montreuil had planned on his escaping all along! Well, perhaps not really. . . . But surely she would allow herself to be co-opted after the fact in his scheme? "You can easily recognize in all this, as I do," he wrote to his notary Gaufridy in a letter that is not entirely cynical or ostensible in intention, "the craftiness of a woman who is as shrewd and intelligent as she is wise; who is as brilliant and sensitive as she is a good mother. She wants to hang on to my tether but she also wants me to enjoy the recovery of my honor, she wants my rehabilitation to be a shining event."[27] A few weeks later, not long before Marais returned to La Coste to arrest him, Donatien again wrote to Gaufridy of his unshakable confidence in this "good mother," of his deep conviction that she "did not hate him": "You can be certain that I am not wrong in this. I have known her much longer than you. Don't be deceived by her: Mme de Montreuil, for personal reasons, must make a show of vengeance and hatred toward me, but underneath it all she will be busy at sorting out my friends from my enemies and one day she will pass on what she has learned, just as she did during that first difficulty. [. . .] I tell you once again, she is a woman who is very subtle and very sly, and I think you have still not fathomed her true nature."[28]

Were the fugitive marquis' stated perceptions of Mme de Montreuil's intentions entirely wide of the mark or merely for show?[29] Judging from the number of times the Présidente went back on her various "final" decisions to wash her hands of her son-in-law, it is clear that she found the social consequences of abandoning entirely her daughter's worthless husband, this father of her darling grandchildren, daunting in the extreme. Hence her continued efforts to work things out behind the scenes with the authorities, even resorting at times to blatant corruption of witnesses to further Donatien's cause. But, unlike the marquis, she was all the time fully aware of how negatively his "case" was perceived by the public and how, even after the long-standing accusations of sodomy and poisoning had been successfully erased by the proceedings in Aix, his own relatives, along with ministry officials and, indeed, the king himself, wanted him locked up, perhaps for a very long time, as an incorrigible recidivist.

It is never an easy matter to determine when the marquis is deceiving himself at the same time as he is obviously trying to deceive others. It seems nevertheless clear that for a time he continued to believe that the great fuss about apprehending him after he escaped from his police escort on the way back from the proceedings in Aix was nothing more than window dressing to mollify the public. Mme de Montreuil herself frequently overestimated his sense of realism, believing, for example, that he fully appreciated the gravity of his situation and the extent of his public disrepute which only a substantial period of incarceration could wash away: "He is too intelligent," she wrote to Gaufridy, "not to foresee, *after all that has occurred since the affair,* and with the minister kept only too well informed by the many complaints that have been lodged, that he cannot count on being freed immediately after his vindication [in Aix]." [30] In fact, given the jurisprudence and penology of the day, her long-term strategy of quietly waiting for the public to "forget" was well calculated to succeed had Donatien chosen to cooperate. Recidivists like the marquis were seen as hybrids of sorts: viewed essentially as a "family prisoner" in the beginning, he was subsequently transformed into something of a "state prisoner," a target of outraged opinion, as public perceptions became more and more a factor in an increasingly communications-sensitive society. He would be expected to go through a correctional process intended not only to reform him personally and to safeguard individual family honor but also to appease the injured sensitivities of a concerned and disapproving society. His sentence had to be indefinite in nature, with no set term, since the time required for reformation and rehabilitation necessarily varied with the individual and could not be determined in advance. There would have to be definite signs of a "cure," of the prisoner's total submission to the purging and renewal process, along with some indication that his change of heart was likely to be sustained for some time. Only then could the father of the nation, the king, standing in for the family but symbolizing as well the larger interests of the state, welcome back the prodigal son. Only then could the public officially "forget" the miscreant. Scandal should have been avoided in the first place (as it had in the Jeanne Testard affair), but once it was out, it simply had to be given a chance to die down.

Mme de Montreuil was clearly much more in tune with these new social realities than Marie-Eléonore had been a decade earlier during the Arcueil affair. As for Marie-Eléonore's wayward son, all his life he would take a special pride in his ability to brush aside what others thought about him or about what he did. Outraged public sentiment, the entire notion of scandal, boiled down to nothing more than "the prejudices of fools," and the prejudices of fools were not his problem; it was *their* problem. "*It is not my way of thinking that has caused my misfortune, it is that of others.*"[31] That most celebrated of imperious Sadean edicts sums up in one bold line both his greatest strength and his most conspicuous weakness. I will come back to this theme.

Not long after Donatien was finally returned to the great keep of Vincennes, Mlle de Rousset, his lively and intelligent friend from La Coste, came up to Paris to lend what comfort she could to Renée-Pélagie in the struggle to gain her husband's release. Now that the legal proceedings in the Parlement of Aix were over—royal annulment of his Marseilles crimes turned out to be a simple affair—the first step was to determine what was the ministry's thinking behind the marquis' renewed detention. Was it all Mme de Montreuil's treacherous doing as Donatien and Renée-Pélagie were convinced was the case? Was there a corrupt conspiracy of some kind between her and the authorities? The answers to such questions were no doubt securely locked away in the minister's private files, and the only way to find out the truth, Mlle de Rousset decided, was to resort to espionage. The remarkable cloak-and-dagger operation, she informed the notary Gaufridy, had been risky in the extreme: "It was not easy to carry out. The person who was fearless enough to do the deed, ran the risk of being sent to the galleys or to prison for life. He brought it off but I was frantic about the operation for days." The clandestine foray had turned up both good and bad news: "We discovered by this bit of derring-do that our dear Présidente is not as guilty as we thought." Mme de Montreuil, it turned out, was not the real cause of the marquis' problems. But Donatien did have some very important enemies nonetheless: "There can be no hope until certain people die and others forget. The notion of *freedom* at this stage strikes me as rather chimerical. It will take a long time." None of this, however, had done much to convince Renée-Pélagie that she should be less optimistic in her hopes: "Despite a thousand proofs to the contrary, Mme de Sade continues to hope and to delude herself totally with respect to present and future prospects."[32]

Two days later, Mlle de Rousset provided Gaufridy with more details garnered by her intrepid agent from Sade's ministry file. Evidently, the French police network had been astonishingly efficient over the years in building up its case against the prisoner: "The charges are serious, very serious indeed; all of which causes me to fear that his captivity will be a long one. Whether true or false, they are nevertheless being used by the minister as a weapon to silence any prominent supporters. M. and Mme de Maurepas, two princesses and several others, after seeing and reading the charges, declared: 'He is precisely where he ought to be; his wife must be mad or as guilty as he is to dare ask for his release. We do not wish to receive her.'" Donatien's Provençal exploits as well as his various Paris adventures, probably going back even before the Jeanne Testard affair, were catalogued in all their real or embroidered splendor in the highly secret file, and despite the fact that the charges of sodomy and poisoning had recently been quashed by the Parlement in Aix, other "unspeakable" accusations, some relating apparently to the La Coste discoveries that three years earlier Mme de Montreuil had asked Gaufridy to "bury one-hundred feet below ground,"[33] were noted in the file. A number of the servants at La Coste had probably talked: "The various police officers who visited the château have filed atrocious depositions. Those persons are accorded credibility. M. de Sade's entire life is written out in an in-folio ledger. (Let us not name him) [has declared][34] that the man deserves to be hanged! Some details that I thought were known only to a few persons are recorded for all to see and, God help us! many other things are listed that need to be kept a deep secret. All of which," Mlle de Rousset concluded, "makes me think that he will be in prison for a long, long time."[35]

The marquis was obviously only at the beginning of his prison ordeal.

VIGNETTES OF VENGEANCE

In Mme de Montreuil's eyes, the circumstances obviously required a careful long-term strategy. Unfortunately, Donatien de Sade had no intention of cooperating with that strategy. He simply could not bring himself to believe that people wanted him to suffer in prison: "All this hush-hush mummery," he wrote knowingly to Gaufridy from La Coste after escaping custody on the way back to Vincennes, "is just another farce [. . .] and they are no more anxious to recapture me than I am to go off and drown myself." [1] In another letter of the same period he warned, in still surprisingly calm and moderate terms, that detention, for whatever reason, was not the answer in his case; it simply would not work—it would embitter him and would rub him the wrong way: "Those who have thought it could do me some good have always been mistaken." Mme de Montreuil might well think it was "very useful and advantageous" for him to accept an additional period of incarceration: "I, on the other hand," he assured Gaufridy, "consider the contrary to be very useful and very advantageous." [2]

All such studied efforts to maintain a detached and temperate tone in his ostensible statements concerning the Présidente disappeared entirely after his recapture and second arrest at La Coste on 26 August 1778. Mme de Montreuil, meanwhile, had also become the object of her own daughter's sworn hatred after a terrible scene during which the Présidente had made it clear, "in an outrageously haughty and despotic manner," that Renée-Pélagie's libertine husband, even after being cleared by the scheduled proceedings at Aix, would still have to return to Vincennes for a time. He would be released, she assured her daughter, but "not immediately." [3]

Renée-Pélagie's furious exchange with her mother had immediate and devastating consequences. Mme de Montreuil now decided—and this time she meant it unconditionally—to withdraw entirely from active involvement in her son-in-law's affairs. She would simply let things take their course. In addition, she decided that she would no longer engage in any form of direct communication with the prisoner. He, after all, had not helped matters by escaping from the custody of a royal warrant: "I owe this to myself," she wrote to her daughter; "I owe it to the minister, to the public and I owe it even to M. de Sade." [4]

And why did she owe it to the minister and *the public* not to interfere? Mme de Montreuil's response to her own question invokes an abstract rationale that would probably not have occurred to Marie-Eléonore, whose principles of belief and action—not unlike those of her son—sprang from the ethos of a simpler age. The world was changing, and the public's view of things was now being recognized as a new force that had to be addressed by high and low alike. The Présidente felt vulnerable on the point: "My easy-going leniency, which has too frequently prevailed until now because of my gullible acceptance of M. de Sade's apparent resolutions and your entreaties, has made me responsible in the eyes of the family and in the public's view for the misfortunes that have resulted from it." And why "to herself"? Obviously, she owed it to herself after Donatien's many "instances of misconduct, his wrongs and insults." Finally, she owed a hands-off policy to Donatien himself: "I wish to be neither his dupe nor his confidante. What was the result of his letting me know of his arrival in Paris, eighteen months ago, twenty-four hours before his arrest? The result was his accusation that I betrayed him! *I betrayed him!* I who knew nothing of his presence in the city, whereas the minister had been aware of it for six days and had even set spies on me in case the marquis tried to make contact!"[5]

Most Sadean scholars have questioned Mme de Montreuil's good faith in all this. Certainly, similar doubts about her sincerity had been uppermost in the mind of Sade's trusted friend, Mlle de Rousset, when she came up to Paris in November 1778 to see what could be done to obtain the prisoner's release. Donatien considered Rousset his closest ally. A notary's daughter, articulate, efficient, and shrewd, she would be ideally suited to unmask the Présidente's evil intentions. Indeed, he thought of this bright Provençal woman as his "most beloved and most worthy friend," an "honest soul," someone to whom he hoped to remain "closely attached for as long as he lived."[6]

It was not long after her arrival in the capital that Mlle de Rousset managed to arrange a meeting with the dreaded mother-in-law. In a letter to Gaufridy, she reveals her surprise at what she learned from the interview:

> Madame de Montreuil is a charming woman and knows how to turn a phrase; she is still very youthful in appearance, more *petite* than tall; her features are pleasing, she has bewitching eyes and an engaging laugh; she is as quick-witted as a sprite with the wisdom and candor of an angel; sly as a fox, however, but agreeable and enticing in her way. Like M. le marquis, she quite won me over.[7]

Their encounter had been a wary battle of wits. "In the confusion of ideas and the heat of battle," Mlle de Rousset nevertheless soon came to the conclusion that "M. de Sade was loved" and that Mme de Montreuil was indeed deeply distressed by her son-in-law's situation. Rousset also learned that Inspector Marais, thanks to the Présidente's intervention, had been punished for the brutality with which he had carried out Donatien's latest arrest at La Coste. Mme de Montreuil had also seen to it that the marquis was more comfortable in his current detention than during his incarceration of the previous year. He was being provided with "visiting and full writing privileges, and all manner of comforts." As for his release, that, contrary to what Donatien thought, did not depend on the Présidente's will in the matter. She spoke energetically to Rousset of having rescued him more than once in the past. He had promised many times to reform: "Oh! If you only knew, Mademoiselle," the Présidente sighed, "all that he had promised me in the past! Here, in this very room, the number of solemn pledges he made!" But surely, Mlle de Rousset had countered, surely the marquis when he made those promises intended to keep them. The man is weak, as you well know, Madame, but now he is much changed: age and misfortune have taught him a lesson. "I only hope so!" the mother-in-law had replied; "But, *tell me, Mademoiselle: would you be willing to answer for him?*" [8]

Ten days later the Présidente gave her own version of the meeting to Gaufridy. It confirmed that she had no intention of standing in the way of any efforts to gain her son-in-law's release. However, she would not herself take any formal steps in that direction, having already been severely criticized for obtaining his release on two previous occasions. She knew, moreover, that for the moment at least, any such efforts would be a total waste of time. The ministry would simply ignore her overtures. In other words, it was not she but the government, with the tacit support of most of the marquis' own family in Provence, that was holding Donatien Alphonse François de Sade a prisoner in Vincennes. [9]

Although that may well have been the reality of the situation, the prisoner's perception of that reality had by now evolved into something quite different. Early on in his imprisonment he had momentarily swallowed his pride and had written pleading, tearful, and quite uncharacteristically penitent letters to Mme de Montreuil, expressing to this woman ("whom I used to call my mother with such pleasure") a remorse he plainly did not feel, at the same time as he invoked a God in whom he definitely did not believe. [10] More heartfelt, however, were the volcanic, demented ragings he addressed at the same time to Renée-Pélagie, screaming out his unshakable belief that he was the victim of a monstrous conspiracy, at the heart of which, manipulating every event and pulling every string, was the most sinister and evil of all women, her mother. Indeed, the Présidente was supremely evil precisely because he now saw her as an all-powerful mother figure who, *if she wished,* could protect him, just as she had protected him in the past. Intermixed with this anger and malaise were probably other elements of primal distress, a deeply buried resentment going back to that time in his childhood when his real mother chose to "abandon" him and turn him into an orphan. Motherhood implied treachery and betrayal. It—and all the orthodox values it claimed to represent—deserved rebuke and vilification. Motherhood became the solitary prisoner's greatest enemy. The mother had deliberately chosen not to save him from his attackers. Once again he, the unfortunate and trusting son, was an orphan betrayed.

This progressive demonization of the Présidente, the prisoner's epic struggle with a maternal she-devil from Hell, monopolizes nearly every page of the Vincennes correspondence. Soon, almost imperceptibly, without generic differentiation, the process would take on a life of its own in the mother-hating execrations of the Sadean novel.

If Sade's letters from Vincennes and the Bastille express one central theme, it is that of heroic rebellion against the institutionalized orthodoxy of maternal values, a revolt grounded in a defiant and triumphant subjectivity. After months of frantic speculation on what might be the prescribed length of his sentence, the marquis finally realized that he was being held for an indefinite term. Why was he there? Presumably to be "corrected" and "changed," to be made into something he was not, to be shaped to fit someone else's mold and subjected to someone else's will. That, he swore, would never, could never, happen. If Jean-Baptiste were alive, he could have told the authorities that they were wasting their time. Yes, son Donatien was "dreadful" in that respect, just like his mother! It is true that from time to time in the past he had expressed remorse, promising to change his ways as he made "full" and repentant confessions to his father. After the Jeanne Testard affair and his first incarceration in 1763, he had even pulled out all the stops in a sniveling letter to the redoubtable Sartine, lieutenant général de police, protesting in tones so remorseful, so penitent, that we scarcely dare to interpret his words for what they really are: pure, unadulterated verbal swill—exquisitely calibrated in dosage, each "effect" calculated right down to the last comma and semicolon. *He does not bemoan his fate. . . . He deserves God's vengeance. . . . He abhors his errors and mourns his sins. . . . He is so thankful to God for bringing about this opportunity for him to stop a moment and examine his conscience. . . .* Fear of dishonor, fear of losing family approval, perhaps even fear of the kind of fate that—in far less exacerbated circumstances—would soon befall the young chevalier de La Barre, motivated this fraudulent plea that ended with a solemn request to see a priest and to receive communion. The holy wafer was now to be put to a very different use. Yes, he wanted to speak to a priest, to profit from repentance and his holy teachings sufficiently to take communion, which he had previously neglected, and that was the cause of all his bad behavior.[11] Mme de Montreuil with some help from Jean-Baptiste had rescued him then, and she had rescued him several times after that, but the clever little tricks he had employed from the very beginning to manipulate her were not working anymore. This cruel mother was no longer willing to pick up and comfort the wailing child, a child whose nature was such that it could respond to a loss of manipulative control only by throwing gigantic tantrums, explosive fits of anger that gathered force and grew into great roaring torrents of rhetorical magma, aimed directly at punishing maternity. Demonization of the mother and punishment of her sex, punishment especially of the unclean whore-mothers whose denunciations had caused him all his problems with the police, becomes, finally, the very essence of the Sadean novel, the true source of its vital fury and excess.

Since the heartless Présidente no longer saw fit to console and pacify the screaming child, that sacred duty fell to her daughter. Renée-Pélagie, faithful and loyal wife, did her best to assume the role of comforting mother. It was a role she would continue to play with a martyr's dedication for at least another decade, until she too finally had the good sense, once the prisoner was freed by the Revolution, to send him on his way. Whether she had ceased to believe in him at that point is not clear, but up until then—and from the very beginning—she had consistently granted him her total and unconditional allegiance. It was early in December 1778, only a few weeks after the prisoner's forced return to Vincennes, that Renée-Pélagie naively informed her mother that the marquis was now fully repentant and had at last seen the error of his ways. The Présidente, so often disappointed in the past, had simply replied, "I want to believe it and I hope it happens." But Renée-Pélagie's mother then went on to point out that things were not that simple: the authorities insisted on judging future probabilities by past certainties, and they wanted firm evidence that the prisoner had indeed seen the light. The mother-in-law herself had tested the ministerial waters and had received a response that was entirely unfavorable. There could be no freedom yet. Time and a cool head—that was the key. There was, after all, no disputing the facts: it was agreed that he had done what he had done. Were his transgressions premeditated, committed in cold blood and with aforethought? If so, he obviously had to be prevented from repeating those acts. On the other hand, if, as he sometimes claimed in his defense, he had been driven to do what he had done by an uncontrollable impulse, by "an untamable imagination," as one friendly magistrate had put it, then it would be to his advantage and benefit "that a few years of detention calm his blood, cool down his imagination, and dissipate, in a word, any fears arising from the thought of his being at liberty." [12]

Renée-Pélagie passed on her mother's carefully weighed and infuriatingly logical assessment of the situation to the prisoner at the first possible opportunity. The effect was immediate and violently explosive. Donatien not only rejected the message; he all but destroyed the messenger. For the next twelve years, Renée-Pélagie's dogged loyalty to her husband was rewarded mainly with humiliating verbal abuse. More important, her message that freedom could come only after fundamental reformation on his part provoked a new rush of defiance and violent fits of rage. When would the world learn, as his parents and his tutor had learned early on, that he was congenitally incapable of bending to the will of others, of receiving any "useful" lessons at all from punishment? "What good did my detention in Pierre-Encize do me? How did I benefit from Miolans? From my first incarceration in Vincennes? The only result has been the corruption of my mind, the overheating of my bile, my brain, and my sexual appetites, all driving me back once more to my errors, if only because of the perverse obstinacy of my nature that will not allow it to *be,* or even *be said,* that punishment can do otherwise than make me worse. Since that is clear, since that is recognized, since it is understood that I would rather die than give proof of the contrary, [. . .] why keep on with it?"[13] The same message is frequently repeated: "Just remember that I would far rather smash my skull against these walls, right here and now, than fail to oblige your loathsome mother to admit one day: *Yes, he was right; I'm sorry. It was not the right way to go about it with someone like him.*"[14]

Loathsome mother: among the mildest of the increasingly violent labels for his hated mother-in-law, spewed out in letters to her unlucky daughter: *prude, fucking tramp, degenerate, odious shrew, monster, termagant, escapee from the Inquisition, escapee from Hell, nature's curse, villainous and sludge-souled old fool, bawd, old harpy and abominable extortionist*—the list goes on, and what he proudly saw as the "perverse obstinacy of his nature," the character trait that had more than once caused Jean-Baptiste to be unpleasantly reminded of Marie-Eléonore, only intensified: "I shall be foolish and heedless as long as I feel the weight of even the lightest chains upon me."[15] That was what the Présidente, "this creature desperate to do evil, this unhappy jade, this imbecile," was refusing to understand!

And, anyway, why were they trying to correct him? What was his crime, after all? The marquis' bad faith, as intrinsic as the obstinacy he took such pride in, rises easily to the challenge of providing an answer, one that modern-day admirers of the marquis' "freedom-loving" integrity, of his "triumphant subjectivity," usually gloss over even though it probably holds the key to his attitude toward women in general and sums up much of the classic Sadean ideology. His "crime" was purely *"a matter of exercising the freedom of [his] conscience"*; it amounted to nothing more than his holding to certain legitimate beliefs and acting on those beliefs. And what were those staunch beliefs and actions? Sade's reply does not disappoint: *"He is unfortunate enough to believe that nothing is less respectable than a whore, and that how we treat whores is of no more consequence than how we go about emptying our bowels.*"[16] It is not the business of the police how we move our bowels. Why should they have any say in how we treat our whores? Why, in any case, so much fuss over what happens to these creatures? Are they not paid for their *pains?* If they do not like their job, why do they stay in the business? "Change professions [. . .] or, if you like that one, endure it, thorns and all."[17] He prided himself on being a careful student of French history, and nowhere could he find in the nation's chronicles a single example of punishment as disproportionate as what he, at that very moment, was being forced to endure. French justice had come to this! *"And all that for whores!"* He would, he vowed, never give in to these crude reformatory tactics, to the imposition of corrective "rigor," come what may. "I tell you again, for the thousandth time, [rigor] is completely useless. You sour my blood, you inflame my brain [. . .], nothing in the whole world can make me renounce *either my habits or my way of thinking.*"[18] Yes, it was a matter of *his way of thinking.* Freedom of conscience and freedom of thought—that is what this was all about. And so he points with pride to his "unyielding resolve, this firmness of character that is part of my self-esteem and pride." No amount of rigor could ever make him submit. Society's censure and severity only increased his determination to resist: "That is my nature and it has never varied," he assured Mlle de Rousset, "not since my childhood—Amblet, who raised me, can confirm it."[19] The "cause" here is very different, but the marquis' rhetoric again reminds us of Marie-Eléonore's defiant tones as she rejects Jean-Baptiste's pressure to make concessions when Donatien's marriage contract was being drawn up. Pressure was the wrong solution to the problem, she too had warned; it would not induce her to change her mind: "There will never be cause for unhappiness with me, the moment you cease grasping me by the throat to make me do what you want."[20]

All of Sade's self-referencing texts on this central issue are designed to place him in a heroic light, but some are more flattering than others in their various representations of his personal integrity. Grandstanding as the champion of conscience and principled intractability now becomes his role of choice. His key theme, however, no matter which dramatic role he adopts, never varies: he, personally, has never done anything wrong (or *very* wrong), and no amount of incarceration will ever make him change. Not only is change for him impossible; it is also morally undesirable, indeed totally so: "Either kill me or accept me as I am for, the devil take me, I shall never change. I have told you, the beast is too old; there can no longer be hope. The most honest, frank, and most sensitive of men, the most compassionate and the most benevolent, I worship my children [. . .], I adore my kin (on my side of the family, that is), the friends I may still have, and, above all, my wife. [. . .] Those are my virtues."[21]

So much for his good side. And his vices? Not unexpectedly, the marquis offers his list with indisputable relish and again with obvious pride: "Imperious, irascible, hot-headed, extreme in everything, with an imagination in the matter of morals that is so disordered the like has never before been seen, an atheist to the point of fanaticism—there I stand before you. And once again, I say: Either kill me or accept me as I am, for I will not change."

Sade returns more than once to the image of "the beast too old" (he really means too fundamentally *worthy*) to be reformed. Not, of course, that he wished to influence his children, for example, with any of his "bad principles." Here again, hyperbole rushes to the rescue. Yes, far better that his children be killed than corrupted! Far better that they die in purity, even by his own hand! "If the choice were either to kill them or to corrupt their hearts I would not hesitate even for a moment, and I almost think that killing them would be the lesser evil."[22] We are not, of course, to lend the slightest credence to such obviously mendacious rhetoric; the statement, like some of Jean-Jacques Rousseau's paradoxical gems in the same vein,[23] is not intended to withstand even the flabbiest attack by either logical analysis or common sense. But the proposition, if made purely for effect, is at least clear: the legitimacy of his intransigence derives from its primary grounding in his fundamental nature; he acquired it, so to speak, with his mother's milk: "Some things are so much a part of our being, especially what is acquired in infancy, that it is never possible to give them up."[24] All efforts to change his fundamental habits had to be resisted since these were so amazingly bound to the physical constitution of his being that "ten-thousand years of detention and five hundred pounds of chain would only increase their force." The Présidente and her magistrate minions could talk all they liked about "cooling down his imagination," of the need to keep him confined until he "matured"; they hoped by their ill-conceived strategy to destroy his sexual urges, obliterating thereby his "overheated" imagination. "What an absurd line of argument, Monsieur!" he protests—rather too much—in a letter to Le Noir, successor to his old enemy Sartine as lieutenant général de police. "An overheated imagination is not the source of my kind of error; the source is, rather, a worn-out sexual appetite." A twelve-year-old child, he insists, could have figured that one out![25] But at the same time, to Renée-Pélagie, he also spoke of the uses and pleasures of intensely cultivating the imagination, of conjuring up new sexual fantasies, of savoring precise memories of past "singularities." The effect was erotically powerful and intoxicating: "I would quite astonish you if I told you that *all those sorts of things* and the memories of them are what I resort to when I wish to deaden the pain of my situation. Our morals do not depend on us, they are determined by how we are put together, by our organic structure. [. . .] When it comes to *those sorts of things,* we can no more adopt a particular taste than we can become straight if we are born twisted, or make ourselves brunettes if we are redheads. That is my eternal philosophy and I shall never retreat from it." [26]

This agreeably wanton recollection of dissipations past, intermixed with active imaginings of unlimited and unrealized sexual fantasies, was taking on a new importance for the prisoner, not only as an aid to his regular onanistic exercises but also as a catalyst for the creative exploitation of his personal conceiving and doing equation. Constrained by physical confinement, the marquis now sought more and more, beyond the solitary relief of his dildos (crudely fashioned wax instruments made from prison candles or the mammoth cylindrical wooden "document" cases unwittingly smuggled in by Renée-Pélagie), a richer fusion of the equation's two elements through the act of writing. Sade the prisoner was on the threshold of becoming Sade the pornographer-ideologue, essentially the writer we know today.

Indeed, it would be more accurate to say that he had already progressed some distance beyond that threshold. The hoary question of whether Sade owed his literary career to his prison experience has, in fact, little pertinence: he himself supplied the answer in a letter from Vincennes to his old tutor Amblet in 1782 when he stated that it was his intention, after his release, to take up *"once again"* what he as a literary artist was best at—that is, "the brushes of Aretino." It is his intention to put aside in future the pen of Molière, his other generic "brush." He reveals that the pen of Aretino, the instrument of licentious prose, had already served him more generously than any of his efforts at dramatic verse. One of his plays, produced in a Bordeaux theater, had achieved only mediocre success, whereas two rather casual pornographic novels "paid for six-months' worth of trifling pleasures in one of the kingdom's principal cities and a two-month tour of Holland [presumably his September–October trip there in 1769], without it costing me a cent of my own money. What a difference!" [27] In short, without his prison experience, Sade might well have continued to churn out even more mediocre dramas than he did, as well as more of the common or garden variety of anonymous hack pornography that circulated so abundantly under cloak and counter in eighteenth-century France. The writing of pornography, whatever other useful functions it served, had the distinct advantage of providing a quick and easy source of funds, a point well underlined by the marquis in a letter to the lawyer Reinaud in 1791 when his first novel, *Justine ou les Malheurs de la vertu,* appeared: "I needed money; my printer asked to have it well *peppered* and I obliged him by making it spicy enough to infect the Devil."[28] That unguarded statement has, it is true, been a source of some distress and embarrassment to an entire cohort of Sade's modern-day celebrants who stoutly insist on their right to confuse literature and pornography: Sade, a porn merchant? A vile calumny! Sade is being purely facetious, protests Maurice Heine who, along with most of the Divine Marquis' aficionados, will not allow his hero to suffer any such hermeneutic indignities.[29] The evidence to the contrary remains, however, as plain and overwhelming as Sade's explicit comment on the subject in the introduction of *Les 120 journées de Sodome:* "Now, dear reader, it is time to ready your heart and mind for the most impure story ever told since the world began. [. . .] No doubt many of the misdeeds you will find depicted here will displease you, that goes without saying; but there are others *that will stir you to the point of costing you some fuck,* and that is all we ask."[30] Accordingly, La Duclos is hardly into her raunchy narrative when she is sternly reminded not to omit any of the juicy particularizing details since it is precisely their abundant inclusion in descriptions of sexual encounters of all sorts that provides the desired "excitement of our senses."[31]

Sade had all the makings of a pornographer before his incarceration in Vincennes and the Bastille, perhaps going as far back as 1763 when he showed the little verses contained in his "unfortunate book" to a shocked Jeanne Testard, and certainly by the late 1760s and early 1770s when he managed to sell the two "well-peppered" manuscripts to underground publishers of the genre, one in Holland and the other probably in Lyons. We have only to look at the hundreds of titles listed in the police files of the ancien régime or catalogued today in the Enfer section of the Bibliothèque Nationale to gain some notion of the sort of novels or private theater "comedies" that the marquis, like scores of other fringe writers of the day, probably turned out at the time. Indeed, it is entirely possible that one of these early anonymous pieces may some day turn up in an identifiable form, at which point it will undoubtedly be added with reverence and full scholarly apparatus to the latest edition of his complete works. Yet another *Venus in Heat,* another *Tittle-Tattle Nuns,* perhaps a *Roving Whore* or an *Art of Fucking,* would not really be so terribly out of place in a last-minute appendix to Sade's corpus, but any such youthful compositions would nevertheless immediately stand out from today's established canon in at least one major respect: Conspicuously lacking would be the vital dimension of frenzied excess and disproportion brought to the marquis' writing by painful isolation behind the thick stone walls of Vincennes or the Bastille, augmented by obsessive autoerotic fantasies and, most importantly, set aflame by the prisoner's burning, passionately fixated hatred of the Présidente and of the magistrates who had seen fit to provide tattle-tale whores the law's protection from his contemptuous and repeated abuse.

Such polemical elements, steeped in mental anguish, unquestionably helped to transform the early society dramatist and casual pornographer into something quite different. They energized his pen with a feverish rage and released from an inner inferno those "furies of vengeance" he refers to in a letter to Amblet of 1782. Let the Présidente beware! She had made the fatal mistake of overlooking her own vulnerability. Had this "monster, this Fury from Hell who defies being *painted* in words,"[32] forgotten, for example, that her persecuted son-in-law was in a position to reveal scandals about her own family that were worse than anything he was accused of? He had not yet tested the avenging power of his "brushes," but he knew already that they would answer the need. His use here of the verb "to paint" is no accident: he was already at work on this sublime project. On his palette of vengeance he had already assembled all the necessary pigments, the "colors of Hell" required to depict this evil matron of darkness and her complicitous underworld. His pen was being readied for an entirely new kind of foray into the world of literature. It had already been tested in a parallel genre, his prison letters, in which he now unremittingly attacked, openly and savagely, the monster-mother, the depraved and villainous Présidente de Montreuil. Writing about her to Renée-Pélagie, he discovers that his slurs and fulminations come to him now with remarkable ease: "No, I do not think it is possible to find in the entire world a creature more abhorrent than your contemptible mother: Hell itself never spews out her like and I am convinced that the phantasms of priests who invented the Furies were modeled on women like her."[33]

As he slaps onto his canvas these blazing "colors from Hell," he describes to Renée-Pélagie a delicious scene he has just imagined. He has actually made a little sketch of it which he will do up properly once he is released: "I sometimes picture to myself your abominable mother before the abscess of her putrid black bile spilled out over me, drop by drop. [. . .] The Présidente can be seen lying *naked* on her back, looking much like the monsters of the sea that sometimes wash up on shore." All his enemies are present at the puncturing of the swollen fetid monster: Le Noir, Rouge-mont,—even Marais "who holds the candle, and from time to time tastes the festering purulence to determine if it is satisfactory." [34] She had much to answer for, this foul creature! Now in his hate-twisted logic he finds it reasonable to assert that it was not he but this she-monster who should have been punished for the entire Arcueil business. [35] Was it not the hated Présidente who transformed "an ordinary tart party" into something crim-inal by buying off the supposedly brutalized victim? Just as it was Sar-tine—"The greatest enemy I have in the entire world, to whom I owe all of my misfortunes"—who was responsible in 1763 for ruining his life in the Jeanne Testard affair, all in order to play the role of "an excellent lieutenant de police who makes exceptions for no one." [36]

But such specific charges against the Présidente do not allow maternity itself to escape the marquis' general and essential indictment. Was she not, after all, the prototype of all mothers, those lubricious matrons of the novels who, without exception, engage in the act of procreation purely for their selfish sexual pleasures? Accordingly, he conjures up a picture of the Présidente's "whoring mentality," her *putanisme,* in a letter to Mlle de Rousset, revealing the peculiarly maternal character of her absolute de-bauchery. Had she not wantonly given herself to all comers? Had she not given birth to as many as *eleven* bastards? Only Renée-Pélagie, of all her children, was legitimate! [37] A few weeks later a revised estimate is provided in a letter to the long-suffering Renée-Pélagie. Now, it seems, the Prési-dente was responsible for presenting to her husband only "seven or eight bastards," but a new and more serious charge is added: the Présidente, like the lowest of procuring bawds, was, in fact, guilty of prostituting every single one of her daughters, including Renée-Pélagie and the young can-oness. It thus did not behoove her to be vexatious in matters of morality, to try to punish or repress sexual singularities in others. Compared with her hideous crimes, his own little failings had been nothing more than faults in his sexual tendencies, beyond his control, but they never did harm to anyone, except, obviously, to a few insolent whores who deserved to be locked up in jail for life as punishment for tattling and whining to the mag-istrate about being abused! [38]

Other essential characteristics of the Sadean mother show up in his portrait of this execrable mother-in-law. Was she not infamously guilty too of a "sanctimonious piety," like those hypocritical, ultradevout mothers who pride themselves on never making mistakes? "In the entire world there is no beast more evil than a sanctimonious old woman." These "religious" women had been the bane of his existence from the time of his childhood:

"If anything, *all my life,* has alienated me from religion, it is the hypocritical piety of old women, *all of whom* heinously combine religious practices with the most odious of vices."[39] The words "all my life" are critically important, for they take us back to the days of a disapproving, fun-spoiling Marie-Eléonore, but events now required that he make a lateral correction in his antimother targeting and shift his aim to the Présidente, "a good Jansenist who disapproves of *molinizing* women" and who—puritanical harpy that she was—claims that her husband "has never *poked* her elsewhere than in her *vessel of propagation* and that whoever strays from that *vessel* deserves to boil in Hell."[40] The prudish matriarch had only to wait! Soon her son-in-law's creative imagination and avenging pen would put her and her kind through torments far worse than boiling in Hell. Even in this "real-life" context of the correspondence, Sade conjures up totally romanesque images of exquisitely brutal tortures that he would like to see inflicted on the Présidente. If he could make laws from his prison cell, he assured Mlle de Rousset, "the first would be to have the Présidente *roasted alive over a slow fire.*"[41] That would pay her back! She would learn how much his hatred knew no bounds:

> Oh! how I hate her! How I hate her, Almighty God! And what a joyous moment it will be for me when I learn that her loathsome life has come to an end! I swear, on the truest of oaths, to give two-hundred gold *louis* to the poor on the very day that happy event occurs, and fifty *louis,* either to the servant who brings me the news, or to the postal clerk from whom I receive the letter of notification. I hereby consent to all forms of torture it shall please God to make me endure if ever I violate this oath, a written copy of which I have carried on my person these past three years. I hereby confess that I have never wished dead anyone but her![42]

By 1783, *Les 120 journées de Sodome* was well launched, and other major writings were in the works. In March of that year, Donatien mentions having sent the manuscript of two completed works to Renée-Pélagie, a comedy and a novel.[43] He was experiencing severe problems with his vision, but the discomfort only added to the force and intensity of his inner phantasms. Scenarios involving imagined punishments of the Présidente, this "repulsive procuress," are now assigned numbers, presenting a structure analogous to the numerical framework of *Les 120 journées.* A precious glimpse of the novelist already at work in the correspondence is the result:

> Being no longer able to read or write, I have been inventing forms of torture for her. Here is the one-hundred-eleventh:

I saw her this morning, in my sufferings; I saw the bitch, yes, skinned alive, dragged over thistles and then hurled into a vat of vinegar. And I said to her:

Vile creature! This is for selling your son-in-law to the executioners!
This is for pimping your two daughters!
This is for having ruined and dishonored your son-in-law!
This is for making him hate the children for whom you sacrificed him!
This is for causing him to lose the best years of his life, when you could so easily
     have saved him after his arraignment!
This is for preferring over him the vile and detestable embryos of your
     daughter![44]
This is for all the evils you have rained down on him for thirteen years, in or-
     der to make him pay for your own stupidities!

And all the while, I aggravated her torments, and I insulted her in her suffering, and I momentarily ceased thinking of my own.
     The pen falls from my hand. I must suffer anew. Adieu, my murderers;
I must go on cursing you.[45]

Sade solemnly promised Renée-Pélagie that his vignettes of vengeance
would more than equal the injuries he had received. He would not be "in
a cold rage," moreover, as he prepared the most bitter venoms required for
the task: "Everything will erupt spontaneously within me, straight from
the heart, pouring out from every wellspring; and be assured that the vipers
I shall release will match those cast in my direction."[46] Already inhabiting
the universe of his own novel, he wrote those words on 8 March 1784, a
week after being transferred from Vincennes to the Bastille where *Les 120
journées de Sodome* was soon completed.
     But even a year before, during what may well have been the peak pe-
riod of his still unchanneled hatred, with the venom of his pen distilled and
concentrated by near blindness, he had delivered up an important trade
secret and identified what would be the key source of the Sadean novel's
unique energy, its very nucleus of excess: "A thousand times worse!" had
become his motto, his direct and final answer to the Présidente and to all
like her who presumed it their right to *correct* him. The passage deserves
the biographer's special attention:

And eleven years of affliction [. . .] are not yet enough to satisfy the voracious beast! [. . .]
     And what does she gain by it? And what does the miserable bitch think
she gains by it? Does she imagine she will reform me with her villainy? Well,
I do hereby swear to her and take my solemn oath that I would have poi-
soned myself three years ago were it not for the unique and consoling hope

of proving to her, *by doing a thousand times worse than I have done,* that her methods are as stupid as she is, and that her advisors are monsters. [. . .]

No, whores are not worth twelve years of torture. [. . .]

Gods of Hell, teach me all your torments, come whisper to me in my innermost being all the odious secrets of your art, let your barbarity be multiplied, inflamed by the venom of this embittered heart! And for my only satisfaction, for my only favor, grant me the opportunity to combine all these torments and to inflict them on this abominable sex which has made a sacrifice of me, and which I loathe!

Oh, powers from Hell, grant me Nero's wish, that all women have but one head and that this head belong to the shrew who tyrannizes me; then grant me the pleasure of chopping it off!

There, now you can see the results of your correction [. . .], of your vile impostures, of your stinking lies! Yes, there are your results! Enjoy them as you await even better! But remember that this is only the desire; remember that, with me, desire translated into effect has always been made worse.[47]

That effect, translated as the violent disproportion and excess of the Sadean novel, clearly found its chief stimulus in the marquis' obsessive and absolute need to wreak vengeance on all maternal authority and on women in general. The essential need was to *defy*, to demonstrate to the Présidente, to the ministry and all the prison authorities, that every attempt to "correct" him, to "cool" his imagination, provoked in fact the opposite reaction. Indeed, such attempts only made him "a thousand times worse." That stubborn defiance—he had already made it clear on earlier occasions—was the most basic part of his nature, of his being; it defined his very essence. He had been like that since childhood. Marie-Eléonore and Jean-Baptiste were long gone, but Amblet was still alive and could testify to his recalcitrance, his immovable determination. De Launay, the governor of the Bastille, would soon learn the same lesson, he who—just ten days before the mob paraded his severed head on a pike through the streets of Paris—had requested the transfer to Charenton of "this being who cannot be brought to submission."[48]

"A thousand times worse." A slogan of heroic defiance? The banner of triumphant individualism? Not really, I think. In a sense, this compulsively exponential translation of *desire* into *effect*, this thousandfold multiplication that drives the Sadean novel, can scarcely be viewed as the autonomous act of "the freest spirit that has ever lived," as Apollinaire was pleased to label his Divine Marquis. The exercise of any freedom implies choice. The compulsive rage and excess of the Sadean novel become, rather, the clinically interesting by-product of a mind shackled by obsession and pathological intransigence—no more "free," in fact, than was the imprisoned author himself behind the grim forbidding walls of the Bastille.

Eighteen

WHEN DO WE BELIEVE HIM?

Though she lived for nearly ten years after its publication in 1791, the Présidente probably never allowed herself the pleasure of reading *Justine* or any other of the Sadean novels that appeared anonymously during her lifetime. Had she done so (and discovering the author's identity would not have presented an insurmountable problem), it is more than likely she would have been able to overcome her abhorrence long enough to grasp some of the hidden reactive processes that helped to sustain her son-in-law's literary creations. Certainly, the Sadean subtext would have held fewer mysteries for her than for Marie-Eléonore, whose influence on the marquis' final elaboration of the central antimaternal theme was probably greater and more deeply seated than the Présidente's but is far less directly discernible. One imagines, moreover, that Marie-Eléonore would have been even more unwilling than the Présidente to peer through the shadows of Donatien's troubled psyche for a long hard look at the incandescent "colors from Hell" that lit up the fertile imagination within. At one time or another she had undoubtedly been forced to come to terms with her son's flagrant delinquencies; however, her ultimate emotional closure with him was likely one of weary, uncomprehending withdrawal. Distance and dissociation had already served her well in dealing with Jean-Baptiste's failings. Her own marital separation, an ultimate gesture of alienation, had no doubt been entirely a matter of her own choosing. Self-exile to a convent residence was the traditionally dignified solution for an injured wife of her class. For an "injured" mother, on the other hand, self-exile involved a far more difficult process of termination. For a long time, she probably continued to respond to filial appeals for material if not maternal support, no matter how patently guileful and disingenuous these were. Donatien was not easy to ignore, and with his cajoling ways he would have been difficult to turn away. Still, it probably came to that point eventually. In the end, Marie-Eléonore must have simply given up on her son, just as she had earlier given up on his father.

Giving up on the troublesome marquis had also been a protracted and problematic operation for Donatien's secondary guardians, the abbé and the Présidente, but they, too, finally managed to beat a dignified retreat. Longest of all to persevere—to the point of martyrdom, almost—was Renée-Pélagie, but even she finally grew tired of serving as her husband's emotional punching bag. Her main purpose during those many years of dancing attendance to her husband's every whim, being always at great pains to soothe his every outburst of anger, his every attack of paranoia, was to rescue him finally from prison. She stuck loyally to that goal for thirteen challenging years. From her letters [1] one gathers that during much of that time she also struggled with an even more complex goal: to understand this strange mercurial man whose destiny was so closely linked to hers but whose nature and true identity seemed such a puzzle. In the end she achieved neither of these objectives, and when Donatien was finally released from Charenton by the Revolution, she suddenly—probably without knowing specifically why—found it impossible to take up her life with him again.

Renée-Pélagie's failed effort to understand her husband can only remind us of the ultimate of all the Sadean puzzles, one that no serious study of the man can legitimately avoid. Who, when all is said and done, was Donatien de Sade? Many different Sades have been invented over the years, [2] and nearly always with passionate hostility toward opposing or even complementary definitions of the man. For many, the marquis is still the most atrociously defamed genius, the greatest and freest spirit, who ever lived; for others, he is a pretentious and fraudulent—even dangerous—pornographer. Some have praised in him the triumphant hero of individualism and subjectivity; others have scorned him as an obvious candidate for safekeeping in an asylum. Is he one of the world's great writers or French literature's most overrated and obnoxious bore? A martyr to freedom of conscience and thought or simply a recidivistic abuser of women? A hero of the Revolution or one of the more opportunistic of the *ci-devant* chameleons whose only creed was to survive? Some speak of Sade as a brilliant precursor of modern psychiatry, of surrealism, of nearly every political *ism,* evil or beneficent, in the contemporary repertory. All of these many Sades—my own not excepted, of course—are the product of one or another kind of reductionism and supported by evidence of widely varying quality. There is a curious irony here since reductionism, always opportunistic and nearly always painfully transparent, is precisely Sade's own favorite attack-defense mechanism when, at different stages of his life, he feels called on to elaborate and present definitions of his protean identity. A middling dramatist—as much in life as in letters—he unfailingly wrote himself into the most guilt-free *beaux rôles,* loudly proclaiming all the while that he was, in fact, consistently playing *himself.* Those roles and their accompanying professions of faith change almost mechanically with each changing scene, and few writers who have indulged in as much dramatic self-referencing have trumpeted a greater number of contradictory personal creeds and escaped so easily the charge of mystification and incoherence.

No modern celebrant has defended the marquis' heroic legend more generously or pointed with greater awe and admiration to the permanent significance of Sade's "preeminent lessons in steadfastness" than Gilbert Lely, to whom all students of the man, friends, foes, and neutrals—Maurice Lever being one of the happy few who has played a leading role in this last group—owe so much. Lely's message, richly poetic in its own right, goes something like this: "The marquis is never willing to disclaim his integral character, anymore than he is prepared to disavow his ethical and metaphysical convictions, no matter what risks such stubbornness inevitably poses for his hopes of freedom."[3] For Lely, Sade was essentially what he claimed he was—a prisoner of conscience, a martyr to free thought. His fanatical atheism was much more than the simple metaphysical rejection of discredited religious dogmas. It was a revolt against all tyrannies and taboos—religious, political, or intellectual: "Sade against God, is Sade [. . .] against anything that in any way attempts to rob man of his essential treasure, his enlightened and glorious subjectivity."[4]

Sade, as many of the grandiloquent pronouncements scattered throughout his prison correspondence suggest, would not have disagreed with Lely's lyrically reverent assessment. Nothing, for example, made him more impatient with Renée-Pélagie than her tearful requests that, "for his own good," he should tone down his verbal abuse of the prison authorities and try to modify "his way of thinking." He found even more intolerable her earnest assurances to the authorities that he would surely *change,* would definitely *reform,* if only he were released, "if he were outside."[5] Such pledges made on his behalf were construed by the prisoner as a supreme insult, a deliberate provocation. Was he, after all, some sort of cowardly slave? Never would he allow misfortune to debase him! The very thought inspires him to declaim his indignation in the style of the great classical tragedians; a line from one of the overlong dramas of the day springs to his mind:

Il n'a point dans les fers le coeur d'un esclave
[Weighed down by chains, but in his heart not a slave] [6]

The prisoner's histrionic posturing on the great stage continues: "And even if these unfortunate chains, yes, even if these chains accompany me to my grave, you will see me always the same. It has been my misfortune to be born with a steadfast soul, *a soul that has never capitulated, and never will capitulate!"* [7] Renée-Pélagie with all her little ideas and silly superstitions simply did not understand. Nothing was to be gained by conforming, by cowering before the authorities. Not only would the effort be wasted; the act would be morally wrong. And then he gives us one of the most memorable passages in his correspondence, one that, had it been authored by anyone other than the marquis de Sade, would assuredly have long since been cast in bronze and given a prominent place of honor on some public monument dedicated to individual human liberty:

> *You say that my way of thinking cannot be approved. Well, what is that to me? He is a fool who adopts a way of thinking for the sake of others! My way of thinking is the fruit of my reflections; it stems from my very being, from the way I am made. It is not in my power to change, and even if I could, I would not. This way of thinking for which you rebuke me is the only consolation I have in my life; it eases all my sufferings in prison; it makes up the whole of my pleasures. I am more attached to it than I am to life itself. The cause of my misfortunes is not my way of thinking. . . . It is that of others.* [8]

Few of history's genuine prisoners of conscience have stated the case more eloquently, and Sade's lofty imperatives seem to stand tall and unassailable in their hermetic splendor. Unfortunately, when it comes time to demonstrate, as Lely and many others have attempted to do, that Sade's was indeed a case of "philosophy in irons" (to use the marquis' own expression), [9] that it was Sade's "uncompromising defence *of ideas* that brought down on him the agonies of imprisonment," [10] the entire statement disintegrates into a vaporous absurdity. The plain truth is that Sade, unlike a fair number of authentic pre-1789 "martyrs" to freedom of thought and expression, was never locked up by the authorities of the ancien régime because of his *ideas.* He languished in prison for having committed *acts* of plain cruelty and vile *conduct* toward his fellow creatures, namely, crimes of physical violence committed during sexual assaults on hapless prostitutes. Such assaults, aggravated by death threats and the element of recidivism, could easily get an offender into similar difficulties today, even in some of the world's more tolerantly enlightened jurisdictions, incurring perhaps for the offender a not dissimilar indefinite sentence to be served in conditions affording relatively less comfort or personal security than the marquis de Sade was in a position to receive as a paying inmate of the French monarchy's most privileged prisons.

Windy bad faith, reinforced by overweening personal arrogance allied to sharp native wit and a fiery partisan style, consistently allowed the marquis to evade any personal sense of guilt for his actions, to deflect all thoughts of remorse, and to set up sham victim scenarios and factitious explanations for what he saw as his persecution. Without exception, all responsibility is always shifted away from himself. Full blame is consistently reassigned to others: it was all Sartine's fault or the Présidente's fault, and earlier still, it had presumably been the fault of Marie-Eléonore, the maternal source of all those "childhood superstitions" that had booby-trapped his life from the beginning. He had occasionally stumbled along the way, to be sure, but it was not his fault; it was the fault, rather, of all the scoundrels who had set so many traps along his path. Thus forearmed, the marquis never allowed himself to view his treatment of a Jeanne Testard or a Rose Keller as anything but a private matter of normal and legitimate self-expression, behavior that amounted to neither more nor less than the rightful cultivation of his "natural and personal" tastes.

On the other hand, an apparently total lack of what one might call sympathetic imagination seems to have prevented the marquis from feeling any symmetrical concern, empathetic or even logical, for the violated "natural and personal" tastes of his victims. What did it matter that he had done this or that to a few "whores"? So much fuss over a few "spankings"! It was, moreover, not *their* rights that had been infringed upon—were they not in the business of getting whipped, threatened, and abused? Rather, it was *his* rights that were now being violated by savagely punitive, power-usurping, upstart magistrates. He had certain tastes in sexual matters; these were *natural,* the proof being that he had them! He had chosen to indulge those tastes and in doing so, aided by the legitimate and *natural* power of his class, his purse, his gender—not to mention his superior daring and wit—he had, again quite *naturally,* coerced his *naturally* weaker victims. Now a contemptible coalition of the weak and the stupid, the slavish herd abetted by a conniving rabble of government ministers and magistrates, was trying to punish him for legitimately exercising those natural rights! They were also making demands that he change his nature, that he sacrifice his individual integrity, but they would never succeed: "These principles and these inclinations are in me to the point of fanaticism, a fanaticism that arises from the persecutions of my oppressors. The more they persist in their oppression, the more deeply my principles become rooted in my heart, and I here declare to the world: *Speak not to me of freedom if you offer it at the cost of my principles. [. . .] Yes, I proclaim it to the world: I would not change, even if the scaffold stood before me.*" [11]

Still pretending that the real issue was good philosophy and not bad conduct, Sade occasionally attempts to co-opt the Enlightenment's pre-1789 reformist agenda to advance his personal cause: "There are jurisdictions in Europe that do not dishonor people because of their *tastes,* that do not throw them into prison because of their *opinions*. It is there that I shall go to live and be happy." [12] He found it easy to overlook the "natural" fact that his status as a privileged and moneyed nobleman had allowed him to benefit time after time from special favor, from the protection of royal *lettres de cachet* and the dispensations of *lettres d'abolition,* whether in comfortably domestic exile or in one of the relatively habitable royal prisons, all of which kept him safely out of the hands of common police justice and out of such unspeakably foul and "dishonorable" jails as Bicêtre. Only well after the Revolution, in March–April 1803 and thanks to Napoléon's totalitarian regime, did his writings cause him to suffer a brief incarceration in that notorious hellhole. But even then, privilege once again was allowed to come to his aid. To avoid the shame of having a relative locked up in Bicêtre, his "respectable" and still relatively well-off family—Renée-Pélagie, two sons, and a daughter—managed to get him transferred to Charenton as a "respectable" and essentially harmless lunatic. [13] At last, "philosophy," disguised as madness, was clapped in irons!

But the big questions still remain: Who was this man, and when can we believe him? So many painfully predictable and transparently hollow protestations and personal credos are scattered throughout the magniloquent—and often magnificent—rhetoric of the marquis' correspondence that it becomes difficult to take at face value even his simplest statements of principle, belief, and intent of any kind. His many suicide threats are a case in point. Can we ever take them seriously? As Jean-Jacques Pauvert has pointed out (though I suspect with considerably more sympathy than I seem able to muster for the Divine Marquis), when Sade threatens to do himself in, when he tells Mme de Montreuil, for example, that he wishes to follow his dear mother, Marie-Eléonore, to the grave, [14] "we do not really believe him." [15] Pauvert suggests that much of our skepticism in the matter is due to Sade's "irrepressible frenzy to live." That is entirely true, and equally plain is the fact that Donatien never showed much inclination to follow Marie-Eléonore anywhere, let alone to her grave! Our main prob-

lem with such direful threats originates, however, in our constant awareness that almost the entire correspondence is cast in that same sublime
mold of fired-up hyperbole. The marquis was so much in the habit of
threatening to kill himself that these threats become, finally, nothing more
than stock items always at hand in a vast arsenal of verbal mannerisms: "If
I am not set free within four days," he writes to Renée-Pélagie from Vincennes, "it is absolutely certain that I shall smash my skull against these
walls." [16] He does not mean it, of course, but the words at least present
some variation on what he had written to the comte de la Tour after escaping from Miolans: "I prefer death to the loss of my liberty." [17] Those are
heroic words, and great patriots in the history of nations have added luster
to the sentiment by actually living up to the promise. But Sade never really means it, personally or politically, and he often wastes such solemn
rhetoric on paltry matters and trivial occasions. To his notary Fage in September 1771 regarding the transfer of funds, he writes, "If the money has
not reached me by 25 September, I shall have no other choice but to blow
out my brains." [18] Almost three decades later, to another notary, precisely
the same formula: "If you do not come to my aid immediately, I shall have
to blow out my brains." [19] Or again, to Gaufridy: "This in all probability
will be the last letter you receive from me, for if I do not receive the money
within two weeks, *I am determined to blow out my brains.*" [20] Or yet again,
regarding money, to Gaufridy: "I give you my word of honor that I immediately grabbed my pistols and had it not been for the intervention of a
friend *I would have blown out my brains!*" [21]

The plain fact is that despite an overall predictability that does little to
enhance his credentials as the "freest spirit that ever lived," we never know
when to believe him. Or is it the case, rather, that we never believe him?
That was finally Jean-Baptiste's most affectionate conclusion: "What he
says and nothing—it all amounts to the same thing!" We do not believe
him when, in a letter that he swears will be "the last that [he] will ever write
to anyone," he also swears to Mme de Montreuil that he would, a thousand
times over, prefer to remain in prison than be a free man separated from
Renée-Pélagie. We do not believe him when he claims that his main reason
for this is his need, awakened by pangs of conscience and deep remorse for
his past transgressions, to repair the injury he has done over the years to his
dear wife. "I have too much to make up for, Almighty God, yes, too much
to make up for!" [22]

We do not even believe him when, on the same subject, he writes quite
the opposite to Renée-Pélagie. In a sense, it is Renée-Pélagie who is the true
martyr of Sade's prison years. And what was her reward for all her faithful

visits to Vincennes and the Bastille, her courageous lobbying of hostile officials, her devoted moral support, the endless errands she ran all over Paris to hunt down the right book, the right jam, the right eau de Cologne, and even the most correctly proportioned and polished wooden *étuis* to serve as his dildos? Most of the time that reward was scornful derision or bullying abuse. Examples abound: "Would that you and your entire loathsome family," he wrote to her on 30 December 1780, "were placed in a sack, all together, and thrown into a deep body of water. Then let someone, soon after, bring me news of the event, and I swear to Heaven that it will be the happiest moment of my life."[23] Or again, a less than gracious request: "Let me have a response to what I ask for in this letter, if you are capable of it, so that I can say at least for once that you were good for something during my detention."[24] We cannot believe he really meant such childishly gratuitous cruelties, any more than we can believe him when he insists on another occasion that in exchange for the privilege of an additional hour of supervised visits with his wife he would gladly give up half of his fortune or even accept an increase of two years in his sentence.[25] We cannot take him seriously when, in a fit of jealous rage provoked by totally paranoid suspicions concerning Renée-Pélagie's fidelity, he urges her to safeguard her virtue for the sake of his own moral redemption: "Guard your virtue, guard it! It is what causes me to blush at my errors, it alone will make me detest them."[26] His *errors?* Are we to presume that the much vaunted, immutable, and personally sacred *principles* and *tastes* professed by this freest spirit who ever lived have now somehow become nothing more than shameful *errors?* Not at all! Confusion arises only if we momentarily allow ourselves to forget that truth, for the marquis is never more than a function of shifting circumstance and the passing moment. For this one time, in this specific instance, for a given tactical advantage, he will concede, to this particular person, that his misfortunes may have been caused by his vices, albeit vices that had to be blamed, of course, on the example of others.

He goes on to warn Renée-Pélagie that if she is unfaithful to him, he will kill himself. Well, "perhaps not kill [himself] . . . , not exactly"; there was a *remote* possibility that "love of life" might make him hesitate: "If love of life were to triumph over the courage needed to kill myself (and I think that it would not), it would only be to plunge me into the wildest dissipations that, one way or another, would bring a quick end to my days." He would simply debauch himself to death! Not the most unpleasant demise, to be sure, for a libertine bent on suicide. He insists that the very idea of any woman being unfaithful to him either in thought or deed is totally repugnant to him: "Once I suspect that a woman has been unfaithful to me, I never see her again." Of course, that solemn statement of "fact" is demonstrably false. He quite routinely, for example, played third and even fourth fiddle in la Beauvoisin's ever-changing ensemble, happily disbursing princely sums for a privilege that—even though it was much shared—he could ill afford. Also false is the claim he makes on another occasion that he has never sexually pursued married women. (As a matter of fact, he seems to have preferred them pregnant!) Nevertheless, he will insist for the moment that if Renée-Pélagie has indeed been unfaithful to him, deceived him, then he might as well be dead: "Oh mighty God! let the gates of my prison remain forever shut! Let me die in my cell rather than learn of my dishonor on leaving here. [. . .]" But if the worst happens, let the world beware! "Let me die here rather than go out into the world to debase myself, to drown myself in the most extreme excesses of the most monstrous crimes, crimes I shall delight in devising in order to forget, in order to be annihilated. Beware! There are none that will be beyond my powers of invention." [27] Cuckoldom would trigger the ultimate Sadean transmutation of conceiving into doing. Imitating in real life the monsters of his fiction, he would stop at nothing.

Clearly, such protestations cannot be interpreted as calmly meditated expressions of the marquis' innermost verities. We must take them for what they are, role-playing formulas, ready-made solos sung on cue by the melodramatist starring in his own *opéra bouffe*.

Was the marquis himself a dupe of his own rhetoric, of the wonderful talent he possessed for extravagant verbal autointoxication? Though a monster of lucidity, he probably did deceive himself unwittingly and uncontrollably at times, and on those occasions both our human and esthetic interest in him threatens to retreat to the clinical level. But for the most part, his hyperintelligent mind is in full control, entirely aware and totally focused, providing an epistolary text that constantly verges on dramatic poetry. He practices his speeches; he deftly calculates the timing, the dosages, the optimum mix of declamation, bluster, and outrage; he listens admiringly with the professional ear of the playwright, modulating the tones, orchestrating the lines; in his mind's eye he observes approvingly every angry gesture. . . . Yes, the role is well written and well played; only the ill-intentioned or the thick-witted will fail to be moved. No matter; he neither lives nor writes for them.

Early success at manipulating and controlling others had brought him the necessary confidence. Even as an adolescent he had gone a long way toward perfecting the art, using as his main subject his overfond father, cleverly positioning himself on Jean-Baptiste's side in quarrels with his less tractable mother. Things did go very sour for a time, even with his father, at which point, momentarily, he cleverly maneuvered himself closer to his mother.[28] Shortly thereafter, he was able to form a far more compatible alliance with his mother-in-law. Manipulating the Présidente in the beginning was easiest of all, especially when he co-opted her support and her own family interests in his money quarrels with Jean-Baptiste. Later, she became just a little too clever for her own good, refusing finally to be duped. But on the whole, controlling others, pulling the wool over their eyes, was mere child's play for him. Any "failures" along the way could easily be accommodated and adjusted by careful application of his revisionist skills, by his instant readiness to employ outrage as an unanswerable debating technique, and, especially, by his unlimited capacity for righteous denial and for shifting blame away from himself. Even "God" (not that he existed, of course) was no match for his talents. Writing to his notary Gaufridy on 29 September 1775, as usual on the subject of money, Sade reveals with supreme arrogance just how lucidly in control he felt he was. Were his business agents, he asks Gaufridy, really such fools as to think that he, Donatien de Sade, could be bamboozled? Did they imagine that he would meekly sit back and accept their explanation for a delay in transferring funds to him? "Truth to tell, I am quite tired of being taken for a dumb animal, tired of seeing a bunch of yokels whom I could quite easily hoodwink if I wanted to, people scarcely out of their village and their cabbage patch, who think they can put one over on me, cloud my vision and make me believe what they want. They think they can do this *to me! To someone who could bamboozle God Almighty if he set his mind to it!*"[29]

Nineteen

HIS FINEST LIE

Manipulation, mystification, and fancy footwork were the marquis' forte in the personal arena throughout most of his life, and one senses that he was justly proud of the fact. However, when it came time during the Revolution to attempt similar triumphs in the public forum, he manipulated and mystified with considerably less skill and success. It is not without reason that Paul Bourdin characterizes Sade's various expressions of revolutionary enthusiasm as his "finest lie," finest even if, as Bourdin concedes, the marquis lacks subtlety in the political arena and tends to be too obvious when he is trying to pull the wool over our eyes.[1] What does show up most clearly in Sade's "revolutionary" words as well as his actions after 1790 is again his characteristic opportunism, now transparently motivated by the need to remain in the good books of the increasingly rabid power brokers of the day.

Unquestionably, the most blatant example of such opportunism is the marquis' fulsome panegyric of Marat, the man whom Gilbert Lely labels appropriately "the most repulsive vampire of the Revolution." No other piece by Sade betrays so clearly his hollowness, his total lack of political integrity. Indeed, as an almost unconditional admirer of the Divine Marquis, Lely concedes that Sade's sycophantic eulogy of Marat is "the most disillusioning" of all his political compositions,[2] redeemable only if it were deliberate parody or satire. But, of course, it is neither. It is instead, to follow up on Bourdin's characterization, Donatien de Sade's biggest—if hardly his "finest"—revolutionary lie. The spectacle of the former *prisoner* de Sade, purportedly an opponent of capital punishment, praising as a "sublime martyr to liberty" the man who more than any other individual of the day had abetted the butchery of over twelve hundred helpless and innocent victims in the prison massacres of September 1792, who at one point called for precisely 260,000 heads to roll to ensure the "despotism of liberty"—that sorry spectacle is surely something more than merely "disillusioning." So too is Sade's toadying defense of the assassinated Marat's thirst for blood: we gag at his tremolo of praise, at the unmistakable ululations of the jackal: "[. . .] slaves accuse you of liking blood! Oh, great leader! it was theirs that you were determined to shed; you were unsparing with the blood of slaves in order to husband the blood of the people."[3] The marquis' fawning sentiments are indeed "disillusioning," and we cannot help contrasting them with those of the poet André Chénier writing at the same time on the same subject. Chénier, arrested and taken to Saint-Lazare prison on 9 March 1794,[4] overlapped Sade's stay there for two weeks before the marquis managed to have himself transferred "for health reasons" to the safe and pleasant "sanatorium" at Picpus where it was his good fortune to escape the Terror. Not so lucky was Chénier who, after four months of the harshest imprisonment, was taken from Saint-Lazare, brutally processed through the usual sham trial, and guillotined at the Vincennes barrier on 25 July 1794, two days before the fall of Robespierre. The decapitated body of eighteenth-century France's finest poet was then carted away in the dead of night to a hastily improvised cemetery, located, ironically, in a field just behind Sade's Picpus prison. There, it was stripped and thrown into a common grave that had been filled in the preceding five weeks with the bloody heads and torsos of more than thirteen hundred other victims. Picpus by then was obviously no longer the pleasantly quiet refuge, the "terrestrial paradise" that the marquis had described when he first joined the other privileged prisoners there several months before ("a fine house, beautiful gardens, select company and amiable women").[5] The stench of the rotting corpses nearby had become overpowering and, worse still, the guillotine now threatened even the prisoners within. But in the end, the marquis' luck held out.

On another plane, however, there is a much more significant Sade-Chénier encounter to meditate than this grisly conjunction of the two men's unequal destinies at Picpus. Less than a year earlier, only days after Sade proudly read out his odious piece on Marat to an assembly of *enragés*, André Chénier, not a hollow man but a courageous opponent of both the aristocratic "red-heeled brigands" and the sansculotte "brigands with pikes," a true martyr to liberty, equality, and fraternity (he would have added truth, justice, and virtue[6]), had penned from his hiding place on the rue Satory in Versailles (coincidentally near the location of one of Donatien's old *petites maisons* on the same street)[7] one of his most powerful political poems, the *Ode* to Marat's young female assassin: "To Marie-Anne-Charlotte Corday." While it is not certain that the fugitive poet specifically had Sade's panegyric in mind as he wrote the opening stanza (political hacks anxious to "lick good Marat's arse"[8] not being in short supply at the time), the shoe in this instance seems to be far too good a fit for Sade not to wear it:

> *Quoi! tandis que partout, ou sincères ou feintes,*
> *Des lâches, des pervers, les larmes et les plaintes*
> *Consacrent leur Marat parmi les immortels;*
> *Et que, prêtre orgueilleux de cette idole vile,*
> *Des fanges du Parnasse, un impudent reptile*
> *Vomit un hymne infâme au pied de ses autels;*
> *La vérité se tait! . . .*
> [Can it be? While everywhere, sincere or feigning,
> The cowardly, the depraved, weeping, groaning,
> Sanctify their Marat among the immortals;
> And, from the gutters of Parnassus, a brazen reptile,
> Prideful priest of this vile idol,
> Pukes out a hymn of infamy at his altar;
> Can it be, that truth holds its tongue? . . .][9]

Of course, the goal was to survive. Sade prudently did, and Chénier, the heroically imprudent lover of truth, did not. It was not, moreover, because the marquis, ever fond of heroic postures, lacked the necessary imagination or dramatic skill to play-act the role of the hero. Given the right circumstances, he could easily have aped even the noble eloquence of Chénier's "Fragments politiques," the last of which was probably composed in the final days of the poet's freedom:

> He is weary of sharing in the guilt of that vast multitude who, in secret, abhor as much as he does, but who, by their silence at least, endorse and encourage atrocious men and heinous acts. Life is not worth so much shame. [. . .]

Chénier goes on to speak of his determination to be among those few who refuse to give up on reason or conscience, and he states his firm resolve to be part of the group about whom it could one day be said, "In those times of violence, they dared to speak of justice; in those times of madness, they dared to scrutinize and question; in those times of the most abject hypocrisy, they did not pretend to be scoundrels in order to buy their own safety by sacrificing oppressed innocence." Finally, Chénier expresses the hope that one day he would be remembered as a true patriot whom "neither a collective madness, nor greed, nor fear, could induce to kneel before the garlanded assassins, to touch hands stained with murder, and to sit at the table where the blood of men is drunk." [10]

"Life is not worth so much shame"! It is not given to everyone to attain such heights of heroic integrity in the face of almost certain death. No goal is more understandable or more human than the goal to survive. Of course, that being said, we are all the more surprised that some of the marquis' truly unconditional admirers seem determined to detract from his extenuating humanity by insisting that all of the glaring contradictions produced by his evolving "political pragmatism" are merely apparent—indeed, that the very incoherence of what he did and wrote during the Terror reflects nothing less than integrity itself, the principled and deliberate expression of his fundamental ideology of freedom.

Sade (politically speaking, neither a democrat nor a humanitarian) probably found only the first term of the revolutionary mantra—liberty, equality, fraternity—much to his liking. In his various author's notes as well as in the dialogues of his characters, both equality and fraternity are roundly condemned as "antinatural." The democratic notion of equality is categorized as essentially nothing more than a "popular prejudice," "the fruit of weakness and of false philosophy" as the statutes of Juliette's Société des Amis du Crime stipulate. Nor can it be objected that this is mere "monster-speak"; Sade reinforces the point by attaching his own earnestly authorial note: "Only the weak will ever be found preaching this absurd system of equality; it can suit only those who, themselves unable to rise to the ranks of the strong, are at least compensated by bringing the strong down to their level; but no system is more absurd or more antinatural, and it will never take root save among the rabble who themselves will renounce it once they have had sufficient time to gild their rags and tatters." [11] Another author's note appended to the text of *Juliette* suggests, paradoxically, that Sade at the beginning of the Revolution probably derived his greatest expectations, his most positive sense of the impending upheaval, and his fondest hopes for "equality" from the thought that, at last, the old feudal nobility, his own caste, would be able to regain the power it had given up over the centuries to the ministerial despotism of a centralizing monarchy. "The equality that is prescribed by the Revolution is nothing more than the revenge of the weak on the strong," he writes in a supporting authorial footnote to Dorval's statement in *Juliette* that "it is no longer the great vassals who rob, it is they who are robbed, and the nobility, by losing its rights, has become the slave of the kings who subjugated them." [12] It was the upstart ministers and the parvenu magistrates of the ancien régime who had caused most of his own personal suffering, and when the Revolution came, the former prisoner of the Bastille was only too happy to see these enemies brutally "leveled down."

But in wanting this, Sade was not being what has come to be thought of as a "revolutionary." The astute observer Zamé in *Aline et Valcour*, a work originally composed in the Bastille, is astonished to discover during an objective fact-finding tour of prerevolutionary France how truly upside down the state of affairs was in that kingdom. His complaint is familiar: "How can it be [. . .] that the nobility of this nation consents to granting authority over itself to a body of magistrates who are no longer from the noble class?" [13] A related passage from the same novel, too blatantly feudal to harmonize with the Republic's agenda of 1795 when in a much sanitized form *Aline et Valcour* finally saw the light of day, was prudently suppressed by the printer at the author's request. Fortunately, a fragment of the repudiated section has survived, and it clearly gives the lie to all of the marquis' opportunistic "republican" protestations. In his heart of hearts, the aristocratic prisoner in the Bastille felt duty bound to die for his king if necessary, but uppermost in his mind was the conviction that his class had allowed itself to be sorely degraded. It had become a coterie of palace slaves, bowing and scraping for favor. France's nobility had to go back to promoting agriculture and living on its lands: "There, this nobility, loved, respected and useful, would at least regain the splendor, [. . .] the esteem, that its servile attendance at the Court has cost it. [. . .] I do not wish to see the nobility rebel, I do not mean it to grow too powerful [. . .], but I also do not want it to demean itself, nor do I want it to be given laws by the first parvenu commoner that the king is pleased to raise up, when it is perfectly capable of giving laws to itself."

Of course, by the time his self-censored novel appeared, France's nobility had long since been abolished, and *citoyen* Sade, play-acting the role of a bloodthirsty sansculotte who had all his life despised the nobility, reluctantly found himself obliged to suppress such dangerously aristocratic remarks, including a cherished passage in this particular note that appositely reviled his old enemy Sartine. The occasion of Sade's renewed anger was the fact that soon after coming to the throne in 1774, the new king, Louis XVI, had appointed Sartine as minister of the navy, a promotion that was not forgotten by the marquis when, more than a decade later (1785) in the original version of *Aline et Valcour,* he had haughtily deplored the former police magistrate's nomination to this powerful post as an example of the ever-diminishing role of France's true nobility in the nation's affairs:

> Who was not sickened ten years ago at the sight of every noble member of the navy from the provinces of Brittany and Provence, a class in which will be found certain gentlemen who can rival in title members of the reigning family itself . . . , who, I ask, was not sickened by the sight of these brave and noble warriors having to wait for grace and favor in the antechamber of a S[artine], this son of a Spanish bankrupt who, starting as a Paris lawyer's apprentice, inevitably rose to become lieutenant general of the Paris police because a pimp was then needed for that post, a vile and base person, and no individual could be found in the capital who was more well disposed to infamy than he?[14]

But if "leveling down" these parvenu magistrates and ministers of the crown was a necessary step in the process of restoring the old feudal nobility to its former glory, the marquis clearly had no wish, before, during, or after the Revolution, to see the masses correspondingly "leveled up." The people, ignorantly superstitious and easily led by crafty priests, can never be trusted, especially when it comes to doing away with religion. For Sade, that was the only truly essential, truly important revolutionary act. "No, no! You will never see philosophy take hold among the masses: their *thick* skulls will never be penetrated by the sacred illuminations of this goddess."[15]

Noirceuil's point in *Juliette* is made even more graphically in *La*

Philosophie dans le boudoir, where we are introduced to Augustin, Mme de Saint-Ange's phenomenally well-endowed gardener whose presence among the list of characters reminds us that the marquis did in fact appreciate a kind of "thickness" in men of the lower classes, if not in their skulls, at least in the supposed dimensions of their sexual organs ("thirteen inches long, by eight-and-one-half in circumference" in Augustin's case, as lovingly measured by Dolmancé just before he sets about reading to the assembled company his famous pamphlet "Français, encore un effort si vous voulez être républicains"). On command of his betters, Augustin executes to perfection those functions the marquis' own sturdy valets used to perform for him in real life (just as their earlier counterparts had similarly obliged Jean-Baptiste in the old days). But when it comes time to hear Dolmancé's tract propounding Sade's most heartfelt revolutionary principles, *centered*—the point cannot be overstressed—essentially on *religion,* not politics, this burly representative of the people is instructed to absent himself: "Leave us, Augustin," Mme de Saint-Ange tells her gardener; "this is not something for you; but do not go very far; we shall ring for you when you are needed again." [16]

Ideally for Sade, the *political,* as opposed to the *religious* revolution, should have come to a tidy halt when the constitutional monarchy was securely achieved. In his *Adresse d'un citoyen de Paris au Roi des Français* (June 1791), he welcomes the demise of the formerly entrenched ministerial despotism, the true source, along with fanatical priests, of all the old political evils. "It is you who will reign from now on, not your ministers," the marquis' pamphlet tells the recaptured Louis XVI on the occasion of his humiliating return to Paris after the disastrous flight to Varennes. The king had foolishly attempted to abandon his loving nation: "You will reign through the laws and in the hearts of your subjects. Oh, how much more splendid will be your authority!" [17] And a little further along in his *Adresse,* Sade makes it explicitly clear that he is not an enemy of either the monarch or the monarchy: "No, Sire, that I am not. No one in the entire world is more deeply convinced than I that France's dominion can be governed only by a monarch. But that monarch, elected by a free nation, must himself be loyally governed by laws." [18]

Not one to worry much about consistency—that hobgoblin of little minds—the marquis would later adopt a series of radically different positions in an attempt to adapt his colors to rapidly evolving events. Although it has been passionately denied, his political opportunism is more than obvious at every stage of the Revolution's unfolding, and even some of the Divine Marquis' most faithful "republican" admirers have reluctantly con-

ceded that his "apparent" monarchism did exist "in the beginning," qualifying it as "a brief and misguided phase in Sade's political evolution." [19] But
in fact there were many such "phases" in Sade's personal Revolution, each
as ephemerally "true" or as "brief and misguided" as the capricious turn of
political events that produced it.

As frequently mocked as the principles of egalitarian democracy in
Sade's various writings—and equally foreign to his basic political thinking—is the third panel of France's revolutionary triptych: fraternity, the
idealistic notion of humanity's natural benevolence and solidarity. Eugénie, the willing pupil in *La Philosophie dans le boudoir,* is sternly warned
against both pity and beneficence. She is even allowed to judge a debate on
the subject between Dolmancé and the Chevalier. Interestingly, the young
Chevalier, though a "libertine and irreligious," capable as well of "every
form of mental debauchery," nevertheless speaks of his own intimate sense
of benevolence: "My heart remains part of me" is his final response in
a complex discussion that almost escapes the simplistic reductionism of
Sade's usual dialectical excursions. [20] Not to worry, though! Dolmancé,
older and wiser, cogently points out that the heart deceives. The so-called
sentimental brotherhood of man is yet another fraudulent invention of the
weak. It is in our nature to be tigers (or sheep!), not brothers. The supreme
law of nature is *égoïsme;* we have no natural social obligations to our fellow
creatures, there is no natural solidarity or fraternity: "One of our greatest
prejudices," Noirceuil informs Juliette, "[. . .] comes from the gratuitous
supposition that there exists a kind of bond between us and other men, a
bond that is, in fact, both illusory and absurd . . . , on which we have based
this notion of fraternity, sanctified by religion." If the strong help the weak,
they are in fact doing something contrary to nature: "charity, far from being a virtue, becomes an authentic vice the moment it leads to our disturbing *the inequality demanded by nature's laws.*" [21] Sade's logic—and it
is patently his, not just Noirceuil's—is impeccable. What is puzzling, of
course, and perhaps this is another of the "ultimate" Sadean puzzles, is that
the marquis' philosophy identifies as *natural* any number of heterocliti-
cal tastes and activities (his frequent example of coprophagia reluctantly
comes to mind), no matter how "abnormal" (i.e., "statistically infrequent")
these may be, whereas the everyday phenomenon of common human em-
pathy, sympathy, or compassion is decreed to be a violation of nature's laws!

But if neither equality nor fraternity was part of the marquis' essential
Revolution, one fundamental and unwavering feature of his revolutionary
thinking—never part of the unwashed multitude's demands—was, without any doubt, the passionate desire to see religion finally wiped from the

face of the earth. Indeed, "Atheist to the point of fanaticism" may well have been the only good-faith assertion among the marquis' vast collection of otherwise hollow slogans, and we experience no difficulty in accepting that it is the real, the integral Sade and not some bombastic *poseur* who shouts out de Bressac's heartfelt pledge in *Justine:* "If atheism requires martyrs, it has only to choose, for I am ready to spill my blood." [22] In his commitment to rid France of all forms of religion, we find none of the marquis' usual equivocation, no apparent incoherence of purpose, and no lack of sustained ideological integrity. In this one respect Sade's Revolution ceases to be a lie, even if, at the same time, it relegates him to the historical fringes of what was an essentially economic and political upheaval. Robespierre, "the infamous Robespierre," [23] by instituting his Cult of the Supreme Being had set the nation on a disastrously "counter-revolutionary" course. Victory in the battle against religion was almost in sight but was now threatened by the Incorruptible's sentimental deism. France had to go the whole way! That, essentially, is the only vital message of Dolmancé's "Frenchmen, one more effort if you wish to become republicans." Europe awaited its deliverance from both the throne and the pulpit. Frenchmen had to realize that it would be impossible to free themselves and the world from the tyranny of kings without at the same time casting off the yoke of religious superstition. [24] Coopting political republicanism at any appropriate stage of the Revolution was merely part of Sade's pragmatic strategy: religion was the real enemy. All of his works preach that same doctrine: "Beyond all question, the first duty of a free government, or of a government that is in the process of regaining its liberty, must be the total destruction of religion's shackles. To banish kings without at the same time destroying religion is to cut off only one head of the hydra." [25]

While Sade's ideological anxieties (and well-grounded fears for his life) were somewhat allayed by Robespierre's death, the danger of a religious revival haunted him even after that happy turn of events: "After so many centuries of error, a ray of philosophical illumination seems to have penetrated the clouds. A nation in renewal seems ready to renounce forever these stupidities. But witness the incredible force of superstition! Here again are those same errors, ready to propagate anew." [26] To stop this retrograde process once and for all, Sade was prepared to go all the way. In *Juliette,* the comte de Belmor suggests how the great goal could be achieved; the method was violent but reliable: "All their priests must be arrested and killed in a single day; all their adherents must be dealt with in the same way and, at the same moment; every last vestige of the Catholic religion must be destroyed." [27] Lest we mistake this statement for nothing more than the hyperbolic "monster-speak" of his fictional character, the author is careful to append a formal note in defense of Belmor's "final solution": "If we compare the torrents of blood spilled by these scoundrels over the past eighteen centuries with the quantity that Belmor's method would shed, we shall see that the means he proposes is far from being as violent as he says, and it is only just. Only after these measures are carried out will there be peace among men." In an earlier authorial note, Sade had already underlined the extreme violence of his anticlerical sentiments: "Who are the most dangerous men on earth, the most vindictive and the most cruel?—*Priests.*—And yet we hesitate to eradicate totally this pestilential vermin from the face of the earth! . . . Obviously, we well deserve all our sufferings!"[28]

The vehemence of such remarks help us perhaps to find some excuse for Sade's fulsome panegyric of Marat. After all, at least a quarter of the twelve hundred helpless prisoners butchered in the September massacres were priests. Indeed, the marquis was under the impression that the total number of victims was much higher: "Ten thousand prisoners perished on September 3rd," he informed Gaufridy. "Nothing can equal the horror of the massacres committed on that day. But they were just."[29] And why, as the manuscript shows, were the words "but they were just" intercalated? More evidence of his usual prudent pragmatism in case his letter was intercepted? A heartfelt addendum inspired by warm thoughts of all those massacred priests? In the case of André Chénier, we would not have to guess.

Once again, when do we believe him?

As a longtime prisoner in the Bastille, transferred to Charenton only ten days before the château was stormed on 14 July 1789, Sade had every reason to rejoice at the fall of the ancien régime, or rather at what would have seemed from his immediate perspective the demise of ministerial tyranny, the long-awaited renewal of the nobility's governing functions and the dawning of a new age of individual freedom. It is also more or less comprehensible that in such cataclysmic times, and according to the vagaries of daily events, he would "adjust"—mechanically, even—his frequently professed "immutable" and "eternal" principles. Not keeping in step was dangerous. Suicide, "noble" or otherwise, was not in his nature. On the other hand, he does seem to have gone farther along the lines of opportunistic toadying than was absolutely necessary. For the sake of his Marat panegyric, for example, he even allowed himself an obsequiously fervent contradiction of perhaps the most fundamental tenet of his moral philosophy: "Egotism, we are told, is the primary motivation for all human behavior; [. . .] Oh, Marat! How your sublime actions place you beyond the rule of that general law!"[30]

Can we even speak meaningfully of Sade's "true" political views? Perhaps the closest he comes to objective sincerity in the expression of these is in his letters to the notary Gaufridy and to several other trusted Provençal correspondents. To the lawyer Reinaud on 22 May 1790, for example, he mentions the possibility of a trip to Provence: "[. . .] if God [a figure of speech!] and the enemies of the nobility [these he saw as *his* true enemies] allow me to live." No *enragé* he: "I assure you that I am only impartial; vexed by my considerable losses, more vexed still to see my sovereign in irons, but feeling little nostalgia, in any case, for the ancien régime; clearly, it treated me too miserably to deserve any tears of regret from me. There you have it, my profession of faith, and I give it to you without fear."[31] He notes, however, that the "democratic gallows" and the "cannibals" of the provinces, not to mention the "thirty thousand armed loiterers" in Paris, were a major worry to him, as was the danger of expressing himself too freely: "One must be prudent in one's correspondence; despotism never opened as many letters as liberty does now."[32]

To Gaufridy a year and half later the marquis revealed that, as with the political situation, his corresponding ideological position had changed somewhat. What did he *really* think of the Revolution? In his direct response to the notary's question, one he describes as "delicate," Sade delivers perhaps one of the most carefully pondered and believable personal statements to be found on any subject anywhere in his entire correspondence, proof that when circumstances warranted he could even play the card of sincerity:

> I am anti-jacobite [Jacobin]; indeed, I have a mortal hatred of them; I adore the King, but I detest the old abuses; I like many articles of the Constitution but others sicken me; *I want to see the nobility restored to its former glory,* because no good has come from its devaluation; I want the King to be head of the nation; I do not want a National Assembly, but rather, an Upper and Lower Chamber, as in England, giving the king limited powers that are counterbalanced by the participation of the nation which is necessarily divided into two orders; the third [the clergy] is useless and I want none of it. There you have my profession of faith. So, what am I? An aristocrat or a democrat? You tell me, dear lawyer, if you please, since I, for one, have not the faintest idea.[33]

But the Revolution soon began to evolve much more rapidly, as did, in lockstep, our hero's succeeding "professions of faith," all buttressed by retrospective claims to long-standing patriotic fervor. Two years after the bloody events of 10 August 1792, *citizen* Sade, now a prisoner of the Terror, swore that he had been a far-seeing sansculotte from the beginning!

Had he not been in the thick of the patriots' attack on the Tuileries, fighting shoulder to shoulder with the brave Marseillais? Did he not at the time "boil with rage" on learning that the "tyrant" Louis XVI and his ignoble spouse would not be put to death *immediately* for their crimes—yes, that very same day?[34] Of course, that particular self-serving chronicle of events, like so many others that he concocted, is totally false. His real feelings concerning the bloody events of 10 August 1792, a day that not only put an end to the monarchy but also saw his relative and patron, the *Monarchien* leader Clermont-Tonnerre brutally hacked to pieces by a street mob, can be found in a letter he wrote to Gaufridy soon after: "The tenth was a day that took everything from me, relatives, friends, family, protection and assistance; three hours ravaged everything around me."[35]

The marquis' years in the Bastille had provided him with what should have been the best of "patriotic" credentials, and on every useful occasion he would point with understandable satisfaction to this proof of right thinking and civic worthiness, much as the celebrated escapee Latude went about displaying his marvelous rope ladder, recovered along with other curious Bastille artifacts when the mob first stormed the gloomy fortress of tyranny. Now as an honored former victim of despotism, attractively self-packaged in a highly sanitized and ideologically correct version of his pre-1789 sentiments, citizen Sade at the height of the Terror informed the world—or rather the revolutionary committee that seemed to be after his head—precisely how he himself, heroically and almost single-handedly, had got the Revolution under way:

By July 1789, I had already suffered through several years of oppression in the Bastille and, quite obviously, my stay there was not of a kind to inspire in me a love of kings. I despised them before I was imprisoned there and I loathed them during all the time I remained. It was there that I witnessed the proofs of their odious treachery. As early as the middle of June, I noticed that the fortress was being stockpiled with arms and that the garrison was being reinforced; I guessed what motives lay behind these deadly preparations and was shocked by them. During my exercise periods in the courtyard, I harangued the soldiers; I asked them if it was their evil intention to fire on the people; dissatisfied with their response, I decided to give warning of their treachery; I called out from my window aperture to the rue Saint-Antoine, shouting through a metal drainpipe. A crowd gathered in the street below, they listened to me, and I repeated three times this operation. A worried Launay wrote to the minister Villedeuil . . . (I have the letter): *If you do not remove Sade from the Bastille, if you do not transfer him to the dungeons of Charenton, I cannot guarantee the security of this place to the King.*[36]

None of that, in fact, was literally true. The Bastille's governor de Launay, faced with one of the marquis' bellowing rages (they had been going on for years) and unable to place him beyond shouting distance of the rue Saint-Antoine where restless crowds had been gathering for several weeks (Louis XVI's prison reforms had several years earlier proscribed the use of the isolated ground floor *cachots*), decided that his only recourse was to transfer the disruptive prisoner—one of eight or nine inmates remaining in the ancient fortress—to Charenton. Sade had launched his shouting campaign, not out of concern for the people or in defense of liberty, equality, and fraternity but because his (entirely exceptional) exercise privileges on the tower platform (where loaded canon were now located) had been suspended and he was unwilling to accept the offered alternative of twice-daily walks in the stifling atmosphere of the prison courtyard below.[37]

Equally untrue was Sade's astonishing claim at the height of the Terror that he was not and had never been an aristocrat:

> I am accused of being a nobleman. The accusation is false. If certain toadies of the old regime, despite my objections, were pleased to append a title to my name, a title that I never possessed, it is no fault of mine. [. . .] By trade, my ancestors have for the most part always been farmers. My father was a man of letters and I followed in the same calling after serving in the military six or seven years during my youth. [. . .] I never once set foot at court, nor did I ever receive from it either grace or favor, pensions or decorations. In short, I defy anyone to produce the slightest proof that attests to my having a noble title, which I hereby swear I have never possessed.[38]

Ironically closer to the truth, though wildly exaggerating the transgressions of the "monster" of Arcueil and Marseilles, were the hostile observations of Jacques-Antoine Dulaure, later a member of the Convention, whose anonymous *Collection de la liste des ci-devant ducs, marquis, comtes, barons, etc.,* published in 1790, pointed out that the self-styled "patriot" de Sade was really just another of those depraved red-heeled aristocrats, rather like a Charolais, or a Fronsac. Dulaure also noted that unlike another of the marquis' counterparts, the notorious fifteenth-century ogre Gilles de Rais, Sade had several times been rescued by royal *lettres de cachet* and protected from common justice. Privilege alone had saved him from the scaffold! So much then for his much vaunted Bastille credentials:

> And this man who was saved from the scaffold by imprisonment, *whose chains were the fetters of favor,* has been confused in our minds, we know not how, with the unfortunate victims who were unjustly incarcerated by min-

isterial despotism. This loathsome scoundrel lives among civilized men and dares with impunity to count himself as one of the nation's citizens.[39]

We are too familiar in our own century with the agonizing moral dilemmas imposed on individual integrity by the vilest forms of political repression not to sympathize with the marquis' increasingly desperate attempts to keep, quite simply and quite literally, his head on his shoulders during those troubled times. Ultimately, the Revolution called on him to play-act a difficult role, his greatest impersonation ever, and he played it, if more and more unconvincingly with each new script, to the hilt. Faced with the need to realign his loyalties after the trauma of 10 August, he became almost overnight a new man. To Gaufridy on 30 October 1792 he wrote, "I am up to my neck, both in heart and mind, in the Revolution!"[40] Whether, as Maurice Lever has suggested, Sade ultimately owed the last-minute escape of that precious neck from the guillotine to successful lobbying in high places by his companion Constance Quesnet, as well as to a number of well placed bribes,[41] or, as Gilbert Lely has indicated, simply to a fortuitous mix-up in the bureaucracy's files,[42] is not clear. Whatever the true explanation, cheating the executioner on the very day of Robespierre's fall from power remains the stuff of great adventure fiction. And equally the stuff of great ironic literature is his candid admission to Gaufridy, once the Terror was safely behind him, that his "national detention, with the guillotine standing before his eyes," had done him "a hundred times more harm than all imaginable Bastilles ever did."[43]

Twenty

FEUDAL RIGHTS AND NATURE'S LAWS

Grandstanding rhetoric, opportunism, or the wise precautions of common prudence notwithstanding, the plain fact of the matter is that the marquis, despite his commitment to the integral destruction of religion in France, never was and never could have been committed "up to his neck," ideologically or emotionally to the *political* Revolution. Essentially a disaffected ancien régime aristocrat steeped in the traditions of the antique feudal style, Donatien de Sade was fundamentally Marie-Eléonore de Maillé de

Carmen's son, born a poor relative of the blood royal princes at the Hôtel de Condé, fiercely proud, willful, and rebellious from the beginning, his self-image nourished and legitimated by a strong sense of caste that was indelibly worked into his being by the stiff-necked precepts of a mother who was herself only too well schooled along such lines by her own mother before her.

As I have already noted, it is precisely this Hôtel de Condé connection and his childhood awareness of it that the marquis evokes most vividly when he speaks of Valcour's "birth" and "origins" in the all-important autobiographical passage of *Aline et Valcour* that he presents to readers in 1795 in the form of a belated *autocritique:* "Born and brought up in the palace of the illustrious prince to whom my mother had the honor of being related. . . ." It was here, very early on ("as soon as I was capable of reasoning"), that Valcour acquired what he calls his "ridiculous prejudice," the absurd belief that nature and fortune had joined together to lavish their gifts on him. This "prejudice," Sade's hero explains, had made him "haughty, despotic and irascible" and encouraged him to think that everything should give way to him, "that the entire universe should gratify my every whim." [1]

The apologetic tone of egalitarian objectivity adopted here should not deceive us. Although begun in 1785 in the Bastille, the manuscript of *Aline et Valcour* was carefully sanitized and prudently adjusted to harmonize with what the author himself describes as the revolutionary "agenda," [2] the political imperatives that prevailed when the book finally appeared, six years after the fall of the Bastille.

There is no doubt at all that, unlike his reformed revolutionary counterpart, the real marquis, born in 1740 into the full privileges of the ancien régime's highest nobility, continued to nourish this "ridiculous prejudice" long after leaving the Hôtel de Condé and well beyond the date of *Aline et Valcour's* original composition. That he did so is not surprising. From all sides, as far back as he could remember, had come easy confirmation of his special status. Even Marie-Eléonore's "rivals," his *secondes mamans,* had always remained a little dazzled by the prestige of the comtesse de Sade's family connections. Mme de Longeville, for example, in a letter of 1753 to her old lover, Jean-Baptiste, alludes to the incomprehensible hesitations of a certain young lady who was apparently reluctant to embark on marriage with one of Marie-Eléonore's nephews: "There is really enough there to turn the head of a young lady from the provinces! To be 'Mme de Maillé,' to be related to the princes of the blood royal and all that is most illustrious, and, at the same time, to be united with the person one loves! What more could she wish for?"[3] Thirteen-year-old Donatien—this "pretty urchin"—had no doubt listened with unquestioning acceptance to such flattering commonplaces during summer holidays spent in the care of one or other of these dear *mamans*. The same superior pedigree distinctions were noted when it came time for him to join a regiment. Sade's surviving army file still retains the special notation that the young officer candidate enjoyed the signal advantage of very distinguished birth in that he had the honor of being related to the prince de Condé "through his mother who is a Maillé-Brézé."[4] For the marquis, a sense of his military rank and of his nobility had always gone arrogantly hand in hand. He attacks, for example, the impertinence of the commandant of the prison château of Miolans who, "employing a tone that *neither my birth, nor my military rank* allows me to accept without challenge,"[5] had dared to turn down one of his special requests. Much of the original version of *Aline et Valcour* had already been written when, as late as June 1788, in an incident already noted,[6] the chevalier du Puget chided the marquis for insulting his fellow Bastille officers because of their supposedly low social origins. Sade's answer to du Puget on that occasion leaves no room for hope that his later egalitarian revisions of *Aline et Valcour* and his after-the-fact attacks on class prejudice are anything more than expedient window dressing. Nature herself has condemned these puffed-up commoners, these disgustingly filthy "toads," to their stinking mire and to the vices of their shameful origins that they can never overcome![7] And it was not only the sham nobility of recent origin, the new nobles whose great-grandfathers were likely to have been the stable boys and footmen of his own ancestors, that attracted Sade's *grand seigneur* disdain.[8] Our haughty aristocrat had only contempt as well for his own lowly "vassals," those beggars at La Coste who "deserved the rack" and who one day might have to be taught a severe lesson for having neglected to show proper deference toward their lord and master.[9]

We can only agree with Maurice Lever that "Sade before 1789 seems very much the archetypal feudal nobleman, proud of his ancestors, jealous of his blood lines and nostalgic for his past."[10] His prisoner status changed nothing—nor, fundamentally, would the Revolution. Sade in Vincennes displayed as much lordly haughtiness as he had previously exhibited outside: "I must have a servant," he complains to Renée-Pélagie. "I was born to be served and I wish to be served."[11] In fact, he saw most members of the French nobility, whether of the sword or the robe, old or new, as beneath him: "I am subject only to the King, I know no other master; I am ready to sacrifice my life and my blood for him a thousand times over if that is his will, but beneath him, I have no superior; between him, his princes, and myself, I see only inferiors and I owe nothing to my inferiors."[12] Clearly the distant origins of that imperious outburst, provoked by momentary displeasure with Renée-Pélagie's "slavish, cringing, style," are to be found more in Marie-Eléonore's blood royal affiliations than in the ancestral charters of Jean-Baptiste's rustic Provence. "See the ministers, Madame, the relatives I have at court, the princes to whom I have the honor of being related"—that is how he phrased his instructions to his devoted spouse from Vincennes in 1783.[13] Unfortunately, Renée-Pélagie herself belonged to a lesser breed, and despite his occasional self-serving protestations of heartfelt affection for her, Sade never really accepted the "vile and mercenary pact" that their marriage represented in his eyes.[14] Energized especially by his hatred of Mme de Montreuil and his bitterness toward Sartine, Sade's scorn for the *noblesse de robe,* the newly minted legal and bureaucratic aristocracy, eventually knew no bounds. He was even politically naive enough to imagine, only six years before the Revolution, that popular opinion was on his side in this, that the general public was outraged at "the villainous deceits perpetrated by the *robe* against the old nobility!"[15] Four years before the fall of the Bastille, he saw his own personal cause as part of the larger struggle to defend France's old feudal aristocracy ("Our cause here is the cause of the nobility") whose very existence was being threatened by the upstart newcomers, "these commoners decked out in ermine," "wrapped in fleurs-de-lys," who were plotting "like an arrogant, insolent and baseborn senate" to usurp the powers and privileges of the nation's legitimate aristocratic rulers.[16] Indeed, so out of touch politically was the marquis that even two years *after* the fall of the Bastille he was still calling for "the restoration of the nobility to its former glory."[17]

At his best, the marquis probably saw himself as a worthy descendant of the Great Condé, seventeenth-century France's preeminent warrior and leader of the *Fronde des princes,* the high nobility's revolt against centralizing monarchical and ministerial authority. After all, was he not also at war with the forces of centralizing authority? Though for quite different reasons, the great general had also been shut up in the royal prison of Vincennes. Interestingly, the commonplaces of historical commentary on the Great Condé's personal belligerence sound only too familiar to students of Sadean biography: *irascible, haughty, peremptory, touchy, impassioned, violent, arrogant, skeptical*—the parallel epithets are striking. The Great Condé had taken similar pride in challenging the patience of men of good will and, although he could not have matched Donatien de Sade's notorious achievements in the darker areas of the human spirit, he did have a goodly number of "impulsive" transgressions to his credit. That kind of aggressive strength was what true heroes, the essential warrior class, were made of, and in his private and intimate historical fantasies the marquis may well have flirted with the notion of an even more direct connection between himself and the princes of the blood. Was it feudal nostalgia, for example, that allowed him to countenance the hypothetical thought that his own mother, "cousin of the Great Condé," might have succumbed at some time in the distantly romantic past to the charms of the famous general's direct descendant, Monsieur le Duc, a Condé prince who had strived to emulate his legendary ancestors and who had died at Chantilly the same year that Donatien was born? The thought of his mother consorting with a noble hero had come up, we recall, in a rather unusual context and was immediately overshadowed by jealous fantasies concerning Renée-Pélagie's imagined adultery with a vile commoner, his former secretary Lefèvre. Significantly, as his mind dwelled on the thought of being cuckolded, it was first the injured sensitivities of the *grand seigneur* rather than a husband's jealousy that ignited his fantasized rage. How degrading it would have been for Renée-Pélagie to satisfy her coarse and vulgar lusts with the grubby "valet" Lefèvre, this "little peasant from my estates"![18]

But it is really to another descendant of the Grand Condé, the notorious comte de Charolais, brother of Monsieur le Duc, that our mind turns most often when we look for parallel *grand seigneur* models in the marquis de Sade's early family background. Apart from the actual contact that obviously took place at the Hôtel de Condé when the celebrated mother-hating ogre became an honorary guardian of Donatien's older playmate, the orphaned prince de Condé, Charolais and his little cousin the marquis finally came to share very similar legends as monsters of criminal debauchery. Contemporaries like the marquis d'Argenson describe Charolais as "a madman with occasional intervals of infuriated lucidity," "a raging lunatic" whose "acts of cruelty and ferociousness [. . .] have endowed him with a widespread reputation as an ogre."[19] Anecdotes illustrating Charolais' brutality are plentiful, and Sade himself in his *"Français, encore un effort si vous voulez être républicains"* tells how Charolais, "who had, for his own amusement, just killed a man," was pardoned by Louis XV with the words "I grant you your pardon, but I also grant a pardon to the one who will kill you in turn." Sade describes the reply as a "sublime remark."[20] The anecdote, familiar as such to Sade's biographers,[21] had actually been a classic in France since the time of the Regency when Barbier first noted it in a journal entry for May 1723 with an attribution to the Regent, the duc d'Orléans: "The comte de Charolois [then 23 years old] is a bizarre character. He has acquired a house at Anet for his parties. One day this month as he was returning from the hunt, he noticed a villager standing in his doorway, still wearing his night cap. With calm deliberation, the Prince announced to his companions: 'Let's see if I can pick that fellow off!' He then aimed and fired, killing the man instantly. The next day, he went to the duc d'Orléans to seek his pardon. Already apprised of the incident, the duc responded: 'Monsieur, the favor you ask is owed you because of your rank and your quality as prince of the Blood Royal; the King grants it, but he will grant the same even more readily to the person who does as much to you.'"[22] The lawyer Barbier, generally a reliable source of current gossip concerning the affairs of the great families of town and court, went on to observe that the Regent's reply on behalf of the thirteen-year-old Louis XV "was judged to be quite excellent and witty," an opinion that reflected, one assumes, the cultivated public's understandable outrage at Charolais' brutality at least as much as its appreciation of stylish repartee. Other examples of the comte's atrocities are catalogued in various underground newsletters and in police reports of the day. With time, the Charolais legend grew even worse. Once sympathetic to the notorious prince, the marquis d'Argenson was prompted in 1750 to note that during the preceding reign, under the old king, Charolais' violence would never have been tolerated.[23] Had the manuscript of *Les Journées de Florbelle* survived the auto-da-fé of Bonaparte's censorship police and the marquis' surviving son, Sade himself would certainly have added much to the evil legend of his infamous cousin whom he included in that major work along with Louis XV as one of history's more notable heroes of perverted lust. Not surprisingly, among Charolais' social entertainments recorded in the marquis' few surviving notes for the lost novel is a "woman hunt," described as taking place in an elegant country park where women were used as live archery targets.[24]

There is little doubt too that the Regent's "sublime remark" figured prominently in this lost text of *Les Journées de Florbelle,* but what seems to have been either generally overlooked or largely misinterpreted in Sade's surviving allusions to the Charolais anecdote is the specific nature of their relevance to his own *grand seigneur* politics. Indeed, Sade's admiring characterization of the Regent's (to avoid confusion, let us call it Louis XV's) remark as "sublime" has a quite different subtext from that which is generally assumed or, for that matter, was implied in Barbier's original observation. The marquis' comment has really nothing to do with punishing Charolais in the usual sense or, indeed, with punishing him at all. Nor does it correspond to the expected reactions of modern cinema patrons as they watch SS Commandant Amon Goeth in *Schindler's List* amusing himself by picking off straggling Jewish prisoners with a high-powered rifle from his balcony in the Plaszow labor camp. The marquis is not concerned in his reference to Louis XV's remark with Charolais' brutal *action* but rather with the wisdom of Louis XV's *reaction*. His admiration for Louis' measured response has nothing to do with putting this ferocious scion of the arrogant feudal nobility in his place. Sade was not interested in putting down the feudal nobility; he wanted, rather, to restore it to its former luster and ancient glory. He is, in other words, standing the conventional interpretation of the anecdote on its head, placing it in the broad context of a discussion that theoretically defends killing, murder even, when such actions by a natural elite, like pruning a tree of unhealthy or superfluous branches, are beneficial: "An individual born without the qualities needed to be useful one day to the Republic has no right to go on living"—such is his metatextual comment in "*Français, encore un effort . . . ,*" in which he opposes all initiatives to establish social institutions for the protection of the unfit, "these vile dregs of human nature."[25] And, of course, the sooner such scum are eliminated the better: "It is unjust to cut short the days of a well-formed individual but it is not unjust, I say, to prevent the birth of a being that will clearly be of no use to the world. The human species must be cleared of weeds right from the cradle."[26] The act of murder, "having regard only to the laws of nature," is not really a crime and is not necessarily harmful to society: "A republican's self-respect calls for a little ferocity; if he softens, if his energy sags, he will soon be subjugated."[27] What is war, after all, if not "the science of destruction,"[28] and the state rewards those who best succeed at it.

So far, one suspects, *Schindler's* brutal SS commandant, sport-shooting at what he sees as verminous subhumans—like Charolais taking potshots at "inconsequential" workmen repairing a distant roof (another of the comte's notable "escapades")—might flatter himself with the thought that he and the famous marquis are roughly on common ground. But Sade has, in reality, a much different "ethical" message in mind. What logic is there, he asks, behind the state's punishment of an individual guilty of doing away with his enemy for a private motive? Murder may well be a horror, but it is a horror that is "frequently necessary and never criminal." The entire universe, the great cosmic jungle, provides myriad examples of this truth. Sade admires Louis XV's reply to Charolais and calls it "a sublime remark" not because it threatened the miscreant Hôtel de Condé prince with royal punishment but precisely because it did *not*. The famous remark clearly recognized, in other words, the working realities of "nature." Capital punishment *by the state* is wrong because it is *unnaturally* interventionist. Private murder, on the other hand, is an entirely different matter and is not to be repressed by institutionalized murder. Logically, if murder is really a crime, then the state has no business committing a like crime to punish it. The real message is that magistrates are superfluous and have no legitimate role here. The resolution of conflicting claims is solely the business of the parties directly involved. The "natural" mediation of the "vendetta" provides the only answer: "We must never impose on the murderer any penalty other than what he brings upon himself through the vengeance of the family or friends of the one he has killed."[29] That, for Sade, was the true "extended" meaning of Louis XV's sublime pronouncement. It correctly set aside, for example, the small-minded and illegitimately interventionist approach of a government administration that had kept him in prison all those years. It correctly damned the Présidente and her interfering magistrate puppets. They had subjected him to long periods of unjust punishment in Vincennes and the Bastille for the trivial offense of "spanking a few bottoms," for roughing up a few prostitutes who were, after all, a kind of subhuman species anyway. They had violated his "natural" rights by attempting to correct his legitimate personal tastes, his individual talents and powers in such matters. They had punished him, as it were, for having blue eyes!

The gypsy chieftain Brigandos in *Aline et Valcour* spells out this central Sadean doctrine in full detail during the course of one of his "mediations." The wise brigand, confronted with the task of adjudicating an attempted brutal rape at pistol point of a thirteen-year-old country girl lured into the woods by a traveler, finds that the traveler's actions were basically within the rules of nature and not, properly speaking, a crime. Innocent as she was, the young virgin had to know that sooner or later "a lass must lose her dearest possession, these things cannot be kept forever."[30] Freed from her bonds, still aching from the would-be rapist's preliminary blows, the juvenile victim listens carefully to the gypsy leader's wise words and is able (with, of course, totally improbable alacrity) to grasp and embrace the essentials of Sadean ethical philosophy. Brigandos decrees that the impetuous young traveler had erred in only one small point of proper procedure; he had neglected to offer the "victim" money! The victim heartily agrees: "If he had talked to me politely, if he had even offered me a doubloon [. . .] he could have done anything he wanted with me." In the blink of an eye a complete solution to the problem is found, and the orderly Sadean universe is soon allowed to continue unfolding as intended. There are no sensitive "protocols of consent" in nature. Compensation is the key. The notion of payment is quickly accepted by the brutalized victim and, of course, *payment,* compensation for injury inflicted, *equals consent.* "Good!"

exclaims Brigandos, "[. . .] the whore is found; all that remains now is to determine the price."

It is then the offending traveler's turn to be heard. He reviews the circumstances that led up to the "crime." The sun was hot. He had encountered this appetizing little pullet along the way, and from the moment he first set eyes on her, nature spoke within him in imperious tones. It is true that he had abused her somewhat as he had initially warmed to his task, but, as everyone knows, "nature, when stirred to anger, is not always delicate." The frightened little creature had resisted and this, of course, had only increased his desire, yes, his *anger,* too. He had indeed been on the point of violating her good and proper but, as everyone would understand, he was only following the dictates of "nature."[31]

The sage Brigandos at this point loses no time in arranging everything. The girl is given the money, and an expeditious pastoral idyll is consummated within the hour to everyone's total satisfaction. Brigandos, the master of mediation, then enunciates his own version of the sublime remark made to Charolais: "The duty of a judge is not to punish; it is to make both parties happy, to the extent that this is possible. [. . .] It is all a matter of determining whether a thing is good or bad in itself and this can be judged only by the effect on the parties. [. . .] A little more good sense here, a little more tolerance there, and everything can always be settled amicably."[32] The young man had experienced "one of those imperious necessities of nature that know no restraint. [. . .] This need, *too violent to be delicate,* had to be assuaged, and to achieve this relief, any object would do."[33]

But what if this innocent little country girl had turned out to be more attached to her honor than to money? Not to worry! Brigandos would have found another commonsensical solution; he would simply have assigned one of his own women to the young rapist for a couple of hours: "We must neither hang nor break on the wheel the man who is hungry; he must simply be fed. Leave aside the rules, pay no heed to the law, respect only man and nature." We now understand that even Charolais' bit of target practice with the unlucky bourgeois in his nightcap could have been completely settled in this "win-win" fashion. Compensation to the dead man's survivors becomes the victim's consent to being murdered. Alternatively, if nature has granted the victim's brothers the necessary status, the individual means and personal determination to carry out retaliatory action, they could legitimately seek proportionate revenge. What must be avoided at all costs, however, is abstract "government" interference, the officious meddling of invariably corrupt, ermine bedecked magistrates perched on their legalistic high horses, insisting on rigorous application of the law at the same time as they solemnly proclaim to the world, "*I am not the one who judges, it is the law.*" Such arrogant, unbending severity, the marquis' spokesman insists, can only end up turning laws and lawgivers into objects of universal disgust and horror.[34]

Sade's purpose here is clear enough. However generalized his conclusions might seem, he is obviously defending his own case. The implicit self-referencing becomes more specific still when he points out that the same principle must hold even if the libertine, carried away by his passion, violently abuses or rapes, obviously seeking "a *victim* in the object that serves him rather than a companion to his pleasures."[35] "There is no need either for laws or punishments. [. . .] Let those who give and those who take do the punishing, each of the other."

It is at this point that Sade supplements the balanced wisdom of the gypsy lawgiver with his own celebrated footnote on prostitutes, summing up his long-held views on the matter and providing at the same time a key to what is perhaps his most coherent theory of politics.[36] This key authorial note also suggests how his moral solipsism, the refusal to accept any social constraints on the expression of his individual subjectivity, forms part of his reasoned defense of the inalienable privileges of the feudal nobility, constantly harassed, he complains, by an insolent "senate," again this "impertinent group of commoners, pretentiously decked out in ermine"—in short, by interventionist magistrates eager to become the vile instruments of social upstarts like the Présidente de Montreuil! Nothing could be more dangerous to the state, for example, than the uncalled-for protection these interfering ministers and magistrates insist on granting to allegedly abused whores: "Only in Paris and London are these despicable creatures protected in this way. In Rome, Venice, Naples, Warsaw and Saint Petersburg, they are asked when they appear before the relevant court whether or not they were paid. If they have not been paid, the court orders that this be done, and that is only just. If, on the other hand, they have been paid *and their only complaint is the treatment they have received,* they are threatened with imprisonment if they persist in belaboring the ears of the judges with such filth. Change professions, they are told, or if that one pleases you, endure it with its thorns."[37]

In a following note, Sade goes even farther. The author of *Les 120 journées de Sodome,* of *La Philosophie dans le boudoir,* of *Justine* and *Juliette,* who spared the public nothing of his most gruesome, stomach-churning fantasies, insists, nonetheless, that any prostitute who tattles anything to the magistrate about her clients, who reveals "dirty" details about what went on, however abusive, criminal, or extreme, even if she herself has suffered those "secret horrors that libertinage engenders," deserves to be punished with the greatest severity. She should be punished, not, he asks us to believe, because it was precisely that kind of testimony from abused women that had caused him no end of trouble with the magistrates, but rather—and here Sadean "bad faith" surely attains one of its numerous peaks—because the scandal provoked by public revelation of such lurid particulars has a potentially corrupting effect on youth! Sade's bad faith becomes all the more apparent when we take note of the fact that, by his own admission, this celebrated hero of free speech, this "freest spirit who ever lived," had participated in (or arranged for) the severe punitive beating of a Bordeaux prostitute in 1773, to "teach her a lesson," apparently, because she had "talked" to the police. Indeed, the marquis' incredibly self-righteous cataloguing of this thuggish and cowardly action has not received the attention it deserves: "A whore whipped, to teach her a lesson about talking and behaving."[38]

It is not difficult to imagine that other examples of his "corrective" brutality inflicted on abused prostitutes may have gone unrecorded. It is only *natural*, after all, that the strong should exact such legitimate retribution from the weak. In a rapidly degenerating topsy-turvy world, he had been punished by upstart magistrates who encouraged these victims to speak out and complain about being abused! Once more, he traces this iniquitous practice back to the pretentious blackguard commoner Sartine, the lieutenant général who had handled the Jeanne Testard business. It was Sartine who, after determining the gravity of the charges by means of his "*inquisitorial* absurdities" (was he not a "contemptible Spaniard," after all?), had officiously insisted that the young marquis de Sade not be let off scot-free merely because of his rank and his youth. Unlike the anecdotal Louis XV who had quite properly abstained from interfering with Charolais' target practice, "this imbecile [Sartine] fancied that he had to camouflage with a varnish of equity the dishonorable function entrusted to him, citing as an excuse for these vexations a love of morals and decency." Sartine, using the absurd argument that the law is supreme and that all are equal under the law, had, in fact, violated the natural laws and eternal verities of the Sadean universe; he had infringed on what could be termed in this instance the "natural inequality rights"—that is, the constituted elitist privileges—of a young nobleman who, moreover, had just returned from the army, where he had been performing with signal merit on behalf of his king the "natural warrior" duties of his aristocratic military caste.

In 1795, citizen Sade, master revisionist and opportunistic revolutionary par excellence, illustrates just how narrow and self-serving his innermost perspectives on the political revolution could be when, still in this key footnote on prostitutes, he translates the Sartine incident and the punishment that had been meted out to him then and on subsequent occasions by magistrates concerned with protecting whores from *his* abuse, into a prime symbolic example of the despotic evils of the ancien régime: "Unhappy Frenchmen! This is how you were once deceived, how you were mocked. . . . This is how, while you sang and danced, and chased after your ladies of pleasure, they placed shackles on your liberty, how they harassed your most basic tastes and fantasies, at the same time as they frustrated your most natural needs; [. . .] and all that under the specious pretext of excellent policing." [39]

Storming of the Bastille, 14 July 1789. (Musée Carnavalet).

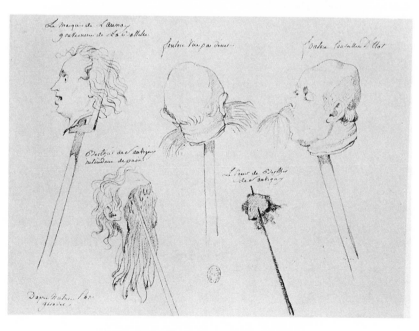

Severed head of De Launay, governor of the Bastille.
(Top left corner; quick sketch "d'après nature" by A.-L. Girodet.)

Detail from a portrait of Jean-Paul Marat (1743-1793) by J.-F. Garneray.

The September 1792 prison massacres, abetted by Marat.

Prison portrait by J.-J. Hauer
of Charlotte Corday (1768-
1793), guillotined 17 July 1793.

Detail from a Saint-Lazare
prison portrait of André
Chénier (1762-1794), by
J.-B. Suvée.

Traîtres regardez et tremblez elle ne perdra son
activité, que quand vous aurés tous perdu la vie

Contemporary sketch of the guillotine.

CONCLUSION

Our itinerary, tracing a line neither straight nor even continuous, has taken us some distance from Marie-Eléonore's matter-of-fact opening letter to Nicolas Berryer, seeking to rescue her unhappy cook from the clutches of the law. The comtesse de Sade, a poor but proud relation of the Condés, princes of the Blood Royal and one of France's most distinguished families, had interceded as a matter of course with the most powerful magistrate in the kingdom. Given the circumstances, the lieutenant général de police could not have been in the least surprised either by the tone or the tenor of her intervention. It exemplified the customary protocols of a disintegrating but still visibly present and powerful feudal society based on seigneurial "protection." Text and subtext of her letter still largely conformed to the political norms of the day. One of hers—a servant as it happens—was in trouble with the law; he had appealed for help to his "family." It was normal for the family, the dominant unit of social identity, to come to the rescue, to protect its own. Of course, appropriate measures would have to be taken by the clan to ensure that the culprit in future remained on the right path, or at the very least—and this was the most essential consideration— out of the limelight of scandal. The magistrate, the state, had no reason to intervene further in the matter.

Nearly two decades later, in 1768, the comtesse de Sade again had occasion to send a letter of rescue to one of Berryer's successors, the lieutenant général de police Sartine. Her intervention, more personal this time, although it exemplified a style of interaction with the administrative authorities that was rapidly losing ground, still largely conformed to traditional norms. A member of her family, of her "race" as she puts it, currently and quite properly detained by *lettre de cachet* in a royal prison and safely protected from dishonorable involvement with common criminal justice as well as from the impertinent meddling of upstart magistrates in the Parlement, was nevertheless being viciously slandered by foreign journalists, a new species of scoundrel who for such insolence—discussing a private family matter in the public arena—deserved to be imprisoned "for the rest of their days." There was not the faintest doubt in Marie-Eléonore's mind that such effrontery, reflecting as it did on the honor of an old noble family, had to be punished with the greatest severity. Her "clan" had no dishonorable stains on its escutcheon to apologize for, and these wretches had to be taught respect for a family that, almost by definition, could not be lacking in honor. Indeed, these nameless beggars, these miserable social vagrants who were attacking her son and who seemed to be operating beyond the pale of any recognized system of civil polity, deserved worse than life imprisonment: they deserved to be hanged! If her son has done something wrong, let him be tried honorably by his peers and in the discreetly respectful manner owed his rank. His honor, the honor of one of France's warrior class, and family honor itself, that supreme motivator and dominant social imperative of the feudal state, hung in the balance.

It was the kind of letter that, by the year 1768 and taken in isolation, already reflected the fading ethos of a bygone age. Not even the king of France had been allowed by recent developments to remain so out of touch in the rapidly evolving political climate of this century of reason and enlightenment. Weeks before, the comtesse had written in that same distressed but haughty style to the minister in charge of the king's household, demanding that her son be given what amounted to even more special treatment than he was already receiving at the royal prison of Pierre-Encize. The insistent tone of her letter was indeed such that the minister had not dared to show it to the king. Times had changed, and His Most Christian Majesty had to pay careful attention now to newly emerging political forces in the land. Faced with the growing public scandal of Arcueil, Louis XV, the minister warned, might be tempted simply to give up in exasperation and hand the marquis de Sade over to the Parlement's jurisdiction, "an option," the minister added with charged understatement, "that would not be to his advantage." In short, by 1768 it was no longer so easy, even through the use of *lettres de cachet,* for the monarchy to protect privileged transgressors from common justice and the equitable application of the law by stubbornly ambitious magistrates responding more and more to widening considerations of social governance. Ministers sensitive to traditional demands for privileged favor had to be careful about the appearance of things and the possible negative reactions of public opinion.[1]

Change was in the air. Communications seemed to be speeding up and spreading out at an uncommon pace, especially the circulation of news and gossip. The domestic press was still heavily censored, but almost every subject was now dealt with by the foreign journals, not to mention the clandestine news sheets that seemed to circulate almost unimpeded in the capital. People talked politics, read published trial briefs of various *causes célèbres*, and grumbled openly in the coffeehouses about all manner of happenings in the increasingly vibrant public sphere. The comte de Charolais, long a frequent target of the underground newsletters, was no more, and his death in 1760 had come not a moment too soon. But now there was much talk about the shocking activities of young Fronsac, the duc de Richelieu's son, and also about an even more fiendish ogre, Charolais' distant relative and successor-villain, the marquis de Sade. Even Donatien's old governess, Mme de Saint-Germain, though totally convinced of the innocence of her dear "child" in the Arcueil affair, expressed concern about what she calls "public ferocity," aroused public opinion that was on the attack and ready to lump Donatien's foolish little escapades in with the genuine horrors perpetrated by the most notorious young rakes of the court.[2] More and more, the Charolais and the Fronsacs had become embarrassing anachronisms within the weakening framework of a society based less solidly with every passing day on its former structure of rigidly constituted inequality. Understandably, the old nobility wanted to continue keeping all such embarrassing matters "in the family." The king, the ultimate father of that family, was happy to oblige whenever possible with a *lettre de cachet* that, in the interests of social stability and family reputation, tactfully imposed what were indeed fetters of favor on privileged delinquents. For the nobility in general, this system of personal justice routinely served as a parallel legal process, attuned to the needs of a class whose highest social imperative was "honor." Incarceration by a royal *lettre de cachet* was quick, efficient, discreet, and honorable. Punishment of the transgressor did form part of the process, but the primary goal of preserving a family's reputation was never lost sight of.

Years before the Revolution finally abolished the *lettre de cachet*, even well before Marie-Eléonore left the scene, fundamental changes taking place within the public sphere had begun to limit severely the effectiveness of such cozy arrangements. Marie-Eléonore, for one, seems never to have become fully aware of that fact. On the other hand, her son, essentially as retrograde and "feudal" in his political outlook as his mother, had spent far too many years caught up in the trammels of this paternalistic and arbitrary system ever to appreciate the fact that, during much of that time, he had indeed benefited from special privilege and the fetters of class favor, legacies of Marie-Eléonore's fast-disappearing world.

Other important legacies associated especially with Marie-Eléonore and her world had a hand in shaping the final destiny of her notorious son, and, in concluding this biographical essay, I must obviously attempt to assess the degree to which its extended if intermittent focus on Sade's parental origins, particularly on the mother, may or may not have helped to throw some light on the nature of the man and his works. Too many of the basic documents concerning Marie-Eléonore's life or the specific nature of her rapports over the years with her son are lacking to allow for much more than plausible speculations about what may have been her primary and most enduring formative influence on the marquis. The precise mixture of nature and nurture that contributed to the unusual makeup of Donatien de Sade will of course never be known. We do know, however, that the theme of mother hatred plays in some central, fundamental way a key role in the inherent emotional workings of both the man and the author who features it obsessively and with maniacal brutality in nearly all of his writings. On the other hand, affection for mothers presents itself very differently and in a warmly positive light in Sade's lifetime attachments to various *secondes mamans* who function as surrogates for the rejected Marie-Eléonore. He displays unquestionably genuine filial affection when he refers to the governess who "raised him" as his "*chère maman*"; the same is true for all the other substitute mothers, including even the hated Présidente in the beginning, as well as Renée-Pélagie, his strangely maternal wife. When she, too, abandons him, the perpetual orphan immediately pleads his undying anguish, but it is not long before he comes up with yet another mothering angel, Constance Quesnet, who comforts him through his twilight years and to the end.

We can, in fact, be certain of little. But even if the precise mechanisms involved remain obscure, it seems evident that most of the marquis' basic mother-centered sensitivities and obsessions somehow got started with Marie-Eléonore and that her early influence in this respect, for good or ill, was crucial. The considered verdict of an exasperated Jean-Baptiste on that point was that Marie-Eléonore's influence was unquestionably all bad: "She is a dreadful woman and her son will be like her." Given the couple's estrangement, the father's testimony has to be suspect; on the other hand, he is the only witness we can quote who had an intimate knowledge of both mother and son. Clearly, his testimony can be ignored only at the biographer's peril.

"And her son will be like her." Jean-Baptiste had made the statement in anger on a particular occasion when Marie-Eléonore was putting on an irritating show of pig-headed determination and "unreasonableness," the sort of perverse behavior he had already found so frequently exasperating in his son as he watched Donatien grow into rebellious manhood. Of course, the comte's own failed and tainted career, culminating eventually in his rejection or marginalization by the highest echelons of a courtly society that had been so dear to his heart, would also have left an indelible imprint of social isolation and loyal resentment on the son's impressionable character. Jean-Baptiste's fundamental ambitions, unlike his son's, had been those of the *noblesse présentée,* the palace groupies who hung about the antechambers of Versailles, Compiègne, and Fontainebleau, alertly trading the latest news and waiting for favors, positions, pensions, decorations, and any other special form of royal recognition. The comte had consistently striven to play on that glittering stage the role of the archetypal, urbanely companionable *honnête homme.* Outward looking, he had come up to Paris as a young man, determined to succeed in the court milieu. During a brief stay in London, he was instantly the "clubbable" good fellow who lost no time, for example, in becoming a Freemason. As a diplomat, he saw social entertainment—always offered at a level beyond his means—as his first duty, and throughout his lifetime he maintained a busy (and very gossipy) social correspondence. Year after year, he did his persistent best to advance his career by haunting the intrigue-saturated corridors and boudoirs of the court. He excelled in jovial networking at social functions, especially at intimate male dinner gatherings where he was always seen as the life and soul of the party.[3]

Jean-Baptiste ultimately failed in his own social ambitions, basically because of personal character deficiencies rather than for lack of talent or effort. He was in most respects very much a man of his milieu and his times. In total contrast, both his wife and his son seem to have shared a basic temperament that was predisposed to alienation and insularity. Neither seems to have been naturally outgoing and gregarious. Timid, yet severe and uncompromising, scorning social equivocation always, Marie-Eléonore finally left her husband for a convent retreat to distance herself from the cynical libertine and shallow wastrel that Jean-Baptiste had become. Her personal solution to the problem of domestic alienation was to cut herself off as a matter of self-preservation. Her son, though he quickly developed close convivial ties with his father and eagerly profited from his sophisticated lessons in life, being dazzled too by Jean-Baptiste's carefree success with the ladies and his easy wit as a writer, was nevertheless even more fiercely uncompromising at heart than Marie-Eléonore. Very much the loner in an era of almost obligatory sociability, an outsider in a society that mocked the socially inept and atrabilious Jean-Jacques Rousseau for taking personal offense at the celebrated line in Diderot's *Le Fils naturel* which held that good men live in society and only the ill-tempered man lives apart,[4] the young marquis never felt comfortable in the crowd. In a letter to Jean-Baptiste, his army commander the marquis de Poyanne faulted the young cornet for neglecting his social obligations to the local dignitaries and senior officers.[5] Donatien himself, describing to Jean-Baptiste his deliberate choice of an unsociable existence in the military, tried to explain the mistrust he felt concerning friends in general: "I have few friends, none at all, perhaps, for truly sincere friends do not exist." Or again: "It is the same with friends as with women: testing often reveals the merchandise to be fraudulent."[6]

Writing to the abbé about the horrors of the Jeanne Testard affair, Jean-Baptiste had included two words in his enumeration of the marquis' misdeeds that really say it all: "extreme debauchery, carried on with cold deliberation, *all alone*." That was not the healthy style of the century's celebrated upper-class rakes and revelers who liked to gather in groups of a half-dozen kindred spirits at one another's *petite maison* to enjoy the best of food and drink in robust good fellowship, razor-sharp banter, and juicy gossip, the whole enhanced by the active participation of a sufficient number of compliant and affable tarts who were joyously passed around along with the bottles. Even sobersided bourgeois philosophers like the alter ego character Moi in Diderot's *Neveu de Rameau* allowed themselves to take such pleasures in an unbridled atmosphere of camaraderie: "Sometimes, *with my friends,* I enjoy a dissolute party, even if things get a bit rowdy."[7] We cannot help recalling here the great encyclopedist's lively account of a youthfully gregarious excursion to a brothel by the famous naturalist Buffon, accompanied by *le petit Président,* the writer-magistrate Charles de Brosses—*petit* in stature, that is—indeed, "scarcely taller than a Lilliputian" but who, when came the moment of truth, suddenly revealed to the astounded professional ladies in attendance "such an astonishing, prodigious and unexpected *thing of merit* that cries of admiration arose from everyone present."[8] Such light-hearted, companionable scenes do not remind us of the marquis' darker *petites maisons* tableaux. Even his tendency to include his valet—a social inferior—as an intimate participant in his debaucheries, sometimes exchanging master-servant roles, was a sign not of sociability (and even less of populism!) but rather of murky disjunction and isolation.

But the marquis shared more than his basic antisocial traits with Marie-Eléonore. The scathing rhetoric, the angry energy he pours incessantly into his letters, reminds us frequently of Marie-Eléonore's brusque and unabashed style and not at all of Jean-Baptiste's elegantly affable epistles to his many distinguished friends (even if, as Baumez discovered, he was considerably less than affable with social inferiors). Most important of all, in addition to providing Donatien with a Hôtel de Condé background and a prince-of-the-blood playmate whom he could pummel at will, Marie-Eléonore probably encouraged in her son her own deeply ingrained sense of haughtiness and high caste. Both mother and son, albeit in very different contexts, are quick to employ the imperious register. Admittedly, our sampling in the mother's case is too limited to be conclusive, but epithets like *beggar* and *wretch* do seem to flow in anger almost as easily from Marie-Eléonore's pen as from Donatien's. The marquis' unfeeling contempt for the unfortunate and the weak undoubtedly had origins far darker and more private than his class-ridden Hôtel de Condé heritage, but that heritage probably played some part nevertheless in reinforcing the executioner-victim structure of the Sadean universe in which nature's elect constantly assert their rights of control and oppression over the frail and the vulnerable. The marquis' childhood lessons in haughtiness and high caste no doubt also contributed to his lifelong determination to seize back for his class the rights and privileges that over the centuries had been usurped by a contemptible coalition of nature's dregs. Somehow, the slaves had managed to trick the true masters. They had caged nature's tigers. Somehow, this scurvy pack of "uncouth, ermine-wrapped magistrates," these "sons of footmen,"[9] had managed to turn nature's laws upside down by making prisoners of the strong and oppressors of the weak. Sade is deadly serious when, through his spokesman Zamé, he maintains that "the legislator must not punish those who seek to achieve happiness at the expense of others." And why is this so? "Because in doing that, man is only conforming to nature's intention."[10] Victims and malefactors are naturally unequal entities; that is how things are supposed to be. Conflicts between the two groups can be resolved, but not through the artificial intervention of magistrate's law. The sage Brigandos has shown us the way of *dédommagement,* indemnification for harm done. Everyone ends up "happy," and the aggressor is never punished. Equilibrium is maintained, and perfect equity is achieved: "One receives the knocks, the other receives the bill for giving the knocks; things are even, each must be happy." Judges have no legitimate role in this exchange: any interference on their part "under the scandalous and vain pretext of *making amends to justice and law*" (how many times had the prisoner of Vincennes and the Bastille heard that pious drivel!) constituted "an atrocious harassment of the citizen."[11]

To lay the full and explicit burden of that self-serving, inverted view of the fitness of things at the feet of Marie-Eléonore would, of course, be nonsensical. The immediate origins of the marquis' negative comments on law and society are the bitter years he spent in prison, stewing in a perpetual rage as sweetly murderous thoughts of Sartine and the Présidente de Montreuil seethed in his brain. But the lion indignantly demanding the lion's share was already present in the nursery at the Hôtel de Condé where, to the proud amusement and mock horror of his mother, the ferocious little cub, sensing the presence of a lamb, was given to thumping and humiliating his passive playmate, scornfully calling the bewildered princeling a "child," ordering the gangly older boy about, and, like the true force of nature that he was, finally taking away his toys.

It seems likely, too, that early disruption of the child's close-knit relationship with his mother, possibly accompanied by a traumatic sense of abandonment and betrayal, played some part in shaping the basic contours of the Sadean universe. The victims in Sade's novels are primarily women, women as a class—virgins, whores, sisters, mothers, and wives—all subjected by the author's inflamed fantasies to every conceivable and inconceivable form of sexual abuse, cruelty, humiliation, and torture. And while it is obvious that the prisoner's need to demonize and defy the hateful Présidente was the most immediate triggering mechanism for much specific antimother violence in the novels—seamlessly transposed from parallel execration in his prison correspondence—it nevertheless remains clear that in real life the basic pattern had been set much earlier, even if (the sufferings of a Jeanne Testard notwithstanding) such early realities were never more than pale approximations of the gothic horrors the marquis eventually depicted in his fictional art. The simple fact is that the Présidente came into his life long after the marquis' perverted taste for "lubricious cruelties" had openly declared itself. He and this latest *maman* were still the best of friends when Jeanne Testard had the misfortune of meeting up with her "bad trick" at the *petite maison* near the rue Mouffetard. We recall too his boast to the terrified victim on that occasion that he had done the same or worse many times before.

Identifying and analyzing in any precise sense the arcane mechanisms that might link Sade's brutally coercive sexual behavior, his "lubricious anger," to mother-related developmental factors, is a question I leave for the most part to those specialists, both medical and literary, who claim particular expertise in the area of developmental trauma. I especially abandon to their care all debate regarding the mysterious workings of the author's "subconscious" and its supposedly determining role in the creative process. The bald fact that the element of sexual violence is present—however disproportionately—both in Sade's life and in his literature obviously invites and justifies a wide variety of investigative techniques. But even if we try to restrict our ambitions to the more classical modes of interpretation, maintaining at the same time a healthy skepticism in the face of attempts to provide precise causal explanations of an author's creative imagination, we can still venture, I think, a few tentative conclusions. Most of these, moreover, are suggested to us by Sade himself and must be taken into account even if few of his self-revelations ever escape the appearance of chronic revisionism and self-serving opportunism.

We have noted, for example, the possible "autobiographical" implications of his comments on the evils that befall the children of unhappy marriages, described as victims of "dissension between the father and the mother." [12] Sade's word "dissension" (*mésintelligence*) covers a broad range of possibilities, and it is not clear that he ever wanted or sought to be more precise in his speculations concerning the reasons that motivated Marie-Eléonore to separate from Jean-Baptiste. In Valcour's autofictional letter to Aline, the hero implies that he was effectively distanced from his family in Paris at an early age when his mother was obliged to accompany his father on diplomatic missions. Orphans, real or "psychological," sometimes feel a need for such exculpatory scenarios, and it is not clear that Sade knew Valcour's to be a basically false explanation of his own Provençal exile. Thanks to the Baumez letters, we now know that Marie-Eléonore, much to Jean-Baptiste's immense relief, spent only a few months away on "diplomatic duty" with her husband during the years that preceded Donatien's departure for Provence, and it is also clear that Donatien's father was offered no further assignments abroad after his return from captivity in late 1745. Meanwhile, difficulties such as Marie-Eléonore's increasingly chronic illness, her unending lawsuit, a troublesome confinement, and the death of her last-born child may have helped to postpone any original plans for the boy's early return. At the same time, the marriage was rapidly disintegrating, and the standard solution of an eventual retreat to the Carmelite convent had no doubt already been envisaged by Marie-Eléonore by the time Donatien finally came back to Paris in 1749 or 1750, precociously wise in the ways of the world after staying with his dissipated uncle for lengthy periods, having already been spoiled rotten by his overfond Provençal grandmother. [13] His most immediate and vital parental resource was now his tutor Amblet. His mother, the woman who had inexplicably "abandoned" him to the care of others five or six years earlier, had become a total stranger. Her convent apartment to which she moved after leaving the Hô-tel de Condé must have seemed to the passionate little meridional an in-tolerable place of austerity and religion, smothered in an atmosphere of in-validism and nauseating piety. It is no accident that he would later describe the Carmélites in *Aline et Valcour* as a "coffin" where people caught up in "dreadful scenes of sorrow" went to be buried alive.[14] The loving and com-forting mother he had known before he was shipped off to his grand-mother's was indeed gone, and in her place was this awkward intruder who somehow made him feel embarrassed and uneasy; perhaps he was troubled by precocious thoughts about how he had been conceived (was it wan-tonly?) *inside* this person, and then afterward thrust back into the world. It did not bear thinking about, a defiling business, so alien to the notions of virginal purity he had once associated with an angelic mother. Indeed, even later on as a grown man he found he could never quite overcome a certain loathing for *that* particular part of the female anatomy. Added to this was an ill-defined dislike of the woman to whom—only to be betrayed—he had once mistakenly entrusted all his love. Now she was little more than a frowning watchdog, not unlike those "Argus-eyed matrons" that become such deserving targets of abusive fathers and sons who in his fiction often ally themselves in common cause. Significantly, in later years he would look back at his parents' separation and see it as having been essentially a cruel and callous *abandonment of the father by the mother,* the father even-tually left to die, poor and alone. It was an image of Jean-Baptiste he identified with closely, and it haunted him to the end of his days.[15]

The kind of mother the mature Sade would have us believe he pre-ferred is well illustrated in comments he made to Renée-Pélagie in one of his prison letters. He had just been reading Diderot's *Père de famille,* more particularly the play's dedicatory epistle addressed to Sophie-Charlotte von Erbach, princess of Nassau-Saarbrück, described by Diderot, one of Sade's favorite authors, as an "enlightened woman and a loving mother." Diderot's summary of her philosophy of motherhood had obviously struck a responsive chord and immediately elicited the marquis' unreserved praise, helping us to deduce how he himself, long after the fact, may have per-ceived retrospectively a basic emotional void in his own childhood: "It is a masterpiece," he informed Renée-Pélagie. "It is an instruction manual for every mother, and it is truly sublime. Go over it with your son, when you can. Diderot is very recognizable throughout."[16]

The key question for us, of course, is do we recognize in this "sublime handbook for mothers" any revealing clues concerning Donatien de Sade's own innermost thoughts on a subject that would play such a central role in his own life and work?

Voltaire, defending Diderot twenty years earlier against the attacks of the *anti-encyclopédiste* Palissot, had also praised the work's dedicatory epistle as a masterpiece of eloquence and a triumph of humanity."[17] But what Sade found so exceptionally praiseworthy in it, one suspects, was its recapitulation of all the good things he found lacking in Marie-Eléonore's behavior toward him as a child. Diderot's first five paragraphs tell the essential story:

> When Heaven granted you children, this is how you spoke to yourself; this is what you said:
>
> My children belong perhaps less to me through the gift of life with which I have endowed them, than they do to the woman who was paid to suckle them. It is by taking care myself of their education that I will be able to claim back from her my rights over them. *It is education that will form the basis of their gratitude and of my authority. I shall, therefore, raise them myself.*
>
> *I shall not abandon them unreservedly, either to strangers or to subordinates.* How could a stranger take the same interest in them that I do? How can a subordinate be listened to by them as I am? If those I have appointed as monitors of my son's conduct say to themselves: "Today, he is my follower, tomorrow, he will be my master," they will over-praise any little good he does; if he behaves badly, they will reprimand him feebly, becoming in that way, his most dangerous flatterers.
>
> It is desirable that a child be raised by his superior, and for a superior my child has only me.
>
> *It is for me to inspire in him the free exercise of his reason; I do not wish his mind to be filled with terrors and superstitions,* like those that haunted men in an imbecilic and savage state of nature.[18]

The nostalgic image of the mother idealized as the warm and ever-present protecting angel, a figure that had disappeared too soon from the emotional landscape of his childhood, probably remained with Sade throughout his life,[19] but there is more than just an implied criticism of Marie-Eléonore's "abandonment" to be read into the subtext of his enthusiastic praise for Diderot's piece. In addition, the marquis would have wanted a mother who was something of a philosopher, certainly someone who would not have fostered in him the religious superstitions that, from his earliest adolescent years, he had made it his chief object to shake off. His ideal mother would not have been that migrainous and moody invalid whose stern reprimands, even if often contradicted by his "tender" papa, only nurtured—to use the words of Diderot's epistle—the growth of "a small, cruel soul" in her child. Marie-Eléonore was simply not cast in that attractive latitudinarian mold. All his life the marquis tended to blame others for his problems, and the belief that Marie-Eléonore had somehow failed him right from the start was probably a significant part of that process. Unlike Diderot's ideal mother, she had not, for example, encouraged in her son "the free exercise of his reason," "a taste for useful things," "sincerity with oneself," or even, as he saw it, the inner conviction that "virtue is everything." She had not instilled in him the lesson "that there is in man's nature two opposed principles: egotism that brings us in on ourselves, and benevolence that takes us outward," and that "if one of these two springs of action were to break, we would end up either wicked to the point of madness or generous to the point of insanity." Nor had she been there when she was needed to curb the unbridled imagination of her son "so that he would feel neither exaggerated fears or unchecked desires." But most of all, we suspect, she had failed him in precisely the same way that, fictionally amplified and distorted a thousand times in the excesses of the Sadean universe, Mme de Mistival is seen as having failed her daughter Eugénie in *La Philosophie dans le boudoir*. The mother, we recall, had talked to Eugénie about God as if he existed, she had told her that fucking was a sin, "whereas *fucking* [is] life's most delicious activity." [20]

This last point, I hasten to add, will not be found in Diderot's public dedication, nor would the great encyclopedist ever have employed Sade's language register to express a similar thought, but the marquis would nevertheless have been even more delighted with Diderot's maternal code had he known that the princess to whom it was addressed had found it necessary to obtain, before agreeing to accept the dedication, the author's voluntary suppression of two "excessively daring" paragraphs that paid special tribute to sensuality and the motivational importance of sexual pleasure in the human reproductive process. [21]

Finally, the last paragraph of Diderot's dedicatory epistle must have interested Sade most particularly, and it brings to mind one of the major constants of the Sadean novel: the punishment of the mother. Those mothers who are negligent in these enlightened duties toward their children should take note that a kind of retributive justice awaits them: "If they are granted the long life they hope for, they in turn will end up as wrinkled children, *pleading in vain for a tenderness they themselves never felt.*" [22] Marie-Eléonore, we imagine, had more than once asked for tenderness from her son, only to be rebuffed with a punishing indifference.

Robbed suddenly of maternal love at the most critical stage of his psychological development, Sade, too, would eventually exact emotional retribution, hitting back both in life and in literature, most specifically and viciously at mothers in his novels and at vulnerable women in his personal life, particularly those lower-class women whose "fallen" status provided a convenient excuse to exercise his penchant for "erotic anger" and violence against them. Confronted here with a shortage of reliable data, we must obviously be reminded again of the dangers of excessive speculation in this area, just as we must remember once more how thorny the question of trying to establish a linkage between the author and his works can be, whether those works be judged masterpieces of world literature or the most boringly repetitive and sophomorically obnoxious examples of pornographic delirium. To posit and defend that linkage is not, I hasten to add, a prelude to censoring the works or even, necessarily, to censuring them. It may well be that the Sadean novel deserves the barbs of parodic humor[23] even more than it merits inclusion in the Bibliothèque de la Pléiade, but it certainly does not deserve burning, anymore than the man himself deserves his widely touted image as a martyr to freedom of conscience.

For the biographer that must remain, I think, the central question—what to make of the man, of Sade the sadist, whose personal involvement in the criminal sexual abuse of women though refracted and magnified beyond measure in his fiction remains nevertheless recognizably traceable therein.[24] Do we simply subscribe to the marquis' own bad faith by dismissing the seriousness of those personal acts, representing them as nothing more than the legitimate expression of individual tastes and personal principles? Sade the man, his devotees insist, was not "sick." Some will concede that there may have been one or two regrettable incidents in his lifetime, but these were much exaggerated and distorted beyond recognition by mercenary "victims" like the "adventuress."[25] Rose Keller, as well as by the police, family enemies, and a gutter press whose libelous ravings launched the unfortunate marquis' evil legend and spread it to the far reaches of the civilized world. Sade was thus primarily a *victim,* punished for courageously choosing the path of personal authenticity in a hypocritically intolerant society. His most zealous defenders go even farther, maintaining that, when one gets right down to the crux of the matter, Sade was guilty of nothing more than of *having thoughts* and of expressing those thoughts in writing: "Let us leave the man in peace; let us judge him as he ought to be judged, by his writing alone!"[26]

But the man who with two pistols at the ready on a nearby table sexually coerced a terrified young woman, threatening to run her through with his sword if she did not carry out what for her were unthinkable and horrifying blasphemies—stamping on a crucifix while uttering certain specific obscenities and indulging in even more curious scatological and "sexual" uses of both crucifixes and sacramental hosts—was surely something more than a noble defender of "man's enlightened and glorious subjectivity"![27] The man who, under the false pretense of offering honest employment, picked up an indigent widow he saw begging for alms outside a church on the Place des Victoires, who later viciously assaulted her, threatening to kill her with a large hunting knife and bury her secretly in a nearby garden if she did not comply with his demands, that man was not really conducting himself like Apollinaire's "freest spirit who ever lived."[28] The man who, not in a ponderous diatribe by one of his fictional monsters but with his own voice in his personal correspondence, states his passionate conviction that the way one treats or mistreats a prostitute "is of no more consequence than the way one empties one's bowels"[29]; who also found it a matter of indifference whether an individual "venerates whores or gives them a hundred kicks in the belly";[30] the man who himself had a prostitute in Bordeaux severely beaten up to teach her to keep her mouth shut about abusive clients; who, again in real life, seems to have "succumbed," to use his own word, to the solicitations of a child prostitute in Naples, one of those "little girls, *four or five years old*" who, in exchange for money, offered their bodies to customers wishing to satisfy "their most debauched desires"[31]—that man was not, by such actions, merely exemplifying the sacred rights of the individual or cherished freedoms of thought, speech, or conscience! "Yes, I am a libertine," Sade confesses in his *grande lettre;* "I have conceived of everything that can be imagined in that genre but I have certainly not done everything I have conceived of and, assuredly, I never shall."[32] Only those readers who have managed to wade through the unending mire of permuted depravities in *Les 120 journées de Sodome* will recognize how absolutely and literally true that statement has to be and, at the same time, how statistically meaningless and fraudulent is its exculpatory restriction to his having done only *some* rather than *all* of the things he has conceived. "I have spanked a few arses, I admit," the marquis confesses on another occasion.[33] The words immediately co-opt and deflect: "spanking" does not suggest bloody excoriations inflicted with hot metal-tipped scourges; especially, it does not suggest highly impressionable victims, terrified by the sight of drawn swords, pistols, and large hunting knives used to carry out a violent and unwanted sexual assault. Sade threatened to murder some of his hired victims during these encounters, of that there can be no doubt; but let us give the marquis the benefit of the doubt and assume that these threats were made only for effect, to provoke terror and tears. Of course, that reassuring minor fact was not spelled out to the victims. In his novels, the marquis allows his monster pedagogues to be more helpful and explicit in this respect: "You must submit in silence to whatever torments I inflict on you, for I must discharge, and I can ejaculate only by torturing you and seeing your tears well up."[34] Here, Noirceuil can afford to open up and wax earnest and professorial, but demystifying these precious rituals in real life would almost certainly lessen the victim's terror and spoil all the fun! Of course, that did not change the fact that it was just a little "spanking," so what was all the fuss about, anyway? And were these women not paid for their *pains?*

Such reasoning is entirely in keeping with the bad-faith arguments of the man who, though he detested magistrates, nevertheless wanted magistrates to punish with the utmost severity any prostitute who had the temerity to complain of abusive treatment and who, in the course of bringing forward her complaints, revealed details of an abusive client's "tastes" and "peculiarities." The terms again provide an example of the marquis' cooptive use of words: his so-called transgressions are nothing more than legitimately eccentric acts of self-expression. "Nowhere is it decreed that one is a rogue because one takes one's pleasure in a *singular* fashion," he assures us. Or again: "We are no more able to adopt *in these matters* such and such a *taste* than we can become straight if born twisted. [. . .] That is my eternal philosophy and I shall never depart from it."[35] Few in this free-spirited age would seriously disagree with that "philosophy," except perhaps to inquire about possible limits, especially when the marquis, speaking through his monsters, fortifies his creed with the much rougher maxim: "Nothing that provokes an erection is villainous, and the only crime in the world is to deny oneself the pleasure."[36]

In their actions, the monsters of the Sadean novels exemplify a complete fusion, a total integration of the marquis' conceiving and doing equation. They *do* whatever can be *conceived.* For them the only crime lies in exercising restraint, in not carrying their excesses through to the ultimate limit. In real life, Sade could experiment with only the limited interplay of imagining and acting out, at times allowing himself, nevertheless, a significant degree of "overlap." But successfully limiting the "nothing is villainous that causes an erection" principle to what tiresome moralists deem to be legitimate self-expression and entirely self-regarding acts can be difficult, especially if such limitations end up spoiling the fun. The marquis himself assures us that consent of the victim spoils the fun. Rape and torture, either in word or in deed, mental or physical, are noted as effective methods for "arousing nature," and we are also told that "nature stirred to anger is not always very delicate."[37] Equality or emotional parity in the sexual act, like consent of the prey, also spoils the fun, as does any concern about *shared* enjoyment for the subordinate "partner" (the marquis would not have used that word!). Noirceuil again makes the marquis' point in earnestly professorial tones: "Try giving pleasure to the object you are using for your gratification and you will soon recognize that it is at your own expense. No passion is more selfish than lust. [. . .] When you have an erection, you must have in mind only yourself; you must always look upon the object you are using as a kind of victim, destined to suffer the rage of this passion. [. . .] The more intense the pain inflicted on the object, the more complete its humiliation, its degradation . . . , the more complete will be your pleasure."[38] Dolmancé, another of the marquis' teaching missionaries, reinforces the same message: "Every man wants to play the despot when he has an erection." To which Sade, concerned with adjusting his text to the ideological fashions of the day, adds a prudent note explaining that he (Sade-Dolmancé) is, of course, not talking about political despotism but only of "the intensely lecherous despotism imposed by the passions of the libertine."[39] The marquis' distinction is, in fact, specious and represents yet another example of his integral bad faith. His real point throughout is that despotism is illegitimate when it is imposed *on him* by the likes of Mme de Montreuil, Sartine, the ministers, and the magistrates. But when he inflicts sexual despotism on *his* weaker victims, it is merely an example of tigers being tigers, of nature's laws unfolding as they should. And in any case, victim's compensation after injury is there to resolve all residual issues.

It is indeed here that the major incoherence of the Sadean ethic becomes most apparent. Whether on a sexual or political plane, Sade seems never to have resolved in his praxis the thorny implications of his moral solipsism, his "*isolisme,*" as he calls it.[40] How, in his scheme of things, do we reconcile the natural rights of the strong with the rights of the others? How do we reconcile the value-neutral "laws of nature" that the rapist, like the tiger in the jungle, "rightfully" exemplifies, with the conflicting claims of his victim? Basically, Sade did not face this problem. He simply dismisses it as *not his problem.* Dolmancé explains: The maxim "do not unto others what you would not have done unto you" is yet another absurd invention of the weak. Yes, of course, the classic objection had occurred to him: "But the others [. . .] may attempt to avenge themselves." Sade-Dolmancé's rebuttal is devastatingly simple and very much to the point: "Fine! Only the stronger of the two will be right!"[41]

This theoretical moral disjunction is carried over to the real-life feelings of the man in ways that are sometimes astonishingly stark and complete. In one breath (let us choose a tiny example, having nothing to do with coercive sex), Sade, the privileged playboy, gambler, and libertine, living habitually far beyond his means and riddled with debt, writes to his notary, begging him to send twelve thousand livres immediately; otherwise, he solemnly (and routinely) assures his correspondent, he will blow his brains out. At the same time, possibly on the very same day, he is capable of scrawling heartlessly cynical instructions to the same notary, across the bottom of a moving and pathetic letter just received from some poor devil who complains, for the *n*th time, that he has not been paid his "pension," a mere one hundred livres of income from funds he has trustingly deposited with the marquis who, notwithstanding his legal and moral obligation, has paid nothing to his distressed annuitant for *six* years in a row! The bored, weary tones of the unfeeling *grand seigneur* are unmistakable, indeed, almost caricatural: "Here is the most boring of mortals who writes the most boring of letters. I beg you, try to get rid of the fellow for me and make him wait, without my having to hear from him again." [42]

Of course, defenders of both the man and his writings usually have little difficulty in finding grounds for general mitigation. The man suffered, after all, many long years of punishment in the prisons of an intolerant society, punishment—let us use Sade's own words—"for not having respected the arse of a whore." [43] "So much fuss over a spanking!" Such has been both the implied as well as explicit verdict handed down on the Arcueil affair by more than one of the marquis' major admirers.[44] Indeed, the remark sums up an entire school of thought and brings us back once more to the central dilemma of addressing the marquis' personal *acts* versus the marquis' *books*.

That dilemma is not easily resolved. There are in today's world too many eager book burners, activist philistines high and low, not to mention suicidal paradise-seeking zealots, for us to lower our guard even slightly in humanity's unending struggle to defend freedom of conscience, as well the individual's freedom of expression in both words and self-regarding acts. No doubt an understandable fear of losing ground in that worthy struggle has encouraged some of the marquis' most eloquent defenders to forego a certain level of objectivity in their assessments of his personal actions, allowing themselves the freedom to blur the distinctions that can legitimately be made between, on the one hand, Sade's inalienable right to think, speak, and write—short of libel—whatever he pleased and, on the other, his real-life behavioral transgressions involving nonconsensual acts of sexual terrorism. Such blurring, however, is indefensible and should be resisted. That Sade was himself a criminal sadist is a plain biographical fact that cannot simply be conjured away.

A recent archival discovery by Arlette Farge,[45] deserving more attention than it has so far received, may prove useful to those among the marquis' admirers who are still inclined to understand and forgive all in their assessments of his personal behavior. Farge's discovery is not a bombshell, not a new Jeanne Testard or Rose Keller affair come to light in the police files of the ancien régime, nor is it the long lost in-folio ledger furtively perused by Mlle de Rousset's daring spy in the offices of the ministry in 1780, wherein were detailed all the "serious, very serious charges" that caused her to fear that her friend Donatien de Sade would be required to languish in prison "for a very long time."[46] It is, in fact, nothing more than a brief and fairly routine entry in the files of *commissaire* Hugues, recording a traffic incident in the district of Les Halles that is not unlike what might be classified today as a nasty case of road rage. But filtering up through the nondescript bureaucratic jargon of the police report can still be heard authentic sounds of a busy eighteenth-century Paris thoroughfare—angry shouting, cries of indignation and shock from the bystanders, the moaning of injured animals, and, finally, dominating the uproar, the vociferous aspersions of a sword-wielding, bullying aristocrat, grievously and criminally at fault, who disdainfully goes about settling matters with his purse. It is as if, quite by accident, captivatingly autonomous fragments of long gone realities have suddenly sprung to life, confronting us with a candid snapshot of the brutish ogre caught in an act of vile cruelty that confirms all too well his evil legend.

My complete transcription and translation of the document reads as follows:

POLICE REPORT, 18 JANUARY 1766

Pierre Lefèvre
Le marquis de Sade

In the year seventeen-hundred-sixty-six, Saturday 18 January at noon, on our premises and in the presence of ourselves, Jean-François Hugues, King's Counsellor and Commissioner at the Châtelet of Paris, did appear Jean Sermaise, Corporal of the Guard at the Sergeants' Gate, who has reported to us that he was summoned to attend at the Place des Victoires regarding a dispute between a gentleman and a coachman, one of whose horses was wounded with a sword; the parties involved having accompanied him back to our premises. And did sign:

Sermaise

Then did appear before us Pierre Lefèvre, public cab driver in the employ of the person Gravelle, coach-hirer established in the rue Saint-Martin at the columbarium opposite the abbey, in whose house he resides, driver of cab Number 65, who has lodged with us a complaint that, being in the Place des Victoires, opposite the house of the notary Renaud, a cabriolet drawn by one horse did suddenly arrive, in which vehicle was a gentleman who, he later learned, was Monsieur le marquis de Sade, and who was accompanied by his servant; the appearer further did state that in order to discharge the passenger who was in his cab, he was stopped opposite the notary's door, thus blocking the cabriolet's passage. At which point the gentleman's servant dealt him three blows with a whip *and his master applied several blows with his sword to the appearer's horses, piercing one of them in the belly with such violence that his sword broke off and he, the appearer, has retrieved the broken tip from the horse's belly and has brought it and shown it to us,* this being the cause that his horse's life is in danger and why, consequently, he did summon the watch and does lodge a complaint regarding the above-cited facts, asking that official record be made of it. [. . .] And did sign:

Pierre Lefèvre

Then did appear before us Monsieur le marquis de Sade, residing in the rue Neuve du Luxembourg, and the aforesaid Gravelle, coach-hirer, who together have agreed on the sum of twenty-four livres for the bandaging of the wounded horse and indemnification for time lost while it cannot be put into service, and for time lost while the cab cannot be used for hire, by means of which they have discharged and acquitted themselves of all claims relative to the wounded horse, the aforesaid marquis de Sade promising to refrain from any actions against the aforesaid coachman whose complaint in this regard is therefore null and void. And did sign:

de Sade
Hugues
François Gravelle[47]

Apart from reminding ourselves that is was indeed a valiant *cavalry* captain who displayed such brilliant swordsmanship in his duel with a helpless horse on that bleak January morning, we should not fail to note the irony of his particular choice of terrain as a field of honor. It would be at this same Place des Victoires that Rose Keller two years later also encountered Monsieur le marquis de Sade, on the lookout for his quarry. In his eyes, the woman begging alms was simply a whore, an object to be used and abused, like the cab horses he speaks of with such strange contempt in a letter attacking several of Renée-Pélagie's relatives and associates. She will, he tells her with icy aplomb, do him the honor of noting that he despises all of those people; indeed, they are beneath contempt, "like cab horses, meant to be beaten or to serve the public at all hours of the day or night." [48] *Meant to be beaten*—yes, and if they block his way, even pierced with such violence in the belly that the tip of the sword breaks off inside. Nature's rages, as the marquis' monsters frequently explain, dictate just such indelicacies. But then, of course, all can be put right again by the *grand seigneur*'s gesture of *indemnification,* twenty-four livres, a *louis d'or,* pretty much the going rate for "special kindnesses"—the cost of the scourges included—in a good Paris brothel of the day.

Of course, some (those who cannot find it in themselves to be sentimental about either horses or whores) may still be tempted to ask, "Why so much fuss over a punctured horse?" And, like the marquis to any bruised and complaining prostitute, they will doubtless also advise the horse to change professions or endure its calling along with the thorns.

Coincidentally, the marquis' prowess at the Place des Victoires also brings us back once more to Sade's Hôtel de Condé heritage and an almost parallel incident in which his distant cousin the comte de Charolais had managed to add a similar degree of luster to his own reputation earlier on in the century. Here, too, a young *grand seigneur*'s road rage was the occasion of a public disturbance. In a journal entry for January 1722, the lawyer Barbier describes how this ferocious prince of the blood, incensed at seeing his carriage blocked by traffic near the Palais-Royal, ordered his servants to take retaliatory action: "the prince's servants got down and set about cudgeling the duc de Luxembourg's coachman and horses." No indemnification seems to have been offered, however. Presumably, the marquis de Sade's later compensatory gesture, not to mention his obvious willingness to do his own puncturing, may be taken as a sign that the century was progressing socially along more egalitarian lines! Charolais' only response to the cries of indignation provoked by his violent actions was the lordly: "Do you not recognize my livery?" [49]

It is highly probable that Donatien de Sade was familiar with that story. Perhaps thoughts of Charolais' imperious performance in a street near the Palais-Royal even crossed his mind momentarily as he proceeded that day to go the legendary ogre one better on the Place des Victoires. A time would come when the revolutionary Dulaure and other publicists would tar him with the same brush, and we wonder whether the marquis himself ever came close to pushing the Charolais parallel farther still, even to the point of committing the ultimate crime that had earned Charolais the Regent's pardon along with the celebrated "sublime remark" that Sade later deemed to be the key to any sensible system of jurisprudence.

Was the marquis, in fact, capable of bridging the gap between conceiving and doing to the extent of committing murder? We have seen him more than once, weapon in hand, threatening to kill his panic-stricken victims and even explaining to one of them how he intended to dispose of her body secretly in a nearby garden. Increasing the sufferer's terror in that way enhanced his sexual pleasure. Whipping, Juliette informs us, is really the libertine's substitute for something much more ferocious and satisfying; when he dares, he does more." One rather doubts that Sade, enterprising though he was, ever *dared* to go farther, even if in the heat of lubricious rage he obviously considered the possibility. His "*Grande lettre*" to Renée-Pélagie specifically sets our mind at ease on the point: "I am a libertine but I am neither *a criminal* nor *a murderer*." [50] We are reassured, but we also know that he allowed himself to get carried away at times and, more important, that he had his own definitions of what constituted both crime and murder. In any case, for Sade, the *crime* of murder, strictly speaking, did not exist. Cornaro in *Juliette* provides a general clarification on the point: "Primitive man has only two needs: fucking and eating; both come from nature. *Nothing man does to satisfy either of those needs can be criminal*." [51] Along much the same lines, Dolmancé's little homily on "cruelty in lubricious pleasures" notes that Charolais, "Condé's uncle," did commit "murders of debauchery." However, no punishment by intrusive laws and magistrates was called for. Such cruelties are *natural:* "Cruelty is simply the energy of a man not yet corrupted by civilization. [. . .] Strike down your laws, your punishments, your customs, and the dangerous effects of cruelty will cease. [. . .] If it is applied to the strong, the strong will repel it; and if it is applied to the weak, thus injuring only those creatures who by nature's laws must yield to the strong, then no harm whatsoever results." [52] It was all so simple, so logical; a mere child could grasp it.

It is, of course, certain that the child born to Marie-Eléonore at the Hôtel de Condé never received such simple, incontrovertibly logical lessons from either of his parents. If Marie-Eléonore did leave any kind of a legacy in the matter, it was transmitted indirectly and without intention. The marquis' strength and energy of purpose focused to the point of intransigence, his willfulness and independence indistinguishable from obstinacy, his class arrogance, and, by way of reaction to his early maternal "betrayal," his "lubricious rage," his libertine hatred of women—those were some of the elements that may have formed part of the son's incidental inheritance from his mother, a legacy that may have helped to lay the foundations on which was eventually constructed not only the quintessentially dreary Sadean universe of executioners and victims but also its pale real-life equivalent of battered whores and punctured cab horses. The linkages we are tempted to perceive between young Donatien's supposed mother-centered developmental trauma and the demonstrably "heteroclitic" realities of his later life, between that life and his literature, are necessarily tenuous and speculative. We would like to know a great deal more about what went on between Marie-Eléonore and her son, especially after he returned from his childhood exile in Provence. More of her correspondence may one day come to light to help to clear up some of these mysteries. But even then, what may well have been the mother's decisive formative influence on her son's life and works would still be difficult to detect and even harder to prove. The wily marquis provides few direct clues that help us to connect Marie-Eléonore in any way to his existence, and it is likely that if he had ever been called upon to comment explicitly on such a question, he would have denied his mother any determining influence whatsoever, just as he insists on denying mothers in general any active or consequential role in the biological production of their child, all part of his need to revile and impugn maternity by reducing it to self-interest and brutish lubricity. The real key to explaining the man, the essential mystery of his overriding hatred for the maternal, as well as his sexual rage against women in general, will probably remain hidden forever. Important clues no doubt lurk in the aversion many of his characters feel with respect to the female sexual organ, variously qualified as an "odious lair," a "stinking" or "ugly" part. The same holds true for such emblems of motherhood as women's breasts: "I can never look upon them without flying into a rage; seeing them provokes in me a kind of disgust, a certain revulsion." So speaks the monster Curval at Silling Castle where "Present yourselves only seldom from the front" was one of the cardinal rules all of the women in attendance were required to obey. We are not, moreover, dealing here only with Sadean "monster-speak": "Ass-fuck, my dear ladies" is the author's own paratextual exhortation to his female readers in a note that enthusiastically recommends "antiphysical sensual enjoyment."[53]

And, of course, there is also the father's all-important legacy. Here, in contrast, we sense that the marquis chooses almost integral transparency when it comes to acknowledging his own awareness of it. Unlike the mother, the father is assigned the role of primary biological creator in the Sadean universe, and Donatien seems never to have been reluctant to acknowledge his major debt to the man he came to know familiarly only around the age of nine or ten. In Jean-Baptiste, the sensitive and already sensual adolescent immediately found a companion, as well as a conniving ally against the estranged mother. Especially, he found in Jean-Baptiste a model and mentor, woefully lacking in personal integrity at times but ever eager to oversee his son's passage to manhood and anxious to shape the boy's precocious tastes in literature and libertinism, areas in which the father's own eclectic triumphs, though substantial, fell far short of the "singularities" the marquis would eventually achieve in each.

Jean-Baptiste's almost excessively visible direct influence on his adolescent son took hold well after Marie-Eléonore's hidden legacy had achieved its defining impact, but it was nonetheless deep and enduring. It was also openly avowed by the marquis with a simplicity and candor that he rarely allowed himself in any of his other personal musings. Too often we find ourselves questioning the sincerity of his various "professions of faith," of his aggressively formal statements of conviction regarding himself or his principles. It is rare that we do not grow uneasy when he takes us into his confidence in this way. The hollowness of his protestations is so frequently betrayed by their studied hyperbole and contrivance; the words often seem copied from the script of a swollen melodrama. But when Donatien speaks directly, as he frequently does, of his love for Jean-Baptiste, of the deep remorse (however short-lived) he feels at having provoked his father's displeasure or disapproval, we believe him. When he tells us repeatedly that none of his misfortunes would have occurred had his father been still alive, we know that he is deluding himself, but we also know that in this regard he probably means every word. We believe him when he speaks of constantly mourning his father's death, even years after that death occurred. Somehow we sense that despite his old quarrels and differences with Jean-Baptiste, Donatien looking back on their relationship—perhaps even at their shared failures—felt an attachment to this man that was closer and more companionable than simple filial love.

Maurice Lever's recent publication of the first volume of the *Papiers de famille* is justly subtitled *Le Règne du père* (*The Reign of the Father*), and his earlier biography has revealed, really for the first time, the full extent of what Lever has called the "intellectual symbiosis," the "affective union" of father and son that played a decisive role "in the young man's imagination and sensibility." [54] We are not in the least surprised, then, that the official inventory drawn up in 1814 at Charenton after Sade's death revealed, among other articles in the late prisoner's possession, a large portrait of his father—in fact, the only large portrait found in the room. For some odd reason (I shall not dwell on the irony), it was also the only picture not in a frame. Listed too are four smaller portraits that the marquis had kept by him until the end. One was a likeness of Louis-Marie, his elder son, his favorite, whose budding literary career was cut short by an enemy ambush in 1809 as he was rejoining his regiment in Italy. Another was a portrait of

Mlle de Charolais, an ancestral cousin, sister of the notorious ogre and one-time mistress of the duc de Richelieu, of the young Louis XV and, of course, of Jean-Baptiste, comte de Sade. A third was of Mlle de Launay, Renée-Pélagie's sister, the canoness who may well have been Donatien's greatest passion. The identity of the person portrayed in the last small portrait will be easily guessed: it was a likeness of his mother, Marie-Eléonore de Maillé de Carman, comtesse de Sade, whose presence in this most private and personal of galleries, even in miniature, can only reinforce our belief that, for good or ill, and despite many appearances to the contrary, she never ceased to be a pervasive force in the deepest and most secret recesses that honeycombed the darkness of the marquis' mind.

CHRONOLOGY

1702   Birth at Mazan, near Avignon, of the marquis' father, Jean-Baptiste-François, comte de Sade (1702–1767), scion of an old Provençal family that claimed kinship with the legendary Laura, the medieval beauty celebrated in Petrarch's verse.

1705   Birth of Jacques-François-Paul-Aldonse de Sade (1705–1777), uncle of the marquis and future abbé.

1712   Birth of Donatien's mother, Marie-Eléonore de Maillé de Carman (1712–1777), related to the Condé branch of the reigning Bourbon family.

1715   Death of Louis XIV; Philippe, duc d'Orléans, becomes regent.

1723   On death of the Regent, Louis-Henri, prince de Condé, duc de Bourbon ("Monsieur le Duc") becomes principal minister.

1724   9 September, Jean-Baptiste arrested by sodomy patrol in the Tuileries gardens.

1726   Cardinal Fleury replaces Monsieur le Duc as prime minister.

1733   13 November, marriage of Jean-Baptiste and Marie-Eléonore in the presence of Monsieur le Duc and his young wife, née Caroline-Charlotte of Hesse-Rheinfeld. The couple take up residence in the Condé palace in Paris, one of the finest of the capital. Marie-Eléonore is appointed Caroline-Charlotte's lady-in-waiting. Sexual liaison between Jean-Baptiste and Caroline-Charlotte begins soon after the wedding.

War of the Polish Succession (1733–1738).

1737   Birth of daughter Caroline-Laure; the child dies two years later.

1739   Jean-Baptiste purchases for the sum of 135,000 livres the honorary office of lieutenant général for the provinces of Bresse, Bugey, Valromey, and Gex.

1740   27 January, death of Monsieur le Duc who leaves a four-year-old son, Louis-Joseph de Bourbon. Monsieur le Duc's notorious brother, the comte de Charolais, is appointed guardian of the boy who later becomes Donatien's playmate.

         War of the Austrian Succession begins.

         2 June, birth of Donatien-Alphonse-François, marquis de Sade (1740–1814), at the Condé palace in Paris.

1741   January, Jean-Baptiste is appointed by his patron the foreign minister Amelot as plenipotentiary to the court of Clement-Augustus, elector of Cologne. He departs for Bonn, leaving wife Marie-Eléonore and son Donatien in Paris.

         14 June, death of Caroline-Charlotte, Monsieur le Duc's young widow.

         Early autumn, Marie-Eléonore joins her husband in Bonn. She returns to the Hôtel de Condé in Paris the following summer.

         2 December, birth of Renée-Pélagie Cordier de Montreuil (1741–1810), Sade's future wife.

1742   August, Donatien, aged two years and two months, physically vanquishes his nearly six-year-old cousin the prince de Condé. The marquis' first recorded diatribe.

1743   29 January, death of Cardinal Fleury.

         31 December, Jean-Baptiste takes unauthorized leave of his post.

1744   April, Amelot dismissed as foreign minister.

         8 August, Louis XV falls gravely ill at Metz; his mistress, the duchesse de Châteauroux (convent friend of Marie-Eléonore), is sent away.

         16 August, four-year-old Donatien is in Avignon, being cared for by his paternal grandmother. Lives at times with his uncle, the licentious abbé de Sade, either at the château de Saumane near Avignon or in the abbatial mansion at Ebreuil near Vichy. Mme de Saint-Germain, an occasional resident of the area, serves as a sometime governess and becomes one of the first of several "substitute mothers" in the marquis' life. (N.B. Almost no information has so far come to light regarding the length of Sade's childhood stay in Provence; on little evidence, it is usually described as lasting from 1744 to 1750.)

         19 November, the marquis d'Argenson is appointed foreign minister.

         8 December, sudden death of the duchesse de Châteauroux.

1745   1 February, following the death of the Emperor Charles VII (20 January), Jean-Baptiste is sent back to Bonn on an inconsequential decoy mission; he is arrested by Austrian troops on 10 February, just short of his destination. Held prisoner in the citadel of Antwerp, he is not released until 24 November.

1746   13 August, birth of Marie-Eléonore's last child, a daughter, Marie-Françoise, who survives only five days; the mother continues to suffer from chronic illness.

         The comte and comtesse de Sade purchase Glatigny, an attractive country residence near Versailles.

1749   January, Jean-Baptiste hires the abbé Jacques-François Amblet to serve as Donatien's tutor; he accompanies the young marquis to Paris, in either 1749 or 1750.

1750   Donatien begins his studies at the Jesuit college of Louis-le-Grand.

1752   Probable year of Marie-Eléonore's de facto separation from Jean-Baptiste. She moves to an apartment in the Carmelite convent on the rue d'Enfer in the Faubourg Saint-Jacques.

1753   September, Jean-Baptiste oversees thirteen-year-old Donatien's social entertainments and presents him with his first little "hideaway" house.

1754   24 May, Donatien is admitted to the elite cavalry training school, les Chevau-légers.

1755   14 December, the marquis assumes the rank of unstipended sublieutenant in the Régiment du Roi.

1756   Beginning of the Seven Years' War.

1757   14 January, gains the rank of *cornette* in the Carabiniers regiment.

         Inspector Louis Marais succeeds Jean-Baptiste Meusnier as head of the Paris vice squad.

1758   23 June, battle of Krefelt; heavy losses suffered by the Carabiniers.

1759   21 April, Sade attains rank of captain in the Bourgogne cavalry regiment; his reputation for unbridled dissolute behaviour is noted.

         21 November, Antoine-Raymond-Jean-Gualbert-Gabriel de Sartine (1729–1801) appointed lieutenant général de police.

1761   1 April, Marie-Eléonore is unable to raise sufficient funds to satisfy her wish to purchase a senior officer commission for her son.

1763   10 February, Treaty of Paris signed; end of the Seven Years' War.

         16 March, Donatien is demobilized.

         April, a passionate affair (and shared venereal infection) with Mlle de Lauris in Avignon.

         17 May, reluctant marriage to Renée-Pélagie de Montreuil, twenty-one-year-old daughter of Claude-René Cordier de Launay de Montreuil,

honorary president of the Cour des Aides (Customs and Excise), and his wife, "la Présidente," Marie-Madeleine Masson de Plissay. The young couple reside with Renée-Pélagie's parents on the rue Neuve-du-Luxembourg (today's rue Cambon).

June, shortly after the wedding, the marquis resumes his libertine pursuits in a newly rented *petite maison* near the rue Mouffetard.

18 October, the Jeanne Testard episode.

29 October, Sade incarcerated by order of a *lettre de cachet* in the château of Vincennes, for "extreme debauchery" and "horrifying impiety."

13 November, a second *lettre de cachet* issued, ordering the marquis' release from Vincennes and discreet exile to the château d'Echauffour, the Montreuils' country residence in Normandy. He is escorted there by Inspector Marais. The entire affair is successfully hushed up.

1764   15 April, Donatien allowed to return to Paris.

Public liaison with the actress Mlle Colet.

Inspector Marais warns the proprietress of a bawdyhouse that the marquis poses a serious physical danger to unprotected prostitutes.

26 June, Donatien goes to Dijon to be received by the Parlement of Bourgogne as lieutenant général of Bresse, Bugey, Valromey, and Gex.

The abbé de Sade begins publication of his *Mémoires pour la vie de François Pétrarque*. Third and final volume appears in 1767.

1765   Sade spends the summer in Provence with la Beauvoisin, high-style tart and Opéra *danseuse*. His debts continue to mount rapidly.

1766   Adds a small house in Arcueil to his already well-stocked inventory of secluded apartments and *petites maisons*. Frequent police reports of his violent and disorderly conduct in the vicinity.

1767   24 January, death of Sade's father, Jean-Baptiste.

27 August, Renée-Pélagie gives birth to a son, Louis-Marie. The prince de Condé (Donatien's former playmate) and the princess de Conti act as godparents.

1768   3 April (Easter Sunday), incident with Rose Keller triggers the Arcueil affair. Intense public scandal spreads even beyond the borders of France. A series of *lettres de cachet* ordering the marquis' detention, initially at the château de Saumur, and subsequently at the château de Pierre-Encize near Lyons, rescue him from the jurisdiction of the common criminal justice system. Liberated 16 November, again by a privileged royal order, he is exiled to his Provençal residence of La Coste.

1769   2 April, granted permission to return to Paris for medical treatment of a fistula.

27 June, birth of second son, Donatien-Claude-Armand; the marquis' mother and Renée-Pélagie's father act as godparents.

25 July and 11 August, Marie-Eléonore's efforts to raise much-needed funds by selling her diamonds to Louis XV are politely rebuffed.

September–October, the marquis visits Holland; composes a short travelogue in letter form (*Voyage de Hollande*). Pays for his travel expenses by selling the manuscript of one of his earliest pornographic works to an underground publisher. Not long after, probably in Lyons or Bordeaux, he sells another "well-peppered" work for an even more substantial sum.

1770   Socially marginalized by scandal, Donatien discovers he is unwelcome at the royal court. More serious still, his attempts to rejoin his regiment are rebuffed; in retaliation, he may have provoked (or threatened to provoke) a duel, thereby necessitating a quick getaway to London to escape prosecution.

1771   13 March, the marquis is authorized to purchase a *mestre de camp* commission (equivalent to colonel) in a cavalry regiment; two months later, in desperate need of funds, he sells it.

17 April, birth of daughter Madeleine-Laure (1771–1844).

Beginning of September, Sade is released from For l'Evêque prison after a two-month incarceration for debt.

Leaves for La Coste with Renée-Pélagie. They are soon joined there by Renée-Pélagie's nineteen-year-old sister, the canoness Anne-Prospère de Launay (1751–1779), who is promptly seduced by her brother-in-law.

1772   27 June, beginning of the Marseilles affair; Sade implicated along with his valet Latour in a major scandal involving five prostitutes; both master and servant are charged with sodomy and poisoning (Spanish fly overdose); the fugitives, accompanied for a time by the apparently still besotted canoness, escape to Italy.

12 September, after being sentenced to death in absentia, the marquis and his valet are executed and burned in effigy at Aix-en-Provence.

8 December, Sade is arrested in the duchy of Savoy at the request of French authorities (urged on by his mother-in-law); he is incarcerated in the citadel of Miolans near Chambéry.

1773   30 April, escapes from the fort of Miolans; travels incognito to Bordeaux, perhaps also to Spain. By autumn he is back at La Coste but lying low.

1774   6 January, thanks to advance warning, the marquis escapes a police raid on La Coste (instigated and heavily subsidized by his mother-in-law); papers compromising future prospects of his sister-in-law the canoness are recovered. The fugitive again takes refuge in Italy.

10 May, death of Louis XV; Sade's outstanding *lettre de cachet* is renewed by the new king.

September, Sade returns to France; is joined in Lyons by Renée-Pélagie who, abetted by the "chambermaid" Nanon, collaborates in the hiring of at least six new servants, including a "boy secretary" and five juvenile girls. Housed at La Coste for the winter, all probably fall victim to the marquis' abuse.

1775   17 July, escaping potential charges of abduction and seducement resulting from the ongoing "little girls' affair," Sade again crosses into Italy. To silence Nanon, Renée-Pélagie has her imprisoned on false charges of theft.

1776   After a year's absence, Sade returns to La Coste; begins work on his *Voyage d'Italie.*

November, Catherine Treillet, twenty-two-year-old daughter of a weaver, is hired in Montpellier.

1777   14 January, death in Paris of Sade's mother, Marie-Eléonore.

17 January, father of Catherine Treillet (now called Justine), enraged by lurid reports concerning his daughter's employer, turns up at La Coste and demands her immediate return. The marquis (imperiously, as usual) rejects the father's demand and narrowly escapes being shot dead.

29 January, Sade leaves for Paris, accompanied by Renée-Pélagie (and "Justine"). Arrives in the capital 8 February. Despite news of mother's death, loses no time in launching a sexual expedition on the town with a like-minded companion.

13 February, arrested by Inspector Marais and taken to the château de Vincennes.

April, compromising paraphernalia and accessories discovered in a secret room at La Coste; Mme de Montreuil (3 June) orders the lawyer Gaufridy to destroy all of the evidence in total secrecy.

31 December, death of the abbé de Sade.

1778   14 June, escorted by Inspector Marais, leaves prison of Vincennes for Aix where he is held in custody until (thanks to Mme de Montreuil's skillful lawyers and the suborning of witnesses) he is cleared (14 July) of the 1772 sodomy and poisoning charges. The *lettre de cachet* requiring his detention in Vincennes remains in force.

15 July, departure from Aix, again escorted by Inspector Marais. The following day, on reaching Valence, the marquis escapes custody. Within forty-eight hours he successfully makes his way back to La Coste.

26 August, in an early-morning raid, the fugitive is brutally arrested at La Coste by Marais.

7 September, Sade is once again locked up in the donjon of Vincennes. Twelve years of uninterrupted confinement will pass, in three different prisons, before he is released.

8 November, arrival in Paris of Mlle de Rousset, an old friend from La Coste. Fruitless efforts by Renée-Pélagie to have her husband freed.

1779   13 May, death of the canoness Anne-Prospère from smallpox; the marquis is not informed.

1780   October, Mlle de Rousset employs an intrepid spy to determine what the police really know of Sade's activities. The file is dense and damning; a lengthy period of incarceration seems inevitable. Contrary to the marquis' passionately unshakable convictions, Mme de Montreuil appears to be not significantly or directly implicated in his continued imprisonment.

1781   22 April, completes his comedy *L'Inconstant;* others plays (e.g., *le Prévaricateur, La Folle épreuve, Jeanne Laisné*) follow in succeeding years. Theater, his first love, will remain a constant preoccupation.

13 July, the prisoner receives Renée-Pélagie's first authorized visit. Violent explosions of contempt and jealousy will be her frequent reward.

1782   12 July, completes the *Dialogue entre un prêtre et un moribond.*

1784   25 January, death at age forty of Mlle de Rousset at La Coste.

Vincennes prison is closed; as one of four remaining inmates, Sade is transferred 29 February to the Bastille.

1785   Completes final draft of *Les Cent Vingt Journées de Sodome;* begins writing *Aline et Valcour.*

1787   8 July, completes *Les Infortunes de la vertu.*

1788   1 October, compiles a detailed *Catalogue raisonné* of his writings.

1789   5 May, meeting of the Estates-General.

4 July, Sade transferred to Charenton after repeatedly causing a disturbance and attempting to stir up the crowd in the rue Saint-Antoine by shouting from his window through an improvised megaphone.

14 July, storming of the Bastille. The governor de Launay and the major de Losme-Salbray are massacred by the rioters; du Puget, the prison's lieutenant de roi and Sade's sometime confidant, escapes, wearing a disguise. The marquis' former cell is ransacked.

4 August, abolition of feudal privilege; 26 August, Declaration of the Rights of Man.

1790   2 April, the marquis is released from Charenton after the National Assembly abolishes (16 March) all *lettres de cachet.*

9 June, Renée-Pélagie is granted a legal separation, plus the (theoretical) return of her dowry amounting to 160,842 livres.

25 August, Sade meets the thirty-three-year-old actress Constance Ques-net (1757–1832). Their association will endure to the end of his life. Con-tinuing efforts to have his plays performed in various Parisian theaters.

Sade establishes his first political contacts with the Club des Impartiaux and a group of moderate constitutional monarchists led by Clermont-Tonnerre, his cousin by marriage; becomes a member of the Section de la Place Vendôme (later renamed Section des Piques).

1791　21 June, Louis XVI and the royal family are arrested at Varennes after a botched attempt to flee the country; Sade composes an essentially monar-chical *Adresse d'un citoyen de Paris, au roi des Français* for the occasion.

Anonymous publication of *Justine ou les Malheurs de la vertu.*

Sade's play, *le Comte Oxtiern ou les Effets du libertinage,* performed at the Théâtre Molière.

1792　The marquis' sons emigrate. La Coste is pillaged.

10 August, invasion of the Tuileries palace by antimonarchist mob. Clermont-Tonnerre is brutally murdered.

2–6 September, horrendous prison massacres; the butchery abetted by Marat.

21 September, the Convention abolishes the monarchy; the Republic is proclaimed.

2 November, Sade composes *Idée sur le mode de la sanction des lois,* inten-sifying his efforts to display himself in radical guise.

1793　20 January, assassination of Le Peletier de Saint-Fargeau.

21 January, execution of Louis XVI.

13 July, assassination of Marat by Charlotte Corday (1768–1793).

17 July, Charlotte Corday tried and executed after a dignified defense.

29 September, seizing the opportunity, citizen Sade presents his *Discours aux mânes de Marat et de Le Peletier;* adopts more and more the public stance of a rabid sansculotte.

16 October, execution of Marie-Antoinette.

10 November, *Fête de la Raison* celebrated.

8 December, despite his best efforts at revolutionary showmanship, Sade is arrested as "suspect" and taken to the Madelonnettes prison.

1794　13 January, transferred to the Carmes prison; 27 January, moved to Saint-Lazare.

9 March, André Chénier arrested and taken to Saint-Lazare prison.

27 March, Sade succeeds in gaining admission "for reasons of health" to an expensive (and relatively safe) "sanatorium" on the rue de Picpus.

8 June, celebration of the *Fête de l'Être suprême;* Robespierre preaches the need for religion in the Republic.

25 July, André Chénier guillotined.

26 July, Sade's name appears on a general list of prisoners indicted for trial, but he is declared "absent."

27 July, fall of Robespierre: end of the Terror.

15 October, the marquis is released from Picpus.

1795   15 January, death of Renée-Pélagie's father.

Publication of *Aline et Valcour* and *La Philosophie dans le boudoir.*

1796   Sale of La Coste; Sade purchases a house in Saint-Ouen.

1797   Brief visit to Provence, accompanied by Mme Quesnet.

1799   (1799–1801), publication of *La Nouvelle Justine ou les Malheurs de la vertu, suivie de l'Histoire de Juliette, sa soeur.*

10 November, Bonaparte's coup d'état; end of the Directoire.

1800   Publication of *Oxtiern ou les Malheurs du libertinage* and *Les Crimes de l'amour* (preceded by *Idée sur les romans*).

18 August, *La Nouvelle Justine* seized by the police.

22 October, the critic Villeterque launches a polemical attack. Sade responds but continues to deny authorship of offending novels.

1801   Death of Mme de Montreuil at the age of eighty-one.

6 March, Sade arrested along with his publisher Nicolas Massé; copies of *Juliette* and *Justine* seized. He is taken to Sainte-Pélagie; the beginning of a thirteen-year period of detention.

1802   Signing of the Concordat; Bonaparte is made consul for life.

1803   15 March, Sade transferred from Sainte-Pélagie to Bicêtre after attempting to molest several young inmates.

27 April, transferred at the family's expense to the asylum of Charenton; Constance Quesnet is allowed to join him in residence there the following year.

1804   Bonaparte proclaimed emperor.

1805   November, citing the pornographic nature of *Justine* and *Juliette,* the atheist-astronomer Lalande makes a point of denying the marquis honorable listing in his second supplement of the *Dictionnaire des Athées.*

1806   30 January, Sade makes a will; names Constance Quesnet as a special beneficiary for having saved him from certain death during the Terror.

1807   5 June, *Les Journées de Florbelle ou la Nature dévoilée,* Sade's last monumental novel, is seized by police; after the marquis' death it will be destroyed at the request of his surviving son, Donatien-Claude-Armand.

1808   15 September, marriage of Donatien-Claude-Armand to his cousin, Louise-Gabrielle-Laure de Sade-Eyguières.

1809   9 June, death of the marquis' elder son, Louis-Marie de Sade, ambushed while on his way to rejoin his regiment in Italy.

1810   7 July, death of Renée-Pélagie at the Montreuil family home in Echaffour where she had been residing with her unmarried daughter, Laure-Madeleine.

1811   10 July, Bonaparte takes part in decision to continue Sade's detention at Charenton.

1812   Completion of *Adélaïde de Brunswick.*

1813   6 May, Sade is ordered to cease all theater performance activities at the Charenton hospice; publication of *La Marquise de Gange;* completion of *Histoire secrète d'Isabelle de Bavière.*

1814   27 November, pays seventeen-year-old Madeleine Leclerc, the rather fragile daughter of a female employee at Charenton, her usual gratuity for their ninety-sixth session of diversified sexual dalliance in his rooms. Sternly warns her not to attend balls, to be faithful to him and submissive.

         2 December, death of the marquis de Sade at Charenton; though sometimes described as "unworthy," his remaining son, Donatien-Claude-Armand de Sade (1769–1847) is present and sees to both a religious burial and the eventual destruction of the major Charenton manuscripts, ironically obeying in that way the marquis' lifelong injunction that children should take no account whatsoever of the last wishes of their parents.

SADEAN CRITICISM
A   P o s t s c r i p t

Sade's negative press, based mainly on amplified rumors concerning the Arcueil and Marseilles affairs, attained hopeless proportions well before any of his writings were published. As early as 1775 he complained to his notary that "not so much as a cat could be whipped in the province without everyone saying: *The marquis de Sade did it.*" In 1790, Sade's "first biographer," the future Convention member, Jacques-Antoine Dulaure (see chap. 19 and *Papiers,* II, 715–717), shows no mercy to the ex-prisoner just released from Charenton, whom he considered to be one of the most vicious surviving examples of the ancien régime's red-heeled monsters, as morally and criminally reprehensible as the medieval ogre Gilles de Rais. French justice had finally punished that perverted Bluebeard, responsible for the murder of hundreds of children, by burning him at the stake in Nantes in the year 1440. Surprisingly, the marquis de Sade, "convicted of the same atrocities," was free to walk about in the streets of Paris and was currently engaged in negotiations to have his plays performed by the capital's leading theatrical troupe!

In fact, Sade had little success in his attempts to convince the actors of Paris that his plays were worthy of performance. On the other hand, his novel *Justine,* published anonymously not long after Dulaure's attack and privately described at the time by the marquis himself as "well-peppered" to increase sales, quickly became a Parisian best-seller and went through several editions before a much-expanded and even more well-peppered version, *La Nouvelle Justine,* appeared at the turn of the century. Well before then, however, rumors disclosing the identity of the anonymous author only helped to reinforce Sade's already well-established legend as a monster. One of Dulaure's former colleagues in the Convention, the celebrated author Louis-Sébastien Mercier, deplored in 1798 the excesses of the free press and noted in this regard that *Justine, ou les Malheurs de la vertu* was on full display in the capital's bookstalls: "The kind of books now sold openly at the Palais-Égalité were assuredly never read in Sodom and Gomorrah," he lamented. As for *Justine*: "Put a pen in Satan's claw [. . .] and he could do no worse" (*Paris pendant la Révolution [1789–1798] ou le Nouveau Paris* [Paris: Poulet-Malassis, 1862], I, 370–371). Some contemporaries saw the work as part and parcel of the recent Terror: "Danton used to read it to get himself aroused," confides Rétif de La Bretonne in 1796 in *Monsieur Nicolas* (*Monsieur Nicolas,* ed. Pierre Testud [Paris: Gallimard, "Pléiade," 1989], I, 1044, 1555–1557]). In *Le Spectateur du Nord* a year later, the emigré writer Charles de Villers mentions Robespierre in a similar context: the *Incorruptible,* it was rumored, used to read a few pages of *Justine*—not to work himself up to orgasms but whenever he found that his blood lust needed fortifying. De Villers, one of the first to introduce Immanuel Kant's philosophy to France, does not guarantee the truth of the anecdote but suggests that its currency was, in any case, the important point to keep in mind: "The story has been circulating in France. People believe it and that alone is sufficient to record for posterity the opinion once held by contemporaries of a work that will surely not survive" (*Le Spectateur du Nord, journal politique, littéraire et moral,* Hambourg, IV [October, November, December 1797], 408–409; see also various excerpts in Françoise Laugaa-Traut, *Lectures de Sade* [Paris: Armand Colin, 1973], and references in Michel Delon's introduction to Sade, *Oeuvres* [Paris: Gallimard, "Pléiade," 1990]).

Villers, as it turns out, proved to be a mediocre prophet. Sade did survive, albeit mainly underground, both the informal and formal censorship measures of the Napoleonic and Restoration eras. It was not long before veiled rumors of his authorship turned into direct accusations in the press. On several occasions, as in his "L'Auteur des 'Crimes de l'amour' à Villeterque, folliculaire" (1800), Sade fought back, drawing on his well-tested reserves of vituperative insult and blustery rodomontade to deny that he could ever have written such an "immoral" work as *Justine*. That particular whipped cat was, however, well out of the bag, and it was not merely right-thinking conservatives or gallophobic émigrés who saw him as "infamous" in this respect. The dean of France's atheists, the astronomer Lalande, himself a notable victim of Napoleon's repressive measures against freedom of expression, felt compelled to point out that the marquis was unworthy of an entry in his Who's Who of honorable unbelievers that proudly listed such old friends and Enlightenment stalwarts as Buffon, Diderot, d'Holbach, d'Alembert, Helvétius, and Condorcet. "I would like to have included M. de Sade," Lalande wrote in 1805; "he has all the requisite intelligence, reasoning powers and erudition but his infamous novels *Justine* and *Juliette* must exclude him from a sect where virtue alone holds sway" (*Dictionnaire des athées, second supplément,* 119).

Although by 1825 the *Biographie universelle* of Michaud (partly as a result of the intervention of Sade's surviving son, Claude-Armand, who had tried to have all mention of his notorious father suppressed) was able to present a considerably more objective account of the marquis' biographical facts, discounting some of the old horror stories and noting that his role in the Revolution had been essentially moderate; the charges against his novels were nevertheless maintained, and Sade's own claim to eventual vindication by posterity (made in his self-authored epitaph) was characterized as a piece of monumental impudence. Scarcely a decade later the word *sadisme* made its first appearance in a French dictionary (Claude Boiste's *Dictionnaire universel,* eighth edition, 1834), accompanied, admittedly, by the notation "infrequently used."

As his personal contribution to modifying that frequency count, Jules Janin in the same year published in the *Revue de Paris* one of the nineteenth century's most influentially negative accounts of the marquis and his works, sparing no effort to evoke for the benefit of his horrified readers an assortment of Sadean tortures, obscenities, crimes, perversions, and blasphemies, capping the whole with a warning that Sade's poisonous books, though forbidden, could be found hidden away in the nooks and crannies of many private libraries ("Le Marquis de Sade," XI, 321–360). As proof of their dangerous nature he cites the tragic case of an adolescent boy named Julien, nephew of a priest of his acquaintance, who aged overnight and was reduced to total idiocy after reading the marquis' atrocious works. Sade's novels, Janin concluded, had killed more children than the infamous Gilles de Rais, and the tragedy was that they would continue to kill such innocents, both in body and soul.

There was plenty of evidence around to suggest, however, that little Julien's reaction to the marquis' poison must have been at best an atypical side effect. In 1839, scorning Janin's bourgeois perspectives, the seventeen-year-old *collégien* Gustave Flaubert, precociously talented and caught up in the current poetic fascination with themes of passion and madness, the Devil, monsters, and death, wrote from provincial Rouen to his friend Ernest Chevalier, a law student in decadent Paris: "Speaking of the Marquis de Sade, my dear Ernest, if you could find me some of that honorable author's novels I would pay you their weight in gold. I have read a biographical article on him by J. Janin which I found revolting,—because of Janin, needless to say, for he rants on about morality, philanthropy and deflowered virgins!" (*Correspondance,* ed. Jean Bruneau [Paris: Gallimard, "Pléiade," 1973], I, 48; 15 July 1839). Flaubert's fascination with Sade, anticipating that of Baudelaire, was not a passing fancy, and he was only one of many in an evolving century of romanticism and rebellion, poetic aestheticism and decadence, to come under the spell of the Divine Marquis' darker attractions. Confirming in a broad sense the claims already made by Janin regarding widespread diffusion of the marquis' works, the critic Sainte-Beuve as early as 1843 took note of Sade's underground influence: "I dare say, and without fear of contradiction, that Byron and Sade (forgive me for placing them side by side) have been perhaps the two major influences on our modern writers, the one openly flaunted and visible, the other clandestine,—but not all that clandestine." ("Quelques vérités sur la situation en littérature," *Revue des deux mondes,* III, 14; as a general reference for this period, see Mario Praz, *The Romantic Agony,* first published in English [London: Oxford University Press] in 1933; also, Claude Duchet, "L'Image de Sade à l'époque romantique," in *Le Marquis de Sade,* proceedings of the February 1966 Aix-en-Provence colloquium, 219–240).

Across the Channel, rather like the young Flaubert yearning to get his hands on de Sade's novels, the poet Algernon Swinburne reminded his friend Richard Monckton Milnes in a letter of 15 October 1861 of a long-standing promise to lend him his copy of the prohibited *Justine.* Already in his twenties and himself a seasoned amateur in the flagellation arts, Swinburne speaks of his eagerness to look at last "upon the mystic pages of the martyred marquis de Sade." Ever since Milnes had made that promise, Swinburne continues, "the vision of that illustrious and ill-requited benefactor of humanity has hovered by night before my eyes, and I run great risk of going as mad as Janin's friend, but with curiosity alone." (*The Swinburne Letters,* ed. C. Y. Lang [New Haven, CT: Yale University Press, 1959], I, 46). Janin's piece, we see, and especially his account of poor little Julien, had remained an important target reference; but despite the verbal horseplay, Swinburne's fascination with the legendary marquis was totally genuine. Indeed, during the following week, he even composed in his excellent French a verse portrait of his hero, entitling it "Charenton, en 1810." The tone of the piece is unreservedly admiring, even reverent. A young man is reading *Justine;* he looks up at the calmly powerful features of this *satyre sublime,* "as one does in prayer."

Swinburne had to wait nearly a year, but, finally, the scene so fondly anticipated in his poem "Charenton" was transformed into reality: the precious multivolume treasure had arrived at last! After reading the several thousand pages of not *Justine,* in fact, but *La Nouvelle Justine,* Swinburne summed up his comments in a letter to Milnes. If I quote it here almost in its entirety, it is because I feel that it deserves attention as one of the most telling pieces of Sadean criticism ever penned, all the more incisive for being the considered and deliberate reaction of a talented, receptive, and honest disciple who all his life continued to be fascinated with the Sadean phenomenon (see also Jeremy Mitchell, "Swinburne—the Disappointed Protaganist," in *Yale French Studies* [1965], 81–88).

And what was that reaction? Not reverence. Not horror, either. Only an incredulous guffaw, a belly laugh so apposite in its expression that we are made to wonder why readers sensitive in matters of style and sense have, in like manner, so seldom dismissed with gales of derisive laughter the infantile excesses of *Justine* and *Juliette,* of *Les 120 journées de Sodome* and *La Philosophie dans le boudoir.* We wonder also why so many solemn critics overdosed on the metaphysics of transgression seem to have forgotten the ludic hyperbole of smutty schoolyard wordplay and possibly their own prurient triumphs in juvenile one-upmanship. Those who have insisted, more and more opaquely, more and more ritualistically, that the emperor is indeed wearing clothes have somehow carried the day, and for far too long.

But let us listen to the monumentally disenchanted disciple writing to his sophisticated older confrere:

> I have just read "[La Nouvelle] Justine ou les Malheurs de la Vertu." As you seemed anxious to know its effect on me I mean to give you a candid record, avoiding paradox or affectation. I would give anything to have, by way of study, six or seven other opinions as genuine and frank as mine shall be.
>
> At first, I quite expected to add another to the gifted author's list of victims; I really thought I must have died or split open or choked with laughing. I never laughed so much in my life: I couldn't have stopped to save the said life. I went from text to illustrations and back again, till I literally doubled up and fell down with laughter—I regret to add that all the friends to whom I have lent or shown the book were affected in just the same way. One scene between M. de Verneuil and Mme. d'Esterval I never thought to survive. I read it out and the auditors rolled and roared. Then Rossetti read out the dissection of the interesting Rosalie and her infant, and the rest of that refreshing episode: and I wonder to this minute that we did not raise the whole house by our screams of laughter.

But on reflection I found the impression left on me to be precisely the same as that of Landor's heroine on her first view of the sea. "Is this the mighty Satyr? *is this all?*" I did think—I did hope that this one illusion might have turned out a reality. Weep with me over a shattered idol! The style of Micawber is inadequate to express my feelings.

Of course the book must be taken on its own grounds; well, assuming every postulate imaginable, I lament to say it appears to me a most outrageous *fiasco.* I looked for some sharp and subtle analysis of lust—some keen dissection of pain and pleasure—*"quelques taillades dans les chairs vives de la sensation"* [a few deft cuts into the live flesh of sensation]: at least such an exquisite relish of the things anatomized as without explanation would suffice for a stimulant and be comprehensible at once even if unfit for sympathy. But in *Justine* there seems to me throughout to be one radical mistake rotting and undermining the whole structure of the book. De Sade is like a Hindoo mythologist; he takes *bulk* and *number* for greatness. As if a crime of great extent was necessarily a great crime; as if a number of pleasures piled one on another made up the value of a single great and perfect sensation of pleasure. You tear out wombs, smash in heads, and discharge into the orifice. Après? [And so?] You scourge and abuse your mother and make dogs tear off her breasts, etc. Après? [And so?] Suppose you take your grandmother next time and try wild cats by way of a change? [. . .] Shew me the point, the pleasure of all this, as a man of genius ought to do in a few touches; *that* will be worth something as a study. [. . .] Take the simplest little example of your way of work. You have, say, a flogging to describe. You go in for *quantity* in a way quite regardless of expense. You lay on some hundreds of cuts, behind and before; you assert that they drew blood; probably they did; that the recipient wept and writhed; which is not unlikely; that the inflictor enjoyed himself and was much excited in his *physique;* which is most probable of all. Well? You have asserted a great deal; prove it now; bring it face to face with us; let the sense of it bite and tickle and sting your reader. Assertion is easy work. Shew us how and why these things are as they are. I on my part assert that you never do this once. [. . .] Why, there is more and better sensual physiology in that little "Manon-la-Foutteuse" [i.e., *Manon Lescaut* (and not Manon-*the Slut*), by Prévost] than in all your great lumbering *Justine. There* one finds some relish in the style, and catches it of the writer. I boast not of myself; but I do say that a schoolboy, set to write on his stock of experience, and having a real gust and appetite for the subject in him, may make and has made more of a sharp short school flogging of two or three dozen cuts than you of your enormous interminable inflictions; more of the simple common birch rod and daily whipping-block than you of your loaded iron whips and elaborately ingenious racks and horses. Will you reply that your critic cannot yet judge you, being too young, too green, and physically fresh to fathom the mystic Apocalypse of Priapus? You shall not get off on that score, M. le marquis; not if I know it. Had you given

me all these strange dishes of yours served up in the right sauce, I should at
once have recognized the value of them: I might have felt doubt, disgust,
aversion for this dish or that, (*notamment,* for the process of tearing one's
mother to rags or beating to death a little girl in the agonies of a head broken open; also, with your leave, for those rank and rancid preparations
which served as *entremets* at the great dinners and suppers of Gomorrah) but
I should have appreciated, admired, tried on the whole to understand and
enjoy your work as great in its own way. But as it is, your book misses aim;
with half your materials another man would have built a better palace of
sin—a fairer house to sweep and garnish for the advent of the seven devils.
You have gathered up and arranged in rows all manner of abominations and
your work is *fade* [dull] after all—flat, flaccid, impotent, misshapen, hung
awry. It might be bound up with Télémaque or Paul et Virginie. [. . .]

As to your horrors—ask people what they remember, as little children,
to have said, heard of, thought of, dreamed of, done or been tempted to do.
Nothing in your books but will find its counterpart or type. (I remember
when I was seven a most innocent little girl of six telling me of a bad dream
that made her unhappy; in that dream there was the whole practical philosophy of *Justine* embodied; God impotent or indignant, virtue trodden under and defiled by vice, and finally the very same climax you make so much
of—*the curse of Rabshakeh.* [See *II Kings,* 18:27; Swinburne apparently did
not share the Divine Marquis' coprophilic interests.] Get along with you!
You call a taste for eating and making others eat foul substances, the supreme excess of libidinous and voluptuous wickedness. Priapus have mercy
on you! Why not say the same of a distaste for honey and taste for mush-
rooms? "Eat, yea eat abundantly," if you like; make others eat if you can and
care; take your fill and hold your tongue. As to your story and the framework of your theories—you *must* know that Justine is a juggler's show, an
ingenious acrobatic performance, and no more. Very ingenious and inventive; many of the tricks and postures (Rodin's, for example, Gernande's, or
Cardoville's) most creditable to a phallic juggler; but who on earth is to
make more than its worth of the very best conjuror's exhibition!

Look here, my friend, Arch-Professor of the Ithyphallic Science as you
are, will you hear the truth once for all? You take yourself for a great pagan
physiologist and philosopher—you are a Christian ascetic bent on earning
the salvation of the soul through the mortification of the flesh. You are one
of the family of St. Simeon Stylites. You are a hermit of the Thebaid turned
inside out. You, a Roman of the later empire? Nero knows nothing of you;
Heliogabalus turns his back on you; Caracalla sniffs contemptuously at the
sight of you; Cotytto veils her face and the Baptae shrug their shoulders;
Venus Cloacina dips down into her gutter, and Priapus turns to a mere fig
tree stump. Paganism washes its hands of you. You belong to Christian
Egypt; you smell of Nitria; you have walked straight out of some Nile
monastery; you are twin brother to St. Maccarius; you are St. Anthony and

his pig rolled into one. It matters little that you have forgotten your own ge-
nealogy, or that you operate rather on the flesh of others than your own.
Your one knack is to take common things, usual affections, natural pleasures
and make them walk on their heads; by the simple process of *reversing*, any
one may write as good a Justine as yours. If you were once cured of that trick
of standing on your head for ten volumes through, and your energies turned
back into the old channel they ran in some centuries since, you would re-
vert to the chain and the top of a pillar and ascetic worship. That is about
your mark, I reckon. We took you for a sort of burlesque Prometheus; you
are only a very serious Simeon Stylites—in an inverted posture. You worship the phallus as those first ascetics worshipped the cross; you seek your
heaven by the very same road as they sought theirs. That is all.

  I drop my apostrophe to M. de Sade, having relieved my mind for good
and all of its final judgment on a matter of some curiosity and interest to
me. [. . .] I have said just what I think in the first words that came uppermost. [. . .] You see that whether it drives curates and curates' pupils to madness and death or not (Janin says it does—and Janin has the lips that cannot lie) it has done decidedly little damage to my brain or nerves; (unless
you think the incoherence of my critical remarks a proof of incipient mania). If you keep *Charenton* "as a physiological extravaganza," perhaps you
will keep this prose rhapsody with it by way of comment and remark, giving as it does a sincere and deliberate opinion of the life's labours of Stylites
de Sade. [. . .] Sancta Donatiane, ora pro nobis!

  Authentic discipleship does not, we see, necessarily commit the acolyte
either to superstitious praise of the master's literary merits or to blind acceptance of bad logic. Given the choice, the marquis, one suspects, would
have much preferred to suffer the more correctly horrified criticisms of a
Jules Janin, even if he had been aware that such a fine critic and poet as
Swinburne, on the slim evidence of eighteen lines of melodramatic verse
(Aline's song before death) in the novel *Aline et Valcour,* considered him at
the same time to be "a good lyrical poet," reminiscent of the early Blake,
"sweet and perfect," medieval too "in grace and quietness of beauty." A far
cry, indeed, from the muffled screams that emanate day after day from behind the grim walls of Silling Castle!

  Criminal or mad? The debate already well begun in the eighteenth
century intensified among the marquis' critics in the nineteenth. For Jules
Janin, Sade was criminal rather than mad; that is always the preferred
diagnosis of the severe moralist. For the more humanistically tolerant, the
other side of the coin is most often preferred. Anatole France, for example,
characterized Sade as *notre fou,* "our madman," and in his preface to *Dorci,*

a benign tale originally intended for *Les Crimes de l'amour* (1800) but removed by Sade himself as more suited to be part of a different collection, he displays the same healthy skepticism about poor little Julien's plight as had Swinburne. He also rejects the worst horror stories still circulating about Sade. Janin's parallel with Gilles de Rais, for example, is described as "extremely unjust." Rais committed real lust murders, whereas Sade only puts them into his noxious fiction, "which is already a bit much." The marquis' indecent whipping of Rose Keller and the cantharides overdose episode in Marseilles (which France, relying on erroneous accounts, mistakenly believed had resulted in unintended fatal consequences for several of the prostitutes) were most assuredly not up to Nero's exalted standards. Sade's madness certainly never led him to commit murder. "Our madman," in short, would never have been very dangerous "if his books had been burned rather than published." Moreover, there are also degrees of sadism to be taken into account: Baudelaire was touched by the phenomenon, but any attempt to compare Baudelaire with Sade would be odious. Baudelaire was a true artist, a genius who had discovered a new and rare form of beauty; his poetry is magnificent and "normal" precisely because in its singularity it is still beautiful. Sade's own literary achievements hardly matched that standard, and France warns his reader that in editing the manuscript he intends to note only its more notable variants, it being unnecessary to treat a text by the marquis de Sade as if it were a text by Pascal. Four years after launching that still famous quip, Anatole France returned to the theme and reinforced the point: There is no doubt, he stated in a journalistic piece of 1885, that Sade's books could be justly described as poisonous in many ways, but surely the most dangerous ingredient they contained was their fatal dose of ennui (*Oeuvres complètes illustrées* [Paris: Calmann-Lévy, 1934], XXIV, 31–46; 372–373).

While increased tolerance in matters of variant sexuality no doubt played a part in the late nineteenth century's growing tendency to apply medical perspectives to the study of Sade and his works, the primary impetus undoubtedly came from the expansion of scientific research into human mental behavior generally. In 1886, the first edition of Richard von Krafft-Ebing's *Psychopathia Sexualis* was published in Germany. Written in Latin and intended for a restricted public, it soon became an influential classic on sexual pathology. Here, finally, the term *sadism,* along with what Krafft-Ebing called its "perfect counterpart," *masochism,* a term coined by Krafft-Ebing based on the form of eroticism described in the popular fiction of Léopold von Sacher-Masoch (1836–1895), achieved, with only passing reference to the marquis' life and writings, its first medical definition and formal taxonomic credentials. Soon after, the word made its debut in English.

In 1904, the Berlin psychiatrist Dr. Iwan Bloch, following up on the German-language biography of Sade he published in 1900 under the pseudonym Eugen Dühren (a study occasionally attacked as gallophobic but superior to anything that had appeared earlier in the genre), added to the marquis' literary as well as medical fortunes by bringing out in a limited edition (one hundred eighty copies) the long-lost novel, *Les 120 journées de Sodome.* The marquis' first and perhaps most extreme "Sadean" work, copied out on both sides of a long scroll made up of small sheets of paper pasted together and unavoidably left behind in his room at the Bastille when he was hurriedly whisked away to Charenton ten days before the ancient prison-fortress was sacked by the mob, finally surfaced as a quasiscientific document! Some well-meaning scholars still view it as such and speak of Sade as a precursor of Krafft-Ebing and Freud, far ahead of his time in providing a comprehensive compendium of sexual aberrations.

Five years later, in the introduction to his anthology *L'Oeuvre du marquis de Sade* (1909), the avant-garde poet Guillaume Apollinaire praised Dühren for his courageous contributions. Although initially only one of several potboiling prefaces he undertook at this time for the Bibliothèque des Curieux's "Les Maîtres de l'Amour" series, Apollinaire's fifty-six-page review of Sade's life and works marks a major turning point in the literary and ideological fortunes of the now irreversibly "divine" marquis. It is with Apollinaire that the twentieth-century phenomenon of Sade's rehabilitation really begins, and the process continues to this day.

Apollinaire saw the problem of editing Sade initially in terms of easing the public's fears. Readers had no reason to be nervous about either the marquis or his writings. All of the many Sadean legends of the past needed correcting. It is doubtful, for example, that any "genuine cruelties" took place at Arcueil. As for the Marseilles affair, that was "even less serious" than Arcueil. Sade got into trouble essentially because he was a political progressive, committed to the cause of the people. Indeed, his role in the storming of the Bastille on 14 July 1789, even though he had been removed to Charenton ten days earlier, may have been the determining factor in the people's success. It is entirely possible, Apollinaire suggests (and totally without tongue in cheek), that his earlier shouting to the crowds in the street below, "along with the papers he threw down at the time from his tower window, describing the tortures inflicted on the prisoners," initially stirred up the crowds and ultimately inspired their victory.

And like his biographical record, the marquis' works also deserved rehabilitation, in spite of "Monsieur" Anatole France's sneering reference to the marquis' merits compared with those of Pascal. Various free spirits, Apollinaire noted, had already pointed out that such scorn was entirely unjustified. In Germany, the lyric philosopher Nietzsche had not hesitated to make room in his own thinking for some of the marquis' more "energetic" ideas. Dr. Eugen Dühren had courageously suggested that Sade's writings were a veritable wellspring of scientific knowledge and innovation. Indeed, no modern thinker doing research on human relationships, no one investigating the "sociology of love," for example, could afford to ignore the principal works of the marquis de Sade. His ideas had already shaped profoundly the thinking of many progressive writers, economists, naturalists, and sociologists, from Lamarck to Spencer. These ideas had disconcerted and frightened people in the marquis' day, but now they were even more pertinent and alive. The time had come to free those ideas that had been too long locked up and smothered in the infamous *enfer* cages of libraries. Sade, the freest spirit who ever lived, had counted for nothing during the entire nineteenth century; it could well be that he was destined to dominate the twentieth.

Apollinaire's message remains entirely familiar to us today, including even the notion that Juliette represents modern woman, still partly undefined in nature but destined to free herself from the trammels of humanity and, in soaring flight, to "renew the universe."

From Apollinaire to the surrealists of the 1920s and 1930s was only a small step, and the link between the two, both personal and intellectual, was provided by Maurice Heine, a dedicated libertarian Communist who devoted his life and resources to researching Sade's biography and studying his works. It is thanks to Heine that the most important of these were made available for the first time to the reading public—notably, an authoritative edition of *Les 120 journées de Sodome* (Paris: Stendhal, 1931–1935), *Les Infortunes de la vertu* (doubly dedicated to Apollinaire and to Heine's companion surrealists in 1930; Paris: Fourcade, 1930), the *Dialogue entre un prêtre et un moribond* (Paris: Stendhal, 1926), and the *Historiettes, contes et fabliaux* (Paris: Société du Roman philosophique, 1926). Heine also carried out pioneering archival research on the Arcueil and Marseilles affairs as part of his preparations for a biography of Sade, a project that was left unfinished when he died at the age of fifty-six in 1940. His spiritual heir, Gilbert Lely, rescued the collected materials and brought out *Le Marquis de Sade* (Paris: Gallimard) under Heine's name in 1950. Two years later, Lely published the first volume of his own massive biography of Sade.

In retracing Sade's twentieth-century rehabilitation, it would be difficult to overemphasize the importance of the Apollinaire-Heine-Lely connection, although Lely himself was finally inclined to minimize Apollinaire's contribution, as well as the part played earlier by Dühren (see *Vie du marquis de Sade,* in *Oeuvres complètes* [Paris: Cercle du livre précieux, 1967], II, 665). At the same time Lely praises Heine for having been the first to establish formally "the incomparable literary, philosophical and scientific superiority of the marquis de Sade," the first to demonstrate—Anatole France notwithstanding—that a text by de Sade "is owed the same respectful treatment as a text by Pascal," the first to defend Sade's memory as "the most lucid thinker of modern times, the depth of whose moral insights was equal in all respects to the genius of Nietzsche" (G. Lely in preface to M. Heine, *Le Marquis de Sade* [Paris: Gallimard, 1950], 11). Heine's own texts follow Lely's prefatory accolades, delivering a message that is equally forthright and uncompromising: Sade is an *absolute,* and those who wish to study his life and works must never lose sight of that "one essential fact." As a thinker Sade never wavers: he looks fearlessly straight ahead and proceeds unblinkingly to ultimate consequences. Whether those consequences upset our prejudices, our preconceived notions, social conventions, or moral laws, is a matter of supreme indifference to him: "He does not, at every opportunity, merely *write* that God does not exist, he thinks it and acts it out constantly, he gives witness and he dies for his beliefs. It is this unshakable conviction, this pride of self, that people have found most unpardonable. And that is precisely when he rises to the greatest heights and when his curses become the equal of prayers" (Heine, 31).

With all that, still according to Heine, Sade has been the most atrociously slandered genius the world has ever seen. The Arcueil affair? It is entirely possible that Rose Keller actually consented to—Heine chooses his words with great care—"an exceptional *aventure galante*" (207). In any case, if Sade was guilty in some way it could only have been of an offense that a modern French police court would classify as minor. Above all, the question must be asked, Why so much fuss over a simple "spanking" (203)?

Other slanders? Sade a pornographer? Heine rejects the charge. Despite the marquis' own explicit statements to the contrary, Sade would not have sold his pen. He did not deliberately "pepper" his texts for money—unless, of course, he did so in times of desperate need (295).

Sade an anti-Jacobin aristocrat at heart? More slander! He may have momentarily lost his way and taken the wrong path at the beginning of the Revolution, but he quickly realized his mistake and shifted to the patriotic side as political events evolved. As a writer, "Sade belonged totally to the Revolution" (277, 321)

That, of course, was also the view taken by Heine's surrealist associates, like him members of the radical Left and happy enough to claim as an ancestor such a splendid apostle of rebellion as the marquis de Sade. "Sade is a surrealist in sadism," writes André Breton in the first (1924) *Manifeste du surréalisme.* Six years later in the *Second Manifeste* he continues to praise the "perfect integrity of the marquis' life and thought," not to mention "his will to total liberation, both moral and social" (*Oeuvres complètes,* ed. Marguerite Bonnet [Paris: Gallimard, "Pléiade," 1988], 329, 827). For the poet Paul Eluard, Sade had suffered in prison nearly his entire life for the sole reason that he had tried "to restore to civilized man the vital force of his primitive instincts" and had fought desperately "for absolute justice and absolute equality." It goes without saying that he was also dedicated "body and soul" to the Revolution. (*L'Évidence poétique* in *Oeuvres complètes* [Paris: Gallimard, "Pléiade," 1968], I, 517 and variant, I, 1496).

The frequency and continuing inflation of such claims, occasionally disrupted by internal party disputes in which attitudes toward Sade sometimes played a significant part (e.g., Bataille versus Breton), continued apace throughout the thirties. After World War II, and especially after 1960, the number of articles, books of criticism, editions, and prefaces devoted to Sade increased almost exponentially. One minor illustration of the phenomenon is especially revealing: In 1960, the useful if somewhat traditional *Dictionnaire des lettres françaises; le dix-huitième siècle,* edited in two sturdy volumes by Cardinal Georges Grente (Paris: Fayard), first made its appearance. It contained a *ten-line* article on Sade, and one is led to imagine that it was only because of the marquis' thriving reputation that the editor was ultimately persuaded to grant even that niggardly amount of space to "the freest spirit that ever lived." Inclusion did not, however, imply recognition, and the author of the article (another bad prophet!), no doubt weighing each word with great care, makes a prediction (my italics): "Whatever the extent of Sade's *current temporary vogue,* his writings are more properly the province of pathological or psychoanalytical studies rather than of literature; they address themselves only to specialists or the curious" (II, 501). It is some indication of what has been happening in Sadean studies since 1960 that the 1995 reissue of the "Grente" (ed. F. Moureau) devotes not *ten* but well over a thousand lines to the marquis de Sade.

A major sign that the marquis' rising star was becoming visible even to the general reading public was the appearance in 1947 of the first volumes of Jean-Jacques Pauvert's edition of Sade's complete works. During this same period, a number of influential studies were published. Jean Paulhan's "Le Marquis de Sade et sa complice" (*Table Ronde,* 1945), in addition to finding Sade's self-portrait concealed in the masochistic personality of his heroine Justine, suggested that in the areas where it seemed most alive and aggressive modern French literature was dominated and determined by Sade. Pierre Klossowski (*Sade mon prochain,* 1947) and Maurice Blanchot ("À la rencontre de Sade," *Les Temps modernes,* 1947, republished in 1949 in *Lautréamont et Sade*) also brought out influential critical studies.

Several major writers of the day were similarly turning their attention to Sade. In 1951, in an era overshadowed by expanding Stalinism, Albert Camus (*L'Homme révolté*) struck a refreshingly discordant note when he revisited a disquieting theme already touched on at the end of the war by Raymond Queneau in the context of the recently defeated Hitler regime: "It is undeniable," Queneau had noted in "Lectures pour un front" for 3 November 1945, "that the world imagined by Sade and willed by his characters (and why not by Sade himself?) is a striking prefiguration of the world ruled by the Gestapo, its tortures and its camps" (*Bâtons, chiffres et lettres* [Paris: Gallimard, 1950], 152). Camus enlarges that debate considerably in his overall assessment of the marquis' literary merit: Sade, despite his occasionally felicitous phrases and despite the exaggerated praise of many recent critics, is a writer of the second rank. He is admired today (and with so much naiveness!) for reasons that have nothing to do with literature. Glorified as a philosopher in chains and as the first theoretician of absolute rebellion, he in fact knew only the logic of his own feelings and the only philosophy he created was a monstrous dream of revenge: "His success in our day can be explained by a dream he shared with contemporary sensibilities: the demand for total liberty, and the dehumanization that is systematically perpetrated by intelligence" (Camus, *L'Homme révolté* in *Essais d'Albert Camus,* ed. R. Quilliot and L. Faucon [Paris: Gallimard, "Pléiade," 1965], 457). Is it a valid defense, Camus asks, to object that Sade's murderous characters, those theoreticians of power bent on enslaving man as an object, are not the author? That Saint-Fond is not Sade? Perhaps not, is Camus' nuanced reply; while it is true that a character is never the author who created him, it is quite likely that an author may be all of his characters at once. In sharp contrast to the surrealist's positive image, a much grimmer representation of the Sadean phenomenon thus emerges: "Two centuries in advance and on a reduced scale, Sade exalted the totalitarian society in the name of a frenzied liberty that rebellion does not in fact demand. With him the history and the tragedy of our times really begin" (*L'Homme révolté,* 457).

In her stimulating essay "Faut-il brûler Sade?" (in *Les Temps modernes,* December 1951, January 1952; later in *Privilèges* [Paris: Gallimard, 1955]), Simone de Beauvoir, took no particular account of Camus' political analysis, obviously based on ideological premises vastly different from her own, but at the same time she does not disagree substantially with Camus' ranking of Sade among the literary stars of lesser magnitude. She notes, however, that Sade had suffered from a conspiracy of silence and had never been officially accorded the place he deserved. Exactly what that place should be is not clear: certainly something considerably less than what Sade's more enthusiastic supporters, reacting to the aforementioned conspiracy of silence, wanted to grant him. Those enthusiasts had injudiciously acclaimed Sade as a prophetic genius. But Sade is not a prophetic genius. Even his admirers have to admit that his work is in great part "unreadable." It escapes a derivative banality (e.g., in its wholesale acceptance of d'Holbach's and La Mettrie's mechanistic platitudes) only to founder in incoherence. Sade basically failed in his attempt to convert his own psychophysiological destiny into a valid ethical choice. As for great literature, the cliché-ridden, repetitive speeches he constantly sandwiches between representational interludes of debauchery rob these of all life and verisimilitude. It is true that sometimes the dull grayness of his work is suddenly illuminated with bright flashes of bitter or arrogant truth, allowing us momentarily to catch sight of a great writer's style; all the same it would simply not occur to anyone to rank *Justine* with either *Manon Lescaut* or *Les Liaisons dangereuses*. In terms of his overall contribution, Sade's chief merit lies in the raw force of his opposition to social abstractions, in his total commitment to the analytically concrete; but neither in his life nor in his works does he overcome the contradictions of solipsism. He failed to see any other solution than individual rebellion. Abstract morality or crime are his only alternatives. He was unaware of "action." Sade in the end provides no revelation, and Beauvoir, politically unwilling to follow the likes of Camus but too clearheaded to confuse Sade with Heine's and Lely's "most lucid thinker of modern times," understandably fudges her conclusion and ends with a commonplace: "The supreme value of his testimony is that he makes us uneasy. He forces us to rethink the essential problem that, in other guises, haunts our times: that is, the true nature of man's relationship to man" (*Privilèges*, 82). She does not recommend (we guessed that would be the case from the beginning!) that we burn Sade. It is far from apparent, however, that she would have gone out of her way to grant the marquis priority status for admission to the Bibliothèque de la Pléiade.

Two additional Sadean events of this period stand out especially and have particular significance. Most notable in the area of publication was Gilbert Lely's two-volume critical biography, *Vie du marquis de Sade, avec un examen de ses ouvrages* (1952, 1957), forming eventually in its definitive edition Volumes I and II of the *Oeuvres complètes du marquis de Sade* (sixteen volumes; Paris: Cercle du Livre Précieux, 1966–1967). Acknowledging his debt to Heine, Lely's dedication reads "To the memory of Maurice Heine, who permanently destroyed the prison in which the marquis de Sade wasted thirty years of his life and where eternal dogs, enemies of love and truth, kept him prisoner after death." Despite the strong lyrical current of unqualified admiration that runs throughout the work, Lely's two volumes contain much original biographical research and a good deal of insightful analysis that together guarantee for his biography the status of an enduring classic.

The other major Sadean "milestone" of the 1950s involves what has come to be known as *l'affaire Pauvert,* the prosecution (1956–1958) of Jean-Jacques Pauvert on charges of publishing obscene pornography—namely, the four titles *La Philosophie dans le boudoir, Les 120 journées de Sodome, La Nouvelle Justine,* and *L'Histoire de Juliette.* Despite the assistance of such expert witnesses for the defense as André Breton, Jean Paulhan, Jean Cocteau, and Georges Bataille, and even though concessive stipulations were made by the publisher, the prosecution was successful. The complete works enterprise suffered only a temporary reversal, however, and after 1960 regained lost ground when the restraining legislation was changed. The broad long-term effects of such legal interventions, paralleled in somewhat similar trials in England (*Fanny Hill, Lady Chatterley's Lover*) and in the United States (*Tropic of Cancer*), ultimately ensured a relaxation of legislated obscenity standards and official censorship. In the decade following, several editions of Sade's collected works appeared, including, in the United States, the publication by Grove Press (1965–1968) of Sade's major novels in the Austryn Wainhouse and Richard Seaver English translations.

In a brief survey such as this, it is not possible to list—let alone do justice to—the many critics and writers who have published on Sade, especially since the 1960s: commentators like Roland Barthes, Angela Carter, Béatrice Didier, Gilles Deleuze, Michel Foucault, Jane Gallop, Marcel Hénaff, Jacques Lacan, Philippe Roger, Philippe Sollers, Chantal Thomas, and many others of equal, greater, or lesser importance who have escaped this almost random pass of the alphabetical scanner. A telephone book approach, attaching to each name an identity tag, an "address" that shows (appropriately in sixties parlance) where each critic "is coming from," and perhaps providing for each a handy quote, the equivalent of a TV news sound bite, would not be very useful. The accumulated mass of critical works is obvious evidence that the marquis' reputation has continued to grow, even if, with some notable exceptions, much of that criticism has tended to tell us more about the critics, their individual poetics, constructs, and problematics, than about Sade himself. Mention should also be made of various collectaneous volumes devoted to Sade, such as *Yale French Studies* (1965), *Tel Quel,* 28 (1967), and *Obliques,* 12–13 (1977). Sade's formal admission to the universities—rarely to the undergraduate classroom but frequently to faculties of graduate research (witness the astonishing average of five theses on Sade completed per year in 1975, 1976, and 1977)—bespeaks the ever-widening acceptance of his academic "credentials," as do also the various distinguished colloquia that have been organized in his honor (e.g., in Aix-en-Provence, 1966, proceedings published as *Le Marquis de Sade* [Paris: Armand Colin, 1968]; at Cerisy-la-Salle, 1981, published as *Sade: écrire la crise* [Paris: Belfond, 1983]). For more bibliographical details on these and other publications, the reader is referred to such useful critical surveys as Michel Delon's "Dix ans d'études sadiennes (1968–1978)" in *Dix-huitième siècle* XI: 393–426, as well as Delon's important introduction to Volume I of the Pléiade edition of Sade's *Oeuvres* (1990). Much useful data will be found in Colette Verger Michael, *The Marquis de Sade: The Man, His Works, and His Critics: An Annotated Bibliography* (New York: Garland, 1986), which contains no fewer than 1,857 classified listings. Françoise Laugaa-Traut's compact and frequently cited *Lectures de Sade* (Paris: Armand Colin, 1973) is also highly recommended.

With notable exceptions, much of the recent critical work on Sade has been marked by a determined rejection of any overall life-and-work focus and by a resolutely "textual" approach. Questions relating to such matters as Sadean madness, morality, or even monotony have been largely banished from interrogations of the "only true" Sadean universe—that is, the universe of discourse where the goddess semiosis and not mimesis most often reigns supreme. When Barthes in *Sade, Fourier, Loyola* already a quarter century ago (Paris: Seuil, 1971) revealed that "shit," when written, has no odor, that Sade can inundate his partners with it but we catch not a whiff of it, he illustrated how language has the power to deny, obliterate, and dissociate reality; libertinage thus becomes a fact of language and no more. We simply bypass the larger moral or even poetic issues—the big questions, as they were once called—and safely make our way to the crossword section.

Which brings me to Annie Le Brun, indisputably one of the more significant figures in recent Sadean criticism, a latter-day surrealist and possibly the marquis' most ardent contemporary champion.

It is not difficult to imagine that a miraculously resurrected Sade (who disliked even the relatively benign "metaphysics" of his own century's *marivaudage*) would be immensely baffled today by some of the more ingeniously arcane psychoanalytical, linguistic, and literary exegesis that has been applied to his writings for the past several decades. On the other hand, it is something of a tribute to Annie Le Brun's *Soudain un bloc d'abîme, Sade* (Paris: J.-J. Pauvert, 1986) and her *Sade, aller et détours* (Paris: Plon, 1989) that I can imagine this same resurrected marquis, after a serious vocabulary upgrade, almost feeling at home with some of Le Brun's conclusions about him. To suggest that does not necessarily mean that I think she is right, either about Sade the writer or about Sade the man; indeed, I find that I disagree with her passionately on many key issues, and notably with respect to the inclusive question of Sade's coherence, his political opportunism, and his bad faith (integral atheism excepted) in general. But at least when I find myself disagreeing with Le Brun (as well as, often enough, with her associate Jean-Jacques Pauvert, who chose Le Brun as his coeditor when he reissued in the mid-1980s Sade's complete works minus the more forbidding prefaces of the Cercle du Livre Précieux edition), I have a strong sense that we are talking more or less about the same man and about the same books, books that I insist on reading as prose— often very boring prose—but that Le Brun basically prefers to read as a form of (sublime) poetry. For Le Brun, it is only the poets—the likes of Apollinaire, Breton, Eluard, and Mandiargues—who have understood Sade, and so she castigates the recent critics, these "modernist pedants" who have seen fit to separate art and life, who have lost sight of the organic bond between truth and the body and have tried instead to enable words to live without things. In her eyes they are guilty of far worse than simply misunderstanding Sade. Their ever-denser networks of interminable linguistic analysis have had the effect of making Sade socially acceptable only at the cost of robbing him of his vital power. Paradoxically, whereas nearly two centuries of opprobrium had simply excluded Sade from the company of men, now textual analysis has succeeded in excluding him from his own self. It is wrong in every sense to declaw the tiger in this way, wrong of Barthes to reduce shit to discourse, and equally impertinent of Foucault to evoke "Sade's *calm and patient* language." Sade, must not be watered down and neutralized, not even, it seems (and here I become profoundly troubled) by the discovery of new facts that might "mislead" the biographer (the intended target is Maurice Lever's recent "scientific" biography) to conclude that Sade was "a man of his times" or, to put it in apposite Galilean terms, to suggest that the Divine Marquis actually orbited around the sun and not the other way around. (See Le Brun's "Avertissement" to the 1992 edition of *Soudain un bloc d'abîme, Sade,* in *De l'inanité de la littérature* [Paris: J.-J. Pauvert, 1994], 273–78).

And speaking of Lever, here is obviously the place to mention the two major post-Lely biographies of Sade, Jean-Jacques Pauvert's three-volume *Sade vivant* (Paris: Laffont, 1986–1990) and Maurice Lever's *Donatien Alphonse François, marquis de Sade* (Paris: Fayard, 1991), each with its particular merits and ambitions. I have referred to both works often enough (as well as to Lever's invaluable two-volume [Paris: Fayard, 1993–1995] edition of the *Papiers de famille*) to be able to dispense with further comment here, except perhaps to state once more what I have underlined repeatedly in the biographical essay to which this postscript is attached—namely, that we are still too ignorant of Sade's basic biographical facts, especially those relating to his early formative years, to hope to even begin "explaining" him. At best we can still only describe his rough contours, and I cannot help thinking that a much fuller description of him would probably be available to us today if even a small fraction of the energy that has gone into textual exegesis in the last fifty years had been diverted to the patient and stubborn gathering of facts, especially missing correspondence, in various scattered archives.

I shall close this postscript by referring to the recent contributions of two American scholar-writers, neither of whom lays claim to special expertise in Sadean studies but whose opposing views help to define for today's readers some of the subject's basic parameters. Both critics employ an accessible scholarly idiom, and both happily eschew the crippling notion that there is no person behind the text. The first is well-known writer Camille Paglia whose book *Sexual Personae* (New Haven, CT: Yale University Press, 1990) presents a massive synthesis and review of the theme of art and decadence in Western culture. Paglia adopts Sade as a patron saint from page 1. In the beginning was nature; not Rousseau's benign and motherly nature of love and equality but the nasty, brutish, red-in-tooth-and-claw nature of the human jungle that is inhabited by fierce hierarchical creatures of lust and raw aggression who settle all matters in terms of power relationships, brute force, violence, and predatory sex. Paglia sees Sade as the uniquely clear-eyed philosopher of that world who, although he tells it the way it is, remains unfortunately "the most unread major writer in western literature" (2). His absence from university curricula is a clear illustration of the timidity and hypocrisy of the liberal humanities: "No education in the western tradition is complete without Sade. He must be confronted in all his ugliness" (235). And why, Paglia asks, has Sade made barely a dent on the American academic consciousness? The answer is *violence:* "It is his violence far more than his sex which is so hard for liberals to accept. For Sade, sex *is* violence. Violence is the authentic spirit of mother nature" (235). Practicing what she preaches, Paglia favors her readers with a few choice examples of Sade's barbaric fantasies—not the worst by far, but certainly bad enough to jolt the sensibilities of even the least squeamish humanities undergraduate who will be astonished to discover what a famous eighteenth-century course-assigned "novelist" was able to imagine doing to the human body with a red-hot poker. (All of which makes one think of some fairly awkward situations arising in the halls of academe.) But Paglia provides two very helpful hints for the easily nauseated, one theoretical, the other practical: "Remember, these are ideas, not acts" (242) and "Don't read Sade before lunch!" (239).

Focusing precisely on that question of *ideas* and *acts,* the second author I have in mind is the distinguished scholar and critic Roger Shattuck, whose recent work, *Forbidden Knowledge: From Prometheus to Pornography* (New York: St. Martin's, 1996), devotes a key chapter to Sade that includes an important history of the marquis' twentieth-century rehabilitation and a very sober examination (using the examples of Ted Bundy and the Moors murders case) of the possible role played by Sade's ideas and depraved narrative scenes in stimulating homicidal madness in vulnerably warped minds. Shattuck's findings are necessarily cautious, but his conclusions regarding the current tendency to classify Sade's works as literary and philosophical masterpieces are unmistakably firm and clear: We should obviously not, to answer Simone de Beauvoir's question, burn Sade; but neither should we glorify him "as a new classic of revolutionary moral liberation" (289). Sade's current reputation violates all truth in labeling criteria. In short, "the divine marquis represents forbidden knowledge that we may not forbid. Consequently, we should label his writings carefully: potential poison, polluting to our moral and intellectual environment" (299).

TWO LETTERS FROM THE COMTESSE DE SADE TO HENRI BAUMEZ

À Paris, ce 7 août 1742

Je suis inquiète de ce que vous me mandez, Monsieur, de l'indisposition de M. de Sade. Il ne me donne aucune de ses nouvelles et je vous suis obligée de m'en mander. N'a-t-il point là fait cure? Je vous recommande toujours, Monsieur, d'en avoir bien soin et de m'en dire des nouvelles exactement. Je ne vous ai point fait réponse à toutes vos lettres à cause de la cherté du port. Je n'ai point ouï dire à M. l'abbé qu'il en ait reçu de vous. M. le maréchal de Maillebois m'a mandé que M. de Sade revenait incessamment et ici on [n']en parle pas. Je voudrais qu'il fût ici à cause de sa santé, et je crains fort que l'air de ce pays-là ne lui soit pas bon. Il devrait me mander s'il veut que j'en parle à M. Amelot car je suis fort inquiète de lui.

Je me suis bien attendue que mes ballots n'arriveraient pas promptement. Dieu veuille encore qu'ils arrivent sans aucun accident. Je crains bien, à moins que l'on n'ait pris des précautions pour cela, qu'ils ne soient ouverts et si cela est tous mes pauvres habits seront gâtés et je ne suis pas en état d'en racheter d'autres.

Vous direz à M. de Sade que j'ai donné à un sellier ma berline et son berlingot lesquels tombaient tous deux en pourriture. Enfin il les a repris pour huit cents francs avec bien de la peine et s'il n'avait pas eu envie de faire plaisir à M. d'Auteuil qu'il espère qu'il lui achètera une voiture pour M. le prince de Condé il ne les aurait pris pour rien car il n'en voulait point. M. d'Auteuil m'a conseillé de garder les deux petits chevaux pour moi et de vendre les deux autres dont on ne m'offre que cent écus. Je donnerai encore cet argent au sellier, cela fera onze cents francs là-dessus et me donnera une berline qui est quasi toute neuve, bien étoffée, et que monsieur trouvera à son retour quand il voudra s'en servir mais il faudra donner encore sept

301

cents francs et ce marché-là au dire de bien des gens que j'ai consultés n'est pas mauvais parce qu'en vérité les deux voitures que j'ai vendues sont infâmes et tombées en pourriture. Je ne sais pas si M. le comte approuvera cela. J'en doute car il n'approuve pas toujours ce que je fais, ce qui me fâche beaucoup, faisant toujours tout de mon mieux. Faites-lui mille tendres amitiés de ma part et mandez-moi des nouvelles de sa santé.

Dites-lui que mon fils a battu le prince de Condé, qu'il s'est emparé de tous ses jouets et qu'il lui disait toujours *Otez-vous de là, Enfant!* Il ne m'a jamais été possible de lui faire appeler autrement. [. . .]

[From Bibliothèque de l'Arsenal, Archives de la Bastille, ms. 11636, ff. 220–221; unpublished; spelling has been modernized.]

Paris, ce 29 août 1742

J'ai fait réponse à votre lettre, Monsieur. Je ne sais pas pourquoi vous me mandez ne l'avoir pas reçue. Je vous suis obligée de me mander des nouvelles de M. de Sade. Je suis ravie d'apprendre qu'il se porte mieux. Je crois cependant qu'il ne se rétablira tout à fait que quand il sera ici et je désirerais bien qu'il y fût. M. Amelot à qui j'ai demandé s'il ne revenait point me dit l'autre jour que ce ne serait pas encore tout à l'heure.

Mais vous avez très mal fait d'écrire à ma belle-mère que M. de Sade était malade. Vous pouviez lui mander qu'il l'était mais non pas de la façon dont vous lui marquez. Il semble, à lire votre lettre qu'elle m'a envoyée, qu'il soit à toute extrémité. Ne vous avisez plus de faire des choses comme cela! La pauvre femme est dans une inquiétude affreuse. Premièrement, si M. de Sade avait été aussi mal que vous le dites à Mme sa mère pourquoi ne m'avez-vous pas mandé son état? Qui est-ce qui s'y intéresse plus que moi et vous me mandez toujours tout le contraire, qu'il se porte bien! Je suis très mécontente de cela, Monsieur. Je ne veux point que vous me cachiez les incommodités de M. de Sade et il ne faut point affliger sa pauvre mère mal à propos comme vous avez fait. Donnez-moi donc de ses nouvelles et rendez-moi compte de son état car la lettre de Mme de Sade, quoique j'en aie reçu depuis de lui, m'a fort inquiétée et il n'y pas à aller par quatre chemins, si sa santé continue à être languissante il faut absolument qu'il revienne. Vous pouvez lui montrer ma lettre et j'attends votre réponse là-dessus.

Faites toujours mes compliments à toutes les dames et les messieurs de Bonn et surtout à Mlle de Nothaft. Mes ballots n'arrivent point et l'on n'en a nulles nouvelles à l'hôtel de Maillebois où ils sont adressés. On ne sait pas seulement ce que ça veut dire. Donnez-vous donc du mouvement pour que je puisse les avoir bientôt et mandez-moi où il faut que je m'adresse pour en savoir des nouvelles. Que Bequelin fasse un peu de perquisition. Il fait un froid affreux et je n'ai pas un habit d'hiver. Me voilà comme j'étais l'année passée. Je me suis bien doutée que cela arriverait comme cela.

Je viens de recevoir votre lettre. M. l'abbé en a reçu aussi une de M. de Sade qui me paraît fort en colère de ce que j'ai pris de l'argent chez M. Lambert pour payer une berline que j'ai. Il m'en fallait bien une. Je ne pouvais pas être ici à pied! Cependant si cela le fâche si fort il n'a qu'à le dire. Je la vendrai. Je ne sais pas [ce] que je lui ai fait mais assurément ces proc[édés] sont étranges. Il aurait bien mieux fait de me garder. Je lui aurais évité beaucoup de fatigues au passage de l'armée. Il aurait fait les honneurs de chez lui le moins mal qu'il m'aurait [été] possible. Mais enfin, telle n'a pas été sa volonté. Je vous suis bien obligée de tout le détail que vous [m'avez f]ait. Il me paraît que cela a été très beau et je ne vois pas que M. de Sade fasse moins de dépense pour ne me pas avoir. Mme de Belle-Isle a mieux fait car elle a rompu sa maison dès qu'elle a su que l'armée passait, et quand M. de Sade en aurait fait autant il aur[ait] très bien fait.

Vous pouvez si vous voulez lui envoyer ma lettre et me mander toujours des nouvelles de [sa] santé car j'en suis inquiète.]

[From Bibliothèque de l'Arsenal, Archives de la Bastille, ms. 11636, ff.246–247; unpublished; spelling has been modernized.]

Notes

All translations in this study are my own. The following shortened forms are used in the notes to cite frequently mentioned works:

B.A.   Bibliothèque de l'Arsenal, Archives de la Bastille

Barbier   Edmund-Jean-François Barbier, *Chronique de la Régence et du règne de Louis XV* (Paris: Charpentier, 1857)

Bourdin   *Correspondance inédite du marquis de Sade,* ed. Paul Bourdin (Paris: Librairie de France, 1929)

CXLVIII lettres   Marquis de Sade, *CXLVIII lettres inédites à Madame de Sade (1779–1785),* ed. Georges Daumas and Gilbert Lely (Paris: Borderie, 1980)

D'Argenson   René-Louis, marquis d'Argenson, *Journal et mémoires du marquis d'Argenson,* ed. E. J. B. Rathery (Paris: Société de l'Histoire de France, 1859–1867)

Debauve   D. A. F. de Sade, *Lettres inédites et documents,* ed. Jean-Louis Debauve (Paris: Ramsay/J.-J. Pauvert, 1990)

De Luynes   Charles-Philippe d'Albert, duc de Luynes, *Mémoires sur la cour de Louis XV,* 17 volumes (Paris: Firmin Didot, 1860–1865)

Laborde   *Correspondances du Marquis de Sade et de ses proches,* ed. Alice M. Laborde (Genève: Slatkine, 1991–).

Lely, O.C.   Gilbert Lely, *Vie du marquis de Sade,* in *Oeuvres complètes du marquis de Sade,* Vols. I and II (Paris: Cercle du Livre Précieux, 1966)

Lettres et mélanges   Marquis de Sade, *Lettres et mélanges littéraires écrits à Vincennes et à la Bastille,* recueil inédit, Tomes I and II, ed. Georges Daumas and Gilbert Lely (Paris: Borderie, 1980)

Lever   Maurice Lever, *Donatien Alphonse François, marquis de Sade* (Paris: Fayard, 1991)

O.C.   *Oeuvres complètes du marquis de Sade,* Vols. III–XVI (Paris: Cercle du Livre Précieux, 1966–1967)

Oeuvres	Sade, *Oeuvres,* ed. Michel Delon (Paris: Gallimard), collection "Bibliothèque de la Pléiade," Vol. I (1990), Vol. II (1995)
Papiers	Maurice Lever, *Bibliothèque Sade, Papiers de famille,* Vols. I and II (Paris: Fayard, 1993–1995)
Pauvert	Jean-Jacques Pauvert, *Sade vivant,* 3 vols. (Paris: Laffont, 1986–1990)

Introduction

1. Michel Rey, "Police et sodomie à Paris au XVIIIe siècle: du péché au désordre," *Revue d'histoire moderne et contemporaine* XXIX (1982): 121.

2. Maurice Lever, *Les Bûchers de Sodome: Histoires des "infâmes"* (Paris: Fayard, 1985), 383.

3. Rey, "Police," 113; Lever, *Les Bûchers,* 190. See also Erica-Marie Benabou, *La Prostitution et la police des moeurs au XVIIIe siècle,* présenté par Pierre Gaubert (Paris: Librairie Académique Perrin, 1987), 83.

4. Barbier, IV, 441, 447.

5. Barbier, I, 425; May 1726.

6. Barbier, IV, 448.

7. See B.A. mss. 10254–10260, unnumbered folios.

8. Framboisier became wealthy; see Camille Piton, ed., *Paris sous Louis XV: rapports des inspecteurs de police au Roi* (Paris: Mercure de France, 1906), I, 20, n.3.

9. B.A. ms. 10260, 13 August 1749.

10. B.A. ms. 10260.

11. See petition of Geneviève Thureau and Jacques Charpentier of 17 May 1749, B.A. ms. 10259.

12. "Interrogatoire subi par Lefèvre par devant le commissaire de Rochebrune, le 10 mars 1749," B.A. ms. 10260.

13. Letter of 29 May 1749, B.A. ms. 10260.

14. B.A. ms. 10260.

15. See letters of 12 and 26 November 1748, 18 December 1749; B.A. mss. 10260, 10258, 10259.

16. Letter of 13 May 1749, B.A. ms. 10260.

Chapter One

1. Pauvert, I, 25, *Une innocence sauvage, 1740–1777.*

2. See also Pauvert, II, *Tout ce qu'on peut concevoir dans ce genre-là . . .* (1989); and III, *Cet écrivain à jamais célèbre . . .* (1990).

3. See *Papiers,* I, *Le Règne du père (1721–1760)* (1993); and II, *Le marquis et les siens (1761–1815)* (1995).

4. Lever, 23; my emphasis.

5. Pauvert, I, 25.

6. Simone de Beauvoir, "Faut-il brûler Sade?" *Privilèges* (Paris: Gallimard, 1955), 14–15. First published in *Les Temps modernes,* December 1951–January 1952.

7. O.C., XII, 24.

8. *Oeuvres,* I, 1106.

9. O.C., XII, 201; to Mlle Rousset (April–May 1779); my emphasis.

10. See chap. 5, p. 65.

11. See chap. 6, p. 77 and n. 19; an undated letter from Mme de Saint-Germain, Donatien's governess at some point during his stay with the abbé de Sade at Ebreuil before his return to Paris with the tutor Amblet in 1749 or 1750.

12. *Papiers,* I, 26–27. It would appear that Maurice Lever is in error when he describes this letter of 17 July 1729 as having been written to Marie-Eléonore rather than to her mother (see *Papiers,* I, 26). Monsieur le Duc married Caroline-Charlotte in July 1728, and Marie-Eléonore's mother was designated her *dame d'honneur* several months before the wedding (see Mathieu Marais, *Journal et mémoires sur la Régence et le règne de Louis XV [1715–1737],* ed. François-Adolphe Mathurin de Lescure [Paris: Firmin Didot, 1864], III, 536). She "resigned" from her position (in fact, she was dismissed; see Lever, 40) in August 1733 (see F.-A. Aubert De La Chenaye-Desbois, *Dictionnaire de la noblesse* [Paris: Schlesinger, 1867], XI, 826) apparently because she had failed to warn Monsieur le Duc about the amorous designs his brother, the comte de Clermont, had on his young spouse. Marie-Eléonore was appointed to the lesser position of *dame de compagnie* only in November 1733 on the occasion of her marriage to Jean-Baptiste de Sade, the future marquis' father.

13. See Robert Shackleton, *Montesquieu: A Critical Biography* (Oxford: Oxford University Press, 1961), 140–141.

14. Puzzlingly characterized as "*jeune,*" though he was fifteen years Jean-Baptiste's senior; also described erroneously as Amelot's "successor" at the ministry of foreign affairs (Lever, 35; *Papiers,* I, 18, n.1).

15. Lever, 35.

16. See B.A. ms. 10255; also Erica-Marie Benabou, *La Prostitution et la police des moeurs au XVIIIe siècle,* présenté par Pierre Gaubert (Paris: 1987), 182–183; Lever, 34–35.

17. D'Argenson, V, 399.

18. See chap. 5, pp. 66–67.

19. Lever, 666, n. 30, states that the marriage took place in 1729, but see n. 12 above.

20. A rumor (unfounded) that Louis XV had himself quietly conquered the young princess was circulating in 1731, according to the Dutch ambassador of the day. See Michel Antoine, *Louis XV* (Paris: Fayard, 1989), 484.

21. Voltaire, *Correspondance,* ed. T. Besterman (Paris: Gallimard, "Pléiade," 1963), I, 433; cited in a letter to the abbé de Sade, 3 November 1733.

22. "Fragment autobiographique," Lever, 41.

23. See *Papiers,* I, 816.

24. Lever, 42.

25. See Barbier, III, 187.

26. D'Argenson, II, 230.

Chapter Two

1. *Papiers,* I; letter to the comte de Sade, 16 December 1736.

2. *Papiers,* I, 33; letter of 27 May 1734.

3. 19 July 1734, *Papiers,* I, 37.

4. *Papiers,* I, 43.

5. 23 January 1741, D'Argenson, III, 260.

6. See G. Livet, ed., *Recueil des instructions données aux ambassadeurs et ministres de France,* XXVIII, Tome II, 159–172 (Paris: Centre National de la Recherche Scientifique, 1963).

7. 17 August 1741; Laborde, II, 135, 140, 153, 162–163.

8. B.A. ms. 11636, f.129.

9. Barbier, III, 194.

10. D'Argenson, II, 407.

11. Barbier, III, 285.

12. See Barbier, III, 286–287.

13. *Papiers,* II, 124.

14. Jean-Baptiste to Amelot, 6 August 1741, Laborde, II, 155.

15. From Brühl, 24 June 1741; Laborde, II, 143; my emphasis.

16. See *Papiers,* I, 77.

17. Like his brother the comte, the abbé occasionally ran into trouble with the capital's vice squad but in less "eclectic" circumstances. See, for example, the report of commissaire Mutel, 25 May 1762 in Lever, 674.

18. B.A. ms. 11636, ff. 220–221; unpublished. For the original French version, see App. III.

19. See de Luynes, IV, 201.

20. "Histoire de Valcour," *Aline et Valcour ou le roman philosophique, Oeuvres,* I, 403.

21. B.A. ms. 11636, ff. 246–247: unpublished. Some words are partially hidden by the wax seal or illegible because of gaps in the paper. For the original French version, see App. III.

22. See the comte's letter of 11 May 1742, erroneously dated 1741 in Laborde, II, 137.

23. *Papiers,* I, 79; 4 January 1742.

24. From Frankfurt, 20 June 1742; Laborde, II, 177.

25. See Jean-Baptiste's letters of 18 and 28 September 1742, B.A. ms. 11637, ff. 147–148, 472–473; also 11636, f. 208.

26. See *Papiers,* I, 132.

27. Mlle Kaukol's brother, presumably.

28. B.A. ms. 11638, ff. 531–532 (draft).

29. *Papiers,* I, 93.

30. Laborde, II, 179; 3 December 1742.

31. Ibid., II, 181–182; 31 December 1742; my emphasis.

Chapter Three

1. D'Argenson, IV, 241.

2. See *Papiers,* I, 111; 18 March 1743.

3. Out of prudence, Baumez declined to carry out these instructions. The newly discovered correspondence between the comte and Baumez reveals many hitherto unknown facts about this Byzantine affair. See B.A. ms. 11638, ff. 519, 504–505; 24 January and 30 May 1744.

4. *Papiers,* I, 165; 3 January [1744].

5. See de Luynes, IV, 201; 13 August 1742: "He resembles neither his father nor his mother, except that he is very blond."

6. *Papiers,* I, 181; 25 May 1744.

7. See B.A. ms. 11638, f. 505; 11637, ff. 292–293; also Laborde, II, 278–280.

8. See Laborde, II, 225, 234.

9. Count Ferdinand von Hohenzollern.

10. B.A. ms. 11637, f. 519; my emphasis.

11. B.A. ms. 11637, f. 28.

12. B.A. ms. 11637, ff. 274–275.

13. B.A. ms. 11638, ff. 504–505.

14. See G. Livet, ed., *Recueil des instructions données aux ambassadeurs et ministres de France,* XXVIII, Tome II (Paris: Centre National de la Recherche Scientifique, 1963), 175–180.

15. B.A. ms. 11637, f. 282. My emphasis. Similar testimonials were written on the same day to Baumez by Esmasle in Liège and Malbran de la Noue in Frankfurt.

16. B.A. ms. 11637, ff. 292–293.

17. *Papiers,* I, 181; 21 May 1744.

18. Ibid., I, 191; 2 June 1744.

Chapter Four

1. See Barbier, III, 538.

2. De Luynes, VI, 43; Barbier, III, 537–538.

3. See *Papiers,* I, 256.

4. Ibid., I, 191; de Luynes, VI, 33.

5. "A Bar-le-Duc, à dix heures, 14 août 1744"; see Jean Hervez, *Les Maîtresses de Louis XV le bien-aimé* (Paris: L'Édition, 1924), 71.

6. Indeed, there is a remote possibility that Mme de Châteauroux was Monsieur le Duc's illegitimate daughter.

7. *Papiers,* I, 242.

8. [Ca. 10 October] 1744; ibid., I, 268.

9. D'Argenson, IV, 40.

10. B.A. ms. 11637, f. 294.

11. Madame Félicité, also known as Madame Sixième, daughter of Louis XV, who died around the end of September 1744 at the abbey of Fontevrault. News of her demise reached Versailles on Saturday, 3 October; de Luynes, VI, 102.

12. B.A. ms. 11636, ff. 216–217.

13. *Oeuvres,* I, 403.

14. *Papiers,* I, 288, 482.

15. Pierre-Charles Fabiot Aunillon, *Mémoires de la vie galante, politique et littéraire de l'abbé Aunillon Delaunay du Gué* (Paris: L. Colin, 1808), II, 107–108. Aunillon (1685–1760) arrived in Bonn on 5 January 1745 and left in October 1747. Judging from the quantity of factual errors it contains, the first volume of Aunillon's *Mémoires* is unquestionably apocryphal. The Cologne journal ("Quatorzième lettre," II, 98–276) is, on the other hand, undoubtedly authentic.

16. See Georges Livet, *Recueil des instructions données aux ambassadeurs et ministres de France* (Paris: Centre National de la Recherche Scientifique, 1963), XXVIII, *États allemands,* Tome II: *L'Electorat de Cologne,* 199.

17. B.A. ms. 11638, ff. 72–75; draft letter dated 3 February 1745. Aunillon's original instructions were to avoid confiding in Baumez (Livet, *Recueil,* 194; Aunillon, *Mémoires,* II, 112), who nevertheless subsequently became his official secretary.

18. *Papiers,* I, 302; letter of 7 February 1745.

19. See Laborde, II, 240; 292–293.

20. Ibid., II, 288.

21. Ibid., II, 289–290; 25 February 1745.

22. See d'Argenson, I, 272; II, 101.

23. *Papiers,* I, 361; letter of 25 September 1745.

24. Ibid., I, 362.

25. Ibid., I, 383.

26. Ibid., I, 410, 414, 421, 428, 454.

27. See, for example, Monsieur le Duc's letter of 8 June 1734, ibid., I, 34.

28. See Frantz Funck-Brentano, *Les Lettres de cachet à Paris: étude suivie d'une liste des prisonniers de la Bastille (1659–1789)* (Paris: Imprimerie Nationale, 1903), #3966. Folios 6–7 of B.A. ms. 11636, containing part of the 1747 police report on Baumez, were published by François Ravaisson, *Archives de la Bastille* (Paris: A. Durand and Pedone-Lauriel, 1883),

XV, 389–392. See also Lever, 669–670. D'Argenson describes Baumez in the harshest terms: "one of the vilest creatures ever to become involved in our affairs" (IV, 244). After noting that Baumez served as his secretary for more than a year, Aunillon states that "his bad conduct, his indiscretions and even treacheries, forced me to send him back to France" (*Mémoires de la vie galante,* II, 112–113).

C h a p t e r F i v e

1. *Papiers,* I, 390.
2. See ibid., I, 506; Mme de Bulkeley to Marie-Eléonore.
3. Ibid., I, 488.
4. Ibid., I, 375; 19 December 1745.
5. Ibid., I, 385.
6. Ibid., I, 388, 391, 401, 409.
7. Ibid., I, 417.
8. Ibid., I, 488.
9. Ibid., I, 289–290. Regarding the date, see the comments later in this chapter.
10. Ibid., I, 522.
11. De Luynes, VI, 193.
12. Lely, O.C., I, 47, n. 3.
13. Lever, 62.
14. Pauvert, I, 36; also 31–32; Lely, O.C., I, 43–47; Lever, 65.
15. O.C., IV, 16.
16. *Papiers,* I, 289.
17. De Luynes, IX, 163: "Thursday, 26 December" [1748].
18. D'Argenson, VI, 106; 26 December 1749.
19. *Papiers,* I, 411–412; [19 May 1746].
20. Ibid., I, 590; [June] 1753.
21. See B.A. ms. 10260 (unnumbered folios).

C h a p t e r S i x

1. Pauvert, I, 25.
2. Lely, O.C., I, 34.
3. *Papiers,* I, 599.
4. Lely, O.C., I, 50, n. 1.
5. *Papiers,* I, 49 [December 1735–January 1736].
6. Ibid., I, 529; 10 October 1750.
7. See Pierre Klossowski, *Sade mon prochain* (Paris: Seuil, 1947), 191.
8. See, for example, *La Nouvelle Justine,* O.C., VI, 435–436; *Histoire de Juliette,* O.C., IX, 40.
9. 25 April 1759, to the abbé Amblet; O.C., XII, 7 .
10. *Aline et Valcour,* in *Oeuvres,* I, 403.
11. Lever, 303; 5 January 1778.
12. Ibid., 75.
13. *Papiers,* I, 612; my emphasis.
14. Ibid., I, 614; 22 September 1753.
15. Ibid., I, 615; 1 October 1753.
16. See his letter to Sartine, 2 November 1763; O.C., XII, 18.
17. *Papiers,* I, 816; 31 December 1758; my emphasis.

18. Lever, 80.

19. Lever, 79; my emphasis. This important letter, described by Maurice Lever as unpublished (678, n. 16) is apparently undated. Lever situates it in the same time period as the comte's September 1753 exchange of letters with Mme de Longeville, just cited. In fact, it may well belong to an earlier period in Donatien's life, perhaps even as early as 1749 or 1750. Mme de Saint-Germain was more than a *seconde maman* in the sense we have been using the term. Thanks to arrangements made by the abbé de Sade, she had come into Donatien's life as a kind of governess even before the arrival in Ébreuil (in 1749, as we have seen) of the tutor Amblet. Sade cites her along with Amblet as a potential witness to his good character during his "earliest childhood years," just as he cites the marquis de Poyanne as someone who could vouch for the virtuous innocence of his adolescence ("Ma grande lettre," to Renée-Pélagie, 20 February 1781, O.C., XII, 277). Mme de Saint-Germain was living at the time near Vichy, not far from Ébreuil where the abbé de Sade took up residence in 1745. Her letter (Lever, 79) refers specifically, moreover, to Donatien's uncle and to the fact that Jean-Baptiste is aware that it is the abbé who has entrusted Donatien to her: "Your brother has been trying to take him away from me these past two weeks. I am frantic. He tells me you are clamoring for him." If this is the case, it amounts to more evidence that Marie-Eléonore did make efforts to see her son during his supposedly uninterrupted Provençal stay.

20. See, for example, *Eugénie de Franval,* O.C., X, 429.

21. See Pauvert, I, 53.

22. *Papiers,* I, 794.

23. Ibid., I, 716; "le 11 octobre" [1756].

24. Ibid., I, 718; 29 October 1756.

25. Ibid., I, 721; 18 November 1756.

26. Ibid., I, 48, 814; see also 721, 1082, 1091. Marie-Eléonore's letter of 25 September 1745 to Jean-Baptiste, prisoner of war (see chap. 4, pp. 56–57) bears the notation "Letter from my mother"; *Papiers,* I, 360–362.

27. Ibid., I, 9.

Chapter Seven

1. See, for example, Léonore in *Aline et Valcour* and Cornaro in *Juliette.*

2. *Papiers,* I, 711; 3 August 1756.

3. Ibid., I, 711; 3 August 1756.

4. O.C., XII, 258; to Renée-Pélagie, 14 December 1780.

5. O.C., IX, 256.

6. Archives Nationales, F⁷ 3126, cited by Lever, 603.

7. See, for example, René Pomeau, *D'Arouet à Voltaire (1694–1734)* (Oxford: Voltaire Foundation, 1985), 39–40. In 1726, Voltaire shocked the mother of Alexander Pope by confiding to her that he had been sodomized by the "damned Jesuits" while a pupil at Louis-le-Grand to such an extent that he felt he would never recover physically from the experience for as long as he lived. (Pomeau, *D'Arouet,* 40, 226).

8. Two surviving fragments of the journal, discovered among the family papers by Count Xavier de Sade, have been published by Georges Daumas. See *Journal inédit du marquis de Sade* (Paris: Gallimard, 1970), 36.

9. O.C., XII, 395.

10. *Oeuvres,* I, 69. Pierre Bayle (*Dictionnaire historique et critique* [Rotterdam: R. Leers, 1697]) devotes a lengthy and curious article to Sanchez. See also Voltaire, *Correspondance,*

ed. T. Besterman (Paris: Gallimard, "Pléiade," 1963–1993), II, 607; V, 586, 619; X, 14. See also the section, "Mariage de l'homme aux quarante écus" in his classic conte, *L'Homme aux quarante écus* (1768).

11. See de Luynes, VI, 235. The duchesse died in December 1744 and left Glatigny to her equerry M. de la Courneuve, who, having decided to stay on at Versailles, then sold it to the comte de Sade.

12. *Papiers,* I, 514.

13. Ibid., I, 693.

14. See ibid., I, 540; Jean-Baptiste to his uncle, 11 November 1752.

15. Ibid., I, 543.

16. Ibid., I, 538; [October 1752?].

17. See "Détail des services," Archives de la Guerre, Lely, O.C., I, 55.

18. See Lever, 82–83; also *Papiers,* I, 715, n. 2.

19. See de Luynes, XV, 156. The *Gazette*'s account on page 1 (*Extraordinaire,* 17 July 1756, "Relation de la prise des Forts de Mahon par l'Armée du Roi, commandée par le Maréchal Duc de Richelieu") also makes clear that "le sieur de Sade" in question was "Lieutenant-Colonel du Régiment de Briqueville."

20. *Papiers,* I, 738–739; April 1757; my emphasis.

21. Ibid., I, 734; March 1757.

22. De Luynes, XVI, 64.

23. Barbier, VII, 54.

24. *Papiers,* I, 764.

25. Ibid., I, 769; 20 June 1758.

26. Ibid., I, 786; 31 August 1758.

27. Ibid., I, 813; 24 November 1758.

28. Ibid., I, 756; 27 April 1758.

Chapter Eight

1. *Papiers,* I, 772.

2. De Luynes, XVI, 480–484.

3. *Oeuvres,* I, 404.

4. De Luynes, XVI, 481–482.

5. See *Papiers,* I, 837, 1 April 1759; I, 853, 4 August 1760.

6. Ibid., I, 839.

7. Ibid., II, 39.

8. Lely, O.C., I, 57.

9. *Papiers,* I, 306.

10. Lely, O.C., I, 58.

11. *Papiers,* II, 36.

12. Lever, 107–108, and *Papiers,* II, 32, identify the recipient as the comte's sister, the abbesse; Pauvert, I, 70, and Laborde, III, 81, suggest that the comte is writing to his mother.

13. *Papiers,* I, 788; letter of 12 September 1758.

14. Ibid., II, 35.

15. Ibid., II, 81.

16. Ibid.

17. Ibid.

18. Ibid., II, 39; 2 February [1763].

19. Laborde, III, 103; Pauvert, I, 76, n. 2; Lever, in *Papiers,* II, 85, suggests a 12 February 1764 dating, but Donatien, mentioned in the letter, could not have been in Paris then.

20. *Papiers,* II, 47.

21. O.C., XII, 15; 6 April 1763; my emphasis.

22. *Papiers,* II, 50.

23. Ibid., II, 55; my emphasis. Cf. Pauvert, I, 83, and Laborde, III, 138–139.

24. The comte to the abbé, 17 March 1763; *Papiers,* II, 43.

25. See Alice M. Laborde, *Le Mariage du marquis de Sade* (Paris: Champion-Slatkine, 1988), 209.

26. *Papiers,* II, 51.

27. Ibid., II, 52.

28. Lely, O.C. I, 82.

29. Ibid.

30. See Jean-Baptiste to the abbesse de Saint-Laurent, Lely, O.C., I, 82.

31. *Papiers,* II, 73; 24 September 1763.

Chapter Nine

1. See Camille Piton, ed., *Paris sous Louis XV: rapports des inspecteurs de police au Roi,* troisième série (Paris: Mercure de France, 1910), III, 244.

2. O.C., XII, 645–647.

3. "Variante"; ibid., XIV, 88.

4. "Projet de Frontispice"; ibid., XIV, 88.

5. Ibid., XII, 18; 2 November 1763.

6. Lely, O.C., I, 109.

7. O.C., XII, 17–18.

8. Simone de Beauvoir, "Faut-il brûler Sade?" *Privilèges* (Paris: Gallimard, 1955), 19.

9. "I who could bamboozle God Almighty if I put my mind to it!"; to Gaufridy, 29 September 1775, O.C., XII, 84.

10. "La Vérité," ibid., XIV, 81.

11. *Papiers,* I, 725.

12. See the comte de La Tour to the chevalier de Mouroux, 17 April 1773; Laborde, VI, 208–209.

13. See, for example, O.C., XI, 408.

14. See Denis Diderot, *Oeuvres complètes,* ed. R. Lewinter (Paris: Club Français du Livre, 1971), VIII, 900.

15. Voltaire, *Correspondance,* ed. T. Besterman (Paris: Gallimard, "Pléiade," 1963–1993), XI, 304; 6 April 1773.

16. Diderot, *Oeuvres complètes,* VIII, 964; XI, 1027.

17. O.C., XII, 306–307 [from Vincennes, 20–25 April 1781].

18. Lely, O.C., I, 114.

19. For a brief juridical account of the La Barre affair, see Dominique Holleaux, "Le procès du Chevalier de La Barre," in Jean Imbert, ed., *Quelques procès criminels des XVIIe et XVIIIe siècles* (Paris: Presses Universitaires de France, 1964), 165–179.

20. 21 January 1764; Lely, O.C., I, 115.

21. De Luynes, VIII, 378.

Chapter Ten

1. Lely, O.C., I, 114.

2. 1 June 1766; ibid., I, 138.

3. On Sade's various residences in Paris at this time, see Bourdin, xvii.

4. See Lely, O.C., I, 201.

5. Although it was Jean-Baptiste's ordinary title, official documents even during the period preceding the father's death in 1767 sometimes refer to Donatien as the "comte" de Sade. Except for a family tradition, Jean-Baptiste, on the death in 1739 of his own father, Gaspard-François, marquis de Sade (sometimes "de Mazan"; see Lely, O.C., I, 28; Lever, 663), might have been expected to adopt the title "marquis."

6. Camille Piton, *Paris sous Louis XV, rapports des inspecteurs de police au Roi* (Paris: Mercure de France, 1906–1914), III, 243–244.

7. Pauvert, I, 171; 30 January 1767.

8. Lever, 156.

9. To Renée-Pélagie, 20 February 1780; O.C., XII, 277.

10. See ibid., XII, 277.

11. 18 March 1768; Piton, *Paris,* III, 287.

12. Ibid., III, 359.

13. See "Pièces justificatives," Lely, O.C., I, 197–222, especially 209–212.

14. Ibid., I, 189.

15. 12 April 1768; ibid., I, 186.

16. 18 April 1768; ibid., I, 224.

17. From Saumur, 30 April 1768; ibid., I, 231.

18. Ibid., I, 224.

19. Ibid., I, 225.

20. Ibid.

21. *Juliette,* O.C., VIII, 444.

22. Ibid., VIII, 433.

23. Lely, O.C., I, 225.

24. See, for example, Piton, *Paris,* I, 306.

25. Lely, O.C., I, 225.

26. 26 April 1768; ibid., I, 229.

27. Ibid., I, 230.

28. See Lever, 189.

29. Lely, O.C., I, 231; 30 April 1768.

Chapter Eleven

1. See report of 22 February 1765, Camille Piton, *Paris sous Louis XV, rapports des inspecteurs de police au roi* (Paris: Mercure de France, 1906–1914), II, 172.

2. Lely, O.C., I, 230; 30 April 1768.

3. B.A. ms. 10252, ff. 25, 107; see also Claude Mauriac's novel *La Marquise sortit à cinq heures* (Paris: Albin Michel, 1961).

4. See "Le Président mystifié," O.C., XIV, 208.

5. Lever, 176–179, and App. IV, 798–806.

6. Gilbert Lely, *Vie du marquis de Sade, avec un examen de ses ouvrages* (Paris: Gallimard, 1957), II, 701–702.

7. Lely, O.C., I, 56.

8. Cited in Pauvert, I, 176, n.1.

9. My emphasis; *Gazette de Leyde. Nouvelles extraordinaires de divers endroits,* 29 April 1768, quoted by Lever, 801–802.

10. *Oeuvres,* I, 403; my emphasis.

11. See Lever, 298.

12. O.C., XII, 473-474.

13. Ibid., XII, 392; my emphasis.
14. Ibid., XII, 459.
15. See F. Bournon, *La Bastille* (Paris: Imprimerie Nationale, 1893), passim.
16. O.C., XII, 458–459.
17. Ibid., XII, 459; my emphasis.
18. *Oeuvres*, I, 403.
19. Governor of the fortress of Pierre-Encize.
20. Lely, O.C., I, 231.
21. Ibid., I, 231; 30 April 1768.
22. Ibid., I, 236; 24 August 1768.
23. Ibid., I, 236.
24. Ibid., I, 237.
25. See Lever, 688, n. 26.
26. Lely, O.C., I, 243.
27. *Papiers*, II, 133.
28. Ibid., II, 131; my emphasis.
29. Lely, O.C., I, 244–245.
30. Laborde, II, 286; Aunillon to d'Argenson, 18 [February 1745].
31. Ibid., 245; see *Papiers*, I, 488.
32. Lely, O.C., I, 242–243.

Chapter Twelve

1. 24 March 1770; Lely, O.C., I, 245.
2. See Lever, 190.
3. See F. Funck-Brentano, *La Bastille des comédiens* (Paris: Albert Fontemoing, 1903), for a description of the range of facilities available to prisoners, depending on their means.
4. See O.C., XII, 104.
5. Pauvert, I, 242.
6. *Les 120 journées de Sodome,* in *Oeuvres*, I, 283.
7. O.C., VIII, 254.
8. *La Philosophie dans le boudoir,* ibid., III, 419.
9. Ibid., III, 431.
10. Ibid.
11. See Lever, 36.
12. See ibid., 807, App. V, "L'Affaire de Marseille devant la presse."
13. Cited in Lely, O.C., I, 326.
14. *Oeuvres*, I, 254.
15. O.C., XII, 51; my emphasis. See also Debauve, 117.
16. 23 February 1777; Lely, O.C., I, 597.
17. See, for example, Pauvert, I, 127.

Chapter Thirteen

1. See App. I, "Chronology."
2. Bourdin, 77.
3. In his uniquely valuable *Correspondance inédite du marquis de Sade,* Bourdin, unfortunately, published only extracts from the collection (subsequently dispersed) of manuscript letters at his disposal.
4. Lely, O.C., I, 581; my emphasis.

5. O.C., XII, 93; to Gaufridy, 21 or 22 January 1777.

6. Ibid., XII, 102; end of January 1777.

7. Ibid., XII, 101.

8. Ibid.

9. Ibid., XII, 106.

10. Bourdin, 80.

11. To Renée-Pélagie, 21 April 1777; O.C., XII, 130.

12. Gilbert Lely, *Vie du marquis de Sade avec un examen de ses ouvrages* (Paris: Gallimard, 1957), II, 70.

13. O.C., XII, 107.

14. Mme de Montreuil to Gaufridy, 13 August 1778; Bourdin, 121.

15. To Renée-Pélagie, O.C., XII, 346.

16. 29 April 1777; Bourdin, 84.

17. Mme de Montreuil to Gaufridy, 2 June 1777; ibid., 85 – 86.

18. Ibid., 93.

19. O.C., XII, 111.

20. Ibid., XII, 121.

Chapter Fourteen

1. See Pierre Klossowski, *Sade, mon prochain* (Paris: Seuil, 1947), App. II, "Le père et la mère dans l'oeuvre de Sade," 189 – 201; Lever, 24.

2. Klossowski, *Sade,* 189.

3. Ibid., 191.

4. See Pauvert, I, 105; Lever, 23.

5. See *Papiers,* I, 721.

6. See Elisabeth Badinter, *The Myth of Motherhood: An Historical View of the Maternal Instinct* (London: Souvenir, 1981) (translation of *L'Amour en plus* [Paris: Flammarion, 1980]).

7. *Le Préjugé à la mode* (1735), Act I, Scene IV.

8. *Oeuvres,* I, 403.

9. O.C., XII, 114; 6 March 1777; my emphasis.

10. Ibid., XII, 113; my emphasis.

11. 22 April 1790; ibid., XII, 469.

12. See the marquis' editorial comment (*Papiers,* II, 15) on a 3 January 1761 letter from the maréchal de Belle-Isle, advising Jean-Baptiste that he should immediately begin arrangements for payment: "My father who had originally applied for it, turned it down after it was granted, and refused subsequently to purchase it."

13. Dossier D. A. F. de Sade, Archives du Service Historique de l'Armée de Terre, Vincennes.

14. Debauve, 175.

15. O.C., XII, 129.

16. To Mme de Montreuil, from Vincennes [February 1777]; ibid., XII, 111.

17. Ibid., XII, 113.

18. *Oeuvres,* I, 1065.

19. Ibid., I, 1083.

20. Ibid., I, 1087.

21. Ibid., I, 1099.

22. Ibid., I, 1094; my emphasis.

23. O.C., XII, 116.

24. Debauve, 151.

25. Ibid., 157; 19 January 1778.

26. Ibid., 160.

27. Ibid., 152.

28. To the Abbé de Sade, September 1765; ibid., 76.

29. The Abbé de Sade to Mme de Montreuil, 1 June 1765; Lely, O.C., I, 138. Laborde, in III, 224, dates the letter as 1766.

30. *Oeuvres*, I, 397.

31. To Renée-Pélagie, July 1783; O.C., XII, 392.

32. Debauve, 76.

33. See letter to Gaufridy, 29 September 1775; O.C., XII, 84. It would appear that Debauve, on the basis of an incorrect catalogue description, cites this letter as two separate fragments, written to Fage, respectively, from Rome, 9 September 1773 and Genoa, 29 September 1773. Debauve, 119–120.

34. See Lely's description of the portrait in Lely, O.C., II, 100.

35. *Lettres et mélanges*, II, 63. The editors include (Plate III) a reproduction of the portrait of Lefèvre, "stained with blood and lacerated by the marquis, with abusive captions in his handwriting."

36. Pauvert, I, 26; my emphasis.

37. *Lettres et mélanges*, II, 63–64.

38. Ibid., II, 67.

39. Jacques François Paul Aldonse, abbé de Sade, *Mémoires pour la vie de François Pétrarque, tirés de ses oeuvres et des auteurs contemporains* (Amsterdam: Arskée et Mercus, 1764–1767), 3 vols.

40. O.C., XII, 180–181.

41. For example, the ten-year-old l'Aigle in *La Nouvelle Justine*, O.C., VII, 277–278.

42. Ibid., VIII, 89–90.

43. See, for example, *Lettres et mélanges*, II, 349; 14 February 1784.

44. *CXLVIII lettres*, 71; 22 January 1781.

45. O.C., XII, 277; 20 February 1781.

46. Ibid., XII, 276–277; my emphasis.

47. Debauve, 426.

48. *Papiers*, II, 414.

49. Lever, 431.

50. Sade to Gaufridy, 25 Pluviôse, an VII (15 February 1799), Bourdin, 430.

51. O.C., XII, 598–599.

Chapter Fifteen

1. O.C., III, 390–391; my emphasis.

2. Ibid., III, 391.

3. Ibid., III, 423.

4. Ibid., III, 428.

5. Ibid., IX, 227.

6. Ibid., VI, 172; my emphasis.

7. Ibid., VI, 174.

8. Ibid., VI, 196.

9. Ibid., VI, 197.

10. Ibid., VI, 217.

11. Ibid., VI, 208.

12. Ibid., VI, 209.

13. *La Philosophie dans le boudoir*, O.C., III, 538—539.

14. *Oeuvres*, I, 102—103.

15. Ibid., I, 103.

16. It should be noted that the antimother diatribes of the 1787 and 1799 versions are entirely missing in the 1791 version, *Justine ou les malheurs de la vertu*, for the simple reason that the victim in the 1791 version, Mme de Bressac, is there portrayed as the *aunt*, not the mother of the young libertine. In 1791 the new press laws were still being tested, and Sade, in this his first published work, was probably not yet prepared to confront the public with such joyously lubricious depictions of matricide.

17. O.C., XIV, 368—369; my emphasis.

18. Ibid., XIV, 369; my emphasis.

19. Ibid., XIV, 361.

20. Ibid., VI, 172.

21. *Histoire de Juliette ou les prospérités du vice*, ibid., IX, 220.

22. Ibid., IX, 225.

23. "L'Auteur des «Crimes de l'Amour» à Villeterque folliculaire," O.C., X, 508, 513.

24. Ibid., XII, 646.

25. *Oeuvres*, I, 1065.

26. O.C., IX, 555.

27. Ibid., IX, 361—362.

Chapter Sixteen

1. Bourdin, xxx—xxxii.

2. See, for example, *Vie*, Lely, O.C., I, 79: "P. Bourdin, who excels in the art of portraiture when the characters he is describing are not beyond his level of understanding."

3. Jean-Jacques Pauvert (*Sade vivant*, I, 128) has underlined the extent to which letters that must have been exchanged between Donatien and Mme de Montreuil are missing: "A remarkable thing, indeed: from 1764 to 1778, we have *no direct trace* of these. We know from Mme de Montreuil's letters to the abbé de Sade, for example, that she often wrote to her son-in-law during this sometimes hectic period. Not a single one of these letters, in a family that kept everything, has come down to us. And the same goes for Donatien's letters to his mother-in-law, letters that were most certainly written."

4. Bourdin, xxx.

5. 16 May 1763; Lely, O.C., I, 88.

6. 2 June 1763; Laborde, III, 166.

7. Ibid., III, 169—170.

8. Ibid., III, 174—175.

9. 20 October 1763; ibid., III, 187.

10. From Echauffour in Normandy, 14 September 1763; ibid., III, 179—181.

11. 16 November 1763; Lely, O.C., I, 114; my emphasis. See also Laborde, III, 194—195. Laborde insists, despite the terms of Jean-Baptiste's letter of 16 November to the abbé, that Sade was guilty of nothing more than "being in possession of *an unfortunate book*" and that it was "his Arcueil house" that was involved (I, 18; see also her earlier work, *Le Mariage du marquis de Sade* [Paris: Champion-Slatkine, 1988] where she also states that the reason behind Sade's 1763 incarceration was simply "*a book* which was in his possession or which he

may even have written" [196–197]. Again the Arcueil *petite maison* of 1768 is confused with the Faubourg Saint-Marceau house of 1763.) The frequent editorial duplications, misreadings, misinterpretations, and plain historical errors in this curious multivolume collection (*Correspondances du marquis de Sade et de ses proches*) only add to our impatience to see the completion of Maurice Lever's projected edition of the complete correspondence. Interestingly, with respect to the Jeanne Testard affair, it seems to have escaped the notice of Sade's biographers that the marquis in his penitent letter to Sartine of 2 November 1763, begging that the true reasons for his incarceration be kept from his family, in fact lies about not having been to his *petite maison,* or at least to Paris, since June, affirming that he had spent the entire three months after that in the country (Lely, O.C., I, 111). Mme de Montreuil's letter to the abbé of 14 September 1763 (Laborde, III, 180) makes it clear that her son-in-law was in the capital during at least part of July and August.

    12. Lely, O.C., I, 115.

    13. Debauve, 177; excerpt from a dealer catalogue description.

    14. 20 May 1765; Lever, 142; Laborde, III, 221.

    15. To Mme de Montreuil, 1 June 1765; Lely, O.C., I, 138.

    16. 1 June 1765; ibid., I, 138.

    17. See O.C., XII, 395.

    18. Lely, O.C., I, 57.

    19. 17 July 1765; Lever, 144; Laborde, III, 228.

    20. Laborde, III, 229.

    21. Letter of 17 July 1765; Lever, 145; Laborde, III, 230.

    22. Laborde, III, 232.

    23. Lely, O.C., I, 128.

    24. 7 November [1765]; Laborde, III, 243; Lever, 149–150.

    25. Lely, O.C., I, 127; Debauve, 83, dates this letter 18 December [1766].

    26. Biographers, for example, have apparently failed to follow up on a puzzling though fairly precise reference to a successfully hushed-up affair that probably took place in Paris in August 1771 but was not directly related to Donatien's incarceration for debt that same month in For l'Evêque. The reference can be found in a letter from the marquis to the notary Gaufridy sent around the end of January 1777 regarding the Treillet affair: "I consider it an extremely serious error not to have notified M. de Castillon [Public prosecutor in the Parlement of Aix]. Mme de Montreuil who likes to be kept informed of the smallest details and who will have to be told about this business, will surely not be pleased. When I had those *difficulties in Paris six years ago* [my emphasis], I recall that her first move was to notify the authorities, and it was because of this that the matter was speedily resolved. In that case, moreover, it was I who did the injury whereas here I am the injured party (and rather acutely so, it seems to me)" (O.C., XII, 104). Bourdin (68) cites the same fragment with a number of minor variants (e.g., "*très grande faute*" for "*bien grave faute,*" "*que l'on dut* l'arrangement" for "*que l'on doit*") and adds the comment "The affair referred to here by M. de Sade is apparently the Keller incident, although it goes back eight years and not six." Lely (O.C., I, 587) cites the entire letter as "unpublished" and gives the source as a "private collection." Surprisingly, he fails to make any comment regarding the event Sade is referring to and makes no mention of any obvious chronological difficulties. That it was the Keller affair seems most unlikely. First of all, the Arcueil incident had occurred nearly *nine* years before, not six, and in her efforts to hush up that affair, Mme de Montreuil's "first move" was not to notify the authorities (that had already been well taken care of by the victim, Rose Keller) but rather, and much to Sade's annoyance, to purchase the victim's silence

at what seemed to the marquis an astronomical price. Maurice Lever also does not specifically comment on Sade's mysterious allusion, but in his narrative of events surrounding the marquis' humiliating rebuff by members of his regiment in August 1770 when, still dogged by the Arcueil scandal, he tried to rejoin it at Fontenay-le-Comte, Lever wonders whether the marquis fought a duel at around this time with the officer who had been instrumental in his rejection and who had even gone so far as to order Donatien's detention (Lever, 190). Lever also quotes (689, n. 12) a letter from Sade to Renée-Pélagie, written from Vincennes in May 1778, in which the marquis alludes to a past action that should still serve to remind everyone that "my life has never been important to me when my honor is being challenged." The marquis, always hypersensitive about the possibility of losing face with his military peers (see, e.g., his memorandum of 18 May 1778 in Lever, 859, #15), seems to be pointing with pride to an incident he provoked by "insulting" someone—in other words, a rather typical dueling scenario. Other fairly obscure events in the marquis' life might also fit—for example, a possible self-imposed exile in England in 1770 ("*six* years" might refer back to late 1770) to escape (like the young Voltaire) the consequences of a dueling threat or even a duel, while Mme de Montreuil worked diligently to gain his pardon back home in an affair of honor. See also Sade's note 59 in *Isabelle de Bavière,* O.C., XV, 496: "I made these notes in 1770 while examining the original documents in the library of the king of England." A parallel note in the same work (XV, 497, n. 64) referring to other historical researches (e.g., in Dijon in 1764) seems entirely credible. Obviously, the entire matter deserves further investigation.

27. 18 July 1778; Bourdin, 111.

28. Ibid., 118.

29. See Lely, O.C., I, 633.

30. My emphasis; 8 June 1778; Bourdin, 104. See also Sade's memo of 18 May 1778, from Vincennes, in Lever, 856.

31. *CXLVIII lettres,* 168.

32. 21 October 1780; Bourdin, 159; see also Mlle de Rousset's letter to Gaufridy of 7 July 1780 (Bourdin, 158) in which she reveals that, thanks to Renée-Pélagie's lobbying, Sade's case has been the object of petitions and letters of recommendation, including some from various princesses to Maurepas, who was examining the dossier.

33. 3 June 1777; Bourdin, 85.

34. I have supplied the words in brackets. The sense, I think, is that someone she hesitates to name (the king?), according to evidence in the file, has offered the opinion that the marquis "deserves to be hanged." Mlle de Rousset's prudently paratactic syntax seems to have been misread (or left unconstrued) by all commentators to date.

35. 23 October 1780; Bourdin, 160.

Chapter Seventeen

1. 8 August 1778; Bourdin, 118.

2. Ibid., 119.

3. 27 July 1778; ibid., 114.

4. 13 August 1778; ibid., 120.

5. 13 August 1778; ibid., 120–121; my emphasis.

6. Sade to Gaufridy, 1 September 1778; ibid., 122.

7. To Gaufridy, 27 November 1778; ibid., 129.

8. Ibid., 128.

9. Ibid., 129; 8 December 1778. New documentation in Lever's recent biography (330–331) also makes it clear that most of the members of Sade's own family, with perhaps one or

two exceptions, fully supported his incarceration, insisting that after so many instances of recidivism it would be irresponsible to turn him loose on society without some kind of moral guarantee that he had indeed reformed. His liberty would have to depend on firm assurances that in future he would be on his best behavior.

10. See, for example, a new letter (Lever, 302) dated 5 January 1778, very much like others of the period but traced in blood.

11. See chap. 9, p. 102.

12. Lever, 352.

13. To Renée-Pélagie, [April 1780]; O.C., XII, 239–240.

14. To Renée-Pélagie, 27 July 1780; ibid., XII, 249.

15. Ibid., XII, 312; to Mlle de Rousset, April 1781.

16. Ibid., XII, 346; to Renée-Pélagie [1781]; my emphasis.

17. Author's note, *Aline et Valcour* in *Oeuvres*, I, 863.

18. *CXLVIII lettres*, 156.

19. April or May 1779; O.C., XII, 201.

20. *Papiers*, II, 50.

21. O.C., XII, 419; to Renée-Pélagie [23 November 1783].

22. Ibid., XII, 371; to Renée-Pélagie [1782].

23. Wishing, for example, that he himself had enjoyed the upbringing afforded the five children he had abandoned, one after another, to the Foundling Hospital, and being well aware at the same time that three-quarters of the children taken there—including no doubt a similar proportion of his own—died in the first year. See Jean-Jacques Rousseau, *Les Confessions,* in *Oeuvres complètes,* ed. Bernard Gagnebin and Marcel Raymond (Paris: Gallimard, "Pléiade," 1959), I, 357–358.

24. O.C., XII, 372.

25. Ibid., XII, 368; 22 October 1782.

26. Ibid., XII, 372; to Renée-Pélagie [1782].

27. Ibid., XII, 347; my emphasis.

28. 12 June 1791; ibid., XII, 488.

29. See Maurice Heine's preface to *Les Infortunes de la vertu*, O.C., XIV, 327.

30. *Oeuvres*, I, 69; my emphasis.

31. Ibid., I, 84.

32. O.C., XII, 348–349; my emphasis.

33. *CXLVIII lettres*, 47; to Renée-Pélagie, 3 July 1780.

34. 30 December 1780; O.C., XII, 261.

35. Ibid., XII, 268; to Renée-Pélagie, 20 February 1781.

36. To Mlle de Rousset, 20–25 April 1781; ibid., XII, 306–307.

37. Ibid., XII, 311.

38. 21 May 1781; ibid., XII, 324; *Oeuvres*, I, 863.

39. My emphasis; to Renée-Pélagie, 26 October 1781; ibid., XII, 339.

40. To Renée-Pélagie, July 1783; ibid., XII, 395.

41. 20–25 April 1781; ibid., XII, 312.

42. To Renée-Pélagie, October 1781; ibid., XII, 334.

43. 18 March 1783; ibid., XII, 379.

44. Namely, by giving preference to family honor and the welfare of his children over his own freedom.

45. "Aux stupides scélérats qui me tourmentent" [February 1783]; O.C., XII, 375–376; my emphasis.

46. Ibid., XII, 434.

47. To Renée-Pélagie, January 1783; *CXLVIII lettres*, 126–127; my emphasis.
48. Lely, O.C., II, 190.

Chapter Eighteen

1. See especially *Lettres et mélanges*, II.
2. See App. II, "Sadean Criticism: A Postscript."
3. Lely, O.C., II, 237.
4. Ibid., II, 251.
5. *Lettres et mélanges*, II, 336, Renée-Pélagie to Donatien, 15 June 1783.
6. N. Peyraud de Beaussol, *Les Arsacides* (Paris: Veuve Duchesne, 1775).
7. To Renée-Pélagie, "Ma grande lettre," O.C., XII, 264, 20 February 1781.
8. To Renée-Pélagie, November 1783; *CXLVIII lettres*, 167–168; my emphasis.
9. *Aline et Valcour,* in *Oeuvres,* I, 660, first note.
10. Lely, O.C., II, 237; my emphasis.
11. *CXLVIII lettres,* 168. Later events, not surprisingly, would prove him wrong: the proximity of the scaffold did indeed have an effect on the immutability of his principles, but that is another story.
12. Ibid.
13. Lever, 594–595.
14. O.C., XII, 113.
15. Pauvert, II, 38.
16. Lely, O.C., I, 597; February 1777.
17. O.C., XII, 60; 1 May 1773.
18. Debauve, 108; February 1771.
19. 10 frimaire, an III (30 November 1794); Bourdin, 362.
20. Debauve, 428; 13 thermidor, an VI (31 July 1798).
21. O.C., XII, 530; 5 May 1793.
22. 2 September 1783; O.C., XII, 401–402.
23. Ibid., XII, 262.
24. Ibid., XII, 436; 8 March 1784.
25. Autumn 1781; ibid., XII, 333.
26. Summer 1781; ibid., XII, 329.
27. Ibid., XII, 330.
28. Marie-Eléonore, for example, apparently enraged Jean-Baptiste early in 1763 by offering, in collusion with Donatien, protection to the marquis' insolent valet Teissier; see Laborde, III, 93, 109.
29. O.C., XII, 84: my emphasis.

Chapter Nineteen

1. Bourdin, xliv.
2. Lely, O.C., II, 378–379. See "Aux mânes de Marat et de Le Pelletier," 29 September 1793; O.C., XI, 119–122.
3. Ibid., XI, 120
4. See App. I, "Chronology." Maurice Lever is mistaken when he states (Lever, 520) that Chénier entered Saint-Lazare prison only on 9 June and that Sade, who had managed to get transferred to Picpus on 27 March, could not have made his acquaintance there.
5. Bourdin, 360.
6. See André Chénier, *Iambes IX,* in *Oeuvres complètes,* ed. Gérard Walter (Paris: Nouvelle Revue Française, "Pléiade," 1940), 193–195.

7. See Bourdin, *Correspondance*, xvii–xviii; Walter, ed., *Oeuvres complètes*, xxv.

8. Chénier, *Iambes II, Oeuvres complètes*, ed. Walter, 188.

9. See *Actes du Tribunal Révolutionnaire*, recueillis et commentés par Gérard Walter (Paris: Mercure de France, 1986), 38. Walter suggests that the reference is to Michel Cubières-Palmézeaux's *Poème à la gloire de Marat*, which antedates Sade's piece by about six weeks.

10. Walter, ed., *Oeuvres complètes*, 692–693.

11. O.C., VIII, 402.

12. Ibid., VIII, 123.

13. *Aline et Valcour*, in *Oeuvres*, I, 631.

14. O.C., XI, 407–408.

15. Ibid., VIII, 478; my emphasis.

16. Ibid., III, 477.

17. Ibid., XI, 72.

18. Ibid., XI, 74.

19. See the pioneering study of Maurice Heine, *Le Marquis de Sade* (Paris: Gallimard, 1950), 321.

20. O.C., III, 526.

21. Ibid., VIII, 172–173; my emphasis.

22. Ibid., III, 116.

23. Ibid., III, 484.

24. Ibid., III, 481.

25. *Aline et Valcour*, in *Oeuvres*, I, 590; author's note.

26. *La Nouvelle Justine*, O.C., VI, 410; author's note.

27. Ibid., VIII, 478.

28. Ibid., VIII, 380.

29. To Gaufridy, [6 September 1792], Bourdin, 323.

30. O.C., XI, 120.

31. O.C., XII, 474–475.

32. Ibid., XII, 475.

33. To Gaufridy, 5 December 1791; Bourdin, 301–302; O.C., XII, 505; my emphasis.

34. See "Rapport de la conduite politique du citoyen Sade," 24 juin 1794, Lely, O.C., II, 337.

35. Bourdin, 322; to Gaufridy, 25 August 1792.

36. "Rapport de la conduite politique du citoyen Sade depuis 1789 aux membres du Comité de Sûreté Générale," 7 May 1794; Debauve, 285.

37. A.N., F[7], 4954[3], pièce no. 9; cited in Lely, O.C., II, 190.

38. Debauve, 288, 293.

39. My emphasis; see Pauvert, II, 557; Lever, 523, 753, n.11.

40. O.C., XII, 522.

41. Lever, 534.

42. Lely, O.C., II, 417.

43. Bourdin, 365; O.C., XII, 547; 2 pluviôse An III (21 January 1795).

Chapter Twenty

1. O.C., IV, 16; *Oeuvres*, I, 403 .

2. *Oeuvres*, I, 1199.

3. *Papiers*, I, 603; 6 August 1753.

4. Lely, O.C., I, 56.

5. My emphasis; O.C., XII, 37; to the comte de la Tour, 28 December 1772.

6. See chap. 11, pp. 123 – 124.

7. *Lettres et mélanges,* I, 131; [June 1788]; Lely had originally suggested a 1787 date for this letter: see O.C., XII, 458 – 459.

8. September 1784 to Renée-Pélagie; *CXLVIII lettres,* 193.

9. See chap. 13, p. 142; to Gaufridy, January 1777; O.C., XII, 101.

10. Lever, 458.

11. February 1779; *CXLVIII lettres,* 22.

12. Ibid., 112; to Renée-Pélagie, 10 May 1782.

13. Ibid., 142.

14. *Aline et Valcour,* in *Oeuvres,* I, 397.

15. *CXLVIII lettres,* 169; to Renée-Pélagie, November 1783.

16. "Article détaché des Nouvelles à la main," (23 July 1785), *Lettres et mélanges,* I, 87 – 88.

17. See chap. 19, p. 231.

18. See chap. 14, p. 165; *Lettres et mélanges,* II, 60, 63 – 64.

19. D'Argenson, II, 403, 406; III, 10.

20. O.C., III, 521.

21. See Pauvert, I, 184; Lever, 59 – 60.

22. Barbier, I, 275.

23. D'Argenson, 29 October 1750; VI, 277.

24. See "Notes pour *Les Journées de Florbelle,*" O.C., XV, 75.

25. *La Philosophie dans le boudoir,* O.C., III, 519.

26. O.C., III, 521.

27. Ibid., III, 517.

28. Ibid., III, 516.

29. Ibid., III, 521.

30. *Oeuvres,* I, 858.

31. Ibid., I, 859.

32. Ibid., I, 860.

33. Ibid., I, 861; my emphasis.

34. *Oeuvres,* I, 862.

35. My emphasis; read, Rose Keller, Jeanne Testard, and how many undiscovered victims?

36. On Sade's use of the principle of "arrangement," see Philippe Roger, "Sade et la Révolution," in *L'Écrivain devant la Révolution,* textes réunis par Jean Sgard (Grenoble: Université Stendhal de Grenoble, 1990), 148 – 150.

37. My emphasis; *Oeuvres,* I, 863, author's note.

38. See the marquis' letter of March 1785, cited by Pauvert, I, 324.

39. *Oeuvres,* I, 863 – 864.

Conclusion

1. Describing to Gaufridy in 1774 the necessary legal moves required to lift the sodomy and poisoning charges at Aix, Renée-Pélagie shows her awareness of how the system of favor worked in the Parlement's courts as well: "We will try to have the main business set aside and to deny everything. [. . .] Much will depend on favor, obviously, but I am assured that it will not be entirely impossible to obtain it"; Bourdin, 15.

2. Lely, O.C., I, 225; to her "Cher papa," the abbé, 18 April 1768.

3. See *Papiers,* I, 67.

4. Act IV, scene 3.

5. *Papiers,* I, 725.

6. O.C., XII, 12; 12 August 1760.

7. Denis Diderot, *Oeuvres complètes,* ed. R. Lewinter (Paris: Club Français du Livre, 1971), X, 342; my emphasis.

8. *Salon de 1767;* ibid., VII, 285.

9. *Aline et Valcour,* in *Oeuvres,* I, 633.

10. Ibid., 673.

11. Ibid., 672–673; my emphasis.

12. See chap. 14, p. 155.

13. *Aline et Valcour,* in *Oeuvres,* I, 403.

14. Ibid., I, 405.

15. See chap. 14, p. 156.

16. 14 December 1780, O.C., XII, 259.

17. To Palissot, 4 June 1760; Voltaire, *Correspondance,* ed. T. Besterman (Paris: Gallimard, "Pléiade," 1963–1993), V, 933.

18. Diderot, *Oeuvres complètes,* III, 260; my emphasis.

19. See, for example, his letter to François Gaufridy of 13 February 1799 regarding Mme Quesnet, O.C., XII, 580; also his letter to Charles Quesnet of 1803, cited in chap. 14, p. 170.

20. *La Philosophie dans le boudoir,* O.C., III, 538–539.

21. For the original version, see Diderot, *Oeuvres complètes,* III, 644.

22. My emphasis; ibid., III, 265.

23. See, for example, Swinburne's comments in App. II.

24. Not to mention, of course, the many fictional scenes that transpose, almost directly, elements such as abused sacramental hosts, trampled crucifixes, whippings, penknife cuts, burning wax, and so forth, from the Jeanne Testard or Rose Keller affairs. See, for example, *Les 120 journées de Sodome,* in *Oeuvres,* I, 329–330; *Justine,* O.C., III, 213; *Nouvelle Justine,* O.C., VII, 295; *Juliette,* O.C., VIII, 410, 433; IX, 206.

25. See Maurice Heine, *Le Marquis de Sade* (Paris: Gallimard, 1950), 207.

26. Camille Schuwer, "Sade et les moralistes," O.C., XI, 49.

27. See Lely, O.C., II, 251.

28. *L'Oeuvre du marquis de Sade, pages choisies,* essai bibliographique et notes par Guillaume Apollinaire (Paris: Bibliothèque des Curieux, 1909), 17.

29. O.C., XII, 346.

30. Ibid., XII, 410.

31. See *Voyage d'Italie,* O.C., XVI, 455; my emphasis. The passage seems to have been strangely neglected by scholars. In "Français encore un effort . . . ," it is made fairly clear that a minimum age cannot be set for *enjoying a girl:* "Surely, he who has the right to eat the fruit of a tree can choose to pick it, green or ripe, according to his tastes" (O.C., III, 503).

32. Ibid., XII, 276.

33. Ibid., XII, 396.

34. Ibid., VIII, 257.

35. Ibid., XII, 372.

36. *Les 120 journées de Sodome,* in *Oeuvres,* I, 283.

37. *Aline et Valcour,* in *Oeuvres,* I, 859.

38. O.C., VIII, 257–258.

39. Ibid., III, 529.

40. *Aline et Valcour,* in *Oeuvres,* I, 577.

41. O.C., III, 437.

42. To Fage; the year is 1771; Debauve, 109.

43. O.C., XII, 345.

44. See Heine, *Le Marquis de Sade,* 203.

45. Arlette Farge, *Le goût de l'archive* (Paris: Seuil, 1989), 84–85 (partial transcription).

46. Bourdin, 160.

47. Procès-verbal du guet du 18 janvier 1766; Archives Nationales, Y 11007 A; my emphasis.

48. July 1783; O.C., XII, 396.

49. Barbier, I, 187; January 1722.

50. O.C., XII, 276; [20 February 1781].

51. Ibid., IX, 513; my emphasis.

52. Ibid., III, 438; see also, O.C., IX, 512–513.

53. See ibid., VIII, 67, 86; also, *Oeuvres,* I, 67, 214.

54. *Papiers,* I, 11.

Index of Names, Titles, and Characters